REPORT

OF THE

HEIGHTS OF BUILDINGS COMMISSION

TO THE

COMMITTEE ON THE HEIGHT, SIZE AND ARRANGEMENT OF BUILDINGS

OF THE

BOARD OF ESTIMATE AND APPORTIONMENT OF THE CITY OF NEW YORK

DECEMBER 23, 1913

HEIGHTS OF BUILDINGS COMMISSION

Edward M. Bassett, Chairman

Edward C. Blum
Edward W. Brown
William H. Chesebrough
William A. Cokeley
Otto M. Eidlitz
Abram I. Elkus
Burt L. Fenner
J. Monroe Hewlett
Robert W. Higbie

C. Grant La Farge
Nelson P. Lewis
George T. Mortimer
Lawson Purdy
Allan Robinson
August F. Schwarzler
Franklin S. Tomlin
Lawrence Veiller
Gaylord S. White

George B. Ford, Secretary

Committees

Executive Committee—Edward M. Bassett, Chairman, George T. Mortimer, C. Grant La Farge, Allan Robinson, Gaylord S. White, Lawson Purdy, Lawrence Veiller, Nelson P. Lewis.

Office Buildings, Hotels and Theatres—Allan Robinson, Chairman, Otto M. Eidlitz, Burt L. Fenner, William H. Chesebrough.

Application of Zone or District Method—Lawson Purdy, Chairman, Nelson P. Lewis, Robert W. Higbie, Edward W. Brown.

Dwellings—All Buildings used for Residence except Hotels—C. Grant La Farge, Chairman, Lawrence Veiller, August F. Schwarzler, Gaylord S. White.

Buildings Used in Whole or in Part for Industry—Gaylord S. White, Chairman, Edward C. Blum, Abram I. Elkus, Franklin S. Tomlin.

Fifth Avenue Conditions—George T. Mortimer, Chairman, J. Monroe Hewlett, Abram I. Elkus, William A. Cokeley.

Staff

George B. Ford, Secretary and Director of Investigations.
Robert H. Whitten, Editor of Report and Special Investigator.
Herbert S. Swan, Statistician and Special Investigator.
Frank Backus Williams, Investigator and Writer on Districting Methods in Europe.
A. E. Heffelfinger, Head Draughtsman.

LETTER OF TRANSMITTAL

December 23, 1913.

GEORGE MCANENY, LEWIS H. POUNDS AND CYRUS C. MILLER, *the Committee of the Board of Estimate and Apportionment on Heights of Buildings:*

GENTLEMEN—At once, after the appointment of the Advisory Commission, we formed in co-operation with your committee a working staff, with George B. Ford at its head. Through the courtesy of the Court House Board, ample quarters were furnished us at 115 Broadway, Manhattan. In general the result of the work of the staff is shown in the charts submitted herewith, and the data contained in the special articles in the appendices. The staff did much additional work in assisting the members of the Commission in all of the matters treated in the report and in making calculations for the use of the committees. We consider that we have been especially fortunate in securing such competent and earnest helpers.

The Commission was divided into committees, as shown on the preceding page, in order that particular fields of work might receive constant attention. The Commission as a whole, however, held all hearings, passed on all the data and formulated all of the conclusions. As the work progressed it became evident that our report should emphasize, first, regulation of high buildings, second, districting, and third, Fifth Avenue conditions. The Commission and its staff gave a great deal of attention to factories and residences, as the charts will show, but we deemed it best to omit making specific recommendations regarding such buildings for the reason that active work is being carried on by the State Factory Investigating Commission and the Tenement House Committee of the Charity Organization Society, and we thought best to center our recommendations on fields covered by no other official bodies in this city. We hope that our data regarding factories and residences will be a help to all students of these subjects. It will be noticed, however, that factories and residences come to the front in our recommendations on districting. Although a large amount of work was done by each of our committees and many committee meetings held, the greatest labor devolved on the Committee on Office Buildings and Hotels and the Committee on Districting. The rule for high buildings was mainly prepared by the Committee on Office Buildings during months of exacting detail work.

The Commission held a long series of conferences at which the opinions of competent specialists were heard and discussed. Some of those who attended had prepared themselves carefully or brought written statements. Many organizations took a great interest in our work, appointed conference committees and in some cases had counsel prepare careful briefs for our consideration. All of the title companies and many of the large lenders on real estate securities freely gave us the benefit of facts, figures and opinions. Owners and managers of buildings, both large and small, developers of vacant land, builders, engineers, architects, insurance men, fire fighters and fire protection experts, housing and factory specialists, lawyers and physicians, city officials having to do with streets, building construction and tenement houses, manufacturers and transportation men attended our conferences and gave us an opportunity to check up from every angle the work of our committees and the staff. We have had the constant and valuable assistance of the Corporation Counsel, Mr. Watson having assigned Louis H. Hahlo to attend our meetings.

Special investigations were carried on in a number of the large cities of our country, Canada and Europe. For official assistance and courtesies in all these cities we wish to express our grateful acknowledgment. Furthermore our staff has corresponded with officials of almost every large city of the world that has taken up the subject of building regulation. Statutes and ordinances were collected and a record of the experience of other cities obtained so far as possible at first hand. The co-operation of other large cities and the great interest that they took in helping us were striking and delightful features of our work. We ought to make specific public acknowledgment of this assistance, for in many cases it consisted not only of furnishing opinions but preparation of material.

A series of public hearings was held in the City Hall, notices thereof being sent to 1325 organizations throughout the city. The daily press also gave notice of these hearings. They were well attended and helped us to obtain the views of everybody who desired to make a contribution of facts or opinions. The Commission has at all times invited correspondence and many valuable suggestions have come to us in this way.

We submit this report with full knowledge that it is not the last word to be said on these difficult subjects. We firmly believe, however, that our recommendations point in the right direction. We carried on our work with much diversity of opinion, as might be expected in a commission composed of men of many different callings. As our work proceeded, however, we became substantially unanimous on the main questions involved. This report is not the result of compromises. Continued study of the facts and conditions brought us to a harmonious and united opinion. Respectfully submitted,

HEIGHTS OF BUILDINGS COMMISSION,
EDWARD M. BASSETT, *Chairman.*

CONTENTS

Appendix IX—Statements submitted to the Commission:

LIST OF ILLUSTRATIONS

DIAGRAMS

MAPS

CHAPTER I—INTRODUCTION

On February 27, 1913, on motion of George McAneny, President of the Borough of Manhattan, the Board of Estimate and Apportionment of the City of New York adopted the following resolution:

"WHEREAS, There is a growing sentiment in the community to the effect that the time has come when effort should be made to regulate the height, size and arrangement of buildings erected within the limits of the City of New York; in order to arrest the seriously increasing evil of the shutting off of light and air from other buildings and from the public streets, to prevent unwholesome and dangerous congestion both in living conditions and in street and transit traffic and to reduce the hazards of fire and peril to life; and

"WHEREAS, Under the provisions of section 407 of the Charter, the height and size of buildings may be regulated by city ordinance, but such ordinance must first have the approval of the Board of Estimate and Apportionment; therefore be it

"RESOLVED, That the Chairman be authorized to appoint a Committee of three members of the Board of Estimate and Apportionment to take this general subject under consideration, to inquire into and investigate conditions actually existing, and to ascertain and report whether, in their judgment, it is desirable to regulate the height, size and arrangement of buildings hereafter to be erected or altered within the city limits, with due regard to their location, character or uses, to examine into the practice and the comparative experience of other cities either here or abroad, and to consider and report upon the question of the legal right of the City of New York to regulate building construction in the manner proposed; and be it further

"RESOLVED, That such Committee may also investigate and report whether, in their judgment, it would be lawful and desirable for the purpose of such regulation to divide the City into districts or into zones, and to prescribe the regulation of the height, size and arrangement of buildings upon different bases in such different districts or zones; and be it further

"RESOLVED, That the Committee, when appointed, may in turn appoint an advisory commission to aid it in its work, such commission to consist of as many members as the Committee may determine, serving without pay, if not already in the employment of the City, but including representatives of each of the several boroughs, and that either the Committee or its advisory commission may hold public hearings in each of the boroughs and may use all appropriate means to bring the subject to the attention of the tax-payers and to other persons who may be interested; and be it further

"RESOLVED, That the Committee be empowered to employ a Secretary, who shall also be the Secretary of the advisory commission, to secure such expert or technical advice as it may require for its proper guidance, and to incur such other incidental expenses as it may from time to time find necessary, such disbursements to be made from the Contingent Fund of this Board, but not to exceed in the aggregate the sum of $15,000; and be it further

"RESOLVED, That the said Committee be instructed to submit if practicable, in advance of any general report that it may make, suggestions or recommendations with relation to the proposed limitation of the height of buildings upon Fifth Avenue, between One Hundred and Tenth Street and Washington Square, in the Borough of Manhattan, and within certain prescribed areas on either side of the said avenue, as proposed in the resolution presented to this Board on May 9, 1912, and now pending; and be it further

"RESOLVED, That such Committee shall submit its final report and recommendations to the Board not later than six months from the date of its appointment, and shall thereupon cease to exist."

In accordance with this resolution, the then Mayor, William J. Gaynor, appointed as the Heights of Buildings Committee, George McAneny, President of the Borough of Manhattan; Alfred E. Steers, President of the Borough of Brooklyn, and Cyrus C. Miller, President of the Borough of The Bronx. Later Lewis H. Pounds, President of the Borough of Brooklyn, was substituted for Mr. Steers, who resigned to accept the position of City Magistrate. The Committee on Heights of Buildings appointed the Advisory Commission which submits this report. Two brief extensions of time were granted by the Board of Estimate and Apportionment. The work of the Advisory Commission was carried on within the appropriation made in the foregoing resolution.

It was not considered practicable to make a preliminary report on Fifth Avenue conditions. The injury that is being done to Fifth Avenue is not an isolated problem, but part of a problem that confronts the entire city. We strongly urge that there be no delay in bringing a remedy to Fifth Avenue, as otherwise an irreparable injury may be done. No other part of the city better exemplifies the harm which follows uncontrolled heights and uses of buildings. The Commission is of the opinion that additional legislation will be required before the city can apply the desired remedy, and that the remedy will be stronger in law if applied not only to Fifth Avenue but to other streets similarly situated.

CHAPTER II—METHODS OF CONTROL

The general problem considered by the Commission comprises the regulation of building heights and open spaces and the location of industries and buildings. Regulations relative to building heights and open spaces may be:

(1) Uniform for all buildings within the city, without distinction as to class or location of building;

(2) Uniform for all buildings of the same class throughout the city;

(3) Uniform for all buildings or for all buildings of the same class in a given district or section of the city.

Uniform regulations for all buildings

The simplest case of regulation is a fixed limit of height applying to all buildings within a city without distinction as to class or location of building. This is the usual and in most cases the first form that height regulation has taken in American cities. No case has been found where the constitutionality of such an ordinance has been directly before the courts, but in other cases the courts have stated that the right to make reasonable regulations of this kind is undoubted: People *v.* D'Oench, 111 N. Y. 359, Nov. 27, 1888; Hudson County Water Company *v.* McCarter, 209 U. S. 349, 355; Welch *v.* Swasey, 193 Mass. 364, 79 N. E. 745, affirmed 214 U. S. 91, May 17, 1909; Cochran *v.* Preston, 70 Atl. 113, 114, June 24, 1908.

Regulations varying with the class of building

Height and court regulation varying somewhat with the class of building is a usual and quite generally approved method. One of the most usual forms of classification is a maximum height limit for buildings generally and a lower limit for tenement houses. In New York City the height of tenements is at present limited to 1½ times the width of the widest abutting street, while the height of other buildings is unlimited. In the second class cities of Massachusetts, no tenement may have more than one legally habitable story for each full 10 feet of street width, unless it be set back from the street a distance equal to the excess of its height over that permitted at the street line. The height of other buildings is limited to 125 feet. In Chicago, the height of tenements is limited to 1½ times the street width while the height of other buildings is limited to 200 feet. In Boston, the height of all buildings is limited with the exception of coal hoists, grain elevators and sugar refineries. The constitutionality of the Boston regulation has been upheld, though this question of exemption of particular kinds of buildings is not referred to in the decision (Welch *v.* Swasey, 193 Mass. 364; affirmed 214 U. S. 91).

A special act of the Maryland legislature passed in 1904 limits the height of buildings within one block of the Washington Monument in the city of Baltimore to 70 feet. Churches are exempted from the provisions of this act. The constitutionality of this exemption was upheld by the Maryland Court of Appeals (Cochran *v.* Preston, 70 Atl. 113). This was on the ground as stated by the court that churches "do not present the same danger from fire to the surrounding buildings as many other structures do, chiefly because they are not likely to become very numerous in any one locality."

Though a number of American cities have made special regulations for tenement houses and the constitutionality of such statutes has been affirmed, the opinions rendered have not considered specifically this question of classification. A case of interest, however, is People *v.* D'Oench, 111 N. Y. 359, decided Nov. 27, 1888, which involved the construction and the constitutionality of a New York statute regulating the height of dwelling houses in New York City. The case came up on an application for a writ of mandamus requiring the superintendent of buildings to approve the specifications and plans for a proposed addition to the Buckingham Hotel. The applicant claimed that the act was unconstitutional, and that even if constitutional, the term "dwelling houses" should not be construed to include a hotel. Judge Earle in delivering the opinion of the Court states that there is "no doubt of the competency of the legislature in the exercise of the police power under the constitution to pass such an act, and the sole question, therefore, now to be determined is whether the act applies to hotels." The Court held that the act did not apply to hotels and its discussion of this question throws some light on the question of equality and classification as applied to building regulations. Judge Earle says (at page 361):

"As simple, private dwelling houses are seldom, if ever, built 80 feet, the main purpose of the act must have been to regulate the height of tenement and apartment houses, which are becoming very numerous in New York, which are usually built in the midst of dwelling houses and in which several families live and carry on all the operations of housekeeping. There is not the same reason for regulating the height of hotels not usually built in the midst of dwelling houses, which are mainly occupied by temporary adult guests, which are under the supervision of one management and which can never become numerous. While stores, factories, warehouses, buildings for offices and numerous other buildings may be erected without any restriction as to height, we can see no reason to suppose that the language used in this act was meant to include hotels, nearly all of which in the city of New York have for many years been erected of greater height than the limit prescribed in the act."

In regulations as to required open spaces about buildings the tendency to apply special regulations to each class of buildings is even more pronounced than in the regulation of height. Thus in present laws in force in New York City, special regulations as to open spaces are applied to each of the following classes of buildings: hotels, office buildings, theaters, lodging houses, dwelling houses, tenement houses.

An objection to height and open space regulation based on class of building is that it may result in a partial defeat of the chief purpose of regulation, which is to better light and air conditions. A tenement house has special restrictions as to height and as to courts but if a factory may be built adjoining such tenement without restriction as to height or courts the chief result may be to insure improved light to the factory at the expense of the tenement. Regulations as to height and open spaces are usually based on the supposition that they will be adequate if all adjacent buildings conform to the same regulations. They assume a reciprocity of limitation and advantage. This reciprocal relation may be destroyed if different types of buildings in the same district are subjected to different regulations as to height and open spaces. While, however, a general uniformity is desirable, such uniformity need not be absolute. Some exemption or special restriction will almost always be required for certain classes of buildings that are not segregated but are scattered throughout the city, such as churches, theaters, schools, hotels, etc. Moreover, considerations of safety may require an absolute height limit for certain buildings, such as factories or department stores, that would be unreasonable if applied to all buildings.

Regulations varying with the particular district

Every large city that has made a serious study of the question of regulating heights and open spaces has been forced to the conclusion that an effective solution cannot be secured without a division of the city into districts and the application of special regulations to each district or class of districts. This subject, together with that of the location of industries and buildings, is treated at length in Chapter IV, Districting.

The general scope of constitutional regulation

It is clear that such restrictions as are enacted must justify themselves as a reasonable exercise of the police power of the state. Under eminent domain the individual is compensated for the taking of his property. Under the police power there is also a constructive taking of property in certain cases, but without compensation to the individuals injured. It is theoretically conceivable that a general plan of building restriction and regulation might be entered upon by resort to the power of eminent domain, but, practically, such a solution is out of the question. The expense and burden of condemnation proceedings and litigation in multitudinous cases would create a tax burden that would increase rather than compensate for the injury to property interests. Moreover, the kinds of regulation under consideration are not such as to justify individual compensation. While they restrict individual liberty to a certain extent they do it in such a way as to conserve individual and public interests and rights. They subject the use of urban land to such restrictions as are appropriate and reasonable in the nature and history of this class of property.

The police power may be used to promote the public health, safety, order and general welfare. Protection of public health, safety and order constitute the police power in the primary or narrower sense of the term.[1]

It is a power so vital as to be undoubted when reasonably and justly applied. The exercise of the police power for the promotion of public comfort and convenience and for the promotion of general social and economic interests under the head of "the general welfare," while upheld by competent authority, will nevertheless be subjected to more careful scrutiny and more strict construction.

The position of the United States Supreme Court in regard to the scope of the police power is well stated by Justice Harlan in C., B. & Q. Railway *v.* Drainage Commissioners, 200 U. S. 561, 592, decided March 5, 1906:

> "The learned counsel for the railroad company seem to think that the adjudications relating to the police power of the state to protect the public health, the public morals and the public safety are not applicable in principle to cases when the police power is exerted for the general well-being of the community apart from any question of the public health, the public morals or the public safety. . . . We cannot assent to the view expressed by counsel. We hold that the police power of a state embraces regulations designed to promote the public convenience or the general prosperity, as well as regulations designed to promote the public health, the public morals or the public safety. . . . And the validity of a police regulation . . . must depend upon the circumstances of each case and the character of the regulation, whether arbitrary or reasonable and whether really designed to accomplish a legitimate public purpose."

Again in Welch *v.* Swasey, 214 U. S. 91, decided May 17, 1909, the same court through Justice Peckham concurs, at page 106, in the conclusion of the Massachusetts Court "that regulations

[1] Freund, Police Power, sec. 10.

in regard to the height of buildings, and in regard to their mode of construction in cities, made by legislative enactments for the safety, comfort and convenience of the people and for the benefit of property owners generally, are valid." Finally in Eubank *v.* City of Richmond, 33 Sup. Ct. 76, decided December 2, 1912, Justice McKenna reiterates that the police power extends "not only to regulations which promote the public health, morals and safety, but to those which promote the public convenience or the general prosperity."

The New York Court of Appeals has taken substantially the same view of the scope of the police power. In People *v.* King, 110 N. Y. 418, Judge Andrews says (at page 423): "By means of this power the legislature exercises a supervision over matters involving the common weal and enforces the observance, by each individual member of society, of the duties which he owes to others and the community at large. It may be exerted whenever necessary to secure the peace, good order, health, morals and general welfare of the community. . . . In short, the police power covers a wide range of particular unexpressed powers reserved to the state affecting freedom of action, personal conduct and the use and control of property."

It is thus seen that the police power is broad and comprehensive. Yet it is by no means unlimited. A controlling limitation is that every resort to it should commend itself to the sober judgment as necessary, appropriate and reasonable, the infringement of private right being not disproportionate to the real public gain.

Freund in his treatise on the Police Power well states that a study of the various cases in which the police power has been applied "will reveal the police power not as a fixed quantity but as the expression of social, economic and political conditions. As long as these conditions vary, the police power must continue to be elastic, *i. e.*, capable of development." If an informed and deliberate public opinion becomes educated to the necessity for the exercise of greater control over the planning and over the building of the city, and that such control cannot be effectively exercised except through the police power, it is clear that the police power is sufficiently elastic to meet the situation. The courts, while naturally conservative, have shown a strong disposition to favor all reasonable regulations for the control of the height, size and arrangement of buildings. As the public necessity for such regulations becomes more clearly apparent, we may expect the position taken by the courts to become more and more clearly defined in support of such control.

Bearing in mind the purposes and objects which justify a resort to the police power our study of the problem of controlling building development will be based chiefly on the following considerations:

(1) *Public safety.*—Protection of property from fire and protection of the occupants of buildings from injury due to fire or panic.

(2) *Public health.*—Importance of light, air and the prevention of congestion, to health and sanitation.

(3) *General welfare.*—(a) The comfort and convenience of the occupants of dwellings, offices and factories, through more adequate provision for light and air and in the case of dwellings through the maintenance of the essentially residential character of the neighborhood.

(b) The safeguarding of existing and future building investment values and the encouragement of an appropriate and orderly building development by such regulations as will prevent the taking from an existing structure of its minimum allotment of light and air and as will tend to maintain the character of a district.

(c) The prevention of street congestion.

Regulations based on street width

Numerous height regulations are made to vary in some measure with the width of the street. In European cities the limitation based on street width is in most cases the fundamental restriction on the height of buildings. In America this restriction at present plays a much less important part. It may be said to be fundamental in the general height restrictions of Washington and to be of great practical importance in those of Boston. It is also a very important factor in height restrictions for tenement houses.

In New York City no tenement house may exceed 1½ times the street width.

In some cases the height allowed is exactly proportional to the street width. In other cases special limits are provided to govern the case of either very wide or very narrow streets. In general, limitations based on street width may be classified as follows:

1. The street width, or some multiple thereof.
2. The street width increased or diminished by an arbitrary unit.
3. The street width increased by the amount of set-back.

The most common limitation on height in Germany is the street width either taken by itself or increased by an arbitrary unit. Special exemptions are, however, frequently made in the case of the narrower streets in the inner city—the street, no matter what its width, being assumed as of a given width. The multiple of the street width is rarely found in Germany, and in no case is it applicable to an entire city. Where utilized, the multiple is generally much smaller than that in American cities. In Breslau, Dantzig and Oberhausen, for instance, it is 1¼ times the width of the street. In Bielefeld, Lübeck and Stettin, it is 1½ times the width of the street. In Boston (except as elsewhere noted), Charleston, Cleveland, Erie, Fort Wayne, New Orleans and Youngstown, on the other hand, the multiple is 2½ times the width of the street. With Washington, these cities are the only cities in America that base the general height limitation of all buildings on the street width. Boston, Cleveland and New Orleans include the set-back in the width of the street. Washington is the only city found that bases the height upon the width of the street diminished by an arbitrary amount. As described elsewhere, the height of buildings on residential streets more than 70 feet in width may not exceed the width of the street diminished by 10 feet. In cities of the second class in New York no building to be used for living purposes, except a hotel, may exceed in height the street width, nor in any case may it exceed 100 feet in height (Laws 1913, ch. 774).

The width of the street would seem to have a certain bearing on most of the purposes for which height limitations are prescribed. It directly affects fire prevention, light and air conditions, and street congestion. It seems to be an essential factor in any thoroughgoing treatment of the problem of height regulation. The courts have sustained height limitations based in part on street width in the following cases: People *v.* D'Oench, 111 N. Y. 359, Nov. 27, 1888; Welch *v.* Swasey, 193 Mass. 364, affirmed 214 U. S. 91, May 17, 1909.

Regulations based on maintenance of a minimum angle of light

A limitation based directly on street width maintains a constant minimum angle of light for the front of the building at the ground floor. If prescribed height is equal to street width this minimum angle of light is 45 degrees; if 1½ times street width, it is 33⅔ degrees; if two times street width, it is 26½ degrees; if 2½ times street width, it is 21⅔ degrees. The converse of this is that the maximum angle of light obstruction will be the difference between the above amounts and 90 degrees, *i. e.*, 45 degrees for height limit equal to street width; 56⅓ degrees for height limit 1½ times street width; 63½ degrees for height limit two times street width; 68⅓ degrees for height limit 2½ times the street width.

From the diagram it is clear that a flat limit of height is not necessary in order to secure a minimum angle of light. If the height limit based on street width is made to apply only to the elevation of the building at the street line and other portions of the building are set back in the same ratio as height limit to street width the angle of light is maintained. If the height limit is twice the width of the street a set-back after reaching the height limit at the street line of 5 feet for every 10 feet of increase in height will maintain the angle of light at 26½ degrees.

Provisions for courts in tenement house and general building regulations are sometimes based in part at least on the maintenance of a minimum angle of light. This basis does not usually appear on the face of the law but has nevertheless been used in determining the prescribed factors. In London, the angle of light is more expressly stated. The rear heights of a building are in general regulated by a line drawn at an angle of 63½ degrees to the horizontal toward the building from the rear line of the lot. That is, a building may not be built so as to obstruct the light of the adjoining lot in the rear at an angle of more than 63½ degrees.

DIAGRAM I

Angles of Light and of Light Obstruction at Ground Floor on Street Front

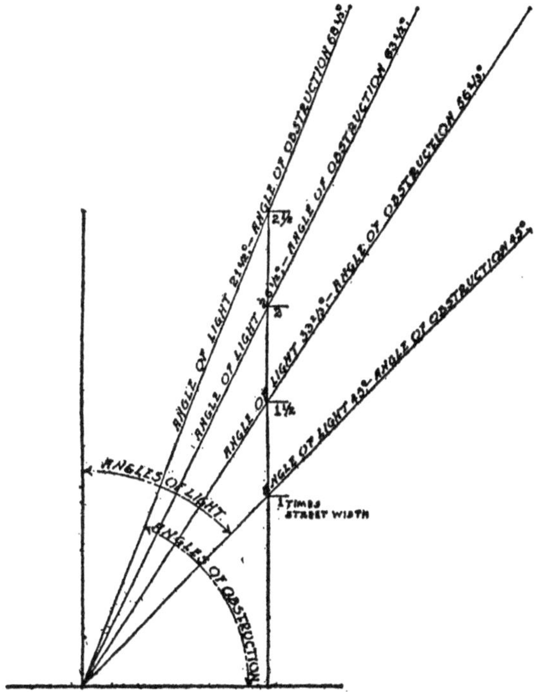

Exceptions to angle of light rule

While light is important it is not the only object that height and court regulations are intended to secure. Air and ventilation are at least of equal importance. It is of course true that if a liberal angle of light is provided it will usually carry with it adequate provision for air and ventilation. If, however, in the case of a court the angle of light is small and the air is not renewed and kept in circulation, the question of ventilation may require separate consideration. This constitutes one reason for a requirement of a minmum open court across the rear of the lot. In the suburbs, moreover, where lower land values make liberal provision for open spaces appropriate, this factor may well be considered apart from the safeguarding of a minimum angle of light.

The diminution of congestion of streets, buildings and districts, is also an important purpose to be served by height and court regulations. Absence of congestion in residence districts makes for more wholesome conditions and favors the physical and civic health and well-being of the community. This purpose, like that of air and ventilation, usually may be provided for by limitations based on angle of light.

Protection against fire is another important purpose that may be served by height and court regulations. If the maintenance of a certain angle of light permits the construction of buildings higher than warranted by considerations of fire prevention and safety to occupants, the simple rule of light angle should be supplemented to provide for such contingency.

A very general exception to the angle of light rule is found in most height regulations based in general upon street width. The rule as to multiple of street width is not applied to very narrow streets in the business center, nor is it applied to streets of more than a prescribed width. In other words, as an exception to the general rule there is a minimum height that will be permitted and a maximum height that may not be exceeded, regardless of street width. It is clear that a general multiple if applied to certain narrow streets in the business center might seriously depreciate land values and interfere with the most beneficial use of the land. Such a result would not be in the public interest and would seem to render the regulation unreasonable and of doubtful constitutionality. As shown more fully below (pages 24-26) reasonableness is largely a matter of degree. There must be some fair relation between the public good to be secured by the regulations and the private injury suffered. Moderation and proportionateness of means to ends is of the essence of reasonableness. It seems that classification or exemption that is essential to the reasonableness of a regulation is itself reasonable.

CHAPTER III—HIGH BUILDINGS

The high building problem is at present confined chiefly to a comparatively small portion of the lower half of the island of Manhattan. The average building height in the Borough of Manhattan is 4.8 stories. Ninety per cent of the buildings do not exceed a height of six stories. The buildings over 10 stories in height constitute only a little over one per cent of the total. Out of a total of 92,749 buildings, there are but 1048 buildings over 10 stories in height; 90 buildings, over 17 stories; 51 buildings, over 20 stories; and only 9 buildings over 30 stories.

The average building height, excluding public buildings and churches, on Broadway, below Chambers Street, is 11 stories; on Nassau Street, from Wall to Frankfort, 8.56 stories; on Trinity Place and Church Street, from Morris to Chambers, 7.8 stories; on New Street, 11.59 stories; on Exchange Place, 14.1 stories; and on Fifth Avenue from Washington Square to 59th Street, 6.4 stories.

TABLE I—HEIGHT OF BUILDINGS IN MANHATTAN[1]

Height in Stories.	Number of Buildings.	Height in Stories.	Number of Buildings.
1	4,598	18	16
2	3,708	19	13
3	5,232	20	11
4	22,526	21	18
5	25,425	22	10
6	21,576	23	3
7	6,774	24	3
8	1,259	26	6
9	413	27	2
10	193	32	1
11	208	33	2
12	150	34	1
13	464	38	1
14	47	40	1
15	27	41	1
16	30	51	1
17	31	55	1

Total number of buildings 92,749

[1] From the building census, January 1, 1913, prepared by Rudolph P. Miller, Commissioner of Buildings.

TABLE II—HEIGHT OF BUILDINGS BY CLASSES IN MANHATTAN[1]

Stories.	Breweries.	Car Barns.	Dept. Stores.	Garages.	Manufactories.	Offices.	Stables.	Stores.	Warehouses.	Dwellings.	Hotels.	Stores, Dwellings.
1........	..	5	..	84	134	113	625	413	238	74	..	24
2........	..	7	1	81	271	93	782	278	254	739	6	313
3........	1	8	..	64	411	85	324	241	146	1,730	16	1,539
4........	3	6	4	38	817	100	219	264	941	15,468	29	4,795
5........	6	..	3	29	1,454	208	143	363	130	13,081	62	9,368
6........	11	..	3	19	1,980	246	106	401	197	8,869	71	9,294
7........	7	..	7	11	1,118	114	45	198	114	1,556	27	3,491
8........	4	..	3	3	383	51	9	46	54	330	30	312
9........	3	..	6	2	178	42	..	31	14	87	20	16
10........	..	..	2	2	47	38	..	5	12	54	21	5
11........	1	..	3	..	86	32	..	1	11	33	15	16
12........	..	..	2	..	76	28	..	..	..	20	13	4
13........	..	..	1	..	232	58	..	..	2	88	53	22
14........	1	..	..	..	6	17	..	..	1	10	7	2
15........	..	..	1	..	3	14	..	..	..	6	..	..
16........	..	..	..	..	5	12	..	..	..	9	3	..
17........	..	..	..	..	12	16	..	..	..	..	2	1
18........	..	..	..	..	..	11	..	..	..	..	5	..
19........	..	..	..	..	3	9	..	..	..	..	..	.
20........	..	..	..	..	2	8	..	..	..	..	1	..
21........	..	..	..	..	3	14	..	..	..	..	1	..
22........	..	..	..	..	..	8	..	..	..	..	2	..
23........	..	..	..	..	1	2	..	..	..	..	..	..
24........	..	..	..	..	..	3	..	..	..	..	..	..
25........	..	..	..	..	..	5	..	..	..	..	..	..
27........	..	..	..	..	..	2	..	..	..	..	..	..
31........	..	..	..	..	..	1	..	..	..	..	..	..
32........	..	..	..	..	..	1	..	..	..	..	..	..
33........	..	..	..	..	..	3	..	..	..	..	..	..
38........	..	..	..	..	..	1	..	..	..	..	..	..
41........	..	..	..	..	..	1	..	..	..	..	..	..
51........	..	..	..	..	..	1	..	..	..	..	..	..
55........	..	..	..	..	..	1	..	..	..	..	..	..
Total.....	37	26	36	333	7,222	1,338	2,253	2,257	1,267	42,154	385	29,202
Average..	5.5	2.7	7.8	2.9	5.9	7.0	2.5	4.0	3.9	4.8	8.0	5.3

[1] From the building census, January 1, 1913, prepared by Rudolph P. Miller, Commissioner of Buildings.

The height of buildings in the district below Chambers Street considered as a whole, is considerably lower than that on the above mentioned streets. The high buildings below Chambers Street are practically all grouped within the area bounded on the east by Pearl and Whitehall Streets and on the west by State, Greenwich, and West Broadway. The average building height in this district, the area of which is a little more than half of the whole territory below Chambers Street, is 6.4 stories.

A classification of buildings according to use reveals the fact that hotels, and not office buildings, possess the greatest average building height. Hotels have an average height of 8.0 stories; department stores, 7.8 stories; office buildings, 7.0 stories; factory building, 5.9 stories; stores and dwellings, 5.3 stories; dwellings, 4.8 stories; stores, 4.0 stories; and warehouses, 3.9 stories. But, of the 90 buildings over 17 stories high, 9 are factory buildings, 10 are hotels and 71 are office buildings. It is clear therefore that while hotels have the greatest average height, the much greater proportion of high office buildings and their concentration in a few areas make the determination of a maximum rule applicable to all buildings very largely a question of determining what rule will be most appropriate for office buildings in the areas of maximum congestion.

Public safety

The Building Code requires that all buildings over 150 feet in height be thoroughly fireproof. The buildings themselves cannot burn because there is nothing combustible in their construction. All high buildings are equipped with standpipes and ample tanks at various levels and many of them with automatic sprinklers. Doors and windows between rooms and between rooms and corridors are fireproof so that fire can be confined to a single room. There are many interesting examples of such fires.

The fact remains, however, that tall buildings are not necessarily safe. The rooms are often filled with highly inflammable material. Unless doors are closed, fire may easily spread to other rooms. The draft up the chimney-like elevator wells may pull the flames across the corridor and the flames, fed by the grease on the elevator guides, may be carried to upper floors. Under such conditions the danger of panic among the employees of the building would be very real and the higher the building the greater the danger.

The fire department cannot fight a fire from the outside more than 85 to 100 feet above the ground. Above that they must rely on the standpipes in the building. If the standpipe does not work or if the fire is so near the standpipe as to render its use impracticable, the fire department becomes helpless. No fatal fire in a modern high building has yet occurred, but it is not an impossibility.

In case of general panic or catastrophe causing the occupants of all offices in all buildings in the high building district to seek the streets at once, a serious situation would present itself. It would be impossible for all the occupants of all the buildings abutting on certain streets to move in the street at one time, even though the street were cleared of all other traffic, pedestrian, vehicular and surface car and absolutely free from all obstructions so that the entire width of the street might be used. The minimum space required by a crowd moving in one direction is five square feet per person. Computed in this manner, Broadway could hold but 96.3 per cent of its occupants; Trinity Place and Church Street 86.6 per cent; Nassau Street 69.3 per cent; New Street 44.5 per cent; and Exchange Place only 37.5 per cent. This being the situation to-day the question arises as to what might happen in case of a general panic should the entire district be solidly built up with buildings of the present extreme heights.

Public health

In areas where high buildings are crowded together most of the rooms even on the street front are inadequately lighted and many are decidedly dark. On New Street and Exchange Place where the office buildings range from 10 to 22 stories high, on a bright sunny day at noon in midsummer it was found that in almost all of the street rooms artificial light was being used next to the windows. The conditions in the interior courts in parts of the tall building district are even worse.

Even with modern artificial lighting of the most approved

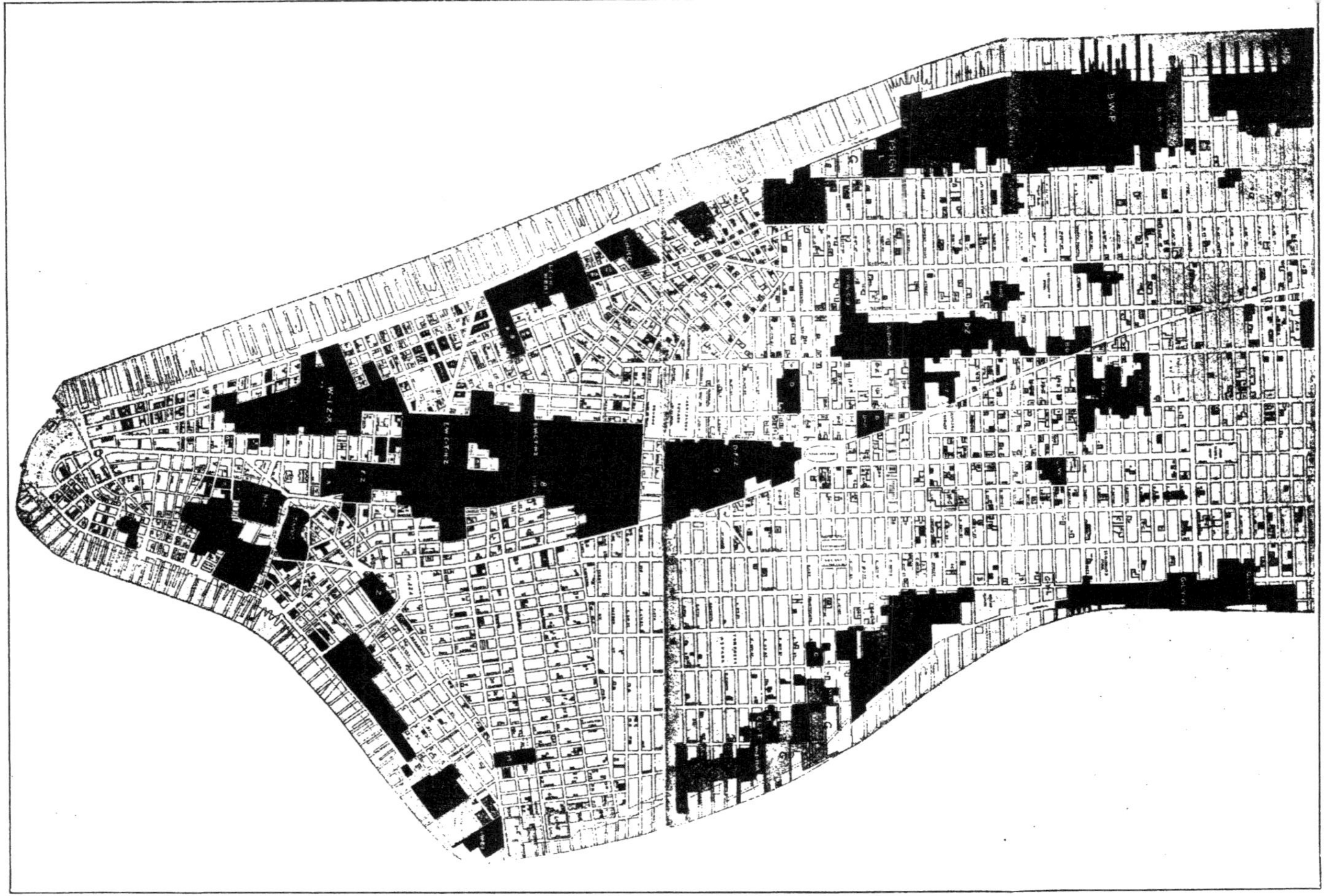

MAP II.—PREVAILING HEIGHT OF FACTORIES IN MANHATTAN.

Shading indicates relative height. The darkest areas indicate a prevailing height of 7 or more stories.

type, the dark offices have caused a great deal of eye strain. Nothing but adequate natural light seems to prevent it. Tuberculosis experts testified to the Commission that they had found many cases of tuberculosis directly traceable to working in dark offices. A noticeable increase in sick leave has been found among the employees of firms that have moved from light to dark offices.

Public comfort and convenience

A number of streets in the high building district are already so congested that pedestrian and vehicular traffic is greatly impeded. Assuming that pedestrians will use sidewalk space only and will move in one direction only, there is room on Trinity Place and Church Street for but 56 per cent of the occupants of the buildings located on those streets;[1] on Broadway, 50 per cent; on Nassau Street, 32 per cent; and on New Street, but 19 per cent. If these same streets should be uniformly built up to an average height of 30 stories, the above percentages would be reduced to: 26 per cent on Broadway; 20 per cent on Trinity Place and Church Street; 11.9 per cent on Nassau Street; 8.9 per cent on New Street; and 8.4 per cent on Exchange Place. It is quite clear that under such conditions the street capacity would be entirely inadequate to take care of the morning, afternoon and noon hour crowds.

Property values

Few skyscrapers pay large net returns. Most of them pay only moderate returns. The cost per cubic foot of tall buildings is greater than that for low buildings. The exact difference can only be approximated because there are so many factors which affect the problem. However, the very tall buildings demand many things out of proportion to their increased bulk. All piping has to be made disproportionately heavier; special pumps and relays of tanks have to be provided, foundations often call for special construction, wind-bracing assumes an important place, long-run elevators are more costly than short-run

[1] This estimate is based on an allowance of five square feet per moving person.

elevators, the extra space taken up by the express run of the elevators is an additional cost. Thus in the aggregate the total cost per cubic foot of a very tall building may be 60 to 75 cents per cubic foot where a low building of the same class would cost only 40 to 50 cents per cubic foot.

The net rentable space on the ground floor is worth on the average as much as that of the third to the eighth floors inclusive. Loss of rentable ground floor space is always serious and must be compensated for in other ways if the building is going to pay. The exceptional size of the columns and the exceptional space taken by pipes and ducts on the lower floors alone, have a serious effect on the net rentable area. However, the great item of waste in the high building is the big loss of valuable renting space on the lower floors due to the dead run of the express elevators to the upper floors. This amounts to from 50 to 65 square feet per elevator per floor. In a 30 story building with 30 elevators this means on the ground floor 1800 square feet given up to elevators and at least as much again given up to the lobby, so that about 4000 square feet is lost. As this ground floor space in such buildings often rents at $20 per square foot, the loss to the building is $80,000 on this floor alone. A 10 story building would save two-thirds of this. The loss on the floors above due to the dead run of elevators also amounts to a surprising total, all of which would be saved in a 10 or 12 story building. This means that tall buildings reach a limit beyond which the loss in space on the lower floors more than counterbalances the profit on the upper floors. Every building according to its shape, size, location, and use has its economic limit.

But even though a high building may pay a moderate net return as long as it is isolated and surrounded by low buildings so that all its floors and offices are light and attractive, the result may be very different after it is surrounded by similar buildings, shutting off light and reducing rentals on the lower floors. As a rule in an area in which high buildings predominate the rentals are lowest and the percentages of vacancies greatest on the lower floors above the second. If before the high building development the owners in such districts could have covenanted among themselves to limit heights and enlarge courts, it would undoubtedly have been to the advantage of all concerned.

The real estate interests which a decade ago were most active in opposing the adoption of a height limit in Boston are to-day among its staunchest supporters. The consensus of opinion among real estate men in Boston is that the height limit, instead of depreciating land values or retarding the improvement of property, has been an unqualified success.

Existing Height and Area Limitations in New York

Height limits

The only direct limitation on the height of buildings in New York is that restricting the height of apartment and tenement houses to 1½ times the width of the widest abutting street. There are of course other provisions in the building code, the city charter, the labor law, and the tenement house law that constitute a very real limitation on the height of buildings, but all of these are indirect limitations. The most important of these provisions are those regarding open spaces and fireproofing.

Open spaces

The open space requirements vary considerably with the type of building. No open space is required in the case of factories, stores and warehouses. Dwelling houses, hotels, lodging houses, office buildings, tenement houses, and theaters are, however, subject to special provisions of varying stringency.

Dwelling houses may cover 90 per cent of the lot area.

Hotels, situated on corner lots and covering an area of not more than 3000 square feet, are prohibited from occupying more than 95 per cent of the lot area above the second floor level. Hotels, situated on interior lots, are prohibited from occupying more than 90 per cent of the lot area above the second story level. An additional 2½ per cent of uncovered lot area must be provided for each and every story over five. The open space provisions with reference to hotels situated on inside lots are tantamount to a maximum height limitation of 41 stories. In the case of a 21 story hotel the open space would equal half of the lot area.

Lodging houses may cover 65 per cent of interior lots and 92 per cent of corner lots.

Office buildings situated on interior lots may cover 90 per cent of the lot area at and above the second floor level. Office buildings situated on corner lots up to 3000 square feet in area may cover the entire lot area.

The amount of open space demanded in the case of apartment and tenement houses is dependent upon the vertical and horizontal dimensions of the building, its interior arrangement and occupancy, the shape and size of the building site, and its location. Tenements situated on corner lots up to 3000 square feet in area may occupy 90 per cent of the lot area. Tenements situated on interior lots more than 90 feet but less than 105 feet in depth may occupy up to 70 per cent of the lot area. Tenements situated on certain other kinds of lots may occupy up to 65 per cent of the lot area.

Theaters and opera houses must be provided with rear and side courts. The width of these courts must be proportioned to the seating capacity.[1]

Height Limitations in American and European Cities

The maximum height limit in America is, as a rule, set so high that it limits the height of buildings only when what might be termed the logical height limit for that particular city or locality has been very much exceeded. In other words, the maximum height limit is no height limit at all so far as most buildings are concerned; it only prevents the erection of a few exceptionally high buildings. It does not limit or condition the character of the great mass of buildings erected even in the central business district. In Boston, Chicago, and Washington, however, the present maximum height limits do constitute a very practical restriction, as evidenced by the tendency in certain districts to build up to the full height allowed by the restrictions.

[1] For a fuller treatment of the entire subject of existing regulations, see Appendix II.

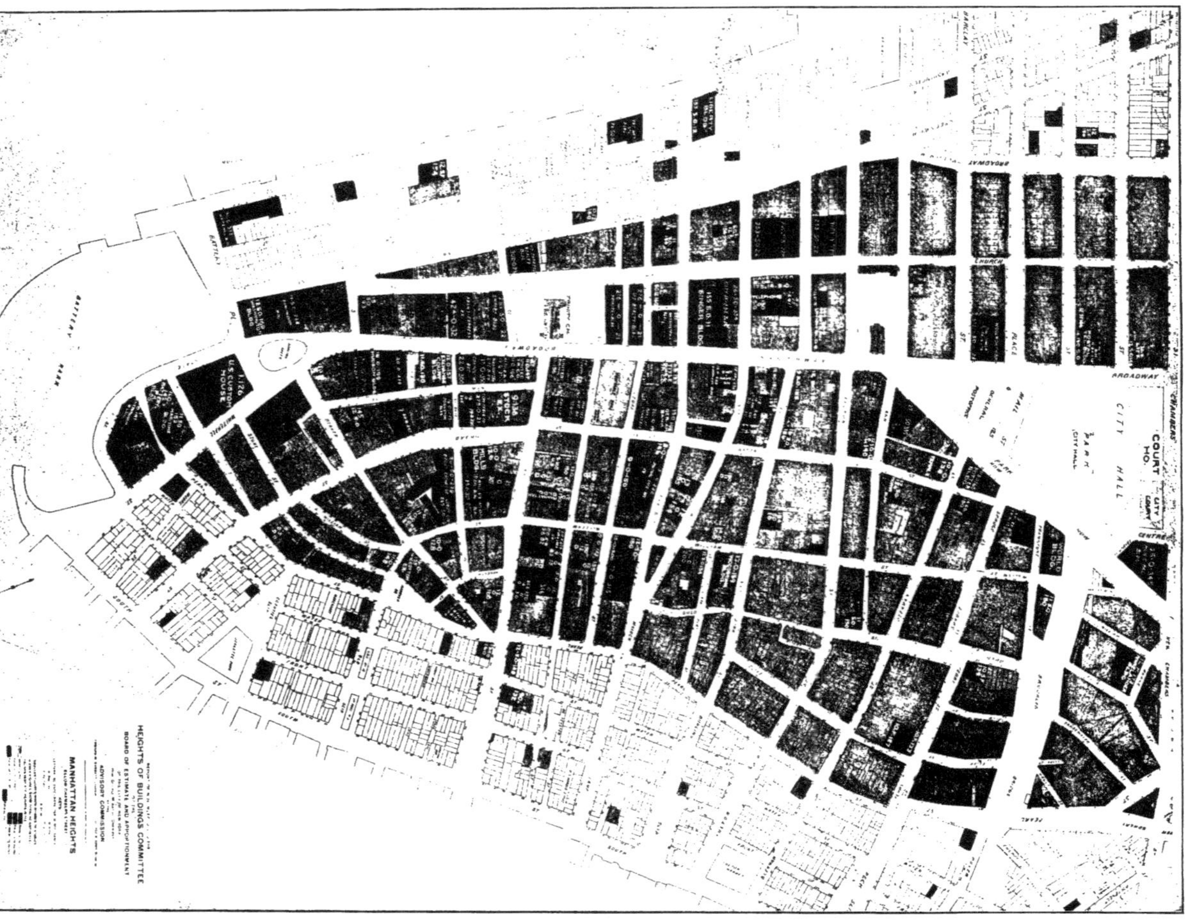

MAP III—DETAILS OF HEIGHTS OF BUILDINGS IN MANHATTAN BELOW CHAMBERS STREET.

Smaller numeral indicates height in stories.
Larger numeral indicates height in feet.

The following is a tabulation of height limits in certain American and European cities:

American Cities

City	Height		City	Height	
Baltimore	175	feet	Portland, Ore.	160	feet
Boston[1]			Rochester[2]		
District A	125	"	Scranton	125	"
District B	80-100	"	Youngstown[1]		
Buffalo[2]			Fort Wayne[1]	200	"
Charleston[1]	125	"	Providence	120	"
Chicago	200	"	Salt Lake City	125	"
Cleveland[1]	200	"	Toronto[3]	130	"
Erie[1]	200	"	Washington, D. C.		
Indianapolis	200	"	Pennsylvania Ave.	160	"
Los Angeles	150	"	Business Streets[4]	130	"
Manchester, N. H.	125	"	Residence Streets[5]	85	"
Milwaukee	225	"	Seattle	about 20	stories
New Orleans[1]	160	"			

European Cities

City	Height		City	Height	
Aix-la-Chapelle	65.6	feet	Hanover	65.6	feet
Altona	72.2	"	Kiel	72.2	"
Berlin	72.2	"	Leipzig	72.2	"
Bremen	62.3	"	London	80.0	"
Breslau	72.2	"	Lübeck	59.0	"
Cologne	65.6	"	Magdeburg	65.6	"
Dortmund	65.6	"	Munich	72.2	"
Dresden	72.2	"	Paris	65.6	"
Duisburg	65.6	"	Posen	65.6	"
Dusseldorf	65.6	"	Rome	78.5	"
Edinburgh	60.0	"	Stockholm	72.2	"
Elberfeld	65.6	"	Stuttgart	65.6	"
Frankfort	65.6	"	Vienna	82.0	"
Halle	59.0	"	Zurich	43.0	"
Hamburg	78.7	"			

[1] Not to exceed 2½ times width of widest street.
[2] Not to exceed 4 times average least dimension.
[3] Not to exceed 5 times least dimension at base.
[4] Not to exceed street width plus 20 feet.
[5] An intermediate height between 60 feet and 85 feet on streets over 70 feet wide—height not to exceed width of street minus 10 feet; 60 feet on streets from 60 to 70 feet wide; and street width on streets less than 60 feet wide.

CHAPTER IV—DISTRICTING

As applied to building restriction there are two general types of districting. Certain localities may be set off as residential or business or industrial districts. Industry and business may, for example, be excluded from the residence districts. The restrictions may go further and attempt to secure a certain type of residence district. The district may be restricted to one family or two family houses. Another type of districting is where different general height and area limitations are applied to all buildings in a particular district. Any thoroughgoing plan for the control of building development must make use of both of these types of districting.

CONSTITUTIONALITY OF DISTRICTING

While the desirability of districting is generally recognized by all students of this subject there is a fear on the part of some that it may be held void as an infringement of the constitutional guarantee of equality. The constitutional guarantee of equal protection of the laws constitutes one of the most important limitations upon the police power. It means that the government shall not impose particular burdens upon individuals or corporations to meet dangers for which they cannot in justice be held responsible, and that all legislative discriminations or classifications shall be justified by differences of status, act or occupation corresponding to the difference of legislative measures.[1] The idea of equality excludes in principle both particular burdens and special privileges, but admits of reasonable classification.[2]

The question what constitutes reasonable classification comes up chiefly in connection with districting. To what length is it permissible to go in the division of the city into districts with varying regulations as to the height, size and arrangement of buildings? Other forms of classification have received quite general acceptance. Thus tenement houses have often been put

[1] Freund, Police Power, page v.
[2] Freund, Police Power, sec. 611.

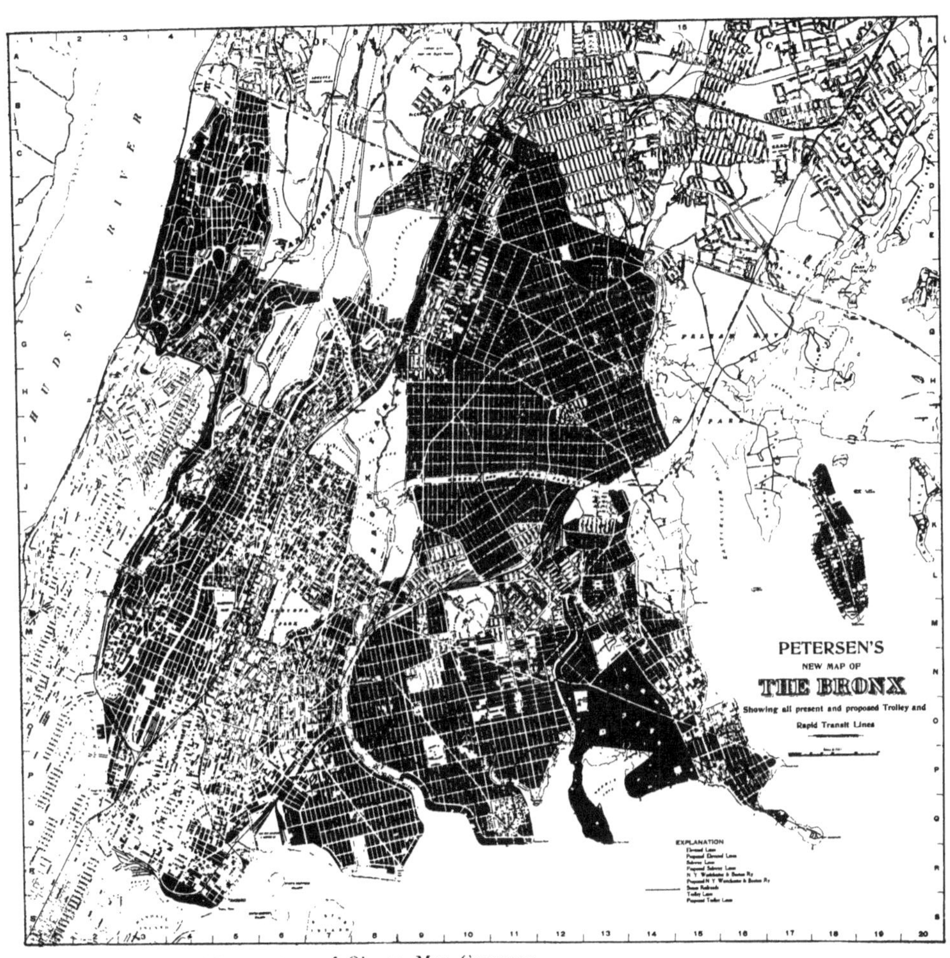

Base map reproduced by courtesy of Ohman Map Company.

MAP IV—UNIMPROVED PROPERTY IN THE BRONX.
Black indicates unimproved land.

in a separate class and subjected to more stringent regulations. This has been justified on the ground of greater importance in relation to public health or safety. Likewise height regulations have been adopted varying according to the width of the street. This is in effect a districting plan. The district changes with each variation in street width. This sort of districting is usual and approved. It may be justified directly on the ground of health and safety. A general plan of districting such as seems needful cannot be justified solely on such grounds. We cannot justify more stringent regulations for dwellings in the suburbs than in lower Manhattan on the ground that light, air and comfort for the residents of the suburbs are of greater public importance than for the residents of lower Manhattan. It seems, however, that such districting can be justified if it can be shown to be essential to the general welfare. If regulations admittedly appropriate and reasonable for suburban areas are admittedly inappropriate and unreasonable for congested areas, the public importance and necessity for districting are clearly shown.

Classification or districting for the purposes of regulation must either be based directly on the purposes for which the police power may be exercised or it must be justified by difference in injury to vested interests. In order to justify more stringent regulations for dwelling-houses in the suburbs than for dwelling-houses in lower Manhattan it must appear either that such regulations for the suburbs are more important to the public health, safety or general welfare than for lower Manhattan, or that while equally important for one or more of these purposes in both districts the suburban regulations would if applied to lower Manhattan interfere so seriously with existing property values as to render them of doubtful expediency or constitutionality. The courts will insist that there be some fair relation between the public good to be secured by the regulation and the private injury suffered. Building regulations must be reasonable in order to be constitutional. There is no absolute standard for all conditions. There must be a reasonable relation between the public object to be gained and the loss of property and liberty suffered. It is clear that any deprivation of individual liberty is a real public loss that must be justified by some greater public gain. It is also clear that extended injury to property interests may cause widespread public loss and consequently should have for its justification as an exercise of the police power some greater public gain. In order to be reasonable there must be a proportionateness of means to ends. This point is dwelt upon at length by Freund in his treatise on the Police Power. He says (sec. 63):

"Leading courts have stated very distinctly that reasonableness is one of the inherent limitations of the police power; so the Supreme Court of Mass.[1]: 'Difference of degree is one of the distinctions by which the right of the legislature to exercise the police power must be determined. Some small limitations of previously existing rights incident to property may be imposed for the sake of preventing a manifest evil. Larger ones could not be without the exercise of the right of eminent domain.' And the Supreme Court of the U. S.[2]: 'A Statute or a regulation provided for therein, is frequently valid or the reverse, according as the fact may be, whether it is a reasonable or an unreasonable exercise of legislative power over the subject matter involved, and in many cases questions of degree are the controlling ones by which to determine the validity, or the reverse, of legislative action,' and in Plessy *v.* Ferguson,[3] in answer to the contention that the principle of separation might be carried to the length of assigning to black and white different quarters of the city for living or different sides of the street for walking, the Supreme Court said: 'The reply to all this is, that every exercise of the police power must be reasonable.' . . . There are few forms of control that cannot become unreasonable by an excess of degree: and there are many cases where no other principle of limitation is discoverable than that of reasonableness."

The districting of a city for building restriction purposes is made necessary by the fundamental characteristic of "reasonableness" which is the essential feature of a valid exercise of the police power. Especially in a great city like New York it becomes necessary that building regulations should vary according to the character of the district and according to the type and

[1] Rideout *v.* Knox, 148 Mass. 368.
[2] Wisconsin M. and P. R. R. Co. *v.* Jacobson, 179 U. S. 287 (1906).
[3] 163 U. S. 537.

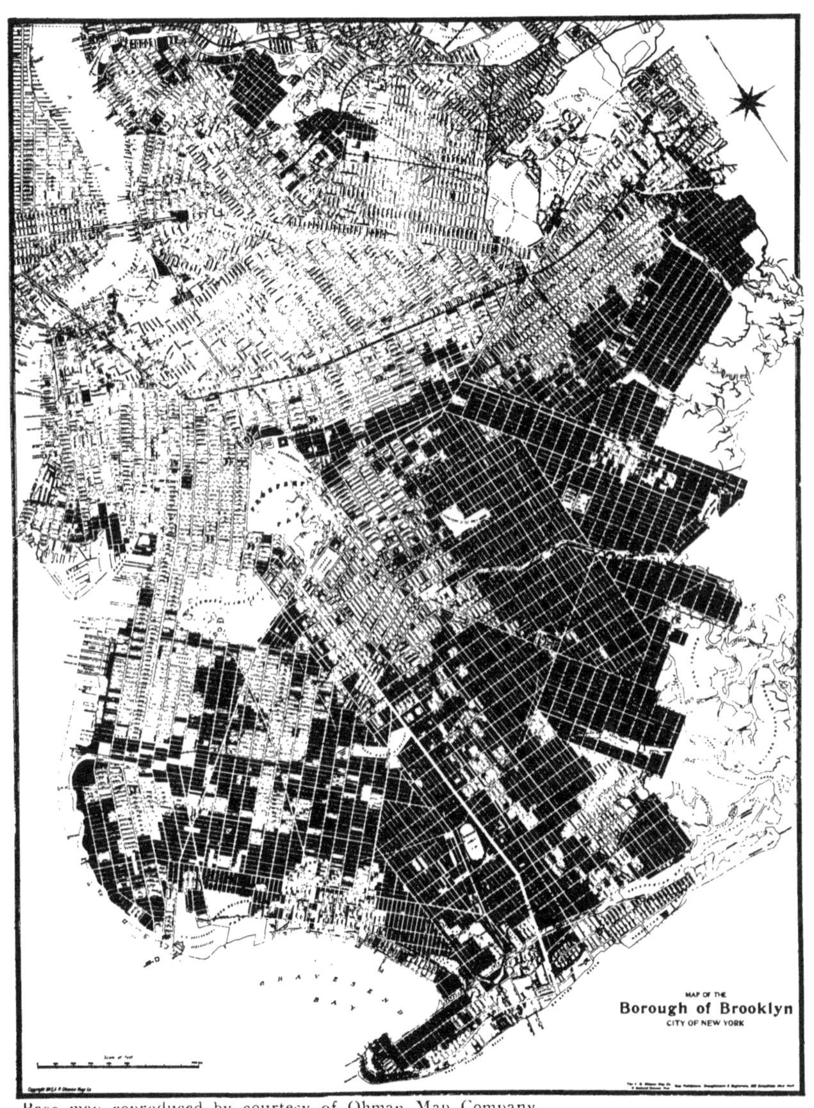

Base map reproduced by courtesy of Ohman Map Company.

MAP V—UNIMPROVED PROPERTY IN BROOKLYN.
Black indicates unimproved land.

use of the building. In certain districts suburban conditions of light and air can be maintained with great public advantage and with slight private loss; in other districts such favorable conditions of light and air while theoretically just as desirable are entirely impracticable and any law that attempted to enforce them would be clearly unreasonable and void.

A classification based on proportionateness of means to ends is recognized in practically all building regulations. General maximum height regulations, for example, apply only to buildings hereafter constructed. In doing so they discriminate in favor of the owners of buildings already constructed. A lopping off of existing buildings in excess of the prescribed height is of no less importance to the health, safety and convenience of the public than the restriction of the height of an equal number of buildings hereafter to be erected. A discrimination in favor of buildings already constructed cannot be justified directly on the grounds for which the police power may be exercised. Such discrimination or classification finds abundant justification, however, when we apply the controlling principle of reasonableness and proportionateness of means to ends. The reconstruction of existing buildings would impose burdens on private owners disproportionate to the public gain. Such regulations would therefore be unreasonable and void. It seems that classification or exemption essential to the reasonableness of a regulation is itself reasonable. This principle constitutes an adequate justification for districting.

While a specific regulation taken by itself may not seem to have a very direct relation to the purposes for which the police power may be invoked, yet when taken as a part of a comprehensive plan for the control of building development throughout the entire city, its relation to such purposes may be unmistakable. Grant that a comprehensive system of districting is essential to the health and general welfare of the city, and it follows that every specific regulation that is an essential part of such comprehensive system is justified under the police power.

Necessity for Districting

In this country comparatively little use has been made of districting. It has been carried out most fully in certain European cities. It is coming to be recognized as essential to well ordered, purposeful, economic and socially beneficial city growth. Haphazard methods of city construction result in a minimum of convenience with a maximum of cost to the public, and, in general, to the individual as well.

The welfare of the people of a city is very largely dependent on the skill and foresight with which the city has been built. Upon this depends their opportunity for agreeable and remunerative occupation, for the enjoyment of leisure and the creation of a home. If factories and offices are dark and poorly ventilated, the worker suffers in health and comfort. If dwellings are huddled together without adequate provision for open spaces and if dwellings, stores and factories are thrown together indiscriminately, the health and comfort of home life are destroyed.

It will pay a city to attempt by every available means to conserve the health and general well-being of its inhabitants. This means increased productivity and increased productivity means higher wages for the laborer, higher profits for the employer and higher rents for the real estate owner.

The need for the creation of special restrictions for special districts is most clearly exemplified in the case of suburban residence districts. Here real estate developers have often found it profitable to secure control of large areas in order by restrictive covenants to insure to intending purchasers of homes the creation and maintenance of a residence section of a certain desired type. The surroundings and neighborhood are all important in securing desirable home conditions. Unless the general character of the section is fixed for a considerable period of years no one can afford to build a home. If he does build, a change in the supposed character of the neighborhood through the building of apartments, stores or factories may render the location undesirable for a home of the character he has built and thus greatly depreciate his investment.

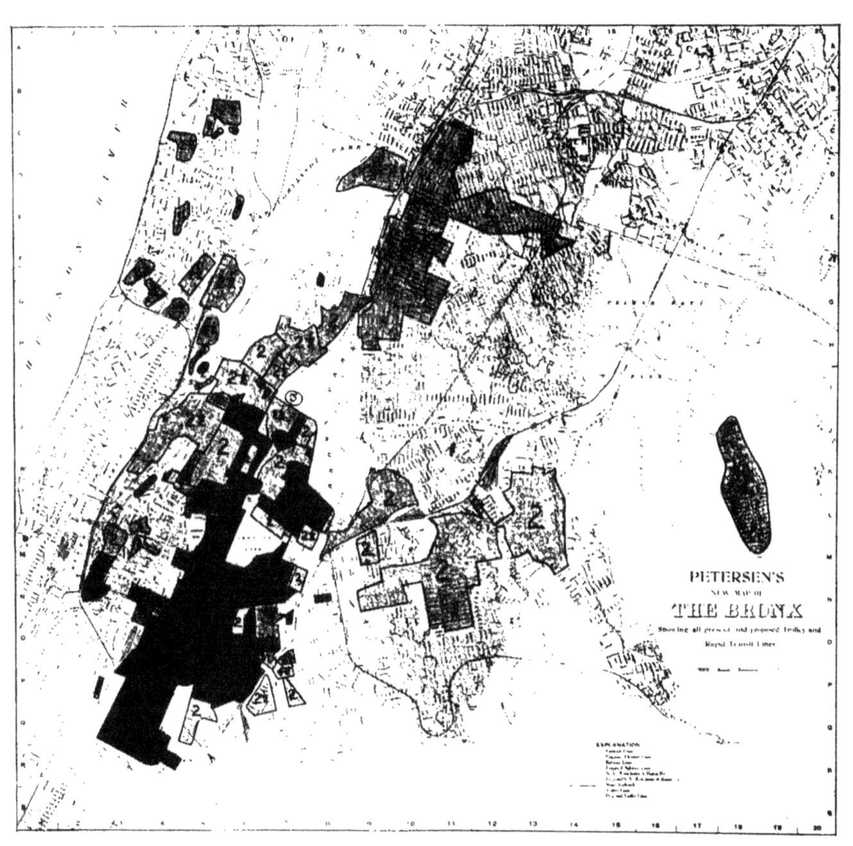

Base map reproduced by courtesy of Ohman Map Company.

MAP VI—HEIGHTS OF RESIDENCE BUILDINGS IN THE BRONX.

Numerals denote height in stories.
Dark shading denotes apartments.

Another general social factor that demands the zoning or districting of the city for building purposes under the police power is the recognized evil of congestion of population as exemplified on the lower East Side. All students of the subject recognize that such congestion of population is a real detriment to the health and civic fitness of the population of the district and a real menace to the welfare of the entire city. The problem is to prevent the repetition of these conditions in other parts of the city. Restrictions that would be upheld as reasonable for the present congested area would be clearly inadequate to prevent the repetition in other districts of conditions almost as bad as those now existing on the lower East Side. The only method by which this can be accomplished is by permitting the creation under the police power of different restrictions for different sections. Surely the prevention of undue congestion of population is a matter of such vital importance to the general welfare that it will justify any reasonable classification of buildings according to type and district; especially if the injury to vested interests resulting from such classification is comparatively small.

Manhattan with its skyscrapers is comparatively undeveloped. It is a fact that a large proportion of the area of lower Manhattan is now so poorly developed that the existing improvements are reckoned of no value for purposes of purchase or sale. The bare value of the land is all that is considered. This means that a large portion of the land of Manhattan is very inadequately utilized. Where space is so scarce this inadequate utilization is a great social and economic loss. This partial development and poor utilization of the land is even more apparent in all the other boroughs. A considerable percentage of the land even in what are considered built up districts, is either vacant or very inadequately utilized. In the suburbs the sprawling character of building development is everywhere apparent. The natural result of a poor utilization of its land area by a city is high rents for occupiers and low profits for investors. It may seem paradoxical to hold that a policy of building restriction tends to a fuller utilization of land than a policy of no restriction, but such is undoubtedly the case. The reason lies in the greater safety and security to investment secured by definite restrictions. The restrictions tend to fix the character of the neighborhood. The owner therefore feels that if he is to secure the maximum returns from his land, he must promptly improve it in conformity with the established restrictions. For example, he will not be deterred from immediate improvement by the consideration that while a detached house is at present an appropriate improvement it is probable that in 10 years an apartment house would be appropriate and that by waiting he will not only be able to reap the advantage of greatly increased land values but will save great depreciation in the value of the detached house due to the fact that it has become an inappropriate improvement for the lot.

The same principle applies in the case of most types of buildings. As a general rule, a building is appropriately located when it is in a section surrounded by buildings of similar type and use, all of which have been constructed with reference to that particular use. Anything that will tend to preserve the character of a particular section for a reasonable period of years, will tend to bring about the uniform improvement of the section. A large proportion of the land of New York City that is now unimproved or poorly improved is in that condition because the owners feel that the character of the section is changing, is bound to change in the near future or that the permanent character of the section is unknown. If restrictions were imposed so that the general character of particular sections could be forecasted with reasonable certainty for a period of years, owners who had been holding back on account of the uncertainties of the situation would find it clearly to their advantage to improve their holdings. The result would be that these restricted sections would be more quickly built up with buildings of similar type and use. This should have the effect of improving living conditions, reducing the cost of living and maintaining real estate values.

Any growing city that fails to control building development must inevitably suffer enormous loss due to building obsolescence. Obsolescence may be defined as lack of adaptation to function. It results from changed conditions and surroundings that render

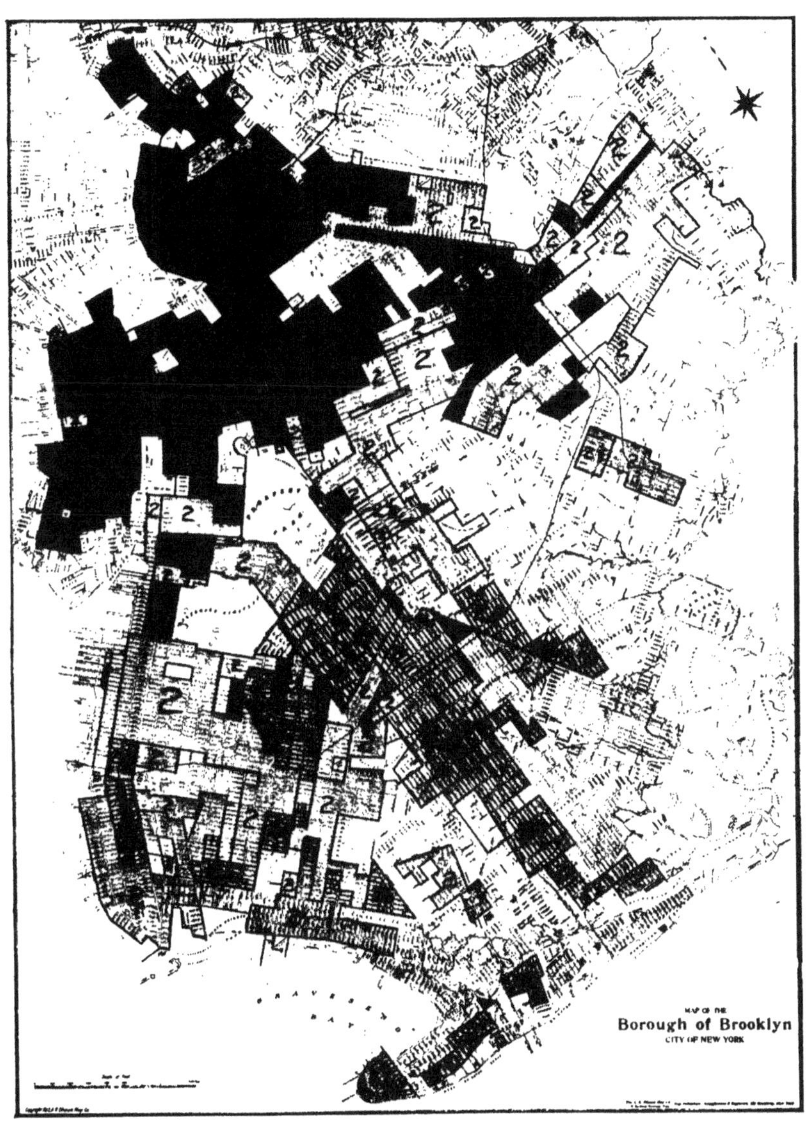

Base map reproduced by courtesy of Ohman Map Company.

MAP VII—HEIGHTS OF RESIDENCE BUILDINGS IN BROOKLYN.
Numerals denote height in stories.

the building an inappropriate improvement for the particular location. The total social loss does not consist merely of the great cost of building reconstruction or of the great decline in the rental value of the inappropriate buildings that are not reconstructed, but there is added to this the social loss due to the retardation of real estate improvements owing directly to the obsolescence hazard.

In a memorandum submitted to the Commission by Frederick L. Ackerman the importance of districting and its superiority over private restrictive covenants is clearly pointed out. Mr. Ackerman says:

" We should not confuse the term 'zoning' with the ideas surrounding the present use of the word 'restriction.' It is true that restrictions upon property are a necessary part of any scheme of zoning, but there is a fundamental difference in the nature of the restrictions. When a group of individuals restrict a section of the city, it is done for the purpose of conserving that section for a particular use. In practice, this object is rarely attained for the simple reason that there are parcels of property within that section which, for one reason or another, are withheld with the result that sooner or later these pieces are used for a purpose detrimental to the adjacent property, causing the restricted property to depreciate in value. Ofttimes the restrictions made by individual owners hamper seriously the growth of a section, and in practice, instead of conserving the section to a better development of the particular activity for which it was intended, these restrictions simply serve as a check upon its development owing to the fact that owners know that sooner or later the restrictions will be removed, when other activities will enter and disintegrate the values. When the city places restrictions over a section, these apply to all properties, with the result that there immediately begins a more permanent development along the lines for which the section is to be used, and properties increase in value.

" We have given too much weight to the ideas surrounding geographical location and have not considered seriously the idea that the value of property depends upon the degree to which a certain section is developed for a certain use. Values appreciate in sections where it is known that the development is to be maintained along definite and well established lines. For instance, the values in office building sections are dependent upon the degree of the development of that section for that particular use. This idea holds in loft, factory, and residential sections, shopping districts, and the like, and experience has taught us that as soon as new elements are introduced into these sections of a nature tending to lower the standard of the section, the values of the properties are correspondingly reduced. There is no economy in the present method of continually shifting geographically the various interests of the city. We should rather foster the idea of developing various sections for a particular use and place a premium upon the erection of permanent, well designed structures within that section, to be used for that particular purpose for which the section is restricted."

Height Districts in American Cities

The chief American examples of districting as applied to the height of buildings are furnished by Boston, Baltimore, Indianapolis and Washington.

Boston

In Boston the entire city has been divided into two districts—District A and District B. In District A, the business section of the city, buildings may not exceed 125 feet in height. In District B, the residential area of the city, buildings may not exceed 80 feet in height except on thoroughfares over 64 feet in width. On such streets, buildings may be erected to a height equal to 1¼ times the width of the street, but no building in District B may be erected to a greater height than 80 feet unless its width on each and every abutting public street is at least one-half of its height. No building, however, in either District A or District B may be of greater height than 2½ times the width of the widest abutting street. This districting has been done under authority of a special act of the legislature through the agency of a commission appointed for the purpose. The regulations, which are considered in detail in Appendix IV, have been upheld by the highest court, both of the State and of the United States.

In regard to the constitutionality of districting, the Massa-

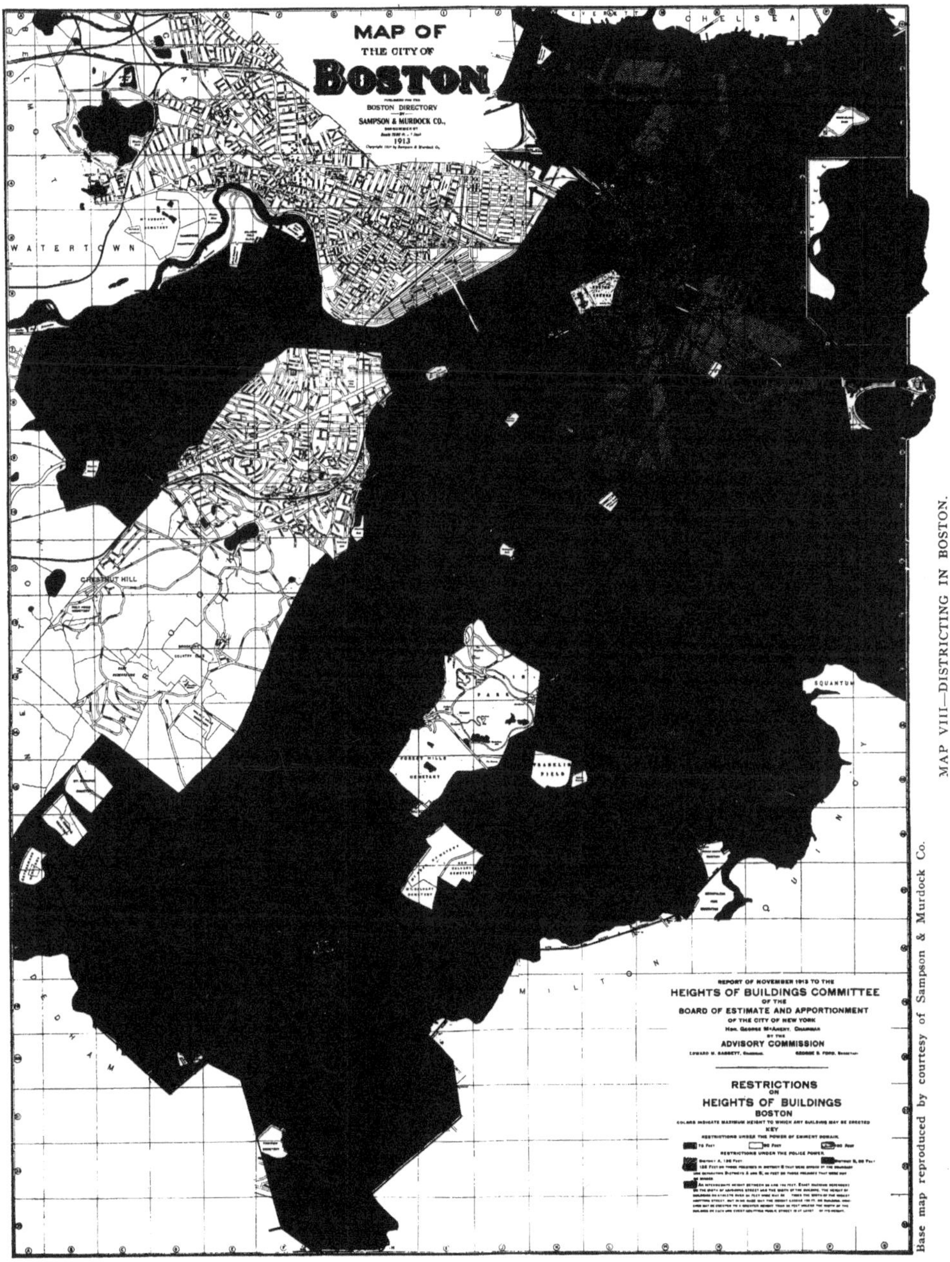

MAP VIII—DISTRICTING IN BOSTON.

Base map reproduced by courtesy of Sampson & Murdock Co.

chusetts court[1] points out that any police regulation must be reasonable "not only in reference to the interests of the public, but also in reference to the rights of landowners." If these rights and interests are in conflict "the opposing considerations should be balanced against each other and each should be made to yield reasonably to those upon the other side." The court indicates that this consideration makes it necessary in considering the height limitation to have reference "to the use for which the real estate probably will be needed." The court calls attention to the fact that the value of land and demand for space in the business district is such as to call for buildings of greater height than in the residential district.

The case was carried to the Supreme Court of the United States and the constitutionality of the act again affirmed. (Welch *v.* Swasey, 214 U. S. 91, 29 Sup. Ct. 567, decided May 17, 1909.) It was contended by the appellant that the real purpose of the act was to preserve architectural symmetry and regular sky line, and that the police power could not be exercised for such a purpose. It was further contended that the infringement upon property rights was unreasonable and disproportional to any public necessity and that the distinction between 125 feet for the height of buildings in District A and 80 feet to 100 feet for buildings in District B was wholly unjustifiable and arbitrary, having no reference to public safety or to any purpose appropriate to the police power. The Supreme Court rejected these contentions, stating that the reasons contained in the opinion of the state court were, in the opinion of the Supreme Court, sufficient to justify the validity of the regulations in question. Justice Peckham, in delivering the opinion of the Court, refers to the justification of the districting provision based on the greater value of land in District A, presented by the state court. He also finds an additional reason for the districting provision in a greater danger in case of fire from tall buildings in a residential district. He says (at page 106-108):

"In this case the Supreme Judicial Court of the State holds the legislation valid, and that there is a fair reason for the discrimi-

[1] Welch *v.* Swasey, 193 Mass. 364, 79 N. E. 745, January 1, 1907.

nation between the height of buildings in the residential as compared with the commercial districts. That court had also held that regulations in regard to the height of buildings, and in regard to their mode of construction in cities, made by legislative enactments for the safety, comfort or convenience of the people and for the benefit of property owners generally are valid. Attorney General *v.* Williams, 174 Mass., 476. We concur in that view, assuming, of course, that the height and conditions provided for can be plainly seen to be not unreasonable or inappropriate.

"In relation to the discrimination or classification made between the commercial and the residential portion of the city, the state court holds in this case that there is reasonable ground therefor in the very great value of the land and the demand for space in those parts of Boston where a greater number of buildings are used for the purpose of business or commercially than where the buildings are situated in the residential portion of the city, and where no such reasons exist for high buildings. . . .

"We are not prepared to hold that this limitation of eighty to one hundred feet, while in fact a discrimination or classification, is so unreasonable that it deprives the owner of property of its profitable use without justification, and that he is therefore entitled under the Constitution to compensation for such invasion of his rights. The discrimination thus made is, we think, reasonable, and is justified by the police power. . . . The reasons contained in the opinion of the state court are in our view sufficient to justify this enactment."

Baltimore

A special act of the Maryland legislature passed in 1904 limited the height of buildings within one block of the Washington Monument in the city of Baltimore to 70 feet. At that time the general maximum height limit for the entire city was 175 feet. The districting act was held to be constitutional by the Court of Appeals of Maryland in a decision of June 24, 1908 (Cochran *v.* Preston, 70 Atl. 113). The appellant in this case claimed that the regulation was an infringement of the constitutional guarantee of equal protection of the laws and due process of law. The statute applied a special rule to a certain small district, and as to that district, provided an exemption in the case of churches. Moreover, the limitation was not uniform for the district, inasmuch as the district was hilly and the statute provided for a uniform limit of height, not exceeding 70 feet "above the surface of the street at the base line of the Washington Monument." Under this restriction a higher building could be erected on lower ground than upon higher ground within the district. The appellant claimed also that the restriction was for the purpose of preserving the beauty and architectural symmetry of the environment of Washington Monument and that in the exercise of the police power, property rights cannot be impaired for purely esthetic purposes. In sustaining the constitutionality of the statute, the court held that its purpose was not purely esthetic, but for the purpose of protecting from fire handsome buildings and works of art in the locality.

The court overruled the objection raised on account of lack of uniformity of application. Owing to the hilly condition of the prescribed territory persons owning property on lower ground would be able to construct higher buildings than those whose property was located on higher ground. This discrimination was also justified on the ground of protection against fire. The exemption of churches from the restriction was also upheld on the ground that churches "do not present the same danger from fire to the surrounding buildings as many other structures do, chiefly because they are not liable to become very numerous in any one locality." On the general subject of regulation the court states that the use of land must be subject to reasonable regulation, in the interest of the general welfare.

Indianapolis

In 1912 the city council of Indianapolis passed an ordinance limiting the maximum height of all buildings erected in the city at 200 feet. An ordinance of 1905 limits the height of buildings erected on Monument Place at 86 feet. Monument Place is the circular street encompassing the Soldiers' and Sailors' Monument. It has a diameter of about 600 feet and an outside circumference of about 1880 feet. The constitutionality of the ordinance has never been tested in the courts.

Washington

Washington is districted for height limitation purposes under an act of Congress applicable to the District of Columbia. The regulations are more stringent than those of any other city in this country with the possible exception of Boston. The limitations in the business section are a trifle more lenient than those in Boston, but in the residence section they are more rigid. All streets are designated as either business streets or residential streets. No building may be erected on a business street to a greater height than the width of the widest abutting street increased by 20 feet, subject, however, to an absolute limit of 130 feet. An exception to this regulation is made in two instances. Buildings on the north side of Pennsylvania Avenue, between First and Fifteenth Streets, are allowed an extreme height of 160 feet. Buildings fronting or abutting on the plaza in front of the new Union Station may not exceed a height of 80 feet. On residential streets the maximum height limit is 85 feet subject to certain provisions. The height may not exceed the width of the street diminished by 10 feet on streets more than 70 feet in width. The height may not exceed 60 feet on streets between 60 and 70 feet in width. The height may not exceed the width of the street on streets less than 60 feet in width. The constitutionality of these regulations does not appear to have been tested.

Regulation of Open Spaces in Richmond, Virginia

By an act of the general assembly of Virginia passed March 14, 1908, councils of cities and towns are authorized, among other things, "to make regulations concerning the building of houses in the city or town, and in their discretion . . . in particular districts or along particular streets, to prescribe and establish building lines, or to require property owners in certain localities or districts to leave a certain percentage of lots free from buildings, and to regulate the height of buildings." (Acts 1908, pp. 623, 624.) By virtue of this act, the city council of Richmond passed an ordinance "that whenever the owners of

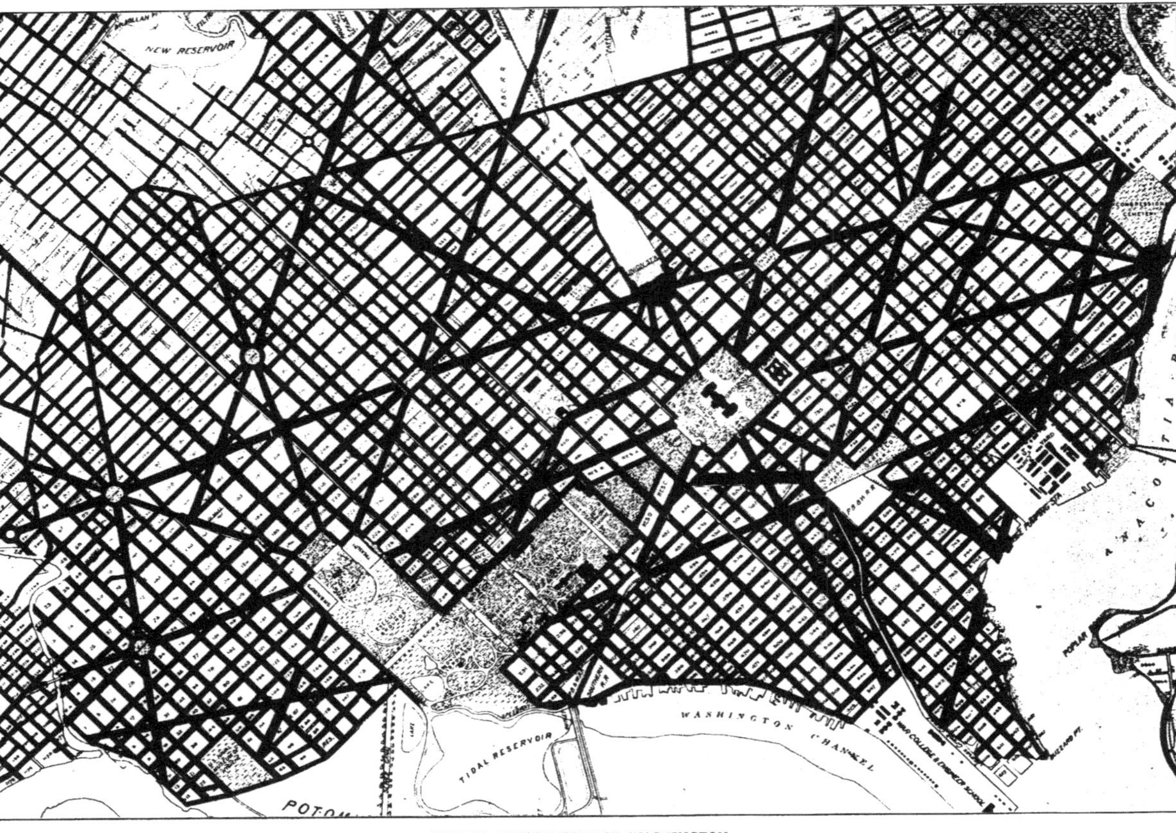

MAP IX—DISTRICTING IN WASHINGTON.

Key to Height Limitations: Olive, 160 feet; red, 130 feet; yellow, 95 feet; green, 90 feet; blue, 80 feet; lavender, 60-85 feet; white, street width.

two-thirds of the property abutting on any street shall, in writing, request the committee on streets to establish a building line on the side of the square on which their property fronts, the said committee shall establish such line so that the same shall not be less than five feet nor more than thirty feet from the street line."

The validity of a building line regulation under the above ordinance came before the Supreme Court of Appeals of Virginia in Eubank *v.* City of Richmond, 110 Va. 749, 67 S. E. 376, decided March 10, 1910. In delivering the opinion of the court Judge Whittle refers to the case of Welch v. Swasey and concludes as follows:

"In the present case the statute is neither unreasonable nor unusual, and we are justified in concluding that it was passed by the Legislature in good faith and in the interest of the health, safety, comfort, or convenience of the public, and for the benefit of the property owners generally who are affected by its provisions, and that the enactment tends to accomplish all, or at least some, of these objects. The validity of such legislation is generally recognized and upheld."

The case was appealed to the Supreme Court of the United States (Eubank *v.* City of Richmond, 33 Sup. Ct. 76, decided December 2, 1913). Justice McKenna in delivering the opinion of the court first comments generally on the police power as follows:

"Whether it is a valid exercise of the police power is a question in the case, and that power we have defined, as far as it is capable of being defined by general words, a number of times. It is not susceptible of circumstantial precision. It extends, we have said, not only to regulations which promote the public health, morals and safety, but to those which promote the public convenience or the general prosperity. But necessarily it has its limits and must stop when it encounters the prohibitions of the Constitution. A clash will not, however, be lightly inferred. Governmental power must be flexible and adaptive. Exigencies arise, or even conditions less peremptory, which may call for or suggest legislation, and it may be a struggle in judgment to decide whether it must yield to the higher considerations expressed and determined by the provisions of the Constitution."

The court found the regulation unconstitutional, its finding being based on the fact that under the ordinance a building line must be established whenever two-thirds of the property owners abutting on any street shall petition the committee on streets to establish such a line. The court holds that an important power of this kind cannot be vested in any number of property owners with power to use as they see fit and presumably in their own interest and not in the interest of public comfort or convenience. Though the particular ordinance in question was held to be unconstitutional, the opinion of the state court and the general treatment of the case by the Supreme Court of the United States give considerable ground for the hope that building line regulations properly based will be held constitutional. This is clearly the view of the matter taken by the city of Richmond, for, following the above decision by the Supreme Court of the United States, it passed another ordinance (April 22, 1913) prescribing the procedure by which building lines may be established in the discretion of the council in particular districts or along particular streets.

Residential and Industrial Districts in American Cities

The legislation of the past few years shows a distinct trend toward the creation of specially restricted residential districts. Legislation has been enacted by New York, Massachusetts, Minnesota, Wisconsin, Maryland and Virginia. Ordinances have been passed in Richmond, Milwaukee, Minneapolis, Seattle and Los Angeles.

New York cities of the second class

The new housing law for cities of the second class, passed by the New York legislature in 1913 (ch. 774) authorized the common council on petition of two-thirds of the owners affected to establish residence districts within which no building other than a single family or a two family dwelling may be constructed. A residence district once created shall continue as

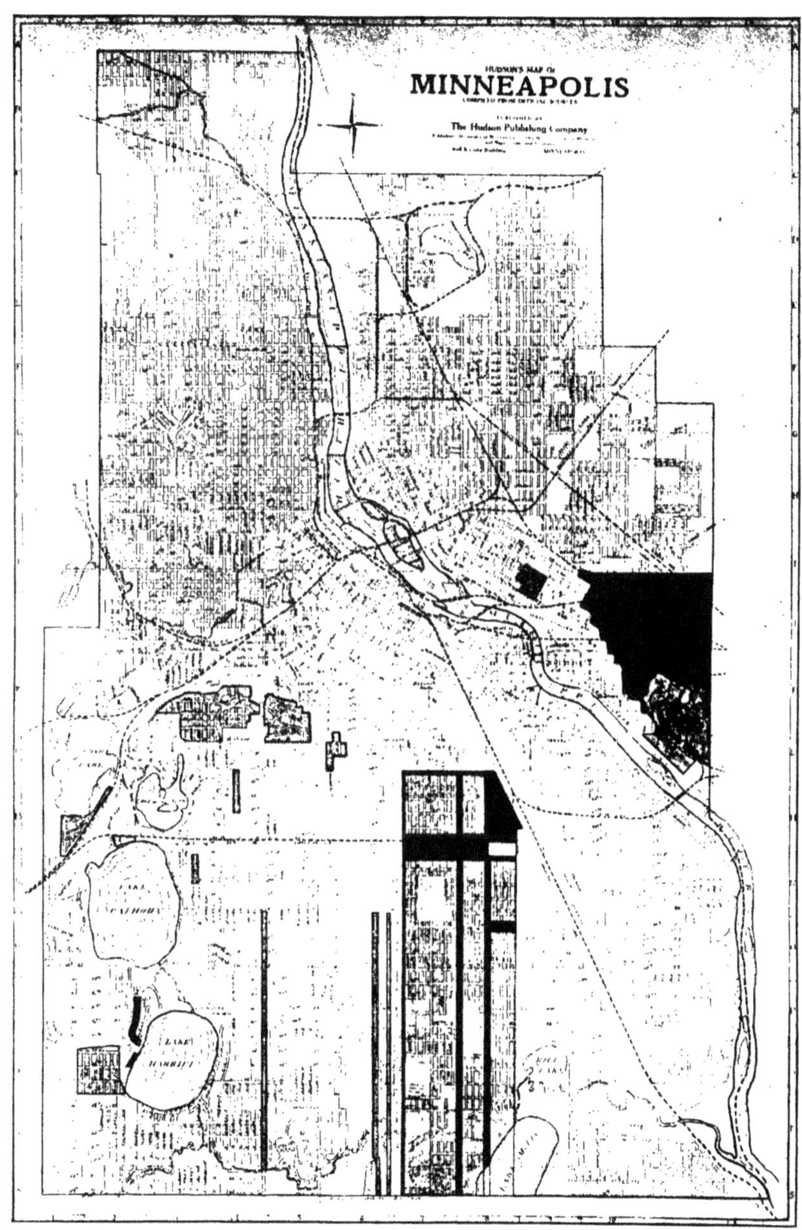

Base map reproduced by permission of the Hudson Publishing Co.

MAP X—DISTRICTING IN MINNEAPOLIS.

Darker shading indicates industrial districts.
Lighter shading indicates residential districts.

such until a like petition shall be presented to and approved by the common council. The unit of area for the residence district consists of the lots fronting on one side of a street between two intersecting streets.

Massachusetts

In 1912 the legislature of Massachusetts passed an amendment to the general municipal act (chapter 334, laws 1912) that permits every city and town in the state, except Boston, to regulate the height, area, location, and use of buildings and other structures within the whole or any defined part of its limits for the prevention of fire and the preservation of life, health and morals. The power extends to all buildings and other structures except bridges, quays and wharves and structures owned or occupied by the national or state government.

Minnesota

The legislature of Minnesota at its last session (laws 1913, ch. 420) passed an act empowering the cities of Duluth, Minneapolis and St. Paul to establish residential and industrial districts. The city council, when petitioned by 50 per cent of the property owners in a district, may by a two-thirds vote designate it as being either a residential or an industrial district. The erection and maintenance of any industrial or business establishment, no matter what its character, may be excluded from a residential district. Even tenements, apartment houses and hotels may be excluded from such a district. In the designation of industrial districts, the city council is authorized to classify the various industries and in its discretion to restrict each class to a definite and limited area. Upon a petition of 50 per cent of the property owners in a district, the council may set aside its original restrictions, and establish an industrial district out of a residential district, or vice versa.

Minneapolis has already taken advantage of this act on several different occasions. The city council has passed ordinances classifying and designating certain buildings, business occupations, industries and enterprises as business industries and defining and designating certain districts in the city as industrial and residential districts, within which such buildings, occupations or enterprises may or may not be maintained or carried on. The question of the constitutionality of these ordinances has not as yet come before the courts.

Wisconsin

The legislature of Wisconsin at its last session passed an act (laws 1913, chapter 743) authorizing cities of 25,000 inhabitants or more to set aside exclusive residential districts. There are at present eight cities in the state of this size—Milwaukee, Green Bay, La Crosse, Madison, Oshkosh, Racine, Sheboygan and Superior.

The common council may set apart portions of the city to be used exclusively for residential purposes and may prohibit the erection and maintenance of factories, docks or other similar concerns within such districts. The council may also restrain the encroachment of business houses upon purely residence districts, and require the consent of the majority of landowners and residents of such districts, before such business is permitted. The power granted may be exercised upon the initiative of the common council, or upon the petition of ten or more residents in the district or block to be affected. The enactment of ordinances excluding factories, docks or other similar concerns from residential districts shall be a final and conclusive finding that factories operated in such districts are detrimental to the health, comfort and welfare of the residents of the city. Milwaukee is at present mapping out residential districts in accordance with this act.

On January 13, 1913, several months prior to the passage of the above act, the common council of Milwaukee passed an ordinance making it unlawful to maintain slaughter houses, rendering plants or rag shops anywhere inside the city limits.

This ordinance also established what is known as "the business section." Businesses within the business section are subject to no restrictions, but outside the business section the ordinance forbids the maintenance of certain businesses unless such business shall first obtain the written consent of two-thirds of all the

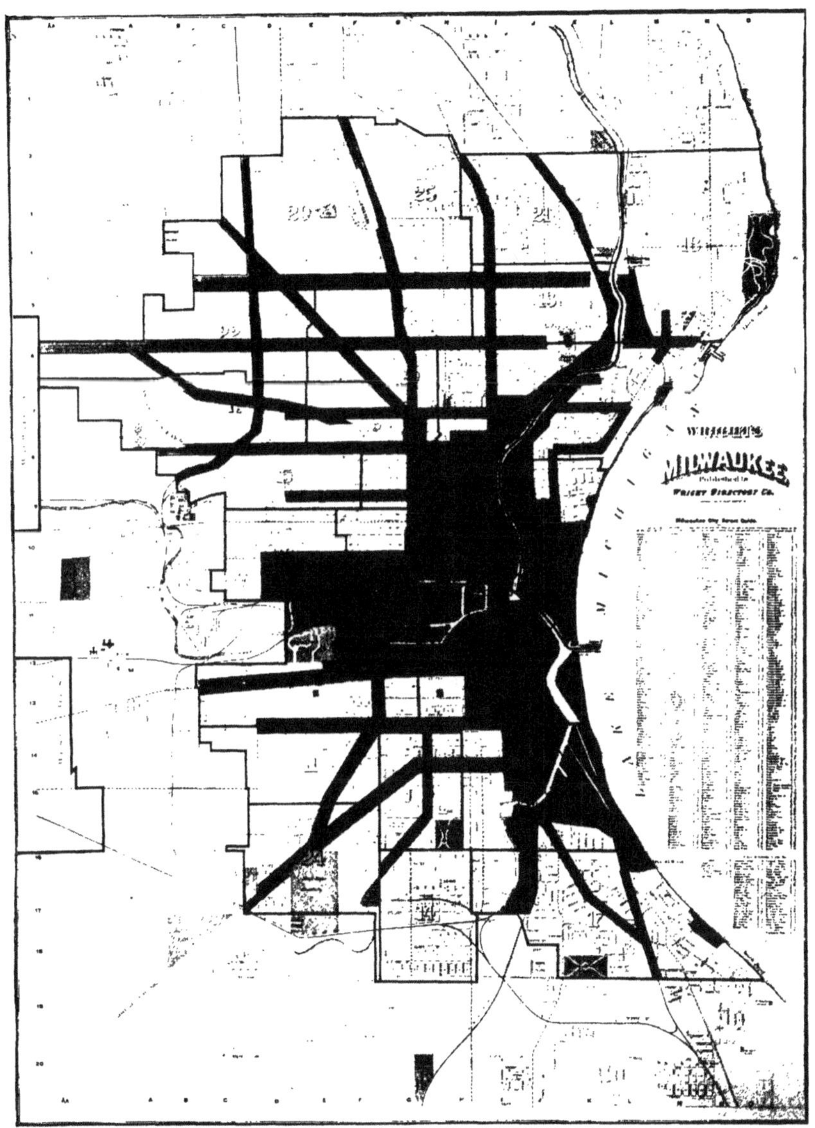

By courtesy of Wright Directory Co.

MAP XI—DISTRICTING IN MILWAUKEE.
Industries are unrestricted in shaded area.

real estate owners within 300 feet of the space proposed to be occupied. The businesses coming within the prohibition are: Livery, boarding or sales stables, gas reservoirs or holders, paint, oil or varnish works, salesrooms or storage rooms for automobiles and garages for the keeping of automobiles for hire. When outside the business section these businesses must be maintained in buildings that conform to the requirements prescribed within the fire district. An ordinance passed on January 11, 1913, imposes similar conditions on garages maintained in certain blocks in the business section that are of a residential character. No garage may be maintained in a block where two-thirds of the buildings in a block are devoted exclusively to residential purposes without the written consent of the property owners on both sides of the street or alley in such block.

Baltimore

In 1912 the state legislature of Maryland passed an act (ch. 693) regulating the erection of dwelling houses in that part of the city of Baltimore known as Forest Park. The dwelling houses constructed in this district, the area of which is about a half mile square, must be separate and unattached buildings. Frame dwellings must be at least 20 feet apart; stone and brick dwellings at least 10 feet apart. The constitutionality of the act has not come before the courts.

The most important classification of buildings according to character and use in the city of Baltimore, as a whole, is that found in section 47 of the building code. This section (subdivisions 12 and 13) limits the location of certain buildings. These buildings are: (1) hospitals and buildings for treatment of the feeble-minded; (2) sanatoriums; (3) livery stables; (4) sale and boarding stables; (5) garages; (6) blacksmith shops; (7) junk shops; (8) brick, tile and terra cotta factories; (9) stoneware and earthenware factories; (10) paint factories; (11) soap factories; (12) candle factories; (13) woodworking factories; (14) the storing and altering of packing boxes on any lot or in any building; (15) lumber yards; (16) planing mills; (17) iron mills; (18) foundries; (19) breweries;

(20) distilleries; (21) packing houses; (22) gas works; (23) acid works; (24) the manufacture of fertilizers.

No permit for the erection of any of the above buildings is given by the inspector of buildings except by the approval of the mayor. In granting his approval, the mayor incorporates such regulations in the permit regarding the location of the building as may, in his judgment, be necessary to safeguard the interests of the public. Permits for such buildings are issued only after 10 days' public notice of the application therefor.

If protests are filed against the granting of the permit, the building inspector holds a hearing. After hearing the protests and considering the rights of the surrounding property owners, the building inspector makes a presentation of the facts to the mayor. Where there is a protest, the permit requires the joint approval of the inspector and the mayor. In granting or withholding their approval to a permit, the building inspector and the mayor are prompted by three considerations: (1) the fire hazard of the proposed building; (2) the effect of the proposed building on surrounding land values; and (3) the effect of the proposed building on the general welfare of the residents in the immediate vicinity.

Seattle

Under the Seattle building code adopted in July, 1913, no building not now used for such purposes may be reconstructed, altered or repaired to be used for any of the following purposes without the consent of the city council and the mayor: (1) confinement of insane children or adults; (2) manufacture of cotton wadding, laps or bats; (3) refining of petroleum or any of its products; (4) distillation of spirits of turpentine or varnish; (5) manufacture of explosives; (6) rendering of fats, lards and like products; (7) hair factory; (8) lime kiln; (9) tannery; (10) refinery; (11) abattoir; (12) glue factory; (13) manufacture of roofing materials of chemical composition; (14) pulverizing charcoal; (15) stockyards; (16) poudrette works; (17) asphalt plant; (18) manufacture of fertilizers; (19) smelter.

Before any ordinance shall be passed authorizing the construction, alteration and repair of any "prohibited" building at least 10 days' notice shall be given by the party applying for the passage of such ordinance by a publication to that effect of at least four insertions in two or more daily newspapers. This notice must specify the lot upon which such building is to be erected, altered or repaired and the purposes for which it is intended to be used in sufficient detail to apprise the property owners in the vicinity of the exact location and nature of the proposed improvement. Notice of such application must, moreover, be conspicuously posted on the property.

In addition to the above, the following buildings are limited as to location: (1) hospitals and buildings for treatment of the feeble minded; (2) sanatoriums; (3) dairies; (4) dog pounds; (5) blacksmith shops; (6) junk shops; (7) rag shops; (8) brick, tile and terra cotta factories; (9) stoneware and earthenware factories; (10) paint factories; (11) soap factories; (12) candle factories; (13) woodworking factories; (14) lumber yards; (15) planing mills; (16) iron mills; (17) foundries; (18) breweries; (19) distilleries; (20) packing houses; (21) gas works; (22) acid works.

No permit is issued for a "limited" building until at least 10 days' notice of the application has been published four times in two or more daily papers and until notice of such application has been conspicuously posted upon the property for a like period of time. If any owner of property within 500 feet of the proposed location files a protest with the superintendent of buildings, the matter is referred to the board of public works for determination, after hearing. Special regulations govern the location of stables and public garages.

Los Angeles

The first districting ordinance in Los Angeles was passed in 1909. The entire city, with the exception of two suburbs, is divided into industrial and residential districts. There are twenty-five industrial districts and one residential district. The residential district comprises the whole districted territory exclusive of the areas within the several industrial districts. It therefore encircles and surrounds many of the industrial districts.

The so-called industrial districts do not fairly indicate the extent of the industrial area of the city. In addition to the industrial districts there are fifty-eight districts, known as "residence exceptions," in the residential district that are exempt from the regulations applicable to the residential district and in which business is permitted subject to certain conditions.

The industrial districts vary considerably in shape and size. The largest district has an area of several square miles. At its greatest dimensions, it measures five miles in length and two miles in width. The smallest district comprises one solitary lot. The combined area of the several industrial districts aggregates not more than one-tenth that of the residential district. The industrial districts are, on the whole, pretty well grouped in one part of the city.

The "residence exceptions" are all small. The largest is about a half mile square. With this exception no "residence exception" covers a greater area than two city blocks. In most instances these districts do not occupy more than one or two lots. The combined area of the fifty-eight "residence exceptions" is probably not more than one per cent of the residential district. The "residence exceptions" are, however, scattered more widely throughout the residential district than are the industrial districts.

In general the distinction between the industrial districts and the residential district is this: All kinds of business and manufacturing establishments are unrestrained in most of the industrial districts, while certain specified businesses are excluded from the residential district. Those businesses not especially excluded are permitted in the residential district. All but the very lightest manufacturing is prohibited in the residential district. The less offensive business and manufacturing establishments excluded from the residential district may be carried on in the "residence exceptions." The owners of sixty per cent of the neighboring

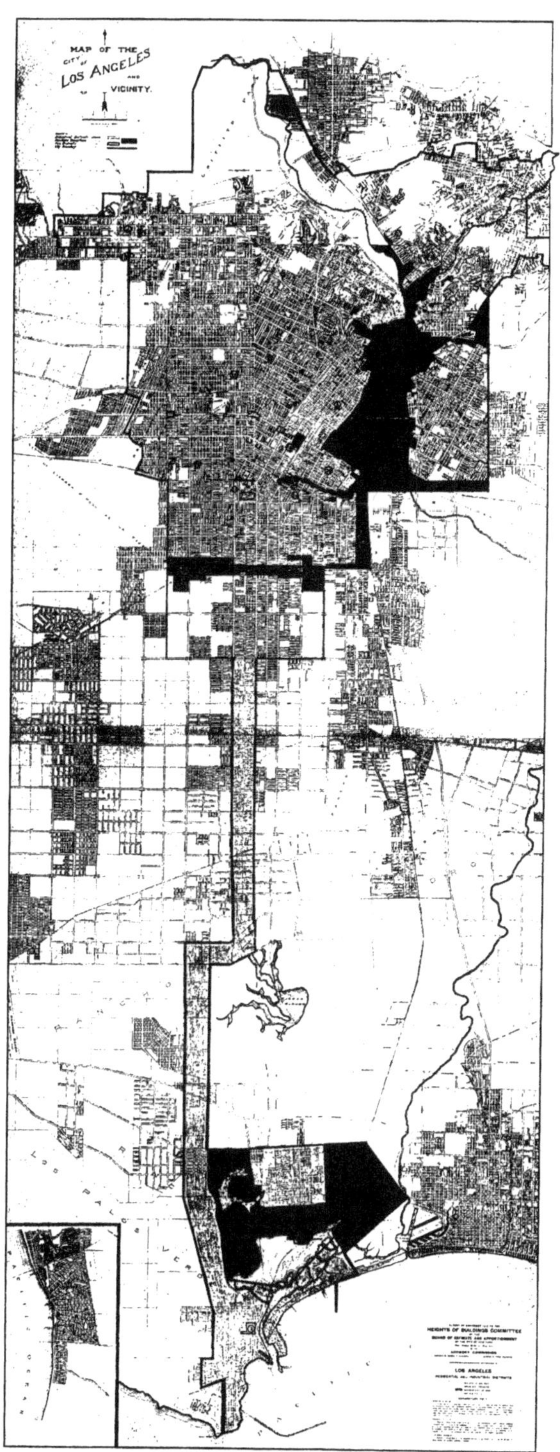

MAP XII—DISTRICTING IN LOS ANGELES.

Dark shading indicates industrial districts and "residence exceptions." Unshaded portion above panhandle, residence district.

property frontage must give their consent to the creation of any "residence exception." (See also Appendix IV.)

The constitutionality of the industrial and residential districts in Los Angeles was sustained by the Supreme Court of California in October, 1911, in the case of Ex Parte Quong Wo, 161 Cal. 220, 118 Pac. 714.

When the city had been districted about 110 Chinese and Japanese laundries found themselves in the residential district. The city immediately undertook to remove them to the industrial districts. The present mayor, Mr. H. H. Rose, then a police judge, upheld the ordinance and sentenced a Chinaman, Quong Wo, to pay a fine of $100 or to serve 100 days in jail. Wo appealed to the Supreme Court of the state, and the ordinance was sustained.

The petitioner, a native and citizen of China, was charged with having maintained and carried on a public laundry and wash house within the residential district. He had conducted such laundry and wash house at said location, occupying the premises under a lease which had two years yet to run.

The court stated that it could not take judicial notice that there had been unjust discrimination in excepting small parcels from the residential district of the city as established by ordinance, and adding them to the industrial district; the presumption being in favor of the legality of the action of the legislative body. That small parcels, consisting of only one city lot, were excepted by the city council from the "residence district" of a city as fixed by ordinance, within which district certain occupations could not be followed, and added to the industrial district, when such parcels were surrounded on all sides by parts of the "residence district," did not of itself show unjust discrimination in excepting territory from the residence district.

The court held that lawful occupations, such as laundry business, might be confined to certain limits in the city wherever such restrictions might reasonably be found necessary to protect the public health, morals and comfort. An ordinance prohibiting the maintenance of public laundries and wash houses in those parts of the city designated as the "residential district" could not be said to be unreasonable and invalid, though large parts of such districts might be sparsely built up, in the absence of facts showing unjust discrimination. Whether restrictions upon the operation of a business in certain portions of a city are reasonably necessary for the protection of the public health, safety and welfare, the court construed as being primarily for the determination of the city council. Such action by the city council, the court held, would not be disturbed by the court, unless the regulations had no relation to the public health, safety or welfare, or unless they clearly invaded personal or property rights under the guise of police regulations.

In Ex Parte Montgomery, 163 Cal. 457, 125 Pac. 1070, the Supreme Court rendered a decision that was almost identical with that in Ex Parte Quong Wo, this time ejecting a lumber yard from the residential district.

In Ex Parte Hadacheck, 132 Pac. 589, decided May 15, 1913, the Supreme Court again sustained the constitutionality of the industrial and residential districts. In this case, the petitioner owned a brick yard in the residential district. He had acquired the land for this brick yard in 1902, before the territory to which the ordinance was directed had been annexed to Los Angeles. The land contained valuable deposits of clay suitable for the manufacture of brick, and was more valuable for brickmaking than for any other purpose. The petitioner had during the entire period of his ownership used the land for brickmaking and had erected on it the kilns, machinery and buildings necessary for such manufacture.

In upholding the constitutionality and ejecting the brick yard from the residential district, the court held that the police power is not restricted to the suppression of nuisances, but extends to the regulation of the conduct of business and to the use of property to the end that public health or morals may not be impaired or endangered.

The court also held that the right of the legislature, in exercising the police power to regulate or in proper cases to prohibit the conduct of a given business, is not limited by the fact that the value of investments made in the business prior to any legislative action will be greatly diminished. A business which, when established, is entirely unobjectionable, may by the growth of population in the vicinity become a source of danger to the health and comfort of those who have come to be occupants of the surrounding territory. If the legislature should then prohibit its further conduct, the proprietor can have no complaint upon the mere fact that he has been carrying on the trade in that locality for a long time. The power to regulate the use of property or the conduct of a business is, of course, not arbitrary. The restriction must bear a reasonable relation to some legitimate purpose within the purview of the police power.

Where a region surrounding a brick yard has become primarily a residential section, and the occupants of neighboring dwellings are seriously discommoded by the operations of the yard, the court held that a prohibition of the business in the district is not objectionable, as being an arbitrary invasion of private right, but is a valid exercise of police power to prevent injury to others.

Where there are reasons justifying the prohibition of a business within an area described in an ordinance adopted by a city, the court states that in determining the validity of the prohibition, it will not consider whether conditions in other parts of the city require a like prohibition, as that presents a legislative question.

Ontario, Canada

The councils of cities having a population of not less than 100,000 may under section 410 of the Ontario Municipal Act pass by-laws prohibiting, regulating and controlling the location or erection of apartment or tenement houses and of garages to be used for hire within any defined area or on land abutting on defined highways or parts of highways. An apartment or tenement house is a building that provides three or more separate suites or sets of rooms for separate occupation by one or more persons. Toronto has, in accordance with these provisions, restricted the character of the development of a large portion of its territory. Apartment houses and garages are excluded from most of the residential streets of the city.

The Municipal Act of Ontario (Sec. 409) empowers the council of every city in the Province to pass by-laws preventing, regulating and controlling the location, erection and use of the following buildings: livery, boarding or sales stables; stables in which horses are kept for hire or kept for use with vehicles in conveying passengers, or for express purposes; stables for horses for delivery purposes; laundries; butcher shops; stores; factories; blacksmith shops; forges; dog kennels and hospitals or infirmaries for horses, dogs or other animals. The erection or use of buildings for all or any of these purposes may be prohibited within any defined area or areas or on land abutting on any defined highway or part of a highway. By-laws of this character may not be passed except by a vote of two-thirds of all the members of the council. Such by-laws, moreover, may not apply to a building which was on April 26, 1904, erected or used for any of these purposes so long as it is used as it was used on that date.

Districting in German cities

Districting is most fully developed in German cities. There it is known as the zone system. The term zone was particularly appropriate in Germany where special regulations were applied to the successive belts of building development surrounding the central walled city. At present, however, in many German cities the districts are not concentric zones, and the system might more appropriately be called the "district system."

The district system is a method of regulating buildings as a part of a general city plan. It has two characteristics: it groups buildings of different classes and it limits the density of buildings progressively, allowing buildings to be higher, and to cover more of the lot, in the centers where land values are greater and business needs require more concentration, and making the requirements more and more severe as the distance from these centers increases.

Under the German rules the height of buildings is invariably

Bauzonenplan von Frankfurt a. M.

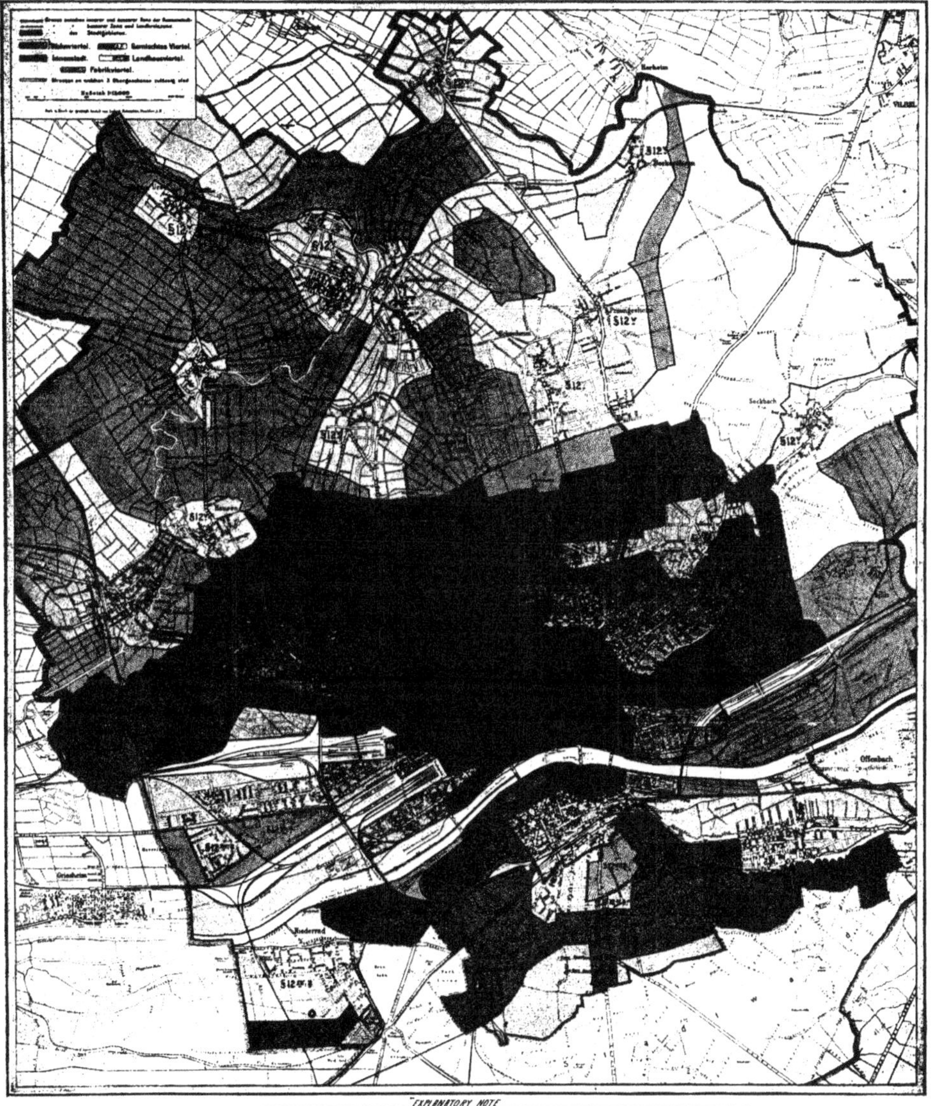

MAP XIII—DISTRICTING IN FRANKFORT.

EXPLANATORY NOTE

DISTRICT—(a)	INDUSTRIAL AND RESIDENTIAL	INDUSTRIAL AND RESIDENTIAL	RESIDENTIAL	INDUSTRIAL AND RESIDENTIAL	INDUSTRIAL AND RESIDENTIAL	RESIDENTIAL	SUBURBAN RESIDENTIAL	RURAL RESIDENTIAL	INDUSTRIAL	STREET ON WHICH FOUR STORIES TO CORNICE ARE ALLOWED
CHARACTER OF BUILDING	BLOCK C	BLOCK C IN STREET WITHOUT FRONT GARDENS, IN OTHERS DETACHED	DETACHED	BLOCK C IN STREETS WITHOUT FRONT GARDENS, IN OTHERS DETACHED	DETACHED	DETACHED, BLOCKS BY SPECIAL LICENSE	DETACHED, BLOCKS BY SPECIAL LICENSE	DETACHED DOUBLE HOUSES BY SPECIAL LICENSE	BLOCK C ONLY OWNER, WATCHMAN ETC. MAY LIVE IN DISTRICT	
MINIMUM OPEN SPACE BETWEEN BUILDING AND SIDE LINE OF LOT (g)		9.8 FEET	9.8 FEET	9.8 FEET	9.8 FEET	13.1 FEET	13.1 FEET	13.1 FEET		
MAXIMUM LENGTH OF BLOCKS IN TERRITORY OF DETACHED BUILDING		262 FEET	262 FEET	262 FEET	262 FEET	262 FEET	262 FEET			
MINIMUM OPEN SPACE — INTERIOR LOT	1/4	4/10 (EXCLUSIVE OF FRONT GARDENS; DOUBLE HOUSES AN EXTRA 107.6 SQUARE FEET, DWELLINGS WITH MORE THAN 4 ROOMS AND KITCHEN AN EXTRA 1/20)		5/10 (DOUBLE HOUSES AN EXTRA 107.6 SQUARE FEET; DWELLINGS WITH MORE THAN 4 ROOMS AN EXTRA 1/10)				7/10	3/10 OF LOT BACK OF BUILDING LINE	
MINIMUM OPEN SPACE — CORNER LOT	1/6	3/10		4/10				7/10		
HEIGHT LIMIT TO CORNICE (c) — IN GENERAL	STREET WIDTH + 6.6–9.8 FEET	STREET WIDTH + 1/3 WIDTH OF FRONT GARDEN		STREET WIDTH + 2/3 WIDTH OF FRONT GARDEN					STREET WIDTH + 6.6 FEET	
HEIGHT LIMIT TO CORNICE (c) — MAXIMUM	65.6 FEET	59.1 FEET	59.1 FEET	59.1 FEET	52.5 FEET	59.1 FEET	52.5 FEET	52.5 FEET	65.6 FEET	
LIMIT OF NUMBER OF STORIES — TO CORNICE	5	4	4	2-3 (d)	2-3 (d)	2-3 (d)	2 (e)	2	NONE	
LIMIT OF NUMBER OF STORIES — ROOF STORY FOR RESIDENCE		1/2	1/2	ALL (f)	ALL	ALL	ALL	ALL		

(a)—INOFFENSIVE INDUSTRIES ARE ALLOWED IN ALL DISTRICTS
(b)—HEIGHT OF ROOF ABOVE CORNICE LIMITED BY AN ANGLE, ROOMS NOT FOR RESIDENCE ALLOWED IN ROOF IN ALL DISTRICTS EXCEPT THE PURELY INDUSTRIAL DISTRICT
(c)—NO OPEN SPACE REQUIRED BETWEEN HOUSE AND SIDE LINES OF LOT
(d)—STREETS 43.9 FEET WIDE AND LESS, 2; OTHERS 3
(e)—STREETS 39.1 FEET WIDE AND LESS, 2; OTHERS 3
(f)—PART OF DISTRICT, BUILDINGS 3 STORIES (EXCLUSIVE OF ROOF) AND MAY NOT CONTAIN INDEPENDENT DWELLINGS
(g)—RECKONED AS PART OF MINIMUM OPEN SPACE

regulated with relation to the width of the street upon which the building is situated; and also, usually, by a maximum which, irrespective of the width of the street, it must not exceed. In many cities, in the zone or zones of greatest concentration, a height a little in excess of the street width is allowed; in the other zones it must not exceed that width, and in the outer zone or zones the maximum limits it to less. Usually, too, there are minimum courts, and all rooms constructed for the residence or long continued business use of mankind must have a window upon a court of at least a specified size. The proportion of the lot that may be covered by buildings, also, is almost invariably limited progressively, buildings on corner lots in each zone being allowed to cover more than those on inside lots. The ordinances in the different cities differ in detail, but in general the system is the same. The provisions of the Frankfort ordinance illustrate it as well as any other:

The old or inner city is the first zone or district. Here the highest buildings are allowed. They must not exceed the width of the street, plus about 10 feet (three meters). Or in any case, however wide the street, about 66 feet (20 meters). This is to the cornice; the roof above this is restricted by an angle, and in no case may exceed about 30 feet (nine meters). The roof is more than mere roof; it is a roof story, in which there are rooms, which, however, may not always be used for residence. The number of stories is also restricted; in this zone it must not exceed five, and the roof story.

Here in the inner city, also, the greatest proportion of the lot may be covered with buildings, three-quarters—for corner lots five-sixths. Factories are allowed, but are not numerous. Solid blocks are permitted. The city here presents the appearance of being fully built up to a fairly uniform height.

The outer city is divided into an outer, an inner, and a country zone, in which the height of buildings allowed progressively decreases, and the amount of the lot that must be left free of buildings progressively increases. In each of these zones are residence, factory and mixed sections. In the residence sections, factories are so discouraged as to be practically forbidden. In the factory sections, situated along the railroads, the harbor, and out of the city in the direction so that the prevailing winds will blow the smoke away from the city, residences are forbidden. In the factory sections, the restrictions on height and amount of lot covered do not become progressively greater. The mixed sections are near the factory sections, and there, too, under certain mild restrictions, many sorts of manufacturing are permitted.

In the residence section a space between neighboring houses of about 10 feet (three meters) in the inner zone and a third more in the outer zone is required. Groups of buildings are, however, allowed with a somewhat less proportionate amount of free space for the group as a whole.

Certain parts of the newly added territory of the city, beyond all the other zones, and forming a zone by itself, have been reserved for a villa section, in which only country houses are allowed.

In all these zones the amount of the lot that must be left free progresses, until, in the villa section, it is seven-tenths of the entire lot. Thus, also, the permissible height decreases to about 53 feet (16 meters) and the number of stories to two. This does not include the roof story and the actual roof, which together, in this zone, must not exceed about six feet (1.8 meter) in height. In no case, however, may the house exceed in height, except for the roof story and roof, the width of the street upon which it stands.

CHAPTER V—FIFTH AVENUE CONDITIONS

The matter of restricting heights on Fifth Avenue was brought up by the Fifth Avenue Association two years ago. In the winter of 1911-1912, Hon. George McAneny, President of the Borough of Manhattan, appointed a commission of seven members, called the Fifth Avenue Commission, of which Mr. Arnold W. Brunner was chairman and Mr. Robert Grier Cooke secretary. In March, 1912, they presented to Borough President McAneny the following recommendations:

"The height of buildings on Fifth Avenue and within an area 300 feet east and west of the avenue should be restricted to 125 feet to the cornice line, with not more than two mansard roof stories additional, the restriction not to apply to steeples, domes, towers or cupolas of fireproof material erected for ornamental purposes."

In May, 1912, Borough President McAneny introduced this resolution in the Board of Estimate and Apportionment, except that as presented the 300 foot area on either side of the avenue was reduced to 100 feet. No action was taken at the time, but the entire question was specifically referred to this Commission in the resolution providing for its appointment.

There is no more striking example of the necessity of districting the city for the purposes of building control than is furnished by Fifth Avenue. The avenue will serve best the interests both of the abutting owners and of the entire city, if it is preserved as an attractive thoroughfare and high class retail center. The highest usefulness of the lower part of the avenue has already been impaired by high buildings, the introduction of factories and the resulting congestion of the street. This congestion of the street with factory workers and with commercial vehicles has destroyed this part of the avenue as a shopping center and has impaired real estate values. The problem is to preserve upper Fifth Avenue from a similar fate.

A high class retail center of the standard required by New York City conditions must be on a broad, attractive thoroughfare easily reached by motor from the high class hotel and residential sections. It must be in large measure free from the congestion with trucks and employees incident to an industrial neighborhood. Fifth Avenue has until recent years fulfilled these conditions to an exceptional degree.

Of the Fifth Avenue frontage between Washington Square and 59th Street one-fourth is devoted to dwellings and three-fourths to business. Hotels occupy 9 per cent of the frontage; stores 11 per cent; stores and dwellings 5 per cent[1]; stores and factories 28 per cent; and stores and offices 21 per cent.

More than half of the 18,193 feet frontage developed with private buildings has a height not exceeding 75 feet. The buildings having a height not exceeding 125 feet constitute 70 per cent of the frontage; those not exceeding 150 feet, 82 per cent; those not exceeding 200 feet, 91 per cent; and those over 200 feet, only 9 per cent.

Fifth Avenue below 12th Street is residential. From 12th Street to 23d Street it is crowded with tall loft buildings, as are also the side streets leading into it. The greater part of these lofts are used for light manufacturing especially of seasonal goods. Their effect on Fifth Avenue is shown by a statement made to the Commission in behalf of the Fifth Avenue Association by Mr. Bruce M. Falconer:

"Many of them are cheap in construction and appearance and are at the same time of considerable height, the highest reaching to about 18 stories. It is anticipated that a height restriction will at least keep down the number of such structures, and if nothing else it would cut down the number of floors and greatly aid the problem of congestion. These buildings are crowded with their hundreds and thousands of garment workers and operators who swarm down upon the avenue for the lunch hour between twelve and one o'clock. They stand upon or move slowly along the sidewalks and choke them up. Pedestrians thread their way through the crowds as best they may. Women shoppers tend to avoid the section in question at this hour. Ordinary business

[1] Only buildings used for *both* store and dwelling purposes are included under "stores and dwellings."

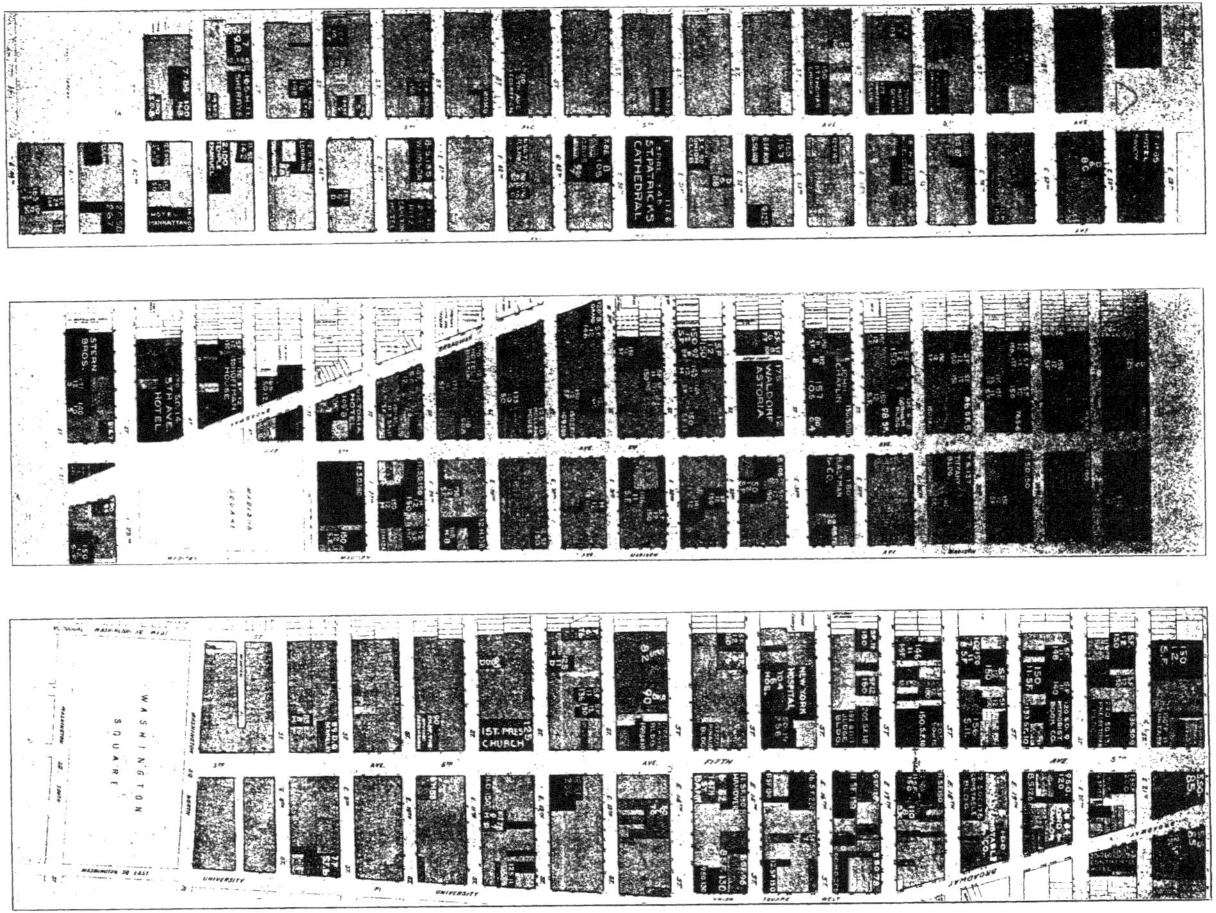

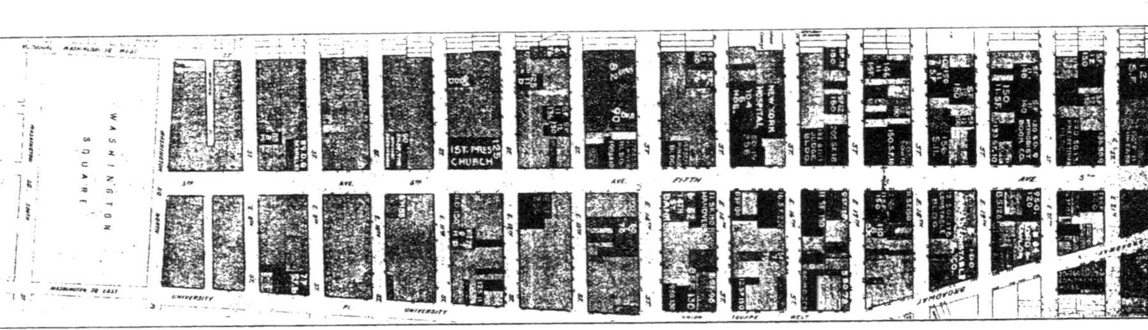

MAP XIV—DETAILS OF HEIGHTS OF BUILDINGS ON FIFTH AVENUE.

Smaller numeral indicates height in stories.
Larger numeral indicates height in feet.

is practically at a standstill until one o'clock, and shopkeepers complain bitterly of financial losses.

"Aside from the obvious discomfort and undesirability of these conditions in themselves, the result of them has been that high-class shops and stores have been driven away from this part of the avenue, property values and rentals have fallen, and the avenue has undergone many changes. But the worst of the matter is that this condition of affairs, at first confined to below 23d Street, has in the last two years been breaking out in the Fifth Avenue district all the way up to 50th Street, and as work ends at the close of the day thousands of these operators pour out upon the sidewalks within a short space of time, and congest the side streets with a steady stream of humanity that moves its way to the East Side."

The highest class of department stores and many first class shops are located between 34th and 42d Streets. Above 42d Street up to 59th Street except for a few tall office buildings, the avenue is devoted exclusively to high class shops and splendid hotels, clubs, churches and private residences.

We concur in the recommendation of the Fifth Avenue Commission that buildings on Fifth Avenue be limited to a height at the building line of 125 feet. For the area on either side of Fifth Avenue, 125 feet should also be the maximum height limit, but in view of the fact that height limitations should bear some relation to street width, we recommend that no building in this area should exceed in height 1½ times the street width. This will mean that on the 60 foot cross streets the height at the building line will be limited to 90 feet. Under the general districting plan which we have suggested (page 69), the entire Fifth Avenue section would be subjected to class D restrictions, *i. e.*, 1½ times street width but not over 125 feet. The section would thus be subjected to the same restrictions that we have considered appropriate for a large part of the Borough of Manhattan.

In addition, we recommend that, under the general control over the location of industries which we are convinced should be exercised by the city, factories should be excluded from the upper Fifth Avenue section.

TABLE III—BUILDINGS ON FIFTH AVENUE BY CLASSES

Stories in Height.	Clubs.	Dwellings.	Hotels.	Stores.	Stores and Dwellings.	Stores and Factories.	Stores and Offices.	Total.	Per Cent.
1	..	..	..	..	..	..	..	..	..
2	..	1	..	..	..	..	..	1	.2
3	2	12	..	1	1	1	1	18	4.3
4	3	59	..	13	10	14	9	108	26.1
5	1	26	1	13	14	45	16	116	28.0
6	1	4	2	7	..	31	6	55	13.3
7	..	..	2	5	4	4	5	17	4.1
8	..	..	3	6	1	6	5	23	5.0
9	..	2	..	..	3	2	4	8	1.9
10	..	..	1	..	..	3	2	6	1.4
11	..	1	2	2	..	15	7	28	6.8
12	..	..	3	..	1	6	2	12	2.9
13	..	1	..	..	1	1	1	3	.7
14	..	..	..	..	..	1	1	2	.5
15	..	..	..	..	..	1	1	2	.5
16	..	..	..	..	..	2	1	3	.7
17	..	..	..	..	..	..	..	..	..
18	..	..	1	..	..	2	1	4	1.0
19	..	..	2	..	..	..	1	3	.7
20	..	..	..	..	..	..	2	2	.5
21	..	..	..	..	..	..	3	3	.7
Total	7	106	17	47	35	134	68	414	100.0
Per cent of total.	1.7	25.6	4.1	11.3	8.5	32.4	16.4	100.0	..
Average stories in height	4.0	4.4	10.5	5.7	6.0	7.0	8.6	6.4	..

TABLE IV—FRONTAGE ON FIFTH AVENUE BY CLASSES OF BUILDINGS

Stories in Height.	Clubs.	Dwellings.	Hotels.	Stores.	Stores and Dwellings.	Stores and Factories.	Stores and Offices.	Total.	Per Cent of Total.
1	..	..	..	..	..	..	..	..	..
2	..	30	..	..	..	..	..	30	.2
3	120	904	..	20	25	22	100	1,191	6.6
4	207	2,164	..	422	220	429	330	3,772	20.7
5	30	828	100	340	351	1,310	597	3,556	19.6
6	95	102	142	253	93	1,042	349	2,076	11.4
7	..	..	255	340	22	172	195	984	5.4
8	..	..	193	491	114	248	227	1,273	7.0
9	..	108	..	..	..	75	252	435	2.4
10	..	..	100	..	..	125	62	287	1.6
11	..	48	143	128	115	911	472	1,817	10.0
12	..	..	335	..	32	226	140	733	4.0
13	..	38	..	..	..	50	92	180	1.0
14	..	..	..	..	..	28	140	168	.9
15	..	..	..	..	..	58	62	120	.7
16	..	..	..	..	..	195	78	273	1.5
17	..	..	..	..	..	..	..	..	..
18	..	..	75	..	..	220	35	330	1.8
19	..	..	308	..	..	..	75	383	2.1
20	..	..	..	..	..	..	115	115	.6
21	..	..	..	..	..	..	460	460	2.5
Total	452	4,222	1,651	1,994	972	5,111	3,781	18,183	100.0
Per cent of total.	2.5	23.2	9.1	11.0	5.3	28.1	20.8	100.0	..
Average frontage height in stories.	4.2	4.3	10.5	6.3	6.1	8.1	10.3	7.5	..

CHAPTER VI

CONCLUSIONS AND RECOMMENDATIONS

The Commission finds conclusive evidence of the need of greater public control over building development. The present almost unrestricted power to build to any height, over any proportion of the lot, for any desired use and in any part of the city, has resulted in injury to real estate and business interests, and to the health, safety and general welfare of the city.

There are many cases where high buildings have destroyed rentable values of neighboring buildings and in turn, perhaps, have had their own rentable values destroyed by other buildings. There are limited areas that seem in process of being smothered by their own growth; light and air are being largely shut off and the streets are becoming entirely inadequate. There are high class business districts such as lower Fifth Avenue that have seen property values impaired by the encroachment of factories. There are high class residence districts in which great property losses have resulted through the coming of stores and apartment houses. There are areas in The Bronx and in Brooklyn where lower East Side conditions of excessive congestion of population are being repeated.

Profiting by past experience we can do much to safeguard the future. We can prevent the repetition all over the city of conditions and evils now confined to comparatively limited areas. Regulations, however, must be carefully devised so as not to interfere unduly with existing property values. We believe that well considered restrictions can be worked out which instead of proving a menace to property values, will in general tend to conserve and in some cases to increase property values. Reasonable restrictions on the use of land will work to the mutual advantage of all owners.

The Commission heard the testimony and opinions of real estate experts, including the heads of several institutions which lend great sums of money secured by mortgages on real estate. This testimony of experienced men supported the opinion of the

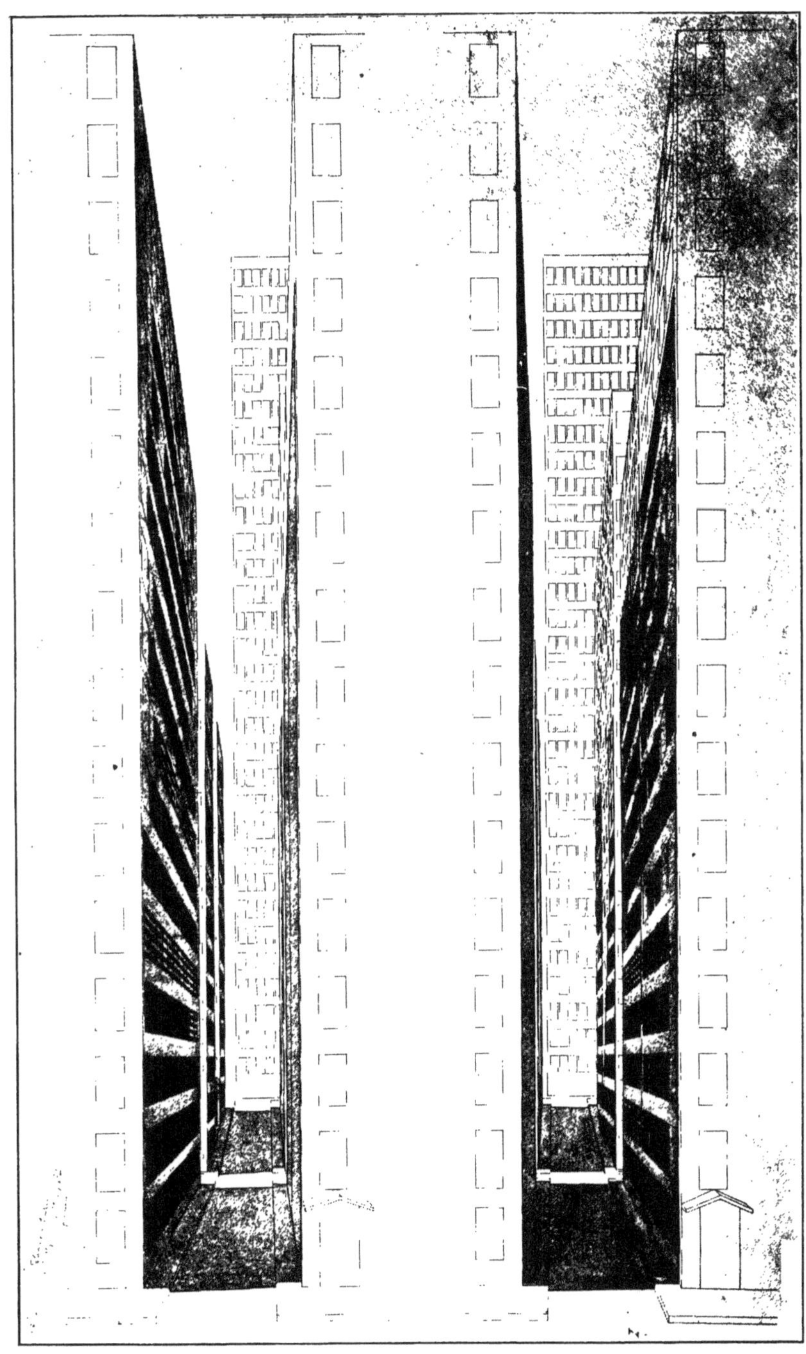

USE OF ARTIFICIAL LIGHT IN OFFICES ON EXCHANGE PLACE FROM BROAD STREET TO BROADWAY.

The black windows indicate where artificial light was being used near the windows at noon on a sunny summer day.

Commission that real estate values will be conserved and rendered far more stable by regulations materially limiting the height of buildings, providing for appropriate yards and courts and restricting various districts against the intrusion of unsuitable industries.

We believe that the state has adequate power to adopt reasonable regulations of this kind. Under the police power the state may adopt any reasonable and appropriate regulation for the promotion of the public health, safety and general welfare. If it is true, as we believe, that the adoption of a reasonable control over building development is essential to the business interests and to the general welfare of the city, we are convinced that the exercise of such control is constitutional. Other American cities have been using the police power to regulate the height and use of buildings. These regulations have in the main been sustained by the courts. New York City has for many years restricted the height, size and arrangement of tenement and apartment houses. We merely propose, for the most part, a more general application and extension of methods of control already in use in the building regulations of this city.

General Restrictions for All Buildings

An urgent problem is the establishment of general regulations that will relieve the situation in lower Manhattan. An occasional building of extreme height is not a matter of great public importance, but when as in parts of the office and financial district such buildings are crowded together, shutting off light and air and congesting the streets, the evil becomes one of grave public concern. The process has now gone far enough to make it plain to any observer that if permitted to continue until the district is uniformly built up with structures of the present extreme heights the situation will be intolerable and injury will be done both to public and private interests.

A building of excessive height is not necessary in order to realize the maximum net return from the land. The tallest buildings often do not pay the best. The entrance hall, elevators, stairs and services take too much valuable space. Even supposing the building can be advantageously rented at the start, its prosperity will probably continue only so long as it is not surrounded by buildings of similar height. When high buildings are crowded together the result is mutually disastrous to all owners. Artificial light must be used on the lower floors even on the brightest day in summer. The darker offices usually rent for much less than those with better light. When such conditions prevail it is clear that a reasonable restriction on height and court area if applied at the start would have been greatly to the advantage of all owners concerned.

Lack of sunlight and the continuous use of artificial light undoubtedly have a direct relation to health, eye strain, and general physical and mental efficiency. Equally injurious is the lack of adequate ventilation due to the opening of work rooms on deep and narrow courts within which any circulation or renewal of air is difficult. The health and comfort of the hundreds of thousands of office employees is a matter of great public importance.

The public also has great interest in the effect which tall buildings have on street conditions. The streets are being darkened and congested. Pedestrian and vehicular traffic is becoming slow and difficult. The street subsurface is becoming overcrowded with sewers, pipes, wires and rapid transit subways; all occasioned in considerable measure by the extreme heights of buildings.

In recommending restrictions we have necessarily been limited by existing conditions as to improvements and land values in the office and financial district. Were it not for the existence of many tall buildings, other and more nearly ideal restrictions could be imposed. The restrictions recommended are designed to secure as much light and air, relief from congestion and safety from fire as is practicable under existing conditions as to improvements and land values. In place of proving a menace to existing values they will tend to prevent future serious injury to such values.

The restrictions recommended are intended to apply, until superseded in part by the districting plan hereinafter proposed,

(A) (B)

USE OF ARTIFICIAL LIGHT IN OFFICES: (A) ON NEW STREET LOOKING SOUTH FROM WALL STREET; (B) ON EXCHANGE PLACE FROM BROAD STREET WEST.

The black windows indicate where artificial light was being used near the windows at noon on a sunny summer day.

to all buildings throughout the city with the exception of tenement houses and with the exception in the case of hotels, lodging houses and theaters of the requirements in regard to courts. Existing requirements as to height and courts of tenement houses and as to courts of hotels, lodging houses and theaters are more stringent than the regulations we propose for general application.

While the restrictions recommended are necessarily somewhat detailed and complicated their general purport may be briefly summarized. They limit height at the street line to twice the width of the street, but such limit shall in no case be less than 100 feet, nor more than 300 feet. After reaching such limit the building may be carried higher by setting the street walls above such limit back one foot for each four feet of increased height. This will permit the building of mansards or of vertical walls if such walls are set back in the prescribed ratio of one to four. No cornice may project into the street more than five per cent of the street width. In order that the proposed height regulations may be effective in securing a maximum of light in the streets, it is obvious that the cornice projection must be limited. Ten foot cornices on both sides of a 30 foot street cut off more light than many feet of increased building height.

Every building may cover the entire lot up to the top of the first story. Above such first story 10 per cent of every interior lot must be left vacant and except on a lot facing on two or more streets such 10 per cent shall be left at the rear of the lot. This will mean as a rule that each owner of an interior lot will leave a 10 foot court across the rear of his lot. This 10 foot court joined with the 10 foot court on the adjoining lot will make a minimum space of 20 feet back to back between buildings. An open court of this kind is of great importance to adequate ventilation. No rear court is required in the case of a corner lot.

In addition to rear courts or the required 10 per cent loss of area there must be a further loss of area covered by the building equal to one per cent of the lot area for each story except the first story. Loss of area occasioned by set-backs of the front walls is included in this one per cent per floor required loss. As the required set-back of front walls on a lot 100 feet deep means a loss of about three per cent per floor, it is only in the case of buildings of unusual shapes that the one per cent requirement would have any practical effect after reaching the height where the required set-back of street walls begins. This requirement is supplemented by prescribing a minimum dimension proportionate to height for main courts other than the 10 per cent rear court. The least dimension of such courts must be not less than six feet and not less than the number of feet equal to 1¼ times the number of stories above the first story. At the twenty-first story the court would have to be at least 25 feet in each dimension. Such courts are included as a part of the one per cent per floor required loss of area. These requirements apply to a corner lot as well as to an interior lot.

Buildings erected on lots of specified shapes and sizes and for which it has seemed that adequate light and air can be secured from the streets, are exempted from the requirement as to the loss in area of one per cent per story, and from all requirements as to courts.

As an exception to all the above height and court regulations a tower may be erected to any height, provided it does not cover more than 25 per cent of the lot, and provided every part of the tower is kept at least 20 feet from the lot and street lines. In the case of a building facing a public park or water front, however, such tower may be placed at the building line. Towers of this kind will not interfere with light and air, and while not attractive investments, will probably continue to be built as in the past from motives other than for rental return.

For plots of normal size, it is estimated that buildings will reach their economic height when through the application of the court and set-back regulations the area of the building has been reduced to about 60 per cent of the area of the plot. This will mean that for buildings on an interior plot on a sixty foot street, the economic height limit will be about 14 to 17 stories. On a corner plot on a 100 foot street, the economic height limit will be probably 16 to 20 stories.

DIAGRAM II

200'-0"
100'-0'
Front Elev.
Side Elev.
Rear Elev.
14
13
12
11
10
9
8
7
6
5
4
3
2
1
15'-0"
120'-0"
14'-0"
12'-0"
12'-0"
12'-0"
16'-0"
Curb Line
60ft. Street
Calculations
Lot Area = 100 × 100 = 10000 sq. ft.
10% of 10000 = 1000 " "
1% " " = 100 " " per floor.
Loss of area 2nd Floor = 1100 " "
" " (100ft.) 9th " = 1800 " "
" " " 11th Floor = 3200 " "
14th Floor:–
Required by 1% + 10% = 2300 " "
Facade Reduction = 1300 " "
Remainder for Court = 1000 " "
1.25 × 14 = 17'-6" least dimension of court.
Area of Building at 14th floor = 68% of Lot.
100'-0
100'-0"
2nd Floor Plan
60ft. Street
15'-0"
65'-0"
15'-0"
14th Floor Plan
Typical Building
on Interior Lot
Fronting on a 60ft. Street.
Scale:– 0 20 40 60 80 100
Date: Nov. 11, 1913.
Drawn by A.E.H.

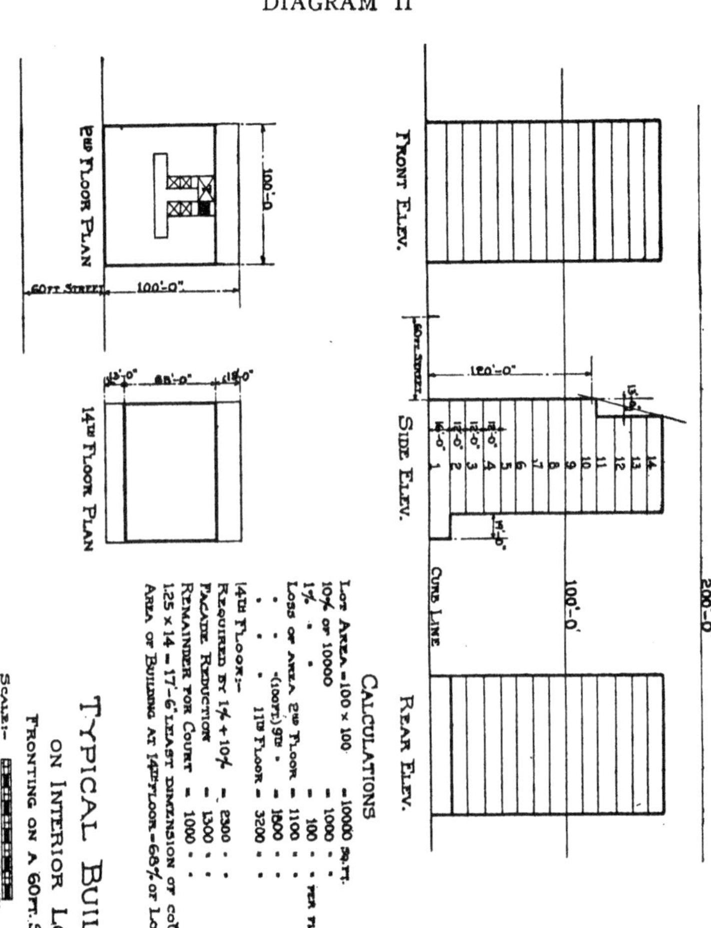

The proposed regulations are in full as follows:

Street walls

1 A. Except as hereinafter provided when the street walls of any building reach a height equal to twice the width of the street, they shall be set back from the street in the ratio of one foot horizontally for each four feet vertically, but the street walls of a building facing on any street, public place, park, or body of water, more than 150 feet wide, including an intervening street if any, must begin their set-backs not over 300 feet above the curb, except as hereinafter provided for towers.

1 B. Street walls if erected on the building line may reach the height of 100 feet on a street less than 50 feet wide before the set-back as stated above must begin.

1 C. When the width of a street varies in a given block the width of the street for the purpose of determining the height of the street walls in said block shall be taken to mean the average width of said street in said block.

2. When street walls are erected inside the building line so that a space intervenes between the street and the wall, the set-back shall begin where such wall intersects the set-back plane as determined by the set-backs in paragraphs 1 A and 1 B and above that point the wall shall set back in the same manner as if the wall were placed on the building line.

3. Where a single building is erected upon a corner lot facing upon streets of different widths, the street of greatest width may be used to determine the height at which the set-back shall begin. The mean level of the curb in such street of greatest width shall be the point from which such height shall be measured.

4. Where a single building not on a corner lot abuts upon streets of different widths the height and set-backs of each street wall shall be determined by the width of the street on which it abuts.

5. No cornice shall project more than five per cent of the width of the street beyond the building line or the plane determined by the required set-backs in 1 A and 1 B.

Courts

6. Every building may cover the entire area of the lot up to and including the tier of beams forming the ceiling of the first story which shall be that story the floor of which shall be not more

than seven feet above the curb level at the highest point of any street on which the building abuts.

7. Except as hereinafter provided on all lots upon which buildings shall be erected, provision for light and air shall be made by leaving yards or uncovered courts above the second story floor level whose least dimension shall be not less than six feet.

8. At any story of a building the least dimension of any court, measured to an opposite wall of the same building or to a lot line, shall equal in feet at least 1¼ times the number of stories from the second floor to and including said story. This provision need not apply to a rear yard as required under paragraph 12.

9. In a court of irregular shape the least dimension shall be taken to mean the least distance between walls or between any wall and a lot line measured on a line erected perpendicular to the center of any side of said court.

10. The provisions of paragraphs 7, 8 and 9 need not apply to a court upon which no office or work room solely depends for access to outside light and air.

11. In every building there shall be a loss in area for each story above the second story floor level of at least one per cent of the lot area, in addition to other requirements hereinafter contained.

12. Except as provided in paragraphs 13 A and 13 B there shall be an uncovered space above the second story floor level between the rear line of every building and the rear line of the lot, which shall contain not less than 10 per cent of the area of the lot and the least dimension of which shall be not less than 10 per cent of the depth of the lot. When the front and rear lines of the lot are not parallel, the depth of the lot shall be taken to mean the average depth.

13 A. The requirements of paragraph 12 shall not apply to a building erected on a lot at the corner of two or more streets.

13 B. When a building is erected upon a lot fronting upon two or more streets but not on a corner, there shall be an uncovered space above the second story floor level equal in area to 10 per cent of the area of the lot.

14. No courts shall be required in a building erected on a three-sided lot in which three sides face upon public streets and in which the length of the shortest side does not exceed 100 feet.

15. No courts shall be required in a building erected upon a three sided lot in which only two sides face upon public streets and in which the length of the third side does not exceed 100 feet.

DIAGRAM III

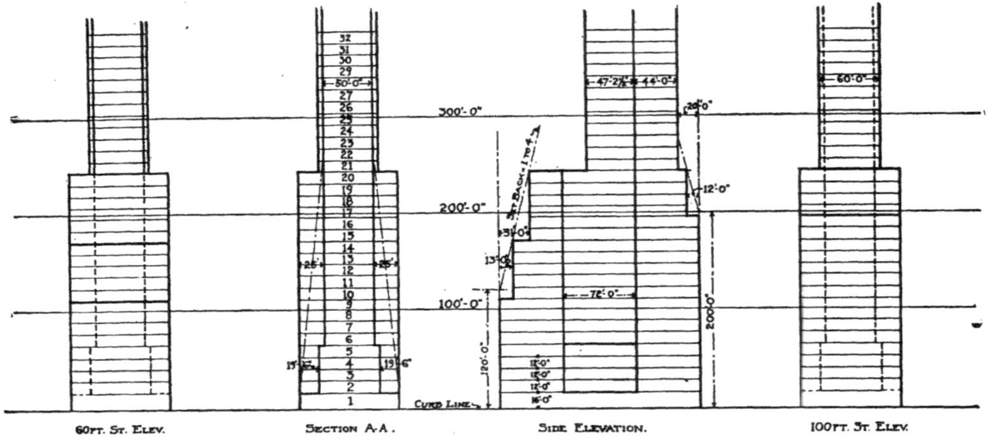

300'-0"
200'-0"
100'-0"

60 FT. ST. ELEV.

SECTION A-A.

SIDE ELEVATION.

100 FT. ST. ELEV.

CURB LINE

SET BACK = 1 TO 4

CALCULATIONS

Lot Area = 100 x 200 = 20000 sq. ft.
10% of 20000 = 2000 " "
1% " " = 200 " " per floor.
Loss of area 2nd Floor = 2200 sq. ft.
" " " (100 ft.) 9th " = 3400 " "
" " " (200 ") 17th " = 5000 " "
" " " (300 ") 25th " = 6800 " "
Tower = 25% of 20000 = 5000 " "
= (60' x 44') + (50' x 47½')

CALCULATIONS (continued)

Courts
Court Area at 9th Story = 2000 + 8 x 200 = 3600 sq. ft.
3600 sq. ft. = 2 courts 72' x 25'. Above the Ninth Story
The Court Area Remains Constant As 1% Losses Are On Facade.
20th Story: Required Loss of Area (10% + 19%) = 5800 sq. ft.
Facade Set Back Reduction = (12' + 31') x 100' = 4300 " "
Court Area = 3600 sq. ft. Total Loss = 7900 " "
20th Story can cover only 60.5% of the lot.
" " is economic height limit.

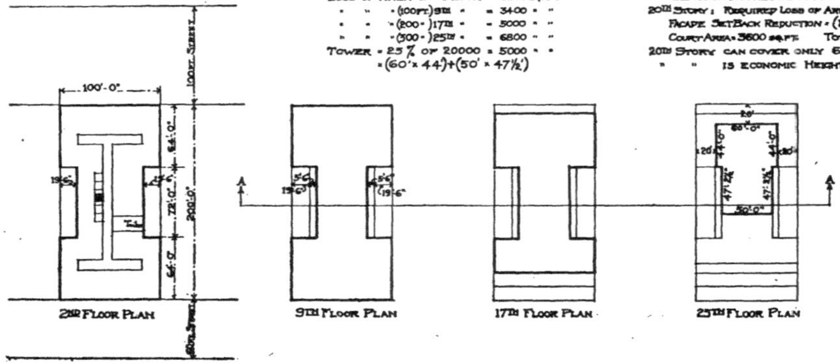

2nd FLOOR PLAN

9th FLOOR PLAN

17th FLOOR PLAN

25th FLOOR PLAN

100 FT. STREET

60 FT. STREET

TYPICAL BUILDING
ON INTERIOR LOT
RUNNING THROUGH FROM ONE STREET
TO ANOTHER PARALLEL STREET.

SCALE: 0 20 40 60 80 100 FT. DATE: FEB. 28, 1914.
DRAWN BY G.B.F.

16. No courts shall be required in a building erected upon a rectangular or trapezoidal lot in which three or more sides face upon public streets, and in which the greatest width of the lot from street to street measured in a line at right angles to either street does not exceed ninety feet.

Towers

17. It is further provided, that, in addition to a building erected as hereinbefore provided, a structure to be called a "tower" may extend without limit above such building and without loss of area, but such tower shall not occupy an area exceeding 25 per cent of the area of the lot, and no part of such tower shall approach nearer than 20 feet to any lot or street line, except, however, that such tower may be built on that building line of a building facing on a public square, a public park, or the water front, with or without an intervening street as hereinbefore defined in paragraph 1 A.

Exceptions

18. The above regulations do not apply to tenement houses and do not apply to hotels, lodging houses or theaters in so far as sections 6-16 in relation to courts are concerned nor do they apply to church spires, belfries or chimneys for power and manufacturing plants. The existing laws and ordinances in relation to tenement houses and hotels, lodging houses and theaters will be continued in force.

Application to Certain Well Known Office Buildings

In the following illustrations the number of the story at which the set-back would begin refers to the building as actually constructed or to the approved plans of a building under construction.

Fifth Avenue building. (*See* Diagram 4)

This structure is 14 stories high, with a two-story parapet, or 196 feet over all. Under the proposed regulation it could go up twenty-five stories, or 300 feet, before it would have to set back from the street front, and might go up five stories, or 60 feet, more in a mansard. The required court under the proposed regulation would be 18 feet narrower all of the way up than the existing court, and at the top, where the existing court is 60 feet wide, it would need to be only 42 feet wide.

Woolworth building. (*See* Diagram 5)

This building is 27 stories, or 360 feet high, before it begins to set back from the street. Under the proposed regulation, if this building were opposite the City Hall Park, it would have to begin to set back at the top of the 23d story level, or 300 feet up, and could have three roof stories. From the 23d story up it could have a tower, 100 feet by 77 feet. The existing tower is 84 feet by 84 feet. The existing court is 36 feet wide all the way up to the 28th story. Under the proposed regulation, the main building would probably stop at the 23d story, and the court for the same depth would have to be 68 feet wide at that level.

Singer building

This building, without the tower, is only 15 stories, or 200 feet high, and 12 stories high before it begins to set back from the street. Under the proposed regulation the building would begin to set back at the 11th story, or 140 feet up, and continue to a height of 16 stories, above which level there might be a tower 90 feet by 70 feet. The existing tower is 66 feet by 55 feet. As to the courts, at the eighth story level only 1692 square feet would be required, and at the 15th story level 3666 square feet would be required. Six thousand four hundred and thirty-five square feet is the area given up in the existing courts.

New Equitable building. (*See* Diagram 6)

On the street the proposed building will be 36 stories, or 496 feet high, with exterior courts on Broadway and Nassau Street, 32 feet wide and 94 feet deep. Under the proposed regulation the building might go up nine stories of the unusual height of the proposed stories before it would begin to set back, and it would be impracticable to carry it above a height of 18 stories. The courts would remain the same as the present courts up to the 14th story, but at the 18th story they would be 12 feet wider. Above the 18th story there could be a tower 115 by 100 feet.

United States Realty building. (*See* Diagram 7)

This building is 21 stories, or 283 feet high. Under the proposed regulation it might go up 12 stories, or 160 feet, before it began to set back, and the probable height under the proposed law would be 15 stories, or 203 feet. There need be no courts in the building.

Whitehall building. (*See* Diagram 8)

This building is 20 stories, or 250 feet high, in one part, and 32 stories, or 405 feet high, in another part. Under the proposed regulation, as this building faces on the water front and on a public park, it could go up 24 stories, or 300 feet, before it would have to set back, and might reach a height of 29 stories, or 360 feet. A tower on the corner 100 by 130 feet would be quite feasible. At the 29th story, if the building covered the whole lot, a court of the same depth as the existing court would have to be 64 feet wide. At the 24th floor the building could occupy about 76 per cent of the present lot area.

Municipal building. (*See* Diagram 9)

This building is 24 stories, or 320 feet high. Under the proposed regulation the building, as it faces a public square, could be 22 stories, or 300 feet high, before it would have to set back, and could be carried up to the 30th story, or 408 feet high. There could be a tower on the building 138 by 110 feet. At the 24th floor level a court, as required under the proposed regulation, would be very nearly the same size as the existing court.

Flat Iron building. (*See* Diagram 10)

This building is 20 stories, or 282 feet high. Under the proposed regulation it could be 18 stories, or 250 feet high, before it would have to set back from the street, and would reach an ultimate height equal to one story more than the present building, or 300 feet. There need be no courts.

Application to Certain Well Known Hotels

Knickerbocker Hotel. (*See* Diagram 11)

This hotel is 15 stories, or 185 feet high, with only 12 stories or 150 feet in height, on the street front. According to the proposed regulation it might be 16 stories, or 200 feet high, before set-backs would be required, with a possible ultimate height of 25 stories, or 300 feet.

Plaza Hotel

The height of this building is 19 stories, or 270 feet, or 16 stories, or 235 feet, before it begins to set back from the street. Under the proposed regulation, as the building faces on a public square and park, it might go to the height of 22 stories, or 300 feet, before set-backs would be required, and a tower on the corner 98 by 98 feet could go to any height.

Biltmore Hotel. (*See* Diagram 12)

The height of the Biltmore Hotel is 25 stories, or 305 feet. Under the proposed regulation the set-backs would begin on the street fronts at the 14th floor level, or 160 feet up. The hotel might go to the same height as the existing building, but it would probably be unprofitable to carry it above 19 or 20 stories, or 240 feet.

Districting

Height regulation districts

The Commission believes that any complete system of height and court restriction necessitates the application of different regulations to different parts of the city. The city should be divided into districts and the restrictions for each district worked out with reference to the peculiar needs and requirements of that particular district. The blanket restrictions which we have recommended for immediate adoption, have as a matter of fact been devised with reference to the needs of the downtown office and financial district—the area of maximum congestion. They have been worked out with a view to securing as much light, air, relief from congestion, and safety from fire as is consistent with a proper regard for the business requirements and existing land values in this area of maximum congestion. They are so liberal as to be of practically no force in controlling actual building development except in very limited areas throughout the entire city. We believe that the needs of each district should be studied

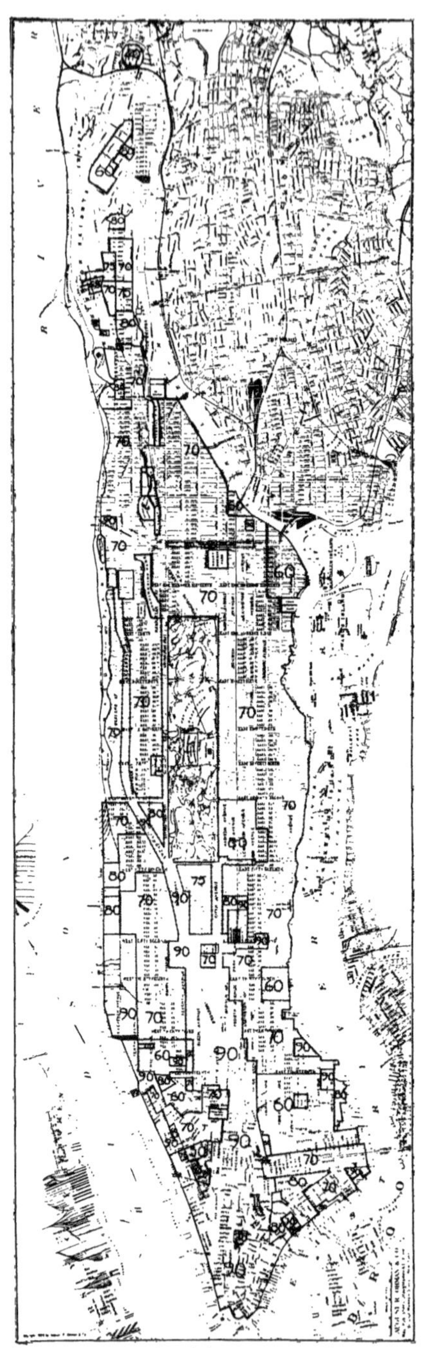

Base map reproduced by courtesy of Ohman Map Company.

MAP XV—PREVAILING PERCENTAGES OF LOT AREA COVERED BY BUILDING IN MANHATTAN.

Numerals indicate percentage covered.

in the same way that we have studied the central office and financial district and restrictions worked out that will best serve the peculiar needs of each district.

Every city becomes divided into more or less clearly defined districts of different occupation, use and type of building construction. We have the central office and financial district, loft districts, water front and industrial districts, retail business districts, apartment house and hotel districts, tenement house districts, private dwelling districts. The character of building appropriate for each district is of course dependent on the character of occupation and use in that particular district. A comparatively high degree of concentration is believed to be important for the facilitation of business in the office and financial district. Certain trades and industries require structures of unusual size or shape. The demand for housing varies with the differing tastes and necessities of the inhabitants of the city. There is a demand for hotels and apartment houses as well as for single family dwellings. Moreover, advantage of location and the resulting enormous difference in land values tend strongly toward differentiation in the character and intensity of use and this and other social and economic factors tend toward a natural segregation of buildings according to type and use. The city *is* divided into building districts. We believe that these natural districts must be recognized in any complete and generally effective system of building restriction.

Height and court restrictions should be framed with a view to securing to each district as much light, air, relief from congestion and safety from fire as is consistent with a proper regard for the most beneficial use of the land and as is practicable under existing conditions as to improvements and land values. The restrictions should be based on the theory that assuming that the entire district should be built up uniformly with buildings of the maximum height and extent allowed, the provision for light and air would be adequate, and the district as a whole would be appropriately improved. The varying district restrictions should also have in view the safeguarding of existing and future investments and the encouragement of an appropriate and orderly building development, by conserving the existing type and character of the district and by preventing the taking from an existing structure of its minimum allotment of light and air.

While we know of no immediate practicable remedy for the existing congestion of population on the lower East Side, we believe that by appropriate restrictions varying with the district, we can prevent the repetition of these conditions in other parts of the city. A few comparatively small districts of the city are already spoiled, but most of the area of the city is still in condition to be greatly helped by appropriate regulations.

The chief American examples of districting as applied to the height of buildings are furnished by Boston, Baltimore, Indianapolis and Washington. In Baltimore and Indianapolis special restrictions have been applied to a single very limited area. In Boston and Washington, on the other hand, the regulations are comprehensive and thoroughgoing. The Baltimore regulations have been sustained by the Supreme Court of Maryland and those of Boston have been sustained both by the Supreme Court of Massachusetts and by the Supreme Court of the United States.

We recommend that the Board of Estimate and Apportionment be empowered by the state legislature to district the city for the purposes of building height and court area restrictions and to apply to buildings hereafter constructed different restrictions in different districts. We recommend that the Board of Estimate and Apportionment, upon receiving such legislative authorization, appoint a commission, which commission after hearings shall recommend to the Board the precise boundaries of the several districts, and the regulations to be applied in each such district.

Such restrictions should secure safety from fire, promote public health and convenience and provide adequate light, air and access. The Board should pay reasonable regard to the character of the buildings existing in each district, the present use of the land and its value based on such present or presently expected use. Restrictions thus imposed would promote the most desirable use of the land of each district and would conserve the

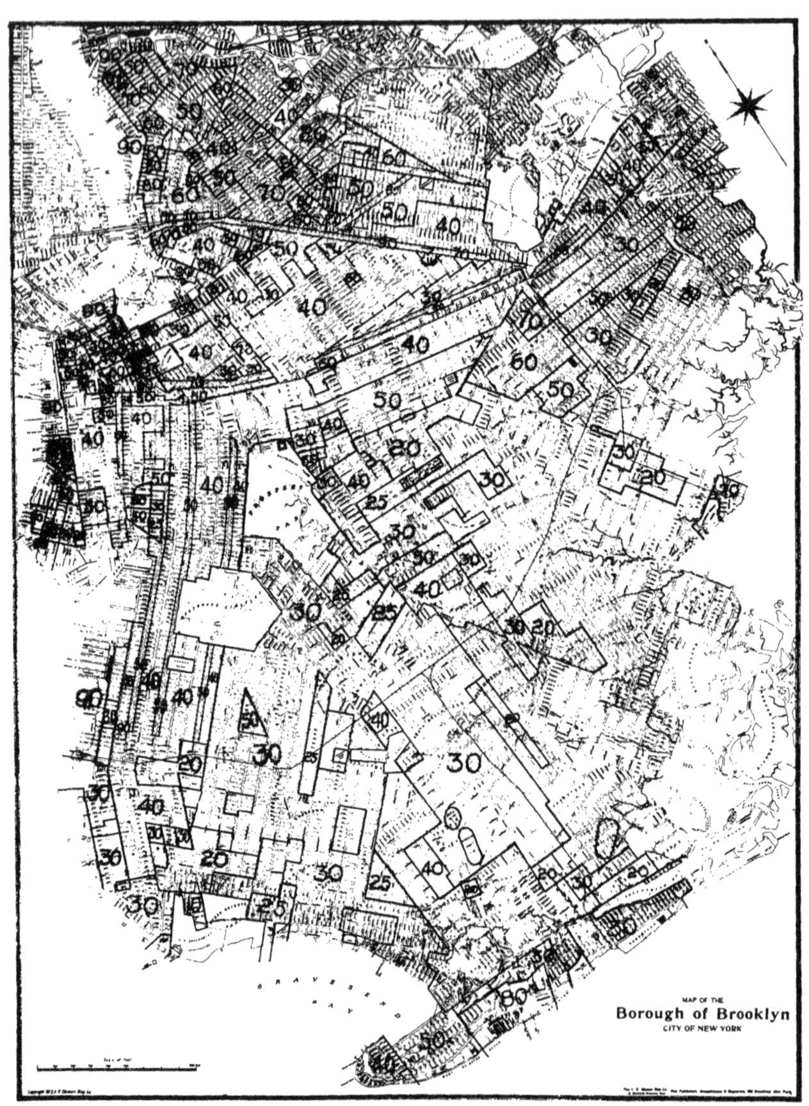

Base map reproduced by courtesy of Ohman Map Company.

MAP XVI—PREVAILING PERCENTAGES OF LOT AREA COVERED BY BUILDING IN BROOKLYN.

Numerals indicate percentage covered.

value of buildings and enhance the value of land throughout the city.

The Commission submits the draft of an amendment to the Charter, to be known as section 242-a, to carry out these recommendations.

While the Commission does not specify the exact number of districts to be created, or the precise restrictions as to height and open spaces to be imposed in each, this question has been considered particularly with reference to height regulations, and certain tentative conclusions are presented merely by way of suggestion and illustration. We suggest that the following eight classes of districts should be provided for:

A districts:

General restrictions recommended for immediate adoption, regulating heights of all buildings.

B districts:

Twice the street width, and not over 150 feet. Set-back one foot horizontally for each two feet vertically.

C districts:

Twice the street width, and not over 125 feet. Set-back same as B.

D districts:

One and one-half times the street width, and not over 125 feet. Set-back one foot horizontally for each 1½ feet vertically.

E districts:

One and one-half times the street width, and not over 90 feet. Set-back same as D.

F districts:

Once the street width and not over 80 feet. Set-back one foot horizontally for each one foot vertically.

G districts: Not over 50 feet. Set-back same as F.

H districts: Not over 36 feet. Set-back same as F.

When the street front of any building shall have reached the height limitation, the building may still be erected to a further height at a point set back from the street to the distance provided by the set-back regulations. The set-back regulations are to be understood to permit vertical walls or pitched roofs or other structures, provided only no part of such structure rising above the height limited at the front wall shall extend above the limit allowed by the particular set-back provision. Where the height limit is the street width or a multiple thereof the set-back provision is designed to preserve a certain angle of light determined for the various classes of districts as herein set forth.

The above eight classes of districts were worked out after careful study of land values and improvements throughout the city. It seemed that every portion of the city could be appropriately placed in some one of these eight classes without sacrificing existing values.

Class A restrictions are the blanket regulations recommended for immediate adoption, and under the districting plan should be confined to the area or areas of maximum business congestion, namely, much of the lower end of Manhattan below Park Place, Broadway to 59th Street, and certain limited areas south of 42d Street.

Class B restrictions limiting height at building line to twice the street width, and not over 150 feet; Class C limiting height to twice street width, and not over 125 feet; Class D limiting height to 1½ times street width, and not over 125 feet, and Class E limiting height to 1½ times street width, and not over 90 feet, are designed to cover most business and industrial districts, and also high class hotel and apartment house districts. Most of Manhattan, small portions of Brooklyn, Queens and The Bronx and no part of Richmond should be included as B, C, D and E districts.

Class F restrictions limit height to the width of the street and not over 80 feet. This permits the erection of a five-story tenement or apartment house on a 60-foot street and a six-story tenement or apartment on wider streets. Class G restrictions limit height at building line to 50 feet. This permits the erection

Base map reproduced by courtesy of Ohman Map Company.

MAP XVII—PREVAILING LAND VALUES IN BROOKLYN.

Numerals indicate prevailing assessed value per front foot for inside lots.

of a four-story tenement or apartment house. It seems that a very small portion of Richmond and Manhattan and very large portions of Brooklyn, Queens and The Bronx should be included as F and G districts.

Class H restrictions limit height at building line to 36 feet. This will mean for the most part the building of one and two family houses, and should be applied to districts where this type of construction is most appropriate. It seems that almost all of Richmond, most of Queens and large areas in Brooklyn and The Bronx can appropriately be included as H districts.

It is understood that a district may be of any required size or shape. Some districts may consist of a single street or portion of a street. When, for example, traffic streets run through areas for which the 36-foot limit is generally appropriate, such traffic streets may be exempted by being included in Class G or F, where the limit is 50 and 80 feet.

In the above illustrations and suggestions in regard to districting the Commission has made no reference to restrictions as to courts and yards, save those contained in the recommendations for Class A, which would prevail for the entire city unless superseded. This is a difficult subject, and in working it out it is possible that it would be desirable to increase the number of classes of districts. It may for example be desirable to divide Class H where the 36-foot height limit obtains into two or more classes with different limitations as to courts and yards. Provision for adequate courts and yards is of the utmost importance in carrying out a well considered plan of building development.

Industrial districts and residential districts

It is clear, however, that any system of building control would be defective unless in addition to regulation of height, yards and courts, regulations be imposed on the location of industries and of buildings designed for certain uses. Height limitations alone will not prevent deterioration of sections owing to the invasion of inappropriate industries or structures. Real estate owners and business men of New York City have suffered enormous losses owing to a failure to protect certain districts from encroachment by factories. Witness the decline in business and property values in lower Fifth Avenue. This is an example of what is occurring on a smaller scale in many parts of the city. Again take the case of the man who builds a home in a district which at the time seems peculiarly suited for single family dwellings. In a few years the value of his property may be largely destroyed by the erection of apartment houses, shutting off light and air and completely changing the character of the neighborhood. When single family dwellings, apartment houses, stores and factories are thrown together indiscriminately, the health and comfort of home life are destroyed and property and rental values are reduced.

As a general rule a building is appropriately located when it is in a section surrounded by buildings of similar type and use. Anything that will tend to preserve the character of a particular section for a reasonable period of years will tend to bring about the uniform improvement of that section. Appropriate improvement is encouraged by the greater safety of investment, and at the same time there is a great reduction in the social loss due to the enormous cost of building reconstruction and the enormous decline in the rental value of the buildings that have ceased to be appropriately located.

We believe that factories should be excluded from the neighborhood of upper Fifth Avenue. The preservation of that thoroughfare as a high-class shopping center is essential to the business prosperity of the entire city. We believe, to the extent that existing conditions will permit, factories and other industries should not be permitted to enter certain residence sections. We believe that in certain districts a man should be able to build a home in a neighborhood of his choice without the hazard that in a few years through the building of apartments or other structures the location will become undesirable for a home of the character he has built, and his property will be seriously depreciated. Reasonable restrictions will tend to stabilize existing districts.

A number of American cities, including Baltimore, Milwaukee, Minneapolis and Los Angeles, have in recent years established residential and industrial districts. Los Angeles has

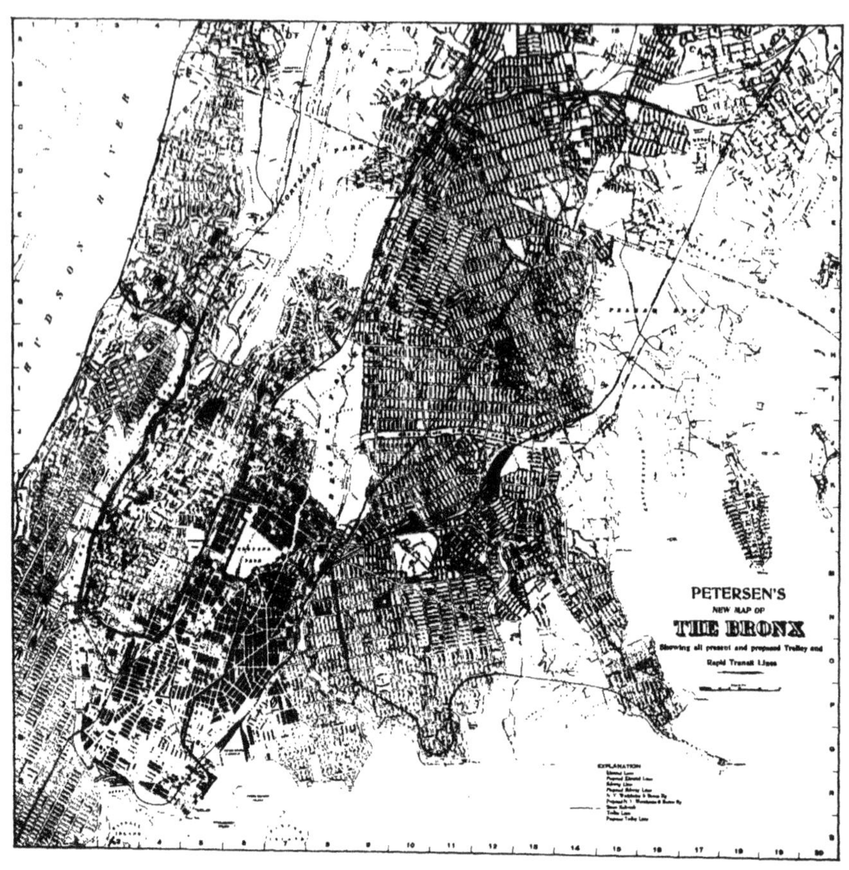

Base map reproduced by courtesy of Ohman Map Company.

MAP XVIII—FIRE LIMITS IN THE BRONX.

Black line indicates fire limits.
Black shading denotes brick buildings outside the fire limits.

enacted drastic ordinances of this character, which have been sustained by the Supreme Court of California. A recent Massachusetts law permits cities and towns to regulate the location and use of buildings. The New York legislature at its 1913 session authorized the creation in all cities of the second class of residence districts within which no building other than a single family or a two family dwelling may be erected.

We recommend that an act be passed by the state legislature authorizing the Board of Estimate and Apportionment to regulate the location of industries and the location of buildings designed for specified uses, and to establish districts for this purpose. In establishing districts and framing regulations reasonable consideration should be given to the character of the district, its peculiar suitability for particular uses, the conservation of property values and the direction of building development in accord with a well considered plan.

The Commission submits the draft of an amendment to the Charter, to be known as section 242-b, to carry out the above recommendations.

With the districting of the city for purposes of height and court regulation the necessity of adopting regulations as to the location of industries and of buildings designed for specified uses will to a considerable extent disappear. The 36-foot height limit (Class H) will serve automatically to prevent the entrance of apartment houses and certain kinds of industry. The height limits suggested for other districts will also tend toward a segregation of buildings according to type and use. Nevertheless it will often be necessary to supplement the height and court restrictions by direct restrictions on the location of industries and of buildings designed for specified uses. For this purpose industrial districts and residential districts should be created, with appropriate restrictions on the type and use of buildings that may be erected therein.

FIFTH AVENUE

The Fifth Avenue problem will be largely solved through the application of the recommendations in regard to districting. We recommend that Fifth Avenue and adjacent territory be subjected to Class D restrictions, *i. e.*, 1½ times the street width, but not over 125 feet. This will limit the height of buildings at the street line to 125 feet on Fifth Avenue and to 90 feet on the 60-foot cross streets. The Fifth Avenue section will thereby be subjected to the same restrictions as to height that the Commission has had in mind as appropriate for a very large portion of Manhattan. In addition, under the system recommended for the regulation of the location of industries, factories should be excluded from the upper Fifth Avenue section. This together with the restriction on height will serve, we believe, to preserve Fifth Avenue as a most valuable asset to the business prosperity of the city.

FACTORIES

We have recommended that the Board of Estimate and Apportionment be empowered to regulate the location of industries and to establish districts therefor. Under such regulations there will be a partial segregation of industries. Certain kinds of industry will not be permitted to enter certain business and residential districts. It is highly important that steps be taken to prevent for the future the serious losses that have resulted to certain sections from the invasion of inappropriate industries.

We have had much testimony as to the depreciation of the value of land and buildings by the intrusion of factories into districts where they are inappropriate. We are deeply impressed also by the danger to life which may arise from the erection of very high factory buildings. This matter, however, is being considered by the Factory Commission and we have therefore made no further recommendations on the subject.

DWELLINGS

The many questions in relation to improvement of housing conditions that would naturally come within the scope of the work of this Commission will we believe be adequately provided for in the working out of the districting plan that we have recommended. Under this plan, four, five or six story tenements and apartment houses will be allowed, according to the character of the particular district. The extreme height, at the street line, for apartment houses will be 125 to 150 feet. Large outlying areas will be made into exclusively residential districts and building construction practically restricted to one or two family houses. Regulations varying with the character of the district will require liberal provision for courts and yards. In short, the housing requirements of the city as a whole will be considered and a plan devised that will work to the mutual advantage of all concerned.

CONCLUSION

The Charter provides that the Board of Aldermen, with the approval of the Board of Estimate and Apportionment, may pass ordinances regulating the height of buildings. We have not construed this as giving authority for districting the city for height limitation purposes. It is probably necessary to secure a charter amendment in order that a thorough plan of building control may be carried out. We have submitted such amendments, which we hope will be enacted by the state legislature during the coming year. A general limitation applicable to all buildings throughout the city can, however, be enacted by the Board of Aldermen and the Board of Estimate and Apportionment under present powers. We earnestly recommend that such action be taken. This will afford immediate relief to an important section of the city and will fit in with any districting plan that is later carried out.

Respectfully submitted by

HEIGHTS OF BUILDINGS COMMISSION,

EDWARD M. BASSETT, Chairman
EDWARD C. BLUM
EDWARD W. BROWN
WILLIAM H. CHESEBROUGH
WILLIAM A. COKELEY
OTTO M. EIDLITZ
ABRAM I. ELKUS
BURT L. FENNER
J. MONROE HEWLETT
ROBERT W. HIGBIE
C. GRANT LA FARGE
NELSON P. LEWIS
GEORGE T. MORTIMER
LAWSON PURDY
ALLAN ROBINSON
AUGUST F. SCHWARZLER
FRANKLIN S. TOMLIN
GAYLORD S. WHITE

GEORGE B. FORD, Secretary

DIAGRAM IV

300 FT.
200 FT.
100 FT.
Curb Line
5TH AVE. FACADE
SECTION "AA"
SECTION "BB"
Lot Area = 51480#
Tower - 25% of 51480# = 12870#
1% " " = 515 ½
Loss of Area 2nd floor = 515#
" " " (100) 8th " = 3605#
" " " (200) 17th " = 8240#
" " " (300) 25th " = 12360#
Present Building is indicated thus
Building according to proposed Code thus
14TH FLOOR LEVEL
Area of Court
Percent of Lot Area.
Present:- 8784# 17%
New:- 7140# 13%
WEST 23RD ST.
WEST 24TH ST.
BROADWAY
5TH AVENUE
2ND FLOOR PLAN
8TH FLOOR PLAN
14TH FLOOR PLAN
32ND FLOOR PLAN
MADISON SQUARE.
THE FIFTH AVENUE BUILDING.
Scale:-
Date:- Nov. 11, 1913.
Drawn by S

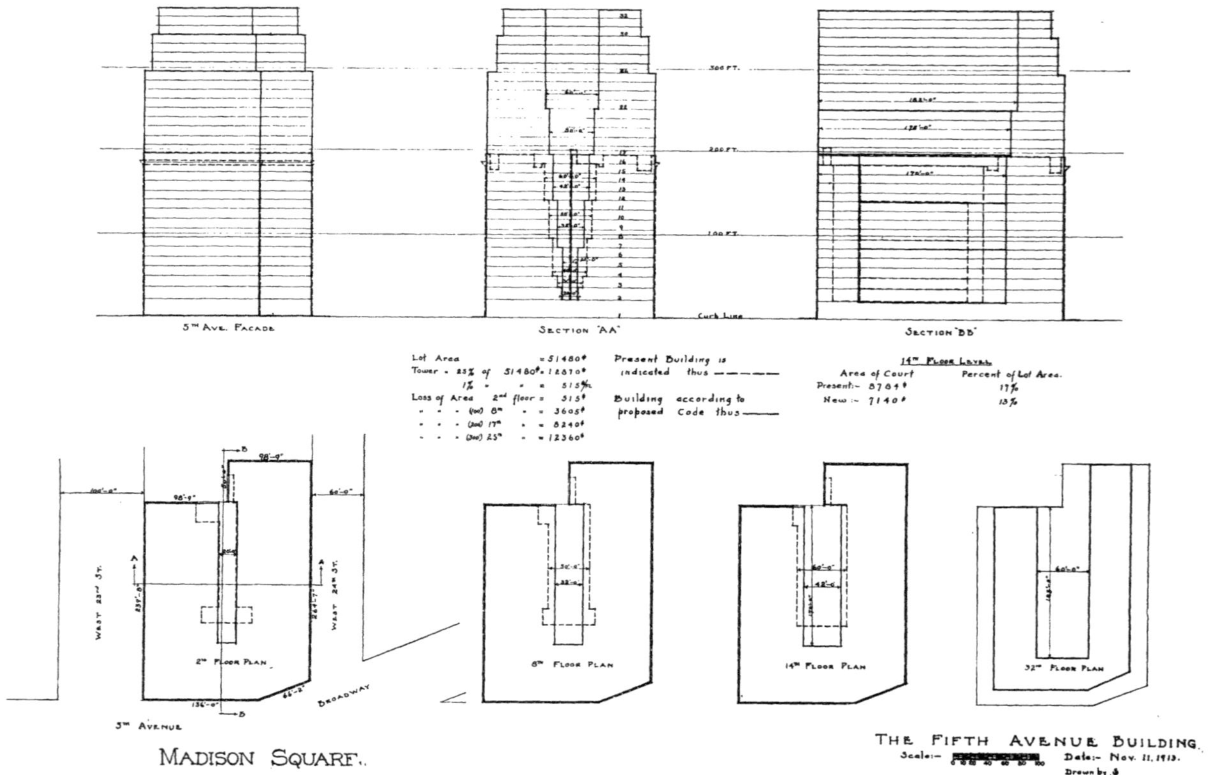

DIAGRAM V

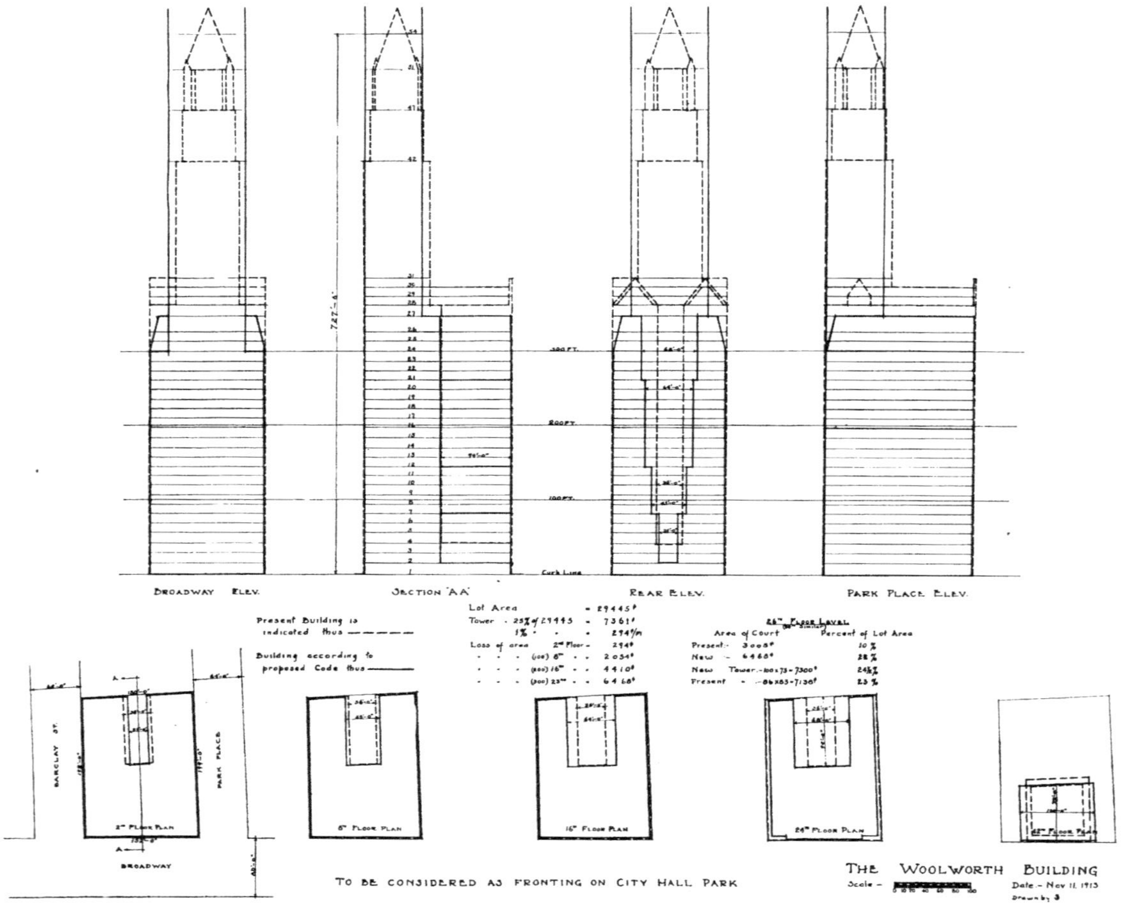

727'-4"

300 FT.

200 FT.

100 FT.

Curb Line

BROADWAY ELEV.

SECTION "AA"

REAR ELEV.

PARK PLACE ELEV.

Present Building is indicated thus ————

Building according to proposed Code thus ————

Lot Area		=	29445°
Tower	25% of 29445	=	7361°
	1% " "	"	294°/m
Loss of area	2nd Floor	–	294°
" " "	(100) 8th	" "	2034°
" " "	(200) 16th	" "	4410°
" " "	(300) 23rd	" "	6468°

26th FLOOR LEVEL (30th Similar)

	Area of Court	Percent of Lot Area
Present:	3008°	10 %
New –	6468°	22 %
New	Tower – 100 x 73 – 7300°	24½ %
Present	" – 86 x 83 – 7138°	23 %

BARCLAY ST.

PARK PLACE

BROADWAY

2nd FLOOR PLAN

8th FLOOR PLAN

16th FLOOR PLAN

26th FLOOR PLAN

42nd FLOOR PLAN

TO BE CONSIDERED AS FRONTING ON CITY HALL PARK

THE WOOLWORTH BUILDING

Scale – 0 10 20 40 60 80 100

Date – Nov 11, 1913

Drawn by 3

DIAGRAM VI

Broadway Facade
Section 'AA'
Pine Street Facade
Nassau St. Facade
Curb Line
300 ft.
200 ft.
100 ft.
Present Building is indicated thus
Building according to proposed Code thus
Lot Area = 48348□
Tower - 25% of 48348□ = 12087□
1% = 483□/m
Loss of area 2nd Floor = 483□
" " " (100) 7th = 2894□
" " " (200) 14th = 4277□
" " " (300) 23rd = 11109□
" " " 37th = 36261□
12th Floor Level
Area of court Percent of L.A.
Present - 3008□ 6% each
New - 2880□ 5% "
Area of court at 9th floor controls the size of court above that point.
Area = 9×483 = 4347□ = 94×50
Nassau St.
Cedar St.
Pine St.
Broadway
Thames St.
8th Floor Plan
7th Floor Plan
14th Floor Plan
23rd Floor Plan
37th Floor Plan
The New Equitable Building
Scale:-
Date - Nov. 11 1913
Drawn by S

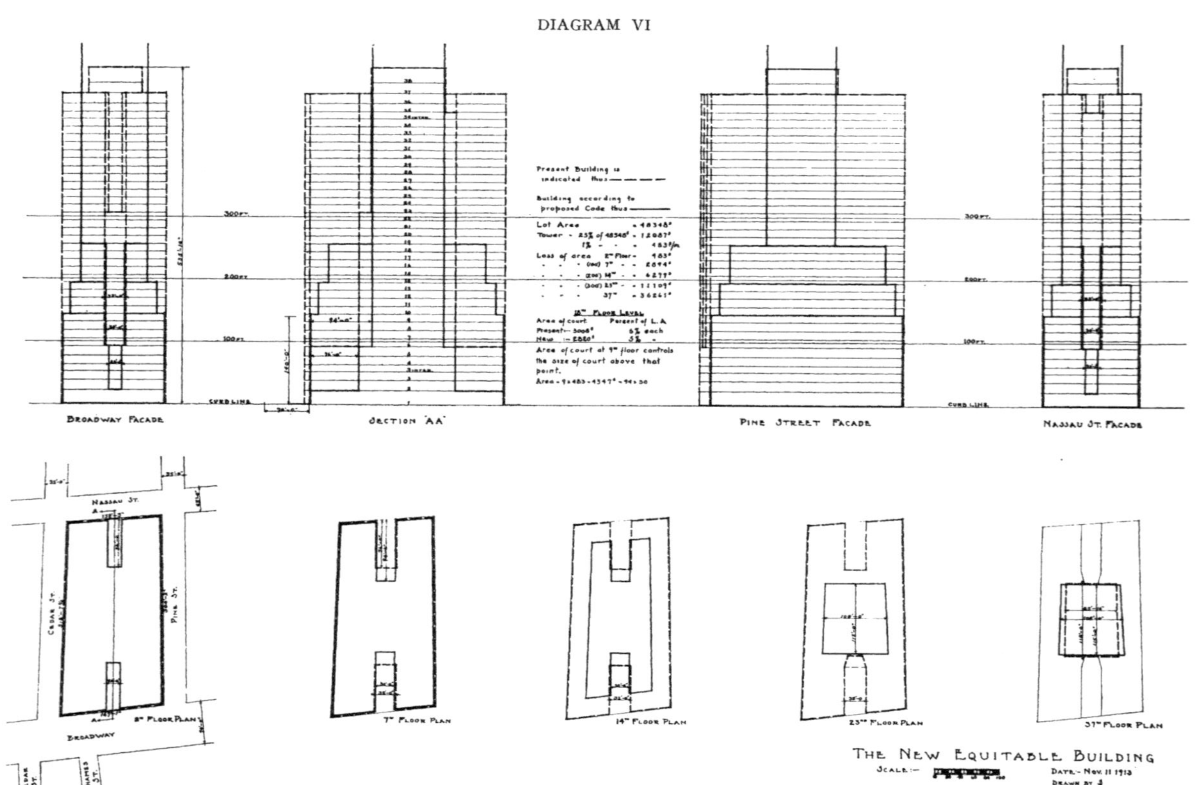

DIAGRAM VII

300'-0"
200'-0"
100'-0"
22
21
20
19
18
17
16
15
14
13
12
11
10
9
8
7
6
5
4
3
2
1
160'-0"
CURB LINE
CEDAR ST. ELEV.
TRINITY PLACE ELEV.
NOTES:-
PRESENT BUILDING IS INDICATED THUS — — — — —
BUILDING ACCORDING TO PROPOSED CODE, THUS ————
COURTS NOT REQUIRED – SEE SECTION No 16 OF THE PROPOSED CODE.
79'-0"
80'-0"
30'-0"
THAMES ST.
269'-7¼"
BROADWAY
61'-0⅝"
2ND FLOOR PLAN
61'-1⅜"
TRINITY PLACE
275'-3⅜"
CEDAR ST.
35'-0"
16TH FLOOR PLAN
22ND FLOOR PLAN
UNITED STATES REALTY BUILDING
SCALE:-
0 5 10 20 40 60 80 100
DATE:- NOV. 11 1913.
DRAWN BY A.E.H.

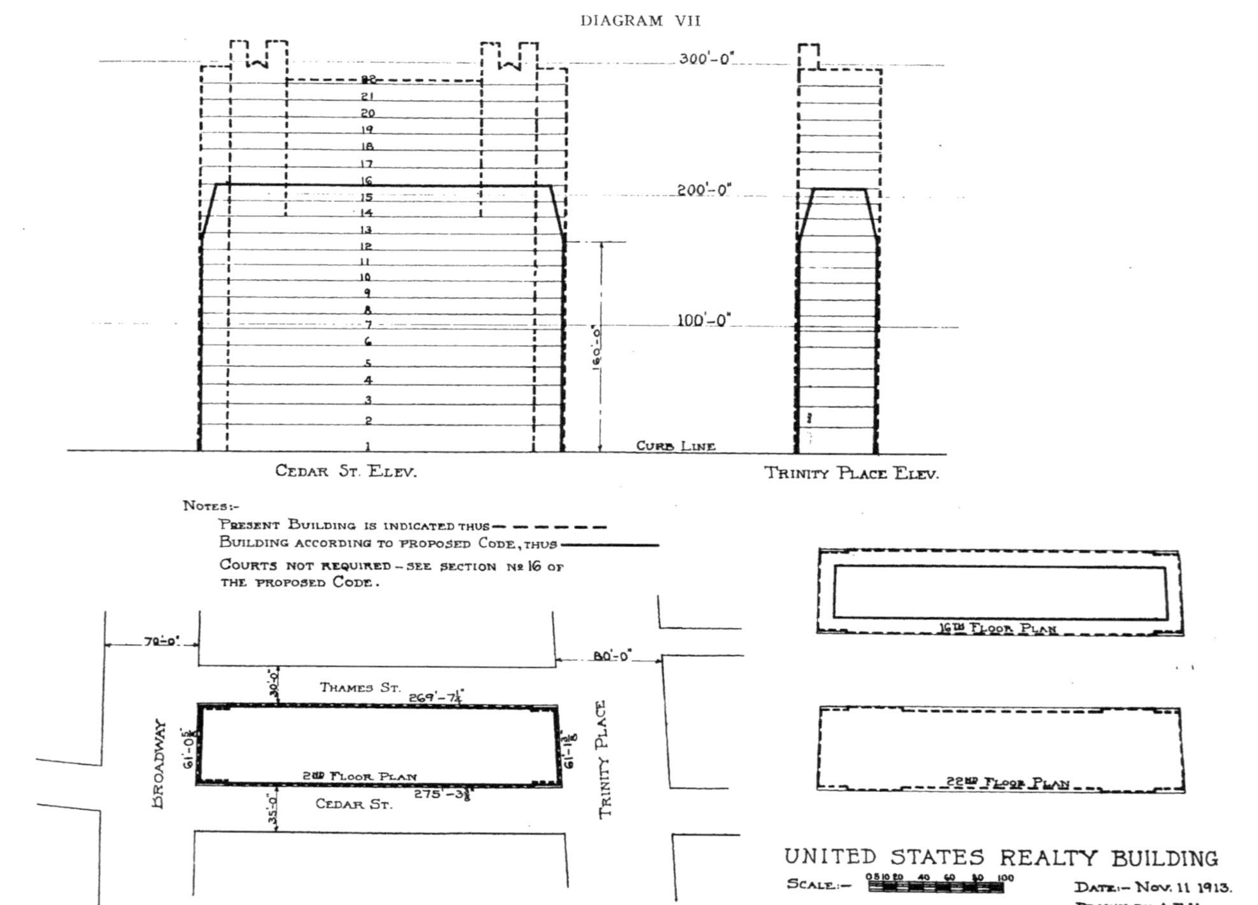

DIAGRAM VIII

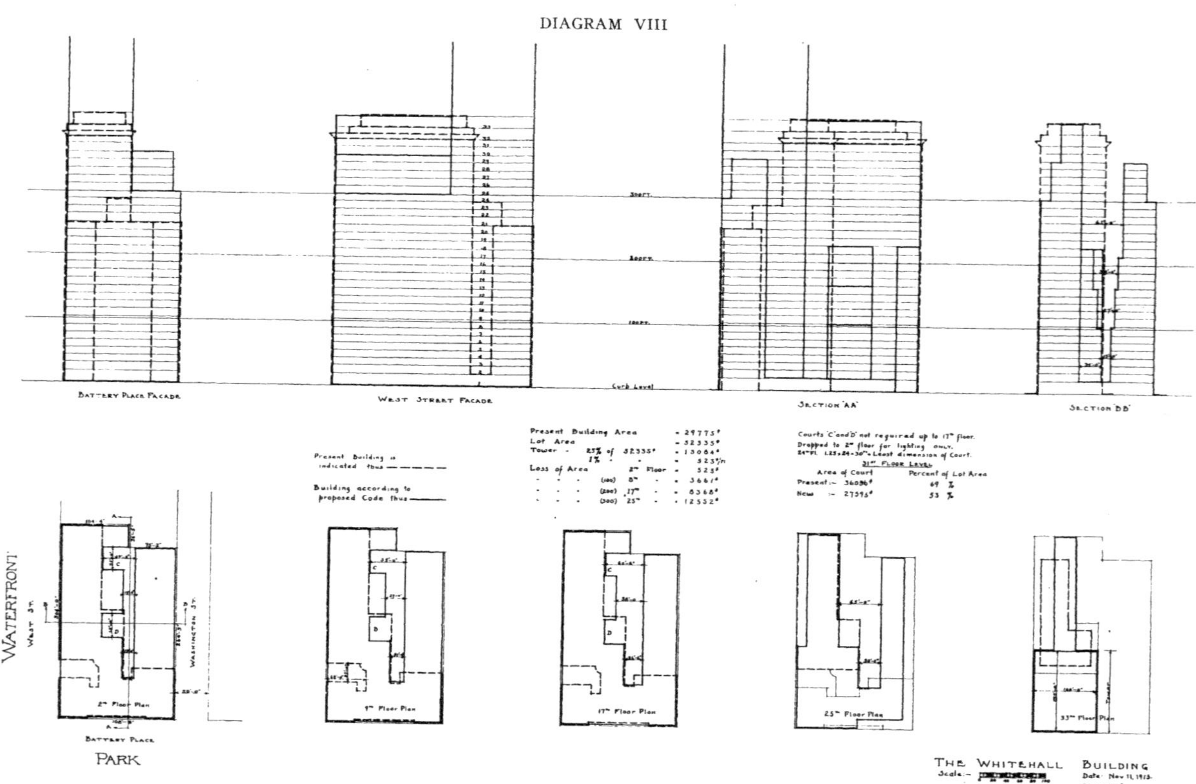

DIAGRAM IX

DIAGRAM X

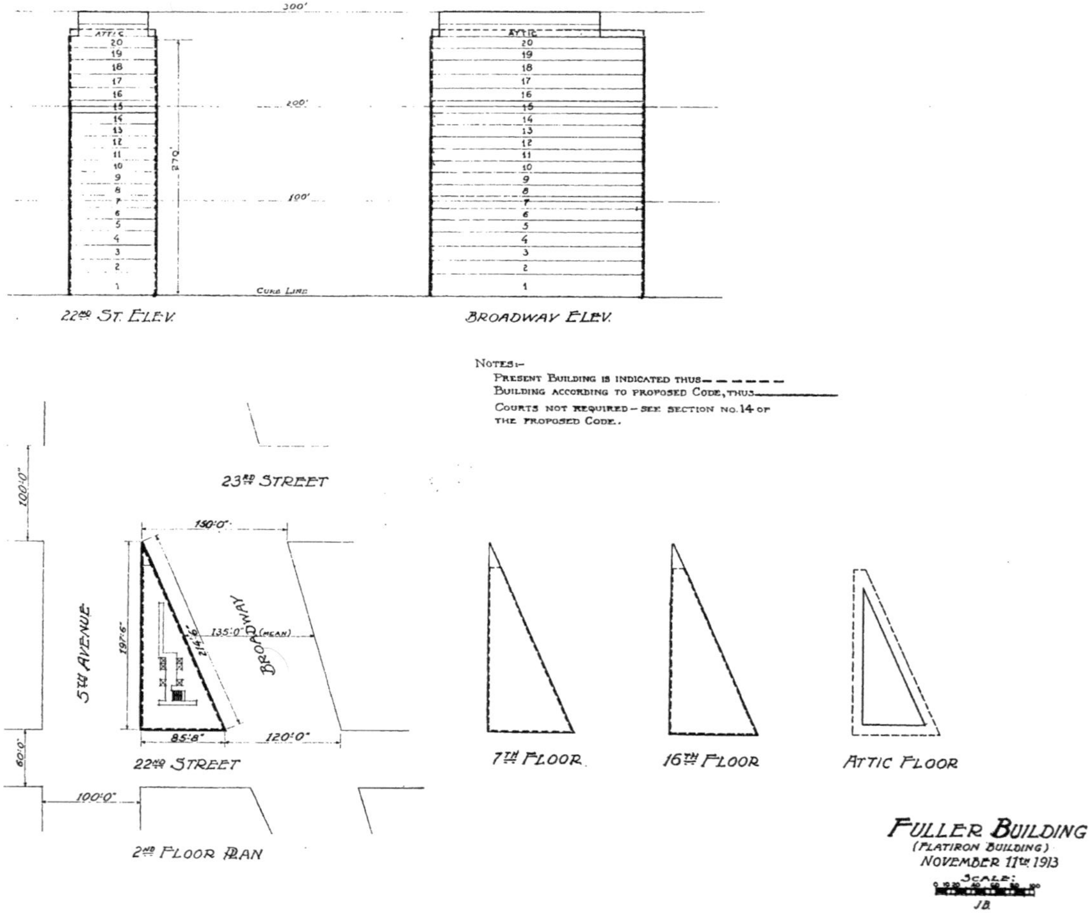
300'
200'
100'
270'
ATTIC
20
19
18
17
16
15
14
13
12
11
10
9
8
7
6
5
4
3
2
1
CURB LINE
22ND ST. ELEV.
BROADWAY ELEV.
NOTES:–
PRESENT BUILDING IS INDICATED THUS – – – – –
BUILDING ACCORDING TO PROPOSED CODE, THUS ———
COURTS NOT REQUIRED – SEE SECTION NO. 14 OF THE PROPOSED CODE.
23RD STREET
5TH AVENUE
BROADWAY
22ND STREET
100'0"
150'0"
197'6"
214'6"
135'0" (MEAN)
85'8"
120'0"
60'0"
100'0"
2ND FLOOR PLAN
7TH FLOOR
16TH FLOOR
ATTIC FLOOR
FULLER BUILDING
(FLATIRON BUILDING)
NOVEMBER 11TH 1913
SCALE:
J.B.

DIAGRAM XI

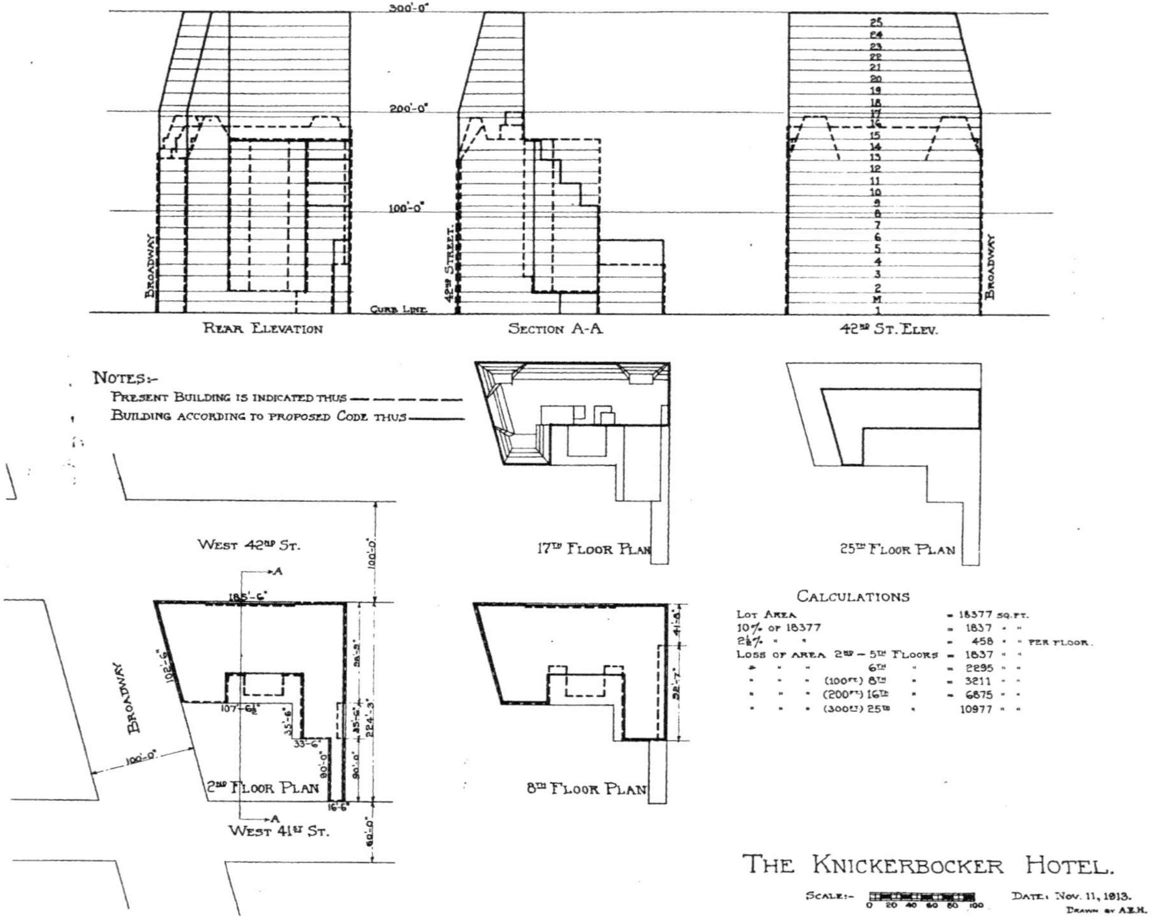

300'-0"
200'-0"
100'-0"
Curb Line
Broadway
42nd Street
Broadway

Rear Elevation

Section A-A

42nd St. Elev.

Notes:-
Present Building is indicated thus — — — —
Building according to proposed Code thus ————

West 42nd St.

17th Floor Plan

25th Floor Plan

2nd Floor Plan

8th Floor Plan

Broadway

West 41st St.

185'-6"
102'-6"
107'-6½"
35'-6"
33'-6"
90'-0"
16'-6"
100'-0"
224'-3"
60'-0"
41'-8"
98'-7"

CALCULATIONS

Lot Area	= 18377 sq. ft.		
10% of 18377	= 1837 " "		
2½% " "	= 458 " "	per floor.	
Loss of area 2nd – 5th Floors	= 1837 " "		
" " " 6th "	= 2295 " "		
" " " (100 ft.) 8th "	= 3211 " "		
" " " (200 ft.) 16th "	= 6875 " "		
" " " (300 ft.) 25th "	10977 " "		

THE KNICKERBOCKER HOTEL.

Scale:- 0 20 40 60 80 100

Date: Nov. 11, 1913.

Drawn by A.E.H.

DIAGRAM XII

300 FT.
200 FT.
100 FT.
Curb Line
160'-0"
135'-0"
81'-0"
70'-0"
Section 'AA'
Vanderbilt Ave. Elev.
Section 'BB'
Present Building is indicated thus
Building according to proposed Code thus
Lot Area = 43311#
10% of 43311# = 4331#
2½% " " = 1083#/FL.
Loss of area 2nd-5th Floor = 4331#
" " " 6th " = 5414#
" " " (100) 9th " = 8663#
" " " (200) 17th " = 17327#
" " " (300) 25th " = 25991#
23rd Floor Level
Area of Court Percent of Lot Area
Present:- 14471# (160×70)+2(65.5×25) = 33%
New :- 13040# (160×81.5) = 30%
Area of court at 13th floor controls the size of court above that point.
Area = 8×1083+4331 = 12995# = 160×81.5
E. 44th Street
E. 43rd Street
Madison Ave.
Vanderbilt Ave.
215'-8"
200'-10"
60'-0"
2nd Floor Plan
9th Floor Plan
17th Floor Plan
23rd Floor Plan
The Biltmore Hotel
Nov. 11th 1913.
Scale

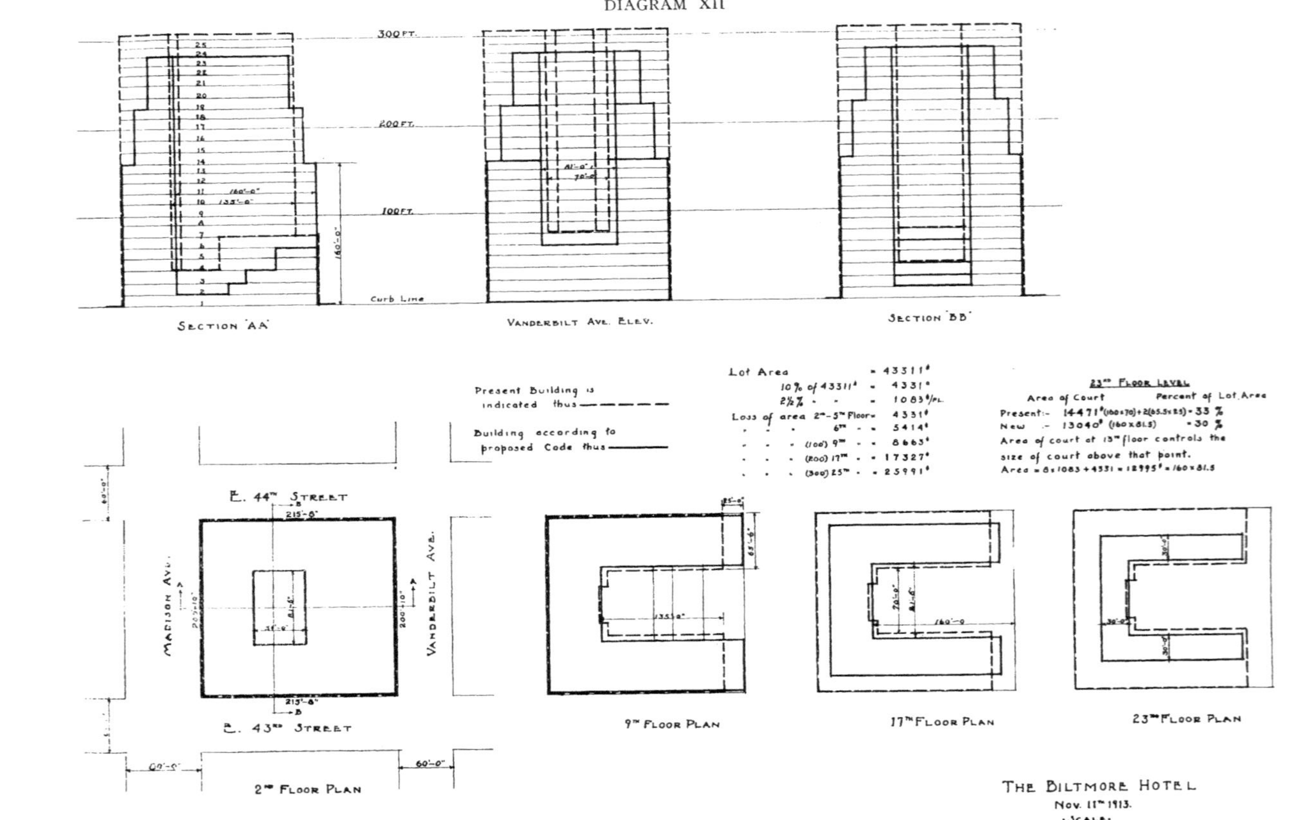

APPENDICES

APPENDIX I

PROPOSED CHARTER AMENDMENTS RELATIVE TO DISTRICTING

Height and open spaces

§ 242-a. The board of estimate and apportionment shall have power to regulate and limit the height and bulk of buildings hereafter erected and to regulate and determine the area of yards, courts and other open spaces. The board may divide the city into districts of such number, shape and area as it may deem best suited to carry out the purposes of this section. The regulations as to the height and bulk of buildings and the area of yards, courts and other open spaces shall be uniform for each class of buildings throughout each district. The regulations in one or more districts may differ from those in other districts.

Such regulations shall be designed to secure safety from fire and other dangers and to promote the public health and welfare including, so far as conditions may permit, provision for adequate light, air and convenience of access. The board shall pay reasonable regard to the character of buildings erected in each district, the value of the land and the use to which it may be put to the end that such regulations may promote public health, safety and welfare and the most desirable use for which the land of each district may be adapted and may tend to conserve the value of buildings and enhance the value of land throughout the city.

The board shall appoint a commission to recommend the boundaries of districts and appropriate regulations to be enforced therein. Such commission shall make a tentative report and hold public hearings thereon at such times and places as said board shall require before submitting its final report. Said board shall not determine the boundaries of any district nor impose any regulation until after the final report of a commission so appointed. After such final report said board shall afford persons interested an opportunity to be heard at a time and place to be specified in a notice of hearing to be published for ten consecutive days in the City Record.

Location of industries and buildings

§ 242-b. The board of estimate and apportionment may regulate and restrict the location of trades and industries and the location of buildings designed for specified uses, and may divide the city into districts of such number, shape and area as it may deem best suited to carry out the purposes of this section. For each such district regulations may be imposed designating the trades and industries that shall be excluded or subjected to special regulations and designating the uses for which buildings may not be erected or altered. Such regulations shall be designed to promote the public health, safety and general welfare. The board shall give reasonable consideration, among other things, to the character of the district, its peculiar suitability for particular uses, the conservation of property values, and the direction of building development in accord with a well considered plan.

The board shall appoint a commission to recommend the boundaries of districts and appropriate regulations and restrictions to be imposed therein. Such commission shall make a tentative report and hold public hearings thereon before submitting its final report at such time as said board shall require. Said board shall not determine the boundaries of any district nor impose any regulations or restrictions until after the final report of a commission so appointed. After such final report said board shall afford persons interested an opportunity to be heard at a time and place to be specified in a notice of hearing to be published for ten consecutive days in the City Record.

NOTE.—The above amendments having been approved by the Board of Estimate and Apportionment were passed by the Legislature, approved by the Mayor and became a law April 21, 1914, with the signature of the Governor.

APPENDIX II

PRESENT RESTRICTIONS IN NEW YORK CITY

By Herbert S. Swan

I—HEIGHT OF BUILDINGS

1. Height of Tenements

Limitations on height[1]

The following three provisions regulate the maximum height of tenement and apartment houses inside the fire limits:

1. The height of a tenement may not exceed 1½ times the width of the widest abutting street.

2. A tenement house of more than six stories in height must be fireproof. The highest tenement in the city, which is situated on Park Avenue, is 17 stories high.

3. All tenement houses, both fireproof and non-fireproof, five stories or more in height exclusive of the cellar, must have the first floor above the lowest cellar, or, if there be no cellar, the first floor above the lowest story, constructed of fireproof material.

Certain other non-fireproof houses must also be provided with fireproof features. Thus every non-fireproof house five stories in height, or four stores in height with a basement above a cellar, and occupied by one or more families on any floor above the first, must have the first floor above the cellar or lowest story constructed of fireproof material.

Definition of height[2]

The height of a tenement is the perpendicular distance through the center of its façade from the curb level to the under side of the roof beams. If the cornice exceeds one-tenth of this height, then the measurement is taken to the top of the cornice.

Where a building fronts on two or more streets of different grades, the measurement is taken on the street having the highest grade. In the case of a tenement on a corner lot formed by the intersection of one street passing under another, the measurement for determining its height and the number of its stories may also be taken on the street having the highest level. No part of the building below the curb level of the highest street may, however, be occupied for living purposes except by the janitor of the building and his family. That part of the building under the level of the highest street must, moreover, be of fireproof construction.

[1] Tenement House Law, secs. 24, 51.

[2] Ibid., sec. 2, subdivisions 7, 12, 15.

Exceptions from height limit [3]

Bulkheads, superstructures or pent houses less than 10 feet in height are not considered in computing the height of a tenement, provided their area does not exceed 10 per cent of the roof area. Elevator enclosures not exceeding 23 feet in height and used solely for elevator purposes are excluded from consideration. Open pergolas and similar ornamentations of roof-gardens or playgrounds also do not enter into the calculation.

In fireproof tenements with one or more power passenger elevators the pent houses and bulkheads may cover 50 per cent of the roof area. But such pent houses must be set back at least 10 feet from both the front and the rear walls of the buildings and at least 3 feet from any court wall. They must have a clear inside height of at least 9 feet from finished floor to finished ceiling, and they may not exceed 12 feet in height from the highest point of the main roof to the highest point of their own roof. They must be entirely of fireproof construction. Such pent houses may not be used or rented as apartments. Their use is limited solely to laundry and storeroom purposes, and to servants' and janitor's quarters.

Wooden tenements [4]

Outside the fire limits wooden tenement houses may be erected subject to the following restrictions:

No such tenement may be more than three stories in height. If three stories in height, wooden tenements may not provide accommodations for more than three families in the aggregate or for more than one family per floor. If two stories in height, such tenements may not accommodate more than four families in the aggregate or more than two families per floor. Their height, moreover, may not exceed 40 feet. The side walls of all wooden tenements must be brick filled.

2. Height of Frame Buildings [5]

Frame buildings may be erected only outside the fire limits.

In those portions of the city outside the fire limits, frame buildings may not be erected to a greater height than three stories, or 40 feet.

Towers, turrets and minarets of wood may be erected to a height of 55 feet. Church spires may be erected to a height of 90 feet.

3. Height of Factories

Fireproof provisions [6]

The height of factories is indirectly limited by fireproofing provisions. All factories over four stories in height must be of fireproof construction.

[3] Tenement House Law, sec. 51.
[4] Ibid., sec. 31.
[5] Building Code, sec. 146.
[6] Labor Law, secs. 79, a-1; f; e-9.

Buildings considered as of fireproof construction need not, however, be wholly of fireproof construction. Thus, the windows may be of combustible material in buildings under 70 feet high unless a neighboring building is within 30 feet or unless the adjoining court or space is less than 30 feet wide. Buildings less than 100 feet in height may be constructed with wooden sleepers, floor finish, and trim.

The industrial board has laid down a rule to the effect that all factories less than five stories and employing more than 25 persons above the ground floor must have all interior stairways enclosed on all sides with fireproof partitions from the basement up. The industrial board has also ruled that such factories must have interior fireproof stairways, regardless of the number of persons employed, if merchandise or combustible material is stored, packed or manufactured in them. An exterior fireproof stairway or a horizontal exit may, however, be substituted for such interior fireproof stairways. If automatic sprinklers are installed throughout the building, the stairways are not required to have fireproof enclosures unless more than 80 persons are employed above the ground floor.

Number of employees per floor limited [7]

The number of persons that may occupy any factory building or portion thereof above the ground floor is limited to such a number as can safely escape by the provided means of exit.

No more than 14 persons may be employed on any one floor for every full 22 inches in width of stairway conforming to the means of exit provided for such floor. No allowance is made for any excess in width of less than 22 inches.

Additional employees permitted in certain cases [8]

1. In buildings where the height between two floors exceeds 10 feet, an additional employee is allowed on the upper of such floors for every additional 16 inches that such height is in excess of 10 feet for every 22 inches in width of stairway leading to the lower floor.

2. Where the stairways and stair halls are enclosed in fireproof partitions, so many additional persons may be employed on any one floor as can occupy the enclosed stair hall on that floor allowing five square feet of unobstructed floor space per person.

3. Where horizontal exits are provided, the number of persons that may be employed on any floor depends upon the number that can occupy either the smaller of the two spaces on such floor on either side of the fireproof partitions of fire walls or the floor of an adjoining or near-by building which is connected with such floor by openings in the wall, between the buildings or by exterior balconies or

[7] Labor Law, sec. 79, e-1.
[8] Ibid., sec. 79, e-3; e-6; e-8.

bridges, in addition to the occupants of such connected floors, allowing five square feet of unobstructed floor space per person. These horizontal exits must, however, be of a sufficient width to allow 22 inches in width of opening for each 50 persons, or fraction thereof, permitted to be employed on such floor.

4. Where an automatic sprinkler system, conforming to the rules and regulations of the industrial board, is installed, the number of employees permitted on any floor may be increased 50 per cent except that this increase may not be applied to the two foregoing provisions.

5. The law also provides that a minimum floor area must be allowed every employee. In fireproof buildings this limit is fixed at one employee for 32 square feet of floor space; in non-fireproof buildings at 36 square feet. These provisions place an absolute limit on the number of persons that may be employed on any floor.

Fire alarm signal system [9]

A fire alarm signal system must be installed in every factory over two stories in height employing more than 25 persons above the ground floor.

Fire drills [10]

Fire drills must be held at least once a month in all factories over two stories high with more than 25 employees above the ground floor.

Exits [11]

Every factory more than one story high must conform to the following conditions:

Every floor area must have at least two means of exit remote from each other. One of them must, on every floor above the ground floor, be either an interior enclosed fireproof stairway or an exterior enclosed fireproof stairway. The other must be either a stairway of the same kind or a horizontal exit.

No point in any floor may be more than 100 feet distant from the entrance of one of these exits.

When a floor area exceeds 5000 square feet, at least one additional means of exit must be provided for every 5000 square feet or part thereof in excess of 5000 square feet. At least one exterior fireproof stairway must be provided in every building over 100 feet in height. This stairway must be accessible from every point in the building.

---

[9] Labor Law, sec. 83, a-1.
[10] Ibid., sec. 83, a-2.
[11] Ibid., sec. 79, a-2.

Width of doorways and hallways [12]

The width of hallways and exit doors leading to the street must at the street-level not be less than the aggregate width of all stairways leading to them.

4. Height of Other Buildings

Fireproofing provision only restriction on height [13]

All hotels, lodging-houses, schools, theaters, jails, police stations, hospitals, asylums and institutions for the care and treatment of persons must be of fireproof construction if they exceed 36½ feet in height.

All other buildings, with minor exceptions, must be of fireproof construction if their height exceeds 75 feet.

When the height does not exceed 12 stories, nor more than 150 feet, the building need not be constructed wholly of fireproof material—the doors, windows, window frames, trims, casings, interior finish, floor boards and sleepers, for instance, may be of wood. When the height exceeds 12 stories, or 150 feet, these must be of fireproof material.

II—SIZE OF NON-FIREPROOF STORES, WAREHOUSES AND FACTORIES [14]

The maximum size of all non-fireproof stores, warehouses and factories is limited in case iron, steel or wood columns or piers of masonry are used in place of brick partition walls. A building extending from street to street is limited to a width of 75 feet and a depth of 210 feet, with a maximum area of 15,750 square feet. A building fronting on three streets is limited to a width of 105 feet and a depth of 210 feet, with a maximum area of 22,050 square feet. A corner building fronting on two streets may not have a greater area than 12,500 square feet. A building located in any other manner may not have a greater area than 8000 square feet. The superintendent of buildings may, however, on considering the location and purpose of a proposed building, allow a greater area than that stipulated above provided its height does not exceed three stories.

III—FIRE APPLIANCES, FIRE-ESCAPES, STAIRWAYS, AND FIRE-PROOF SHUTTERS AND DOORS

Standpipes [15]

Every building exceeding 85 feet in height, but not more than 150 feet, must be provided with a four-inch standpipe running from cellar to roof. In buildings exceeding 150 feet in height such

[12] Labor Law, sec. 79, a-4.
[13] Building Code, sec. 105.
[14] Ibid., sec. 32.
[15] Ibid., sec. 102.

standpipes must be at least six inches in diameter. If any part of the building extends from street to street or forms an L shape, standpipes must be provided on each street frontage.

Water-tank on roof[16]

Every building exceeding 150 feet in height must be provided with auxiliary fire apparatus, consisting of water-tank on roof, or in cellar, standpipes, hose, nozzles, wrenches, fire-extinguishers, hooks, axes and such other appliances as may be required by the fire department. All of these must be of the best material and of the sizes, patterns and regulation kind used and required by the fire department.

Pumps and elevators[17]

A steam or electric pump and at least one passenger elevator must be kept in readiness for immediate use by the fire department during all hours of the night and day, including holidays and Sundays, in all buildings exceeding 150 feet in height.

Perforated pipes and automatic sprinklers[18]

Buildings over 150 feet in height used or occupied for business or manufacturing purposes must be provided with 2½-inch perforated iron pipes placed on and along the ceiling line of each floor below the first floor, and extending the full depth of the building. This perforated pipe must be provided with a valve placed at or near the standpipe so that water can be let into it when deemed necessary by the firemen. When the building is 25 feet or less in width, two lines of perforated pipe must be provided. Where the building is more than 25 feet in width an additional perforated pipe shall be provided for each 12½ feet, or part thereof, that the building is wider than 25 feet. Automatic sprinklers may be installed in lieu of such perforated pipes.

Stairways[19]

Stores, factories, hotels or lodging-houses, covering a lot area exceeding 2500 square feet, but not more than 5000 square feet, must be provided with at least two continuous lines of stairs remote from each other. Such buildings, furthermore, must have at least one continuous line of stairs for each 5000 square feet of lot area in excess of that required for 5000 square feet of area. When a building covers more than 5000 square feet of area, the number of stairs shall either be increased in this proportion or as will meet the approval of the commissioner of buildings.

---

[16] Building Code, sec. 102.
[17] Ibid.
[18] Ibid.
[19] Ibid., sec. 75.

Fire-escapes and stairways [20]

Fire-escapes, stairways or other means of egress in case of fire shall be provided as directed by the tenement house department for tenements and the fire department for other buildings, as follows:

1. Every tenement house exceeding one story in height.

2. Every building more than three stories in height occupied and used as a hotel or lodging-house.

3. Every boarding-house having more than 15 sleeping-rooms above the basement story.

4. Every factory, mill, manufacturing or work shop, hospital, asylum or institution for the care or treatment of individuals.

5. Every building three stories and over in height used or occupied as a store or workroom.

6. Every building in whole or in part occupied or used as a school or place of instruction or assembly.

7. Every office building five stories or more in height.

Exits in theaters [21]

Every theater erected for the accommodation of more than 300 persons must have at least one front on the street. This front may not have a smaller width than 25 feet.

Suitable means of entrance and exits must be provided in this front. Theaters accommodating 300 persons must have at least two exits and those accommodating 500 persons three exits. These exits must be at least five feet wide. Theaters accommodating more than 500 persons must have additional exit facilities—every additional 100 persons or portion thereof in excess of 500 must be provided with 20 inches of exit width.

Distinct and separate places of entrance must be provided for each gallery above the first.

In addition to these entrances and exits, emergency exits into side and rear courts or into the side street must be provided. There must be at least two such exits with a minimum width of five feet on each side in each tier of the auditorium including the parquet.

When a theater is located on a corner lot, that portion bordering on the side street and not required for the uses of the theater may, if such portion be not more than 25 feet in width, be used for offices, stores or apartments. This permission may, however, not interfere in any way with the required emergency exits. The wall separating the auditorium and the portion so used must be of fireproof construction to the roof.

[20] Building Code, sec. 103.
[21] Ibid., sec. 109.

Fireproof shutters and doors [22]

Every building more than two stories in height above the curb level, except dwelling houses, hotels, schoolhouses and churches, must have doors, blinds or shutters made of iron built into the wall on every exterior window or opening above the first story, excepting on the front openings fronting on streets which are more than 30 feet in width, or where no other buildings are within 30 feet of such openings.

IV—PROVISIONS REGARDING OPEN SPACE

There are no statutory or other legal provisions restricting the percentage of lot area that may be covered by stores, factories, warehouses, etc. Such buildings may cover 100 per cent of the lot area in the case of all lots.

Open space about private dwellings [23]

No private dwelling house may occupy more than 90 per cent of the lot area.

Open space about hotels [24]

Hotels situated on corner lots and covering an area of not more than 3000 square feet are prohibited from occupying more than 95 per cent of the lot area above the second story level.

Hotels situated on interior lots and not more than five stories in height are prohibited from occupying more than 90 per cent of the lot area above the second story level. An additional 2½ per cent of uncovered lot area must be provided for each and every story over five. In the case of a 21-story hotel this space would equal half of the lot area.

Where a hotel occupies a number of lots, the arrangement and distribution of the open space must be such as in the opinion of the commissioner of buildings will secure both light and ventilation.

The board of examiners, however, has the power to modify these provisions. In some cases this modification amounts to a repeal of the Building Code. An instance of this is the McAlpin Hotel on 34th Street and Broadway. The lot area of this hotel is about 31,000 square feet. The bureau of buildings insisted the building should cover only 51 per cent of this area above the first story. The owners appealed to the board of examiners and received permission to cover 83 per cent of the area above the first story.

Open space about office buildings [25]

Office buildings erected on interior lots may not cover more than 90 per cent of the lot area at and above the second story floor level.

[22] Building Code, sec. 104.
[23] Ibid., sec. 8.
[24] Ibid., sec. 10.
[25] Ibid., sec. 11.

The Building Code sets no limit on the area that office buildings on corner lots of not over 3000 square feet may cover.

Open space about frame buildings [26]

A space of at least 3 feet must intervene between a frame building and the rear and side lot lines unless the space between the studs on any such side be filled solidly with not less than 2½ inches of brickwork or fireproof material.

Open space about theaters [27]

Every theater or opera-house erected for the accommodation of more than 300 persons must be provided with an open court, in the rear and on the side not bordering on the street in the case of a corner lot, and in the rear and on both sides in the case of a lot having but one street frontage. The width of these courts must be proportioned to the seating capacity of the theater. The court must have a minimum width of 10 feet where the seating capacity is less than 1000; of 12 feet where the seating capacity exceeds 1000 but is less than 1800; and of 14 feet where the seating capacity exceeds 1800.

These courts must extend the full length and height of each side and the rear of the building where its sides or side or rear does not abut on a street or alley. They must be the same width throughout.

Though these are the legal provisions with reference to open space about theaters, they are very seldom applied in practice. In building a theater it is customary to appeal to the board of examiners for a modification of these regulations. The board, as a rule, gives a more or less favorable ruling on these appeals.

Open space about lodging-houses [28]

No lodging-house may occupy more than 65 per cent of the area of an interior lot, unless, in the opinion of the superintendent of buildings, a larger area might be permitted without prejudice to the light and ventilation of the building, when it may cover 75 per cent.

On corner lots such buildings may not cover more than 92 per cent of the lot area above the first story. A lodging-house on a corner lot may not be erected nearer than five feet to the rear boundary.

The interior courts or shafts may not be less than two feet four inches in width. This provision applies to both interior and corner lots.

In computing the amount of a lot area covered by a lodging-house, no cognizance is taken of courts or shafts possessing an area of less than 25 square feet.

---

[26] Building Code, sec. 146.
[27] Ibid., sec. 109.
[28] City Charter, sec. 1315.

Shafts and courts of a smaller area than 10 square feet may be covered.

Buildings erected on same lot as lodging-houses

No building may be erected on a lot already containing a lodging-house unless a space is left between such building and lodging-house. When such building is one story high this space must be at least 10 feet in width; if two stories, 15 feet; if three stories, 20 feet; and if over three stories, 25 feet. The width of this space may, however, be lessened or modified if, in the judgment of the bureau of buildings, the thorough ventilation of the space is not impaired.

Only buildings possessing an open space with a width of 10 feet in the rear may be converted to lodging-houses.

Open Space About Tenement Houses[29]

The amount of open space demanded in the case of apartment houses and tenements is a variable quantity. The area required in any particular case is dependent upon several different factors: on the vertical and horizontal dimensions of the building; the interior arrangement and occupancy of the building; the shape and size of the building site; and the location of the building site. The following five provisions are the most important:

1. Tenements situated on corner lots may occupy 90 per cent of the lot area.

2. Tenements situated on interior lots more than 90 feet but less than 105 feet in depth may occupy 70 per cent of the lot area.

3. Tenements situated on interior lots more than 105 feet in depth may occupy 65 per cent of the lot area.

The above three provisions do not, however, apply to tenements erected on lots not exceeding 100 feet that run through from one street to another.

4. Tenements situated on interior lots not exceeding three stories and cellar in height, and which are not occupied or arranged to be occupied by more than six families, or by more than two families on any floor, and in which each apartment extends from the street to the yard, and which are provided with inner courts with bathroom extension, may occupy 65 per cent of the lot area.

5. Tenements situated on interior lots, not exceeding four stories and cellar in height, and which are not occupied or arranged to be occupied by more than eight families, or by more than two families on any floor, and in which each apartment extends from the street to the yard, and which are provided with inner courts, may occupy 72 per cent of the lot area.

Tenements situated on interior lots less than 90 feet in depth, if

[29] Tenement House Law, secs. 62, 63.

provided with a sufficient number of legal-sized courts, are not required to leave any specific percentage of the lot area vacant.

The exact distribution and arrangement of the open space demanded for tenements is controlled by that provision in the law which requires every room, including water-closet compartments and bathrooms, to have at least one window opening directly upon the street or upon a yard or court of specified dimensions. No apartment, moreover, of three rooms or less may extend in depth from the street or yard, as the case may be, for a greater distance than 18 feet without the intervention of an inner or outer court.

The total window area of each room, except water-closet compartments and bathrooms, must be at least one-tenth of the superficial area of the room. No window may be less than 12 square feet in area between the stop-beads.

The following table shows the minimum size demanded for the different kinds of courts:

		Courts situated on lot line		Courts between wings or parts of same building or between different buildings on same lot	
Height of buildings in feet	Yard, interior lot, depth in feet	Outer court, width in feet	Inner court, dimensions in feet	Outer court, width in feet	Inner court, dimensions in feet
36	10	5	11 x 22	10	22 x 22
48	11	5½	11½ x 23	11	23 x 23
60	12	6	12 x 24	12	24 x 24
72	13	6½	12½ x 25	13	25 x 25
84	14	7	13 x 26	14	26 x 26
96	15	7½	13½ x 27	15	27 x 27
108	16	8	14 x 28	16	28 x 28
120	17	8½	14½ x 29	17	29 x 29
132	18	9	15 x 30	18	30 x 30
144	19	9½	15½ x 31	19	31 x 31
156	20	10	16 x 32	20	32 x 32

Yards [30]

Every tenement must be provided with a yard extending across the entire width of the lot. For a 60-foot building on an interior lot the minimum depth of this yard is 12 feet. The depth of this yard must be increased one foot for every additional 12 feet of height of building, or fraction thereof, above 60 feet. For every decrease of 12 feet in height it might be diminished one foot in depth. It must, however, have a minimum depth of 10 feet.

In the case of a corner lot the depth of this space must be at least 10 feet. But where the lot is less than 100 feet in depth the depth of the yard need not be more than 10 per cent of the depth

[30] Tenement House Law, secs. 52, 53, 54, 55.

of the lot, provided the yard is never less than five feet deep nor less than the minimum width of an outer court situated on the lot line as described below.

In the case of gore-shaped corner lots where the width of the lot at the rear lot line is greater than the width at the front and the average width of the lot does not exceed 50 feet, the average width through the center is taken for the purpose of determining the area of the yard.

Where a corner lot exceeds 50 feet in width, the excess over 50 feet is considered in the same manner as an interior lot.

Tenements on lots running through from one street to another and over 70 and less than 105 feet in depth must have a yard through the center of the lot.

This yard may never be less than 12 feet in depth. Its depth is regulated according to the height of the building, as in the case of other yards. Where such a lot is over 105 feet in depth, the yard left through the center may not be less than 24 feet in depth. The depth of this yard must be increased one foot for every additional 12 feet of height of building, or fraction thereof, over 60 feet.

Where a single tenement runs through from one street to another and also occupies the entire block, no yard need be provided. Where a single tenement is situated on a lot formed by the intersection of two streets meeting at an acute angle, the yard need not extend across the entire width of the lot, provided it extends to a point in line with the middle line of the block.

Outer courts

1. *Courts situated on lot line*

An outer court of a building 60 feet in height situated on the lot line must be at least six feet in width. Such a court in a tenement more or less than 60 feet in height has its width graduated on either a progressive or a regressive scale—the width of a court of a 60-foot building being the basis for this graduation. If the building is higher than 60 feet, the width of the court is increased six inches for every 12 feet of additional height, or fractional part thereof, above 60 feet; if the building is less than 60 feet in height, the width of the court is diminished six inches for every 12 feet of height below 60 feet.

2. *Courts situated between wings or parts of same building, or between different buildings on same lot*

An outer court of a building 60 feet in height situated between wings or parts of the same building, or between different buildings on the same lot, must be at least 12 feet in width. Such a court in a tenement more or less than 60 feet in height also has its width graduated on either a progressive or a regressive scale—the width of a court of a 60-foot building being the basis for this graduation.

If the building is higher than 60 feet, the width of the court is increased one foot for every 12 feet of additional height, or fractional part thereof, above 60 feet; if the building is less than 60 feet in height, the width of the court is diminished one foot for every 12 feet of height below 60 feet.

3. *Other provisions*

Where the depth of an outer court is less than the minimum width prescribed in the above table, then its width may be equal to but not less than its depth, provided the width is not less than four feet in the clear. This exception also applies to offsets and recesses in inner and outer courts. No window, except that of a water-closet compartment, bathroom or hall, may face on any court less than six feet wide.

When an outer court changes its initial horizontal direction, or any part of such court extends in a direction so as not to receive direct light from the street or yard, the length of such portion of said court may not be any greater than its width.

4. *Exceptions from general provisions* [31]

An exception from the above table is also made in the case of outer courts for tenements not exceeding four stories and cellar in height and which are not occupied or arranged to be occupied by more than eight families exclusive of the janitor's family, or by more than two families on any floor, and in which the apartments extend through from the street to the yard. Where the outer court of such a tenement is situated on the lot line and does not extend from the street to the yard, and if its length does not exceed 36 feet, its width need not be more than four feet. Where the court of such a tenement is situated between wings of or parts of the same building, or between different buildings on the same lot, and if its length does not exceed 36 feet, its width need not be more than eight feet.

An exception is also made in the case of outer courts for tenements not exceeding five stories and cellar in height and which are not occupied or arranged to be occupied by more than ten families, exclusive of the janitor's family, or by more than two families on any floor, and in which the apartments extend through from the street to the yard. Where an outer court of such a tenement is situated on the lot line its width may not be less than five feet in any part measured to the lot line nor less than ten feet in any part measured to the nearest opposite wall. Where an outer court of such a tenement is situated between wings or parts of the same building, or between different buildings on the same lot, its width measured from wall to wall may not be less than 10 feet in any part. These provisions apply, however, only in case the length of the court does not exceed 50 feet.

[31] Tenement House Law, sec. 57.

Inner courts

An inner court of a 60-foot building so situated that one side is on the lot line must have a minimum width of 12 feet and a minimum length of 24 feet in every part. For every 12 feet of increase, or fraction thereof, in the height of building the width and length of such court must be increased six inches and one foot respectively; with every 12 feet of decrease in height the width and length may be decreased six inches and one foot respectively.

The least horizontal dimension of an inner court of a 60-foot building not situated upon the lot line but inclosed on all four sides must be at least 24 feet. For every 12 feet of increase, or fraction thereof, in the height of building each horizontal dimension of the court must be increased one foot; for every 12 feet of decrease in the height of building each horizontal dimension may be decreased one foot.

Exceptions from general provisions [32]

An exception is made to the above rule in the case of tenements situated on interior lots not exceeding four stories and cellar in height, and which are not occupied or arranged to be occupied by more than eight families, or by more than two families on any floor, and in which each apartment extends from the street to the yard, and which do not occupy more than 72 per cent of the lot area. An inner lot line court of such building need not be more than eight feet wide nor more than 14 feet long. An inner court, however, which is not situated on the lot line but inclosed on all four sides must be at least 14 feet in each dimension.

An exception is also made in the case of tenements situated on interior lots not exceeding three stories and cellar in height, and which are not occupied or arranged to be occupied by more than six families, or by more than two families on any floor. In such buildings a bathroom extension may be erected in inner courts situated on the lot line, provided such extension has no window facing an opposite building, and provided its maximum width does not exceed 4½ feet nor its length 7 feet, and also provided the width of the court is not reduced by such extension to less than 3½ feet. Inner lot line courts in such tenements occupying not more than 65 per cent of the lot area must have a minimum width of 4 feet measured from the lot line to the opposite wall of the building and a minimum width of 8 feet measured from wall to wall. The length of the court must be at least 12½ feet. An inner court of such tenement not situated on the lot line but inclosed on all four sides must have a minimum width of 8 feet and a minimum length of 12½ feet.

Offsets and recesses are permitted in inner courts that are not less than 10 feet wide.

---

[32] Tenement House Law, sec. 58.

Cutting off court corners[33]

Both outer and inner courts may have their corners cut off, provided the running length of the wall at the angle of the court does not exceed 7 feet. In outer and inner courts of a less size than the minimum prescribed for tenements 60 feet in height the running length of the wall containing windows in the angle of the court must not exceed 4 feet. An inner court less than 8 feet in width may not, however, be reduced by having its corners cut off.

Buildings on same lot with tenement houses[34]

If a building is placed on the same lot as a tenement, an open space must be provided that conforms to the following regulations:

Where either building is 60 feet in height the space must be 24 feet from wall to wall. The space must be increased 1 foot in depth for every 12 feet of increase, or fraction thereof, in the height of such buildings. It may be decreased 1 foot in depth for every 12 feet decrease in the height.

No building of any kind may be placed upon the same lot as a tenement so as to decrease the minimum legal size of any court or yard.

Rear tenements[35]

No separate tenement may be erected upon the rear of a lot 50 feet or less in width where there is already a tenement on the front. Nor may any tenement be erected on the front of such a lot already having a tenement in the rear.

---

[33] Tenement House Law, sec. 59.
[34] Ibid., sec. 61.
[35] Ibid., sec. 60.

APPENDIX III

THE GERMAN ZONE BUILDING REGULATIONS

By Frank Backus Williams

In the solution of municipal problems no nation to-day has progressed so far as Germany; and no contribution to this end is more widely or favorably known than the zone system of building regulations which was there first conceived and applied.

The method of the construction of cities may be divided into two parts: city planning, and regulation of building in accordance with the plan.[1] The city plan lays out the streets, sewers, parks, transit system, and other features of the city; the building regulations prescribe and limit the character, location and intensity of building in accordance with the plan. Thus the city plan locates the principal business and traffic streets, and gives them their direction, breadth and depth of lot; while the building regulations prescribe what kind of buildings may be erected on these streets, how much of the lot they may cover, and how high they shall be. Both the plan and the regulations are necessary to the completed street; to the construction of the city, as a whole, and each of its parts.[2]

The zone system is a method of regulating building under the city plan.[3] It originated in Germany and receives the name because most of the cities were walled cities and grew in zones. It has two characteristics: it groups buildings of different classes, and it limits the density of building progressively, allowing buildings to be higher and to cover more of the lot in the centers where the land values are greater and business needs require more concentration; making the requirements more and more severe as the distance from these centers increases.

Originally, the business center was, roughly speaking, bounded by a circular line where the old walls had been, within which the land was dearest. After the walls were thrown down, development and dear land came in belts or zones, the land becoming cheaper and less intensely used as it was farthest from the old city. The system might more properly be called the " district system." In many German cities where it is to-day applied there are several centers of concentration and dear land; and the different requirements vary in severity according to conditions which change in no very precise proportion to distance from a center.

The zone system was first advocated by the veteran city planner Baumeister in the '70's, but was first actually carried out in Altona

[1] As to the jurisdiction of the City, the State, and the Empire, see page 108.
[2] As to jurisdiction in these matters, see p. 108.
[3] As to the basis of authority to issue building regulations, see p. 110.

in 1884. The noted Franz Adickes was at that time its mayor. In Germany a new mayor is usually obtained by advertisement, and a man who has made a marked success in a smaller city is often employed by a larger one when in need of a new incumbent. So, in 1890, Adickes became mayor of Frankfort.* In 1891 he introduced the zone system, and it has been in force there ever since. From Frankfort it spread to other German and to Swiss and Scandinavian cities and is now the prevailing system in these countries.

Under the German rules the height of buildings is invariably regulated with relation to the width of the street upon which the building is situated; and also, usually, by a maximum which, irrespective of the width of the street, it must not exceed. In many cities, in the zone or zones of greatest concentration, a height a little in excess of the street width is allowed; in the other zones it must not exceed that width, and in the outer zone or zones the maximum limits it to less. Usually, too, there are minimum courts, and all rooms constructed for the residence or long-continued business use of mankind must have a window upon a court at least that size. The proportion of the lot that may be covered by buildings, also, is almost invariably limited progressively, buildings on corner lots in each zone being allowed to cover more than those on inside lots. The ordinances in the different cities differ, of course, in detail; for not only the cities themselves are different, but the judgment of the city fathers varies as well. In a very general way, however, the system is the same. The provisions of the Frankfort-on-the-Main ordinance illustrate it as well as any other.[4]

The old or inner city is the first zone or district. Here the highest buildings are allowed. They must not exceed the width of the street, plus about 10 feet (3 meters), or in any case, however wide the street, about 66 feet (20 meters).[5] This is to the cornice; the roof above this is restricted by an angle, and in no case may exceed about 30 feet (9 meters). The roof is more than mere roof; it is a roof story, in which there are rooms, which, however, may not always be used for residence. The number of stories is also restricted; in this zone it must not exceed five and the roof story.

Here, in the inner city, also, the greatest proportion of the lot may be covered with buildings, three-quarters—for corner lots five-sixths. Factories are allowed, but are not numerous. Solid blocks are permitted. The city here presents the appearance of being fully built up to a fairly uniform height.

* Unless otherwise explained, Frankfort wherever used in Appendix III means Frankfort-on-the-Main.

[4] The zone regulations are issued by the "building police" (see p. 110), and are a part of the code of ordinances covering also structural requirements, rules with regard to the occupation of buildings, and all other matters relating to building, many of which here are regulated by different authorities and issued separately.

[5] On streets less than about 30 feet (9 meters) wide, a height of about 36 feet (11 meters) is permitted.

The outer city is divided into an outer, an inner, and a country zone, in which the height of buildings allowed progressively decreases, and the amount of the lot that must be left free of buildings progressively increases. In each of these zones are residence, factory and mixed sections.[6] In the residence sections, factories are so discouraged as to be practically forbidden. In the factory sections, situated along the railroads, the harbor, and out of the city in the direction so that the prevailing winds will blow the smoke away from the city, residences are forbidden.[7] In the factory sections, the restrictions on height and amount of lot covered are mild and do not become progressively greater. The mixed sections are near the factory sections, and there, too, under certain mild restrictions, many sorts of manufacturing are permitted.

In the residence section a space between neighboring houses of about 10 feet (3 meters) in the inner zone and a third more in the outer zone is required. This is generally used for a broad walk with green grass bordering it on each side of the high fence that divides the two lots. Groups of buildings are, however, allowed with a somewhat less proportionate amount of free space for the group as a whole.

Certain parts of the newly added territory of the city, beyond all the other zones, and forming a zone by itself, have been reserved for a villa section in which country houses only are allowed.

In all these zones the amount of the lot that must be left free progresses, until, in the villa section, it is seven-tenths of the entire lot. So, also the permissible height decreases to about 53 feet (16 meters) and the number of stories to two. This does not include the roof story and the actual roof, which, together, in this zone must not exceed about 6 feet (1.80 meters) in height. In no case, however, may the house in this zone exceed in height, except for the roof story and roof, the width of the street upon which it stands.

The building regulations in Germany are at best complex. For instance, the height of a dwelling house is determined by a maximum; by the width of the street; by the width of the side street (if it is a corner building); by the distance the building extends along the side street; by the width of the court; by the height of the rear building.[8] This is true of practically all ordinances—some have many other provisions. Height is only one of many factors—such as length, depth, minimum courts of various sorts, light angles, etc. All these factors vary, both absolutely and proportionally, in each zone, and all must be included in any calculation of house dimensions in the different zones.

---

[6] In many cities there is only a provision establishing a protected district, in which offensive industries cannot be carried on.

[7] This is under an amendment of 1912. The prohibition of residence in the manufacturing section exists in very few if any other cities.

[8] The ordinances universally provide that the height on the principal street may be retained on the side street for a certain distance.

For many reasons the ordinances are becoming more and more complicated. On the map of Dresden, for instance, the building zones are kaleidoscopic. This is, however, a complexity growing apparently out of the character of the city, and not out of theoretical considerations. Many small communities have from time to time been absorbed by the great city; in them, in miniature, are the same conditions as exist in Dresden itself. The provisions of the ordinances of Dresden, its inner and its progressively outer districts, must be applied to each of these minor communities. The result is of interest to us in New York as an application of zoning to very complex conditions.

The complications of the newest regulation for Düsseldorf—1912—are of a somewhat different nature. There, also, the effort is to fit the zoning provisions to the actual, or perhaps to the desired, conditions. They have, therefore, five zones, which, together, cover the entire city. There are, also, building classes, twelve in number. These classes may be applied to any part of any zone, even to so small a portion of it as a part of a street.

The result of the class regulations is usually, but not always, to affect the extent in height or area, or both, of the use of the land, and therefore the value of the territory to which it is applied. That effect is sometimes to increase, sometimes to diminish, it. The classes sometimes, however, simply prescribe the size or character of the house or the extent of the use of the house. The total result is to increase very considerably the complications which in the older and simpler ordinances were not small.

This, as we have seen, is admitted and justified on the ground that in this way the provisions are made more closely to fit the circumstances and guide the development. As the classes may be applied to such portions of the zone as to the building police seem fit at such times as they see fit, and may from time to time be changed or abrogated, the building police are in this way given considerable power.

The same result is obtained in other cities by making for a given territory strict requirements and then allowing the building police to authorize other methods of construction when it seems to them best. Thus, in Essen, in their ordinances of 1907, in Zones 4a and 5a and District A, only single houses, 20 or more feet apart, may "as a general rule" be built; but the police may authorize double houses, groups, etc. Of course, practically everybody applies for permission to build double houses or groups, so as to utilize his land to the greatest extent and obtain the greatest income. The result obtained and no doubt desired is that the authorities can in each case dictate what shall be built and often the exact architecture. The influence of the authorities is for simplicity and a harmony in the appearance of the houses of a street or block. In this way the cost to the owner is often lessened and his house made more valuable. But all cities do not have such men as Beigeordneter (vice-mayor) Schmidt as architectural dictator.[11]

In their effort to fit the provisions to the circumstances, some German cities go even further. They have no zone ordinances at all—each new district as it is laid out and streets built receives its special rule for each street and house. Thus, Leipzig had in August, 1913, ninety-seven districts—I understand they have more now—in which there are different heights of buildings and many variations as to the amount of lot that may be covered with buildings.

Another tendency in modern building ordinances is to make rules for streets in addition to rules for districts. It is recognized that the chief business streets should receive different treatment from the minor business and residence streets, and the chief traffic streets different treatment from either. The allowed height and the amount of the lot allowed to be covered increases with the importance of the street and decreases very greatly the moment the principal street is left behind. Usually one more story is thus permitted, and a considerable portion of the lot may be built over. This tendency can be seen in the ordinances for Cologne and Düsseldorf, and is increasingly emphasized each year. It was also introduced, in 1912, into the Frankfort ordinances.

The Munich ordinance, passed in 1904, goes even further. It disregards the zone or district system altogether, regulating entirely by streets and their differences; or rather, perhaps, it recognizes the fact that streets *are* districts. This system was adopted in 1912 by Karlsruhe, where sixteen classes of streets were created.

The tendency, however, is not always toward greater complexity. As a general thing the earlier ordinances require, in the successive zones, districts or classes, a decrease both in the height of buildings and in the amount of the lot that they cover. Many newer ordinances recognize the fact that intensity of use is the product of two factors—height and amount of lot covered; and allow, if the height is less, that more of the lot be built over. There are also ordinances which in part adopt a rule based upon the proportion of the cubic mass of the building to the size of the lot.[12]

---

[11] For an instance of administrative control of street architecture in Essen, see p. 100.

[12] Chemnitz, ordinance of 1912, Landespolizeibezirk, Berlin, parts of Charlottenburg, Deutsch-Wilmersdorf, Schöneberg, Neukölln, Lichtenberg, Boxhagen-Rummelsburg and Stralau, lying outside Ring railroad; part 5 (Small houses). Ordinances of March 26, 1912. Suburbs of Berlin, section 67 (factories); Ordinance of January 30, 1912.

Land owners do not, in Germany, rely entirely upon the building ordinances enacted by public initiative. There, as here, land is sold by large proprietors and development companies, subject to severer or different conditions than those of the ordinances. The object there, as here, is to create a neighborhood of an especially desirable character. Often these conditions are, at the owners' request, introduced into the ordinances and become public law, as well as private covenant. In rare instances the proprietor obtains

The provisions of ordinances which we have been examining are, evidently, utilitarian. They originated chiefly as measures of fire protection. The height allowed was that to which water could be thrown to put out the flames; the court was prescribed of such a size that a fire engine could turn in it; the space between the houses was required so that the apparatus could reach the building in the rear and was called a "fire lane." Regulations of this character are now retained almost entirely for a different reason, also utilitarian—that of providing light, sun, and ventilation.[13]

The regulations are not, however, entirely on this basis, and never were. They have always shown a certain regard for appearances. A wall that can be seen from the street must be finished to some degree like a façade; painting in harsh colors is forbidden. The law has universally and for many years forbidden "gross disfigurement" of the street; some of the South German states long ago went further; and many statutes passed within perhaps six or eight years do the same.[14] Not only is disfigurement that falls short of gross now forbidden, but a certain conformity to the architecture of the street may be required. The law specifically states, however, that the builder shall not be put to any substantial increase of expense thereby.

The parts of the ordinances that are avowedly utilitarian, too, show at times the influence that artistic considerations have upon the people of Germany and their rulers. The height regulations, producing a uniform sky-line, exist in part because the modern German likes such a sky-line and dislikes an exposed party wall. The rules with regard to roofs are another example. The roof

---

the consent of the authorities to have the conditions only a matter of public law, so that it will not be difficult later to do away with these conditions if desired. Usually, however, proprietors are afraid to trust merely the public law and desire to be protected in addition by private covenant.

Vienna, by an interesting and logical extension of the principle of building ordinances, regulates also the subdivision of land into building lots, in order that each lot may be and remain of such form and size as a proper house erected under the building regulations requires.

[13] See p. 110; also p. 114 et seq.

[14] Prussian Landrecht, I, 8, secs. 66, 71.

So the Polizeistrafgesetzbuch (police law) of December 26, 1871, Article 101, of Bavaria, provided: "In the interest of beauty, building police provisions can be passed by local ordinance. Changes in building plans for this reason must not, however, materially increase the building cost."

The Bavarian law, referred to above, has been amended as follows:

Law of May 5, 1890, art. 8 (to be found in Gesetz- und Verordnungsblatt, p. 223).

Law of June 22, 1900, secs. 3 and 4 (same, p. 483).

Law of July 6, 1908 (same, p. 353).

Other states have passed laws as follows:

Prussia. Law against disfigurement of streets, places and prominent country objects, of July 15, 1907.

Baden. Building law of September 1, 1907, sec. 33.

Duchy of Anhalt. Building law of June 19, 1905.

Kingdom of Saxony. Law against disfigurement of city and country, of March 10, 1909.

story, with dwelling or storage rooms in it, is almost universal. This is because the ordinances allow a certain height and number of stories, plus an ample roof besides; and the builder, to gain the additional rentable space, invariably builds an ample roof as he is encouraged to do. This, although not the origin of roof stories, is given in Germany as the principal reason for their retention; for the German loves a large roof, and it is thus obtained at no increase of expense to the builder or land owner.

The ordinances universally allow projections in the interest of variety. These projections may be into the street, or into the front or side or rear spaces required by law; or above the height limit. They are strictly limited both in amount of projection and extent of cubic space.

Much has been done in the cause of beauty by continental cities at public expense. Not only are beautiful public buildings erected, and given suitable site and setting, but in the sale to private individuals of the extensive lands belonging to them cities impose servitudes to secure correspondence and harmony for an entire street or square. Many of the features we admire in Vienna are thus obtained. Paris has done more by this method than any other city and from the most ancient times.[15]

Germany by administrative methods does much to induce and compel private builders to respect and produce a harmonious "street picture" as well as to secure tasteful single houses. There exist in many Prussian cities departments called "Bureaus of Building Advice"; and there are similar departments, under other names, in most of the states. To these bureaus builders are required to submit their plans. Improvements are merely indicated by the bureau—care is taken not to interfere with the business of the architects. Both tact and compulsion are used in varying degrees in different cities.

A story illustrating methods sometimes employed is told of Beigeordneter Schmidt of Essen. A builder—so the story goes—submitted the sketch of a façade to Schmidt and asked for a permit to erect the house. Now in Essen, as in most of Prussia, no man may build upon an unfinished street without express permission of the authorities; and in practice no street is ever legally finished until the last house on it is built. The result is that the discretion of the authorities to allow a given house to be erected is uncontrolled. Schmidt looked at the façade and saw that it was *bad*—bad in itself and utterly out of harmony with the street picture which Schmidt had been so carefully creating. Now it so happened—not to put it too bluntly—that the street upon which the builder wished to erect the house still lacked an infinitesimal bit of curbing; and Schmidt, turning to the builder, said: "I'm sorry; the street isn't finished."

[15] For a list of servitudes with date, text, drawings, etc., see Recueil d'Actes Administratifs et de Conventions relatifs aux Servitudes Speciales d'Architecture, Paris, Imprimerie Nouvelle, 11 Rue Cadet, 1905.

EFFECT OF HEIGHT LIMIT ON UNIFORMITY OF CORNICE LINE IN VIENNA.

After waiting a month the builder applied again, only to be met with the answer " the street is still unfinished."

Then he began to complain, loudly, and all over town, until a friend took him aside and whispered in his ear: " You fool; give him a decent façade and the street will be finished." And it was; and the plan, after a few suggestions from the Bureau of Building Advice, was approved, and a building permit issued.

The " unfinished street " is by no means the only " hold " the German official has; and this power is often used in the interest of beauty. In Essen the result is one of great harmony and good taste, often obtained at a saving to the builder, who, for instance, is persuaded to sacrifice some bit of ugly, useless, expensive ornamentation. Schmidt still shows in his city-planning lectures a house of some time ago so decorated, which, he says, the builders of Essen now beg him not to exhibit any longer, because they " don't build that way any more."

In some cities the zone boundary is in the center of the street, in some in the middle of the block. The expedients for softening the transition from one zone to another are many. In Essen the zone divisions run through the center of the street, but the houses in the zone of less intensity may be built to the same height as the houses on the other side of the street, the percentage of the lot to be covered remaining subject to the rule of the zone in which the buildings are situated. In the new ordinances for Cologne intermediate zones are in many cases introduced to make the passage less abrupt. Sometimes a natural or historical boundary, such as a river, the old city walls, turned into boulevards, the Ring-railroad in Berlin, are used; or a broad street with trees is planned, thus creating an easy transition. Often no such device is considered possible. The border line is recognized to be a difficulty.

Regulation in favor of light, air and sun is regarded as necessary, not alone in residence but in business apartments and rooms. The ordinances invariably make this requirement applicable to all rooms for the continued occupation of mankind.[16]

The effort is made, as a rule, to encourage neighboring builders so to construct their buildings as to throw their courts and yards together; and a slightly less court space is allowed on a builder's own land if their common use for light and air for all is secured by agreement of record to which the public authorities are a party.

This system I have outlined we are accustomed to call the zone system. We have seen that in many cases the zones are really districts, and that for this reason the name is not quite correct. The tendency in Germany to regulate by streets, as we have seen, has

[16] A series of reports of the Prefecture of the Seine (Direction of Municipal Affairs; Bureau of Hygiene for Paris), issued in 1907, 1908 (two reports), 1909, 1910, 1911 and 1912 (Imprimerie Chaix, rue Bergère, 20), and covering the years 1894 to 1912, shows the connection between tuberculosis and high buildings and small courts; and between tuberculosis and the place of work.

rendered the name still more inaccurate. To-day Germany is more apt to speak of the "graduated" ("Staffel" or "abgestufte") ordinances and point out that the regulations are graded in their requirements as to density of population; as to intensity of industrial use; as to size or character of streets, etc.—all in steps or degrees, but not at all in zones, or exactly in districts.[17] So the density or size of house in proportion to lot is graded, but by streets. So the industrial use of land is varied—in places all industries being permitted, in some only those having no disagreeable sound or smell, in some only the smaller industries, in some none at all; so streets vary from chief traffic and business streets all the way to small residence streets, not exactly by districts but rather by use or character.

The zone system has been introduced gradually. In some cities it is quite recent. It is still easy to talk with the men who drew and secured the adoption of zone provisions in some of them.

It is recognized as necessary in such cases that land values shall be respected, and no regulations adopted that shall make it impossible for an owner to build upon his land a building which will pay a fair return upon that value.[18] Often many temporary provisions are adopted to prevent such a loss. This is sometimes done by allowing new buildings in certain cases to be rebuilt for a certain length of time to the old height or to the old surface or cubic content. More often there is a provision for the granting of licenses to erect in disregard of certain provisions of the ordinance, as, for instance, in cases where lots are especially narrow or shallow or for other reasons a profitable building could not otherwise be built.[19]

What is the effect of the zone system upon German cities—upon living and business conditions, upon the price of land and upon rents? This is what we want to know and shall find difficult to ascertain and state. The zone ordinances are a part only of the city-planning ordinances and practice, and city planning is only one of many factors in city life. Administration, too, has a very considerable influence. Let us first, therefore, see what has occurred, without trying in every case to treat zoning as a separate factor; and then let us try to estimate its importance and effect.

Many of the features of German cities—the parks, the boulevards, the wide streets—are due to the city plan. The building regulations are responsible for the fact that upon the building lots themselves, as the street plan creates them, there is less concentration, less congestion. The zone system by exacting progressively less height and more free space as the centers are more and more left behind increases greatly this characteristic. The advantages are very great. The average amount of light and air is high, and special districts of great congestion are avoided to a much greater extent

[17] "Staffel" is South German dialect for "Stufe" (step) and the South German points to the fact as proof that the modification originated there.

[18] This is not always true of changes of ordinance, or land not upon any street. See p. 113.

[19] As to licenses, see p. 111.

than in this country. The fact that all these advantages are so obvious and need so little comment must not lead us to give them the less weight.

Some of the disadvantages, too, are apparent. A city widely spread out has longer streets, but the streets have only the same amount of use spread over their greater extent, and might often be narrower or at least have less surface expensively finished for traffic. This is too little remembered in Germany, and the result is higher cost for abutters and taxpayers and higher land prices and rents. But traffic streets and residential streets are being more and more differentiated, the former being of ample breadth, the latter much narrower. German cities are not, however, more decentralized as a rule than ours, and this is because the city does not as a general thing lay out a street until such time as it is needed for buildings, in solid continuation of the existing city.

The building and zone regulations have increased street costs in another way. In most cities more or less considerable portions are laid out under the rule that a space must be maintained between the building and the boundary of the lot, varying from 3 meters (about 10 feet) to as much as 8 or 10 meters. Under the zone regulations this side space is at a minimum in the inner zone and increases progressively. That this gives light and air and also increases the length of the street fronts and the sewers, gas pipes, water pipes, etc., at the expense of the abutter and with an increase in land prices, is obvious.[20]

In general, and aside from these obvious influences of the zone regulations, what is their effect upon land prices?

In Germany restrictions on intensity of building are advocated,

[20] The result of this side space system upon the character of building varies as the character of the development does. In a fashionable neighborhood or a middle-class neighborhood quite in the suburbs it has not affected the form of the buildings unfavorbly or had any generally recognized and conceded disadvantages whatever. Where, however, the side space requirement has been made in the more crowded parts of the city, where land is dearer, it is generally thought to have produced deep buildings, rear buildings, long ells, side wings—all without a sufficient increase in light and air on the sides. The total result, therefore, by substituting narrow caverns between the houses for abundance of free space back of them is regarded as bad. The modern building ordinances are therefore using side space requirements very much less, and not at all, unless the space that may be required is ample. Thus, double houses and groups of houses are often allowed with certain restrictions and positive requirements, even where a side space zone or class exists; and a front garden space or a rear building line so drawn as to leave the entire interior of a block in one open space is substituted; a break or two for the passage of air through the block being regarded as highly desirable and required in many cases.

These changes in ordinance are partly to cheapen and encourage the building of single houses; or more often of houses for small dwellings, as houses in which more than one family live and the number and size of the rooms are small are called in Germany. These ordinances are not made to encourage or allow the "tenement barrack" or large tenement house, as the older ordinances certainly did. The result is to lessen the side space requirements and decentralization.

as a general thing, for the express reason that they keep down land values. Do they? All Germany is fighting over the question.[21]

The effect of limitation on the height of buildings or the amount of the lot that may be covered by them seems to me scarcely to merit philosophical discussion in such profound terms as are used in Germany, or mathematical formulæ of such length. It is clear that if on Lot A I may build four stories, and on Lot B only two, Lot A, other things being equal, will be worth more, since it will bring in a greater income. Things are by no means always equal in Germany; the two-story districts are created for people who want separate houses and are able to pay accordingly; or else they are farther out where land is always used less intensely. But assuming that we fix by our regulation the relative prices of Lots A and B, we have not determined the basis for their absolute price. This level is fixed by supply and demand as a whole. By cutting off two stories in one part of town you have not decreased the need of dwelling in the town as a whole. These stories or their equivalent must have some foundation to rest upon; if they cannot be placed on top of another building, they must be built upon the ground and probably farther from the center. The total demand remains the same, and more land is needed to satisfy it. Thus, outlying land is more quickly marketed. In this way land owners as a body are perhaps rather benefited than injured, for carrying charges which so often turn profit into loss are saved. Regulations limiting the amount of the lot that may be covered and requiring given amounts of land to be open for access of sun and air would evidently have the same effect as limitations on the height of buildings. The same reasoning applies to business property, except that there a larger degree of concentration is needed for business convenience.[22]

There is often a financial gain through regulation to both land owners and purchasers. In so far as the factory by intruding upon the residence injures the residence without benefiting itself there is mere waste. In so far as the character of localities is preserved, destruction and rebuilding are rendered unnecessary. Both these results have apparently been in a measure attained, for instance, in Frankfort. And it is an interesting fact that average residence, factory and mixed district property in Frankfort the same distance from the center are of about the same value. Business locations in the heart of the old city are often of course much higher than either. As a general thing the relative prices of land are affected at once by a change from one zone to another. This is shown clearly in Berlin, where a series of land value maps—the Müller maps—are issued.

Where, however, concentration has reached a certain point, newer and stricter regulations have not, in my opinion, injured real

[21] As to land values, see also p. 112.

[22] Ibid.

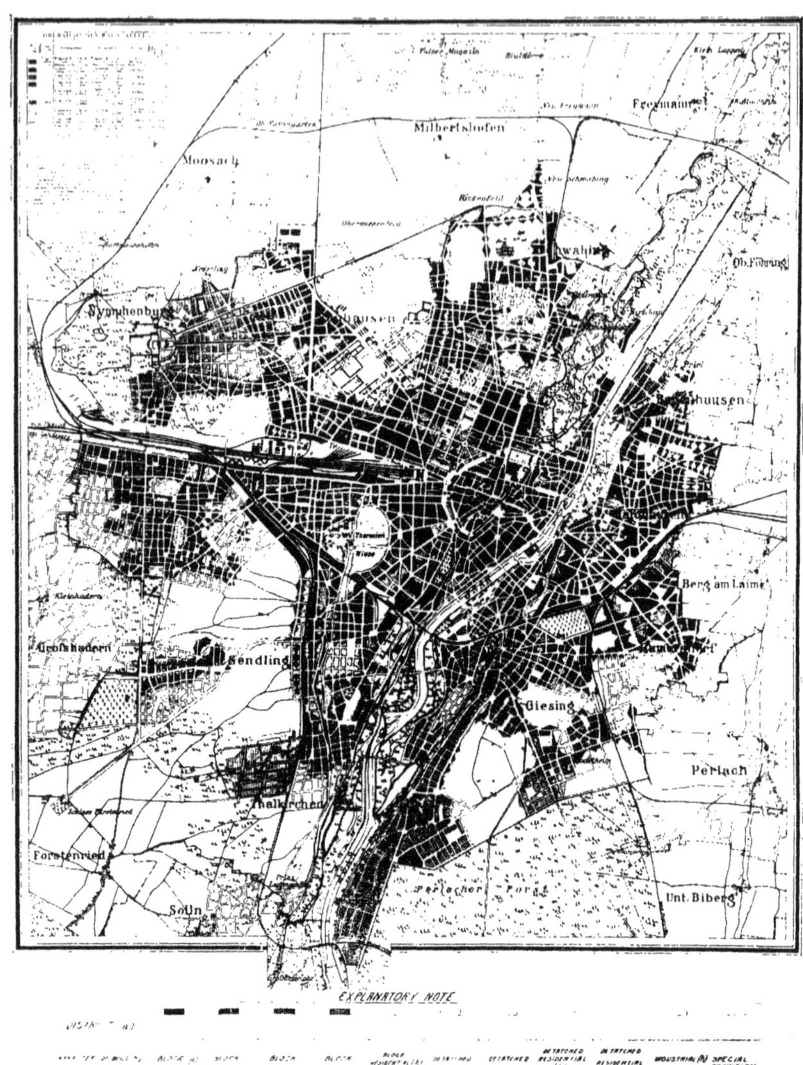

EXPLANATORY NOTE

Character of building	Block (g)	Block	Block	Block	Block residential	Detached	Detached	Detached residential (h)	Detached residential	Industrial (h)	Special provision
Minimum [illegible] width between house and side line of lot						23 feet	29.5 feet	32.8 feet	32.8 feet		
Maximum length of blocks (b)						147.6 feet	147.6 feet	118.1 feet	118.1 feet		
Minimum open space (c), interior lot	[illegible]	1/3	1/3	1/3	1/3	1/3	1/3	1/3	1/2		
corner lot	(e)	1/6 1/5	1/4 1/3	1/6 1/5	1/4 1/5	1/4 1/5	1/6 - 1/5	1/6 - 1/5	1/6 1/5		
Height limit to cornice (d)	Varying, see (d)	59.1 feet	59.1 feet	49.2 feet	39.4 feet	65.6 feet	59.1 feet	49.2 feet	39.4 feet		
Maximum number of stories to cornice (f)	5	4	4	3	2	4	4	3	2		

(a) For corner lots with street fronts in two districts the rules of the district of interest building govern for the entire lot
(b) Allowed only by agreement of neighbors and when also in accordance with city plan
(c) Open space, the front gardens in front of building line, and open side spaces so far as either are required by law are not reckoned as part of required minimum open space
(d) Height should not exceed, to cornice, width of street + width of front gardens or 72.2 feet, but if street is less than 39.4 feet wide that height may in all cases be 39.4 feet, roofs above these limits must be within a given angle
(e) May be less than that of interior lot by an amount fixed by authorities in each case
(f) Rooms allowed in roof for residence in houses if not more than four stories to cornice to half area of floor below
(g) No open space required between house and side lines of lot
(h) All industries are permitted anywhere within the city limits [illegible] districts in which [illegible] are however permitted. Residence are permitted anywhere within the city limits. In the industrial district, the authorities may [illegible] exemptions from main provisions of the building ordinances to industrial buildings

MAP XIX—DISTRICTING IN MUNICH.

estate values. There is undoubtedly a tendency to reckon value and rental by cubage—especially, perhaps, where a new restriction is proposed. But light and air have a well-established market value. In some of the central and older parts of Berlin undue concentration and consequent lack of these necessities have, apparently, hindered the growth of real estate values and rentals relatively to other parts of this central and very valuable district, and the new regulations requiring more open space upon reconstruction have not checked the rise here of values, much less lowered them. The newer buildings also rent with sufficiently greater readiness and increase of rent to more than pay for the loss of area that may be built over.

There is in Germany a " Protective League of Land and House Owners," with headquarters in Berlin and branches or affiliations throughout Germany.[23] Many changes in ordinances are strongly opposed by the league.[24] Relative to this change, however, I have the opinion of one of the founders of the league, who is well informed and would be likely to be conservative in these matters, that the stricter regulations for central Berlin, now several years old, have not injured land owners in this part of town as a whole or the individual land owners who have been compelled to rebuild in accordance with their terms. I also was told by an officer of the league in Cologne that the newer and more generously planned parts of the city were competing so strongly with the older parts that land values had fallen there. This is suggestive to us in New York, where concentration, in places, has gone so far beyond anything in Germany; and yet our average density is less than theirs.

What effect has the zone system on business, living conditions and rents? We have already considered the obvious advantages of light and air, so important and so quickly and simply stated. Manufacturing interests do not complain. Business men object to some of the rules with regard to occupation of buildings and their use. In Berlin the Protective League complains, for instance, that the prohibitions against the business and residence use of roof stories is often wasteful and extreme. It seems strange to allow the roof stories to be built and then forbid any proper use of them. One suspects the German in this case of an undue respect for decentralization as a mere matter of statistics, especially as the roof story usually has an attic or other air space over it. The German would think a condition of things, however, under which his light and air could be taken away by a sky-scraper across the street unbearable. At present, in German cities, business as well as residence districts are low. The maximum in Berlin, for instance, is five stories. There is a movement to allow higher buildings in the purely business districts. Such districts as yet hardly exist. There are only isolated houses and parts of streets in which there are

[23] A similar organization exists in Vienna.
[24] See p. 113.

business buildings in which no people live; but the number is increasing. It seems certain that no such movement will be successful in the immediate future, and even the proposed changes, so far as they are practically made, go no further than suggesting the allowance of one more story, perhaps on corners or opposite open places.

There are many modifications and adaptations permitted for business buildings. For instance, the required court may in Berlin be roofed over to the height of the first story and to half its extent; other cities allow even more.

The complaint is made all over Germany that there are so few single houses, and that the German must live in large tenement and apartment houses. This is caused partly at least by the building regulations, which are to a great extent the same for large and small houses. The result is that the small house is made unnecessarily expensive. The ordinances require: too high rooms; too strong construction; too wide and dear stairs; too thick walls; too expensive sewer and street construction; too expensive fire protection.

There is a tendency to insert in the ordinances modifications in these respects in favor of the small house, but it is not general or far-reaching enough. There is also a tendency to allow double houses and groups, in the case of small houses, more freely than in other cases. The danger and bad effects of uniform requirements for small and large houses are not unknown to us.

It has been impossible for me to see how zone regulations properly drawn discriminate against the small or the single house. The discriminations in Germany seem to be clear mistakes which the Germans are seeing and remedying. The system does, however, uniformly and universally bring about less congestion and more light and air.

In the matter of rent paid and accommodations obtained, it may at first seem a simple matter to compare Germany and other nations. I do not know, however, of any such comparison that is at all complete or reliable. It is my impression that the Berlin workmen pay less absolutely and in percentage of income than in Vienna, which is zoned,[25] and in Paris, which is not;[26] and that he is better housed

[25] Vienna fixes a limit of height of buildings to the cornice of 25 meters. In dwellings, only five stories are allowed for residence; but cellar dwellings are permitted to a certain extent and two cellars for many other purposes. The ground floor also may be divided. Studios too are allowed in the roof.

At least 15 per cent of the lot must be left uncovered, with certain exceptions.

These are the conditions of the innermost zone. The ordinance does not provide for zones, except that it is held to give the authorities large administrative power. Under this power Vienna, in fact, is completely zoned, height being regulated with relation to the width of the street. The authorities have for 20 years been attempting to pass a new ordinance. The drafts provide for a zone system.

[26] Paris also regulates the height of its buildings with relation to the width

than the workmen in either city. These conditions depend upon so many causes that any such comparison is of very little value as a factor in any judgment upon the zone system. The only way in which the essentials of the system can affect rents is through the price of land—if indeed rents can be so affected. We have seen that it cannot with any positiveness be said that the zoning system does increase land prices.[27]

A very real objection to the building regulations that zoning increases is the extreme complexity thereby created. To this reference has already been made (page 96). This splitting up of land would, it would seem to me, make land less available and marketable. I have not found any proof of this in Germany. There are, however, obvious bad effects of this complexity. An architect must devote his greatest study to the question how by a proper combination of the various complexities, often contradictory, he can get the most building on a given lot in a given situation on a given street, in a given zone or class. The unscrupulous architect devotes himself to the problem of cheating the ordinance; and subsequent changes in their details prove that he is at times successful. Nevertheless, and with all study and effort, there can be no certainty that there has been secured that fullest use and profit out of the land which every owner is seeking for.[28]

The complications do not produce much litigation. Whatever difficulties occur are generally disposed of by administrative methods. The building inspector has great power and in case of appeals is seldom overruled. In Berlin the inspectors hold weekly meetings and discuss and settle doubtful questions in the ordinances. A change of opinion in these meetings is often equivalent to a change in the law.

This complexity has also led, as we have seen, to the provision in all the ordinances for granting permits to be relieved of provisions of the ordinance.[29] Many of the permits might, it would seem to me, be reduced to administrative orders; but builders, architects and officials are unanimous in saying that this is not true at all, and that special permits and a considerable latitude in the granting of them is absolutely essential to prevent most unfortunate results. A simplification of the ordinances would certainly reduce such a necessity to a minimum if it did not overcome it altogether, and would probably render such changes in ordinances which are now frequent less necessary. It would seem, too, as if a simple ordinance might be so drawn as to make the total cubage of building on the lot clear and definite. If the architect and builder, as well as the owner, knew that, with all his calculation, only a given cubage could be

of its streets and by a maximum of 20 meters. Mansard and roof are limited by an angle. There are also minimum courts.

[27] See p. 102 et seq.

[28] The Berlin Ordinances, etc. (with drawings).

[29] As to licenses, see p. 111.

obtained, evasion of the ordinance and clever manipulation of it would be robbed of all reward. Thus, many of the provisions of the ordinances, most making for complication and many of the most frequent causes for changes in ordinances, would be done away with, and thus ordinances much and permanently simplified. This is especially important in zoning ordinances, as each variation of zone means complications, not only more numerous but more complex by the added zone features and variations of the regulation.

The underlying principle of the zone system is that building regulations, to be effective, must be progressive. A great and constantly increasing majority of German cities have adopted that principle. It varies in different cities; criticism of its details and administration is widespread; its final form in Germany is still uncertain; but of the principle there is practically no criticism. It is regarded as the only possible method of obtaining results of value.

GERMAN LAW AND ADMINISTRATION

1. City Planning and Home Rule

Germany, like the United States, is a federal government. The construction of cities is almost exclusively within the jurisdiction of the separate states. The only imperial statute of importance is the Reichsgewerbegesetz (Imperial Business Law) of June 21, 1869, as amended from time to time, under certain sections of which (see sec. 16; also 17 to 27, 49, 147) a special permit may be required for the erection of factories which are noisy or emit a disagreeable smell, excessive smoke, etc. It was decided in Prussia, in 1889, by the Ober-Verwaltungs Gericht (Upper Administrative Court), volume 18, page 302 (No. 46), that this statute did not deprive the states or cities of the power to require permits, or limit them in their regulation of such industries, whether more or less severe, and whether by zones or otherwise. This was one of the first decisions in Germany upholding zoning.

No doubt the law, and certainly the practice, with regard to state and city regulations in these matters is the same in other states as it is in Prussia.

The extent to which cities in the matter of their construction are self-governing is a matter of state law, and varies in the different states.

Some matters are universally regulated by law, or royal order, uniformly for the entire state. Thus, Prussia has its Baufluchtliniengesetz (building line statute) of July 2, 1875, generally called in English, town or city planning law. It treats not only of building and street lines, but of expropriation, of street costs and their payment, and other matters. Other states, such as Wuerttemberg (Building Ordinance of July 28, 1910), Saxony (General Building Law of July 1, 1900, as amended May 20, 1904), Hessen (Gesetz betreffend die allgemeine Bauordnung—Law relating to General

Building Ordinance—of May 27, 1881), Brunswick (Gesetz betreffend Bauordnung—Law relating to Building Ordinance—of March 13, 1899), and Anhalt (Building Ordinance of July 19, 1905, to be found in Anhalt Gesetz Sammlung—Collected Laws—No. 1226), by statute, and Bavaria (Building Ordinance of February 17, 1901, August 3, 1910), and Baden (State Building Ordinance of September, 1907), by royal order, have regulations uniform for the entire state, containing not only these matters, but also very general building regulations, leaving it to the cities, to some extent, to pass additional building regulations. All the states issue orders, in general form, for the construction or occupancy of public buildings, such as schoolhouses, and semi-public ones, such as theaters. The cities universally have a greater or less measure of home rule in the matter of the regulation of city construction. City planning proper under the state law or regulation is almost universally regulated and carried out by the cities themselves. Building or zoning regulations are issued sometimes by officials of the state, as in Berlin; sometimes by a city official, like the Bürgomeister, but under state orders and control, as in Cologne; sometimes by city officials, as in Frankfort-on-the-Main, and, generally, in South Germany. In Vienna the building regulations also are state law.

Some of the free cities, such as Bremen and Hamburg, are both states and cities.

Home rule for cities does not, however, mean quite the same in Germany as it does (or would, if we had it) in America. The building code of ordinances is universally subject to the approval of the administrative authorities appointed by the ruler of the state; the city officials having charge of these matters are partly or entirely subject to similar confirmation (which, however, is very rarely refused). The administrative acts of these city officials are also in these matters, as in many others, subject to appeal to the state administrative officials or bodies, also appointed wholly or partly by the ruler of the state.

2. Divided Authority

Thus, by law in many cases, the making and executing of the city plans, and the issuing and enforcing of the regulations for building under it are in charge of different officials; and as a matter of practice these powers are not united where this is permissible. Essen is an exception—a bright and shining one.

This division has generally, and rightly I believe, come to be regarded as unfortunate. A one-family house calls for a one-family house lot. A manufacturing district must be both planned and regulated with that aim in view. It is difficult to secure this unity under divided administration.

3. THE BUILDING POLICE, AND THE "POLICE POWER"

The body which issues and executes building regulations is called "building police." There are many other kinds of police in Germany—for instance, Fire, Health, and Charity, as well as Safety, Police, as "police" in the popular use of the term with us are there called.

The power of the "building police" to issue building regulations has a different basis in the various states. In Prussia it is founded in large part upon two very general statutes giving them power to provide for and protect the public health, order and safety, and their upper courts limit and interpret the power very much as our courts would under similar circumstances.[30] In other states, as a general thing, it is founded upon statutes which give the building police wider powers and define them more explicitly.

Zone building regulations had not been issued in Germany to any extent until 1891.

The first decision, or at least one of the very early decisions, upholding such regulations was rendered by the Prussian Oberverwaltungsgericht (Supreme Administrative Court) in 1894 (volume 26, page 323, of their reports). It was with regard to a zone building ordinance, for a part of the suburbs of Berlin, of December 3, 1892. (See Amtsblatt der Regierung zu Potsdam of December 10, 1892, for the ordinance, which has since been amended.) The headnote reads:

> "Borders of the right of limitation of building freedom by police ordinances; especially the provision for single districts limiting them to country house development."

The ordinance contained provisions limiting building in certain districts to three-tenths of the lot and two stories. The owner of a lot asked for a permit to build more intensely and was refused. The matter was taken to the highest court having jurisdiction in these Prussian matters, the "Oberverwaltungsgericht."

The decision begins by citing the prior decision (just cited) sustaining the power of the building police to pass zoning regulations with regard to factories which are noisy, emit smells, smoke, etc.

The court then goes on to say that zoning is a proper method of

---

[30] Allgemeines Landrecht, sec. 10, II, 17:

"The taking of necessary measures for the preservation of the public peace, safety and order, and the guarding of the public or members of it from threatened danger, is the duty of the police."

Gesetz über die Polizei-Verwaltung (Law with regard to Police Administration), of March 11, 1850, section 6:

"Among matters of local police regulation are:

"a. Protection of persons and property.

"b. Order, safety and ease of communication on public streets, ways and squares, bridges, banks and waters. . . .

"f. Care for life and health.

"g. Protection against fire danger by building operations. . . .

"i. Anything else that in the especial interest of the local communities, or things belonging to them, ought to be regulated by the police."

passing building regulations; that this implies that they shall vary in severity; that, as a part of a general scheme, this portion of the ordinance was a proper exercise of the power of the building police. Other zoning ordinances, among them Frankfort-on-the-Main, with its residence, factory, and mixed sections, were mentioned with approval.

The owner contended that the ordinance was not a proper police regulation, but class legislation, passed, not from considerations of health, but to create a wealthy colony. The court held that the ordinance might well be in the interest of health and safety, and that its necessity and fitness to accomplish such results were not within the jurisdiction of the court.

The same court (volume 37, page 401, No. 67) decided, in 1900, another point of interest to us.

The ordinances for Hessen-Nassau forbade, in a given section, the erection of anything but "country dwelling houses." An owner in this district was therefore refused a permit to erect a storehouse. The court held that the refusal was unauthorized. The building police may forbid any building for an industry likely to cause smell, smoke, noise, etc., on sanitary grounds; they may, perhaps, forbid "gross disfigurement" of the street; but there was no proof that the building was objectionable on either of these grounds.[31]

To the same effect is a decision by the same court (volume 57, page 461, No. 104), in 1910, with relation to a similar ordinance of Frankfort-on-Oder. The court held that such an ordinance was not a provision to promote the public health, as it was not shown that a storeroom or carpenter shop there would produce smell or sufficient noise to affect health or comfort.

It is a matter of surprise to many of us how similar the questions arising under these building ordinances are to questions in our courts, and to what a degree the German courts consider these questions and decide them on the same grounds that we do.

4. Licenses

Exemptions from building ordinances are universally provided for. Generally, certain classes of cases are specified in which the local building police may grant them; and certain further classes, in which the higher state authorities only may issue them. Sometimes the state authorities are allowed to grant exceptions to all the provisions of the ordinance. In cases where they are granted by the local building police there is always an appeal to the state authorities, with further appeals ultimately, as a general thing, to the king, duke or other ruler, or his minister. Where the city does not control the building police, it often may appeal. Often abutters and all others affected may also be heard.

[31] Under Prussian Landrecht (State Law), I, 8, secs. 66, 71. The present statute gives the police more power in this direction. (See p. 99).

There is a tendency to formulate and lay down rules for these exceptions. For instance, if a monumental private dwelling is allowed to exceed the height limit, it is not allowed to go beyond the regular number of stories; the extra height shall not be an increase of rentable space. If a store is allowed to cover more of the ground floor than the ordinance provides, it is on condition that the total cubage on the lot shall not be increased, but that the cubage above the given floor shall be by that much lessened. If a charitable corporation is allowed to construct small dwellings in the roof story, contrary to the provisions of the zone in which its building is situated, it must leave a given extra space (fixed by contract with the building police) for front garden, court or children's playground.

5. Land Values, and Administration

If we should take the opinion of the Germans themselves as to land prices and rents as affected by land prices, we should indeed pity them. The Social Museum in Frankfort has just won distinction by issuing a pamphlet on "The Need of Small Dwellings in Frankfort." The cause of this shortage and high rents was, it was claimed, the high price of land, partly due to the restrictions upon it. Just prior to 1910, building there had almost stopped. The inner zone, where the restrictions were less, was practically full, and no one would build in the outer zone, where the limitations on height and amount of lot that could be covered with buildings were greater, and where, therefore, it took more land for a house of the same size not so high and therefore with less rentable space.

On the demand of philanthropists, land owners, business men and builders, in which the Social Museum joined, these restrictions were lessened in 1910, so that, at current prices for land in the outer zone, a building high and large enough to be profitable might be built. Very few have been erected; the financial situation is bad in Germany as elsewhere.

Frankfort is cited as a case where regulation did not keep prices down. There were, however, other causes given for the higher land prices. Dr. Adickes, as mayor of Frankfort, it is said, built too wide streets, for which the abutters had to pay, and bought land for the city too extensively, thus lessening the supply.[32] The city owns a third of all the possible building land within its limits, and a few large institutions and wealthy private persons hold another third. It is also said that he paid too high prices for the land he bought for the city, thus, in a third way, increasing land values. Adickes is ill and out of office. The new administration stands for economy; the splendid results he obtained remain. To us the modi-

[32] The Prussian "City Planning Law" (see p. 108) does, it is true, limit the amount of street the abutter is obliged to pay for to 26 meters (about 85 feet), 13 to the abutter on each side; but under the Lex Adickes, by which a redivision of land can be compelled, he must pay more; and often, also, the city refuses to lay out the street at all unless he, with the abutter on the other side, pays for it all, however wide.

fications of 1910 would hardly seem a basis for quite so much discussion. Even now, in this outer zone, houses cannot be built quite so high as the street is wide; and half the lot must be left free of buildings. There were, however, certain restrictions upon the building of tenements, intended to encourage single houses, that were practically repealed. In this connection it is interesting to note that in 1910 the Imperial Government, in its exhaustive study of the building regulations (Beitrage zur Arbeiterstatistik No. 11, Wohnungsfürsorge), a portion of which is translated herein, pages 115 to 119, refers to the question of the effect of these regulations upon prices of land and rents as unsettled.

Another cause given for high land values is the prohibition of so-called "wild building." In Germany streets are laid out only in continuation of the solidly built existing city, and only when the street is at once needed for building purposes. This is especially true of most of Prussia, but exists to a considerable extent in all Germany and in Austria. The purpose of this system is to prevent undue cost of construction, repairs and police. The result, it is claimed, is to reduce the supply of "building ripe" land to a mere fraction of the potential supply, and thus, it is claimed, to raise prices. The cause of higher prices oftenest given, and most strongly denounced, is speculation. Any discussion of this subject would, however, lead us too far afield.

6. Changes in Ordinances

The most extreme case of a change of ordinance, I am informed, is the amendment of September 6, 1912, to the regulation of March 15, 1910, with regard to a part of Charlottenburg ("Westend," so-called), changing the regulations from those applying to Berlin proper to, in small part, those of Class A, and in great part, Classes C and D of the suburbs. In Berlin proper five stories and the use of perhaps 75 per cent of the lot is allowed. In Class A, four stories and half the lot; in Class C, three stories and three-tenths of the lot; in Class D, two stories and three-tenths of the lot are the limits. The result was to destroy about three-quarters of the market value of this land.

The tract was undeveloped. There were streets all around it, but none within its borders. There was only an old castle in it.

The justification of the change given by the officials is that the land was not on any street; and, not being "building ripe," the prices that had developed were purely speculative. A state official concerned in a similar change in the ordinance relating to another suburb of Berlin said to me in relation to it: "It was raw land. There was not a single street on the whole tract. All the sales were pure speculation. They must take their chances as to the ordinances they will get, and they knew it when they bought. We can't make our rules to fit their prices; let them fit their prices to our rules."

No doubt the official responsible for the change in the ordinance of Charlottenburg (Westend) would say much the same thing.

However, to avoid complications like these, the latest practice is to pass as early as possible some severe regulation allowing, perhaps, two stories, and two or three tenths of the lot to be covered, with regard to all outlying land about which there is any uncertainty; with the idea that in places, perhaps, a more intensive use may later be allowed. This is called keeping the land "in hand."

In Germany under the zone system, as everywhere, location is the chief factor in fixing land prices. There are great variations in value in the same zone. In Frankfort, a city in 1910 of 414,406 inhabitants, the highest price ever given for land was 3000 marks a square meter (about $66.33 a square foot). This was considered exceptional; a normal value for the best business location in the inner city is perhaps 2000 to 2500 marks ($44.22 to $55.27) a square foot. Business locations may be obtained in this zone for as little as 350 marks ($7.74) a square foot, and land may be had for 150 marks ($3.32) a square foot.

The best residence property in the inner residence zone is worth about 120 marks a square meter ($2.65 a square foot).

In Berlin, the only German city that can be compared with New York, there is the same variation. Greater Berlin has about 3,260,000 inhabitants. As much as 7000 marks a square meter ($154.77 a square foot) has been given for land in the best business location in the inner city. A normal price is 3000 marks ($66.33) a square foot. It is interesting to note that land only two houses removed from Friedrichstrasse and Leipzigerstrasse is worth only 1000 marks ($22.11) a square foot and less.

It is well known that a lot in New York City 25 feet broad by 100 feet deep, at the corner of Wall and Broad streets, is valued at $1,250,000, or $500 a square foot. There is no such valuation in any German city.

HOUSING IN GERMAN CITIES[a]

In 1910 the German Imperial Statistical Office issued, in its series of Workmen's Statistics, a volume of Housing in German Cities. It contains probably the only collection of German building laws, orders and ordinances in existence. The collection covers 106 cities, including all cities and city states (like Bremen and Hamburg) that, according to the census of December 1, 1905, had more than 50,000 inhabitants; and also a number of cities that, in relation to housing, were of special interest.

In the preface (page v) the following passage indicates the

[a] Beïtrage zur Arbeiterstatistik, No. 11; Wohnungsfürsorge in deutschen Staetten. Kaiserliches Statistisches Amt; Abteilung für Arbeiterstatistik; Berlin, Carl Heymann's Verlag, 1910.

basis which, in the opinion of the imperial government, underlies the main provisions of the German building ordinances (the italics are mine):

"From the building police regulations substantially the following provisions were chosen: Height of buildings (front and rear buildings), number of stories, permissible area to be built over and size of court, space between buildings of adjoining proprietors, dwelling rooms in general, roof and cellar rooms, water-closets, also such provisions as contain modifications lessening the requirements with regard to the construction of small houses, one-family houses, etc. *These are essentially health measures.*"

A translation of a portion of the introduction (pp. 1-9) follows:

"A number of German states (Bavaria, Württemberg, Baden, Hessen, Brunswick, Anhalt) have issued general building regulations for their entire territorial limits. In these states the provisions of the separate states, contained in the state building regulations, may be enlarged or in certain points changed as local conditions may require. . . . In Prussia there is no state building ordinance. . . . At present, with the exception of a few general principles of the Allgemeine Landrecht (General State Law), I, 8, secs. 33 et seq., building police law will be found in the building police ordinances of the cities that, in accordance with the law of March 11, 1850, sec. 6, and the Allgemeine Landesverwaltung (law with regard to general state administration) of July 30, 1883, secs. 137 et seq., are passed generally by the local police, with the consent of the Magistrat, Bürgomeister, etc. . . .

"A majority of the cities have passed so-called zone building ordinances. The principle of the zone building ordinance is that for particular, especially outlying, districts of the city, graduated, materially severer provisions exist than for the city center. The graduations are principally in the provisions with regard to the amount of the lot that may be covered with buildings, their height and number of stories. . . .

"Other cities have not, indeed, passed a zone building ordinance—*i. e.*, did not, on passage of the building ordinance, divide in a systematic manner the entire territory of the city into zones—but, nevertheless, by the passage of amendments for given districts, have provided a less intensive use of the land for building purposes. The introduction of such restrictions on building for separate parts of the city, through a zone building ordinance or through amendments, may have as its object to secure to them a villa or country character, or it may have come from the intention to force back the large tenement house, and, through introduction of low building, to provide healthier and cheaper dwellings. Which of these motives was determining in any case in the passage of building ordinances, and how these intentions have resulted in fact, could not here be shown.

"Here reference is also made to the graduated building provisions which contain less severe requirements for 'small buildings,' 'small dwelling houses,' 'one and two family houses.' The less exacting provisions are principally with relation to the use of building materials, the amount of the lot that may be covered, the clear height of dwelling rooms, etc. Such graduations and milder provisions have chiefly been adopted by the following cities: Königsberg, Posen, Bromberg, Breslau, Magdeburg, Halle, Altona, Dortmund, Frankfort-on-the-Main, Düsseldorf, Elberfeld, Oberhausen, Rheydt, Neuss, Coblence.

"Of the health provisions of the building ordinances with relation to the building itself, those with relation to the height of buildings, the number of stories, the amount of lot that may be covered, or size of court, the space between neighboring buildings or open or partly open building, have been chosen for detailed presentation.

"Next come the provisions with relation to height of buildings, since, in connection with the provisions with regard to the distance of the building from buildings opposite, they determine the share of light and air for the inhabitants of the building in question. With regard to the relation of the height of buildings on the street to their distance from opposite buildings, the usual provision is that the height of the building shall not exceed the breadth of the street. This provision, for instance, is also that of the state law for the cities here considered. So, according to the Bavarian Building Ordinance (Royal Ordinance with relation to building of February 17, 1901), 'the height of private buildings, whether newly erected or raised by addition of stories, may not exceed the breadth of the street, including the sidewalk and any front garden' (set-back).[84] According to the General Building Law for the Kingdom of Saxony of July 1, 1900, 'the height of buildings shall not, as a general rule, exceed the breadth of the street, including any front garden.' The same provision is found in the state building ordinance of Baden and in a building ordinance for the duchy of Anhalt. In accordance with the state building ordinance for Hessen (Gesetz, betreffend die allgemeine Bauordnung, vom 27 Mai, 1881), however, 'the greatest permitted height of private dwellings shall not, as a rule, exceed the width of the street, including the sidewalk and the front garden, by more than 2 meters.' In accordance with the state building ordinance for the duchy of Brunswick (Gesetz, betreffend Bauordnung für das Herzogtum Braunschweig, vom 13 Marz, 1899), 'the height of buildings to be erected on the street shall not exceed the width of the street by more than 4.5 meters.'

"The provision that the height of buildings shall not exceed the street width is found as the fundamental provision in the majority of the building ordinances of the cities here considered. In addition, there is usually given a fixed measure as the greatest measure of the height of buildings, for which regularly the height of the building is reckoned from the ground to the upper edge of the roof cornice. There will be found also in the cities with zone building ordinances sharper provisions for the outlying zones. So in Posen the height of buildings in general must not be greater than the established street breadth; but, nevertheless, in the first building class, at most 20 meters; in the second, 17.50 meters; and in the third, 15 meters. Similar graded provisions with the fundamental provision that the building height shall not exceed the street breadth are in force, among others, for Königsberg (for streets less than 7 meters in breadth, always 7 meters high), Breslau (Zones II, III and IV), Kiel, Flensburg, Hagen, Frankfort-on-the-Main (outer city, with a street breadth up to 9 meters, always 9 meters), Cassel, Düsseldorf, Essen, Cologne (Zones II, III and IV), Mannheim, Freiburg. The fundamental principle that the height of buildings shall not exceed the street breadth is in force also in Berlin and its suburbs, Görlitz, Königshütte, Gleiwitz and Beuthen, Luneburg, Pforzheim, and the Bavarian and Saxon cities.

"In a number of cities on streets of a given breadth or less the height of buildings may exceed that width; but on streets of more than that width the height may not exceed it. This width is:

City	Meters	City	Meters
Spandau	10	Münster	15
Potsdam	10	Bielefeld (outside the walls)	10
Brandenburg	10	Wiesbaden	11
Frankfort-on-Oder	10	Duisburg	15
Stettin	15	Barmen (2d zone)	14
Bromberg	11	Saarbrücken	12
Magdeburg	11.50	Grand duchy Saxony	11
Altona	11	Brunswick (outer city)	9
Hanover	10	Bremen	11
Dortmund	15	Metz	15
Bochum	13.50		

[84] Since materially amended. See p. 108. This provision, however, has not been changed.

"In a number of cities the breadth of the street may be exceeded by a given measure. This is true principally of the cities in Württemberg, where the street width generally may be exceeded up to 4.5 meters; also of the cities in Hessen, where it may as a rule, or from a given breadth on, be exceeded up to 2 meters.

"In a still further number of cities, in so far as the street breadth reaches a fixed minimum, the height of buildings may exceed the street breadth by a fixed measure in addition to that excess. Thus the height of buildings in Cologne (first zone), with a street breadth of more than 8 meters, may exceed 11.50 by as much as the street width exceeds 8 meters. Bonn, Mülheim-on-the-Rhine, Coblence and Colmar have somewhat similar rules.

"Further, in a number of cities, the building height may exceed the street width as a rule, or from a given street width on. So in Danzig, with a street width of over 12 meters, the height of the buildings may be 1¼ the street breadth. In Hanover, with a street width up to 10 meters, the building height may also equal 1¼ the street breadth. In Osnabrook, with a street width up to 8 meters, a building height 1½ times the street width is allowed. In Lübeck, up to a depth of 20 meters behind the building line, a building height of 1½ times the street breadth is allowed. In Barmen, in the first zone, with a street width over 10 meters, a height of building of half the street width plus 9 meters is allowed; in the second zone, with a street breadth of from 10 to 14 meters, a height of half the street breadth plus 7 meters is allowed.

"As above stated, a majority of cities have established a maximum for height of buildings beyond which nothing may be built.[35] In the cities with zone building ordinances this height grows less in the outer districts. So far as relates solely to the respective first zones, it appears that a maximum height of 22 meters (a greater measure does not occur in the cities here considered) is allowed in the following cities: Berlin, Charlottenburg, Schöneberg, Rixdorf, Deutsch-Wilmersdorf, Lichtenberg (the five last-named places in so far as their territory lies within the ring railroad), Breslau, Altona, Kiel and Cassel; the Bavarian cities; the Saxon cities—except Dresden, Zittau and Grimmitschau—Mayence and Rostock.[36] Königsberg has a maximum height of 21 meters.

"A maximum height of 20 meters exists in Danzig, Stettin, Posen, Königshütte, Gleiwitz, Reuthen, Magdeburg, Erfurt, Flensburg, Hanover, Harburg, Dortmund, Gelsenkirchen, Frankfort-on-the-Main (inner city), Düsseldorf, Duisburg, Elberfeld, München-Gladbach, Cologne, Bonn, Mülheim-on-the-Rhine, Aachen, Stuttgart, Ulm, Heilbronn, Karlsruhe, Mannheim, Brunswick,

"The maximum height of 19 meters is fixed for Wiesbaden, Freiburg, Bremen; of 18.50 meters for Mühlhausen-in-Alsace; 18 meters for Charlottenburg, Schöneberg, Rixdorf, Deutsch-Wilmersdorf, Lichtenberg (so far as this city lies outside the ring railroad), Brandenburg, Frankfort-on-Oder, Görlitz, Liegnitz, Halle, Osnabrook, Münster, Bielefeld, Essen, Barmen, Crefeld, Coblence, Saarbrücken, Zittau, Crimmitschau, Lübeck.

"A maximum of under 18 meters exists in Hagen, Solingen, Rheydt. . . .

"The number of stories allowed in cities with zone building ordinances grows less from the interior to the outskirts. A few cities make the number of the stories dependent upon the street width. This is true of Harburg, Bochum, Münster, Barmen, Pforzheim. . . .

"In many cities both the amount of the lot that may be covered and the minimum size of courts is fixed . . . For corner lots . . . there are provisions that allow an intenser use. In the building ordinances that provide for a division by zones the provisions with regard to the amount of the

[35] Except, generally, public buildings, monumental buildings, etc.; and turrets and other ornamentation to a limited height and amount.

[36] On page 420 of this work, however, it appears that in Hamburg the maximum is 24 meters; and so it apears from the building ordinances, edition of 1909.

lot that may be covered are throughout so graded that in the outer districts only a small part of the surface may be used for buildings. In the following summary only the first, or, inner, zone will be considered:

"As the proportion of the lot that may be built over in a majority of cities, three-quarters of the entire lot is fixed. In this class belong Königsberg, Danzig, Spandau, Potsdam, Brandenburg, Frankfort-on-Oder, Breslau, Görlitz, Liegnitz, Halle, Altona, Kiel, Flensburg, Dortmund, Gelsenkirchen, Bochum, Frankfort-on-the-Main (inner city), Duisburg, Elberfeld, Barmen, Remscheid, München-Gladbach, Solingen, Rheydt, Neuss, Cologne, Bonn, Mülheim-on-the-Rhine, Aachen, Coblence, Saarbrücken, Karlsruhe, Constance, Darmstadt, Offenbach, Worms and Brunswick, as well as, generally, the Bavarian cities.[87]

"A still greater use of the lot for building (and indeed to four-fifths) is allowed by Giessen, Lübeck, Mühlhausen-in-Alsace and Metz.

"A lesser use of the lot than in the foregoing cities (and indeed up to seven-tenths) is provided in Stettin, Posen, Bielefeld (in the case of lots inside the old walls), Bautzen. Up to two-thirds may be covered in Bromberg, Königshütte, Gleiwitz, Beuthen, Magdeburg, Erfurt, Hanover, Harburg, Lüneberg, Münster, Hagen, Oberhausen, Munich, Zittau, Rostock, and in the duchy of Anhalt. Up to half may be so used in Charlottenburg, Schöneberg, Rixdorf, Lichtenberg (in so far as these five cities lie outside the ring railroad and so far as building Class I is concerned).

"In a number of cities the amount of lot that may be covered is so fixed that the lot is divided into strips. This is true, for instance, of Berlin, Charlottenburg, Schöneberg, Rixdorf, Deutsch-Wilmersdorf, Lichtenberg (so far these cities lie within the ring railroad). The first strip that, measured from the building line, extends to the depth of 6 meters may be fully covered; the second strip, that extends to a depth of 32 meters, may be built over in Berlin to the extent of seven-tenths, in the rest of the above named cities, of sixty-five hundredths, of the lot. A similar division into strips, although to different limits, exists in Osnabrook, Cassel, Wiesbaden, Dresden.

"In Essen the amount of the lot that may be covered is fixed with relation to the number of stories. Thus, in Zone I, with two and three story houses 75 per cent of the surface, with four-story houses 70 per cent, may be built over. In a few other cities (Solingen, Bonn, Mülheim-on-the-Rhine) in certain zones the extent of surface that may be built over is dependent upon height.

"In Stuttgart, Ulm, Heilbronn, Freiburg, Pforzheim, Heidelberg minimum requirements exist only with regard to the height, while actual provisions with regard to the amount of the lot that may be covered are lacking. There are in them all provisions with relation to the distance between front and rear buildings; also 'must a certain amount of the lot, with a given relation to the height of the buildings, remain uncovered.' . . . In Ulm, 'in Class I of the new building lands, a court must be left behind the front building equal to half the height of its rear side.' . . .

"In Freiburg a portion of the lot, undivided and in one piece, of at least 50 square meters must be left free of buildings when there are buildings of three or less stories upon it, and for every additional story 20 square meters more are required. Pforzheim demands a court of 30 square meters, by 3.60 meters least breadth; Heidelberg, one of 60 square meters.

"In the cities that, in addition to provisions with relation to the proportion of the lot that may be covered, have at the same time rules with relation to the size of the court, the least surface that is demanded is, in the majority of cases, given; sometimes in terms of minimum square surface, while other cities simply give the minimum breadth or length of the court. In general, a court of about 40 square meters is required by Danzig, Stettin, Görlitz, Liegnitz, Dortmund, Aachen, Coblence, Bautzen; 30 to 36 square

[87] In Görlitz and Liegnitz in the case of lots whose depths from the neighboring border does not exceed 35 meters.

meters are required by Posen, Cassel, Harburg, Bielefeld, Oberhausen (for lots of less than 108 square meters), Rheydt, Neuss; 50 square meters are required in Spandau, Potsdam, Brandenburg, Frankfort-on-Oder, Halle, Remscheidt (for lots of less than 200 square meters), Dresden. Berlin demands a minimum court of 80 meters by 6 meters least dimension. In Magdeburg, in the old city, a free uncovered court of 10 by 10 meters minimum measurement must be left." . . .

APPENDIX IV

BUILDING RESTRICTIONS IN VARIOUS CITIES

By Herbert S. Swan

LONDON[1]

Definition of height[2]

In ascertaining the height of a building it is measured from the level of the footway immediately in front of its center to the top of the parapet. The top of the external wall is taken if there is no parapet, except in the case of the gabled buildings, where the base of the gable is taken. If there happens to be no footway, then the level of the ground before excavation is taken in its place.

General limit, front height[3]

Except by the consent of the council, no building not a church or chapel may be erected or increased to a greater height than 80 feet. This limitation, however, is exclusive of two stories in the roof and of ornamental towers, turrets or other architectural features.

Roofs may not incline from the external or party walls upward at a greater angle with the horizon than 47 degrees in the case of buildings of the warehouse class and at a greater angle than 75 degrees in the case of other buildings. This provision does not apply to towers, turrets or spires.

Where any existing building forming part of a continuous block or row of buildings exceeded this height January 1, 1895, there is nothing to prevent any other building in the same block or row belonging on the same date this act was passed to the same owner from being carried to a height equal to but not exceeding that of the existing building.

Buildings over 80 feet in height on January 1, 1895, may be reerected to their height on that date.

As regards the possibility of the council consenting to the erection of a building having a height greater than 80 feet, Mr. Cubitt says, page 93: " Possibly if the excess were only a question of a few feet there might be no difficulty in obtaining consent, but if the increase in height were very considerable it is very doubtful whether the application would be granted. It must be remembered that the tendency has been toward a reduction in the height of London buildings. At the time of the passing of the 1894 act a height of

[1] References: London Building Act, 1894, 57-58 Vict. C. CCXIII, and Horace Cubitt, Building in London (1911).

[2] London Building Act, 1894, sec. 5, div. 21.

[3] Ibid., sec. 47.

90 feet was allowed under the provisions of the London County Council (General Powers) Act, 1890."

Limit on certain streets[4]

A special provision is made for buildings on streets formed or laid out after August 7, 1862, and less than 50 feet in width.

In the case of such streets the height, unless the council otherwise consents, may not exceed the distance of the front or nearest external wall of the building from the opposite side of the street. The only exception from this regulation is that existing churches and chapels may be raised to a greater height. A building situated on a corner plot has its height regulated by the width of the wider street to a depth of 40 feet back from such street.

Special limit on the height and open space of "domestic" buildings[5]

The act divided buildings into three classes:

1. Domestic buildings (dwelling-houses and buildings not included in the other two classes). Sec. 5(26).
2. Public buildings (churches, chapels, schools, colleges, hospitals, workhouses, public theaters, public halls, public concert rooms, public lecture rooms, public libraries, hotels, lodging-houses, home refuges or shelters, etc., with contents exceeding 250,000 cubic feet or sleeping accommodations for more than 100 persons). Sec. 5(27).
3. Warehouses (warehouses, manufactories, breweries, distilleries, and any other building with contents exceeding 150,000 cubic feet that are not included in either of the two preceding classes). Sec. 5(28).

"Domestic" buildings with habitable basement erected after January 1, 1895[6]

An open space aggregating not less than 100 square feet, and exclusively belonging thereto, must be provided in the rear of each "domestic" building having a habitable basement and erected after January 1, 1895. The space, which need not necessarily adjoin the rear boundary of the premises, must be free from any obstruction whatever.

A basement is a story having its floor at a greater distance than 4 feet below the level of the adjoining pavement. The space, however, is not required to be at basement but at pavement level.

"Domestic" buildings erected on streets laid out after January 1, 1895[7]

Every "domestic" building erected after January 1, 1895, and abutting upon a street formed or laid out after the same date is subject to two special requirements with reference to open space.

[4] London Building Act, sec. 49.
[5] Ibid., sec. 5 (26, 27, 28).
[6] Ibid., sec. 40.
[7] Ibid., sec. 41.

1. *The fixed minimum*—An open space in the rear with a minimum width of 10 feet must extend throughout the entire width of the building. In no case may this space have an area aggregating less than 150 feet. The act does not define the width of a building when its front and rear widths differ.

There seems to be some question whether this space has to be continuous in its extent. Mr. Cubitt, for instance, is of the opinion that space A and B in Diagram XIII would satisfy all the requirements of the act.

DIAGRAM XIII

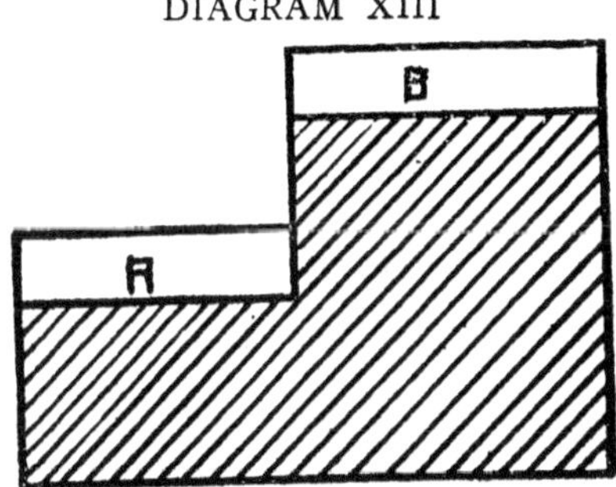

The space may be provided above the level of the ceiling of the ground story or at a level of 16 feet above the adjoining pavement level in two instances.

a. Where there is a basement directly and sufficiently lighted and ventilated by the open space irrespective of any uses to which the ground story is appropriated; or

b. Where there is no basement story but where the ground story is not constructed or adapted to be inhabited.

When the space is provided at a level of 16 feet above the adjoining pavement, it may be used for lantern lights. When it is provided at pavement level a water-closet, earth-closet, or privy and a receptacle for ashes, and enclosing walls not exceeding 9 feet in height may be erected.

2. *The variable minimum, the diagonal line, rear height*—The open space demanded in any particular case depends quite as much upon the *diagonal line* as upon the foregoing requirements.

The diagonal line is drawn as follows: An imaginary horizontal line drawn at right angles to the roadway is projected through the frontage center of the building until it intersects the rear boundary of the plot. From this point of intersection a second imaginary line is drawn in the direction of the building. This line is a diagonal line in the same vertical plane as the first and inclined at an angle of 63½ degrees to it. No part of the building may extend above the diagonal line except chimneys, dormers, gables, turrets or other architectural ornaments aggregating in all not more than one-third of the width of the building.

The horizontal line is drawn at the level of the pavement unless the site inclines toward the roadway. In that case it is drawn at the same level as the point which it intersects on the rear boundary. When the pavement in front of the building is not all on one level, the mean level is taken.

Where the boundary of the space at the rear of the building is not parallel with the rear wall of the building, then the horizontal line is to be drawn to a point situated at the mean distance of the boundary from the rear of the building, whether such point be beyond the boundary line or not. From this point the diagonal line must be drawn.

When the land at the rear of a building and exclusively belonging thereto abuts immediately upon a street, a diagonal line may be drawn upon the horizontal line at the center of the roadway of such street and it is unnecessary to provide any open space at the rear of the building. The roadway furnishes the level at which the line is drawn.

When the land at the rear of a building and exclusively belonging thereto abuts immediately upon an open space which is dedicated to the public or the maintenance of which as an open space is secured permanently or to the satisfaction of the council by covenant or otherwise, the diagonal line may be drawn from the horizontal line at the farthest boundary of the open space and it is unnecessary to provide any open space at the rear of the building. The farthest boundary of the open space furnishes the level at which the line is drawn.

Buildings on corner sites, or on sites abutting on a street and an open space not less than 40 feet wide, the permanent maintenance of which is secured, are allowed, despite the ordinary diagonal line provisions to have their return fronts carried up the full height of the front elevation for a distance of 40 feet, or for such less distance as the requirements for open space at the rear may demand.

The council, moreover, may in the case of these corner buildings, if it sees fit, permit the building to be erected on part or all of the space in the rear to a height not exceeding 30 feet, if it is satisfied that such buildings will be placed so as not to interfere unduly with the access of light and air to neighboring buildings.

In exceptional cases where, owing to the irregular shape of the land, the ordinary provisions of the law relative to space and diagonal level cannot be applied, the council may allow such modifications as it sees fit, provided it is satisfied that these modifications will not unduly interfere with the access of light and air.

Notwithstanding all these provisions it is provided that any part of a domestic building may extend above the diagonal line provided the council or tribunal of appeal shall be satisfied that an open cubic space of air will be provided at the rear of such building equivalent to the open cubic space which would have been provided at the rear of such building if such diagonal line had been drawn from the ground level in the manner previously provided for, and if no part of the building had extended above such diagonal line except as permitted under the preceding provisions of the section. This exception presumably refers to chimneys, dormers, etc., not exceeding one-third of the width of the rear elevation.

This allows the upper portion of a building to project considerably beyond the diagonal line, so long as an equivalent cubic air space is provided by setting back either the whole or some portion of the building to a greater extent than the ordinary provisions of the act require. (See Diagram XIV.)

Nothing in section 41 applies to houses abutting in the rear on the River Thames or on a public park or on an open space of not less than 80 feet in depth which is dedicated to the public or the maintenance of which as an open space is secured permanently or to the satisfaction of the council by covenant or otherwise.

In the case of a shallow lot, the diagonal line will evidently not only limit the rear but also the front height of a building.

"Domestic" buildings erected on streets laid out before January 1, 1895 [8]

The requirements with reference to height and open space of domestic buildings erected on streets laid out before January 1, 1895, are the same as those for buildings erected on streets laid out after that date with one exception: the diagonal line is drawn at a level 16 feet above the level of the adjoining pavement.

Limit on courts within a building [9]

1. *Ventilation of courts enclosed on every side*—In the case of a court enclosed on every side, constructed for admitting light and air to a "domestic" building if its dimensions are such that its depth, from the eaves or top of the parapet to the ceiling of the ground story, exceeds the length or breadth, adequate provisions for the ventilation of such court must be made and maintained by the owner by means of a communication between the lower end of the court and the outer air.

2. *Habitable rooms in court enclosed on every side*—The height of any portion of a building opposite to a portion containing habitable rooms lighted solely by a court is limited by this section. No habitable rooms may be constructed if lighted only from a court enclosed on every side, unless the width of the court is equal to half the height of the wall on the opposite side measured from the level of the sill of the window which lights the habitable rooms to the eaves or top of the parapet of the wall.

A court, however, whose greater dimension does not exceed

[8] London Building Act, sec. 41.

[9] Ibid., sec. 45.

DIAGRAM XIV

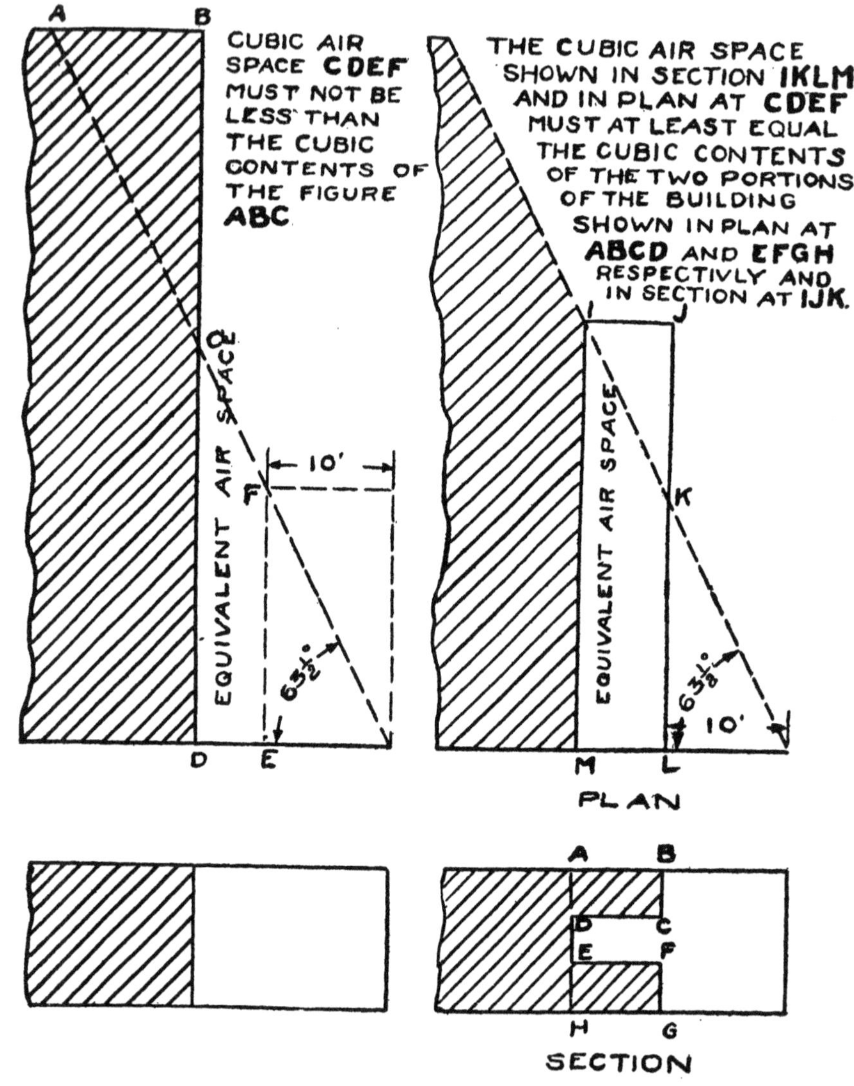
A
B
CUBIC AIR SPACE CDEF MUST NOT BE LESS THAN THE CUBIC CONTENTS OF THE FIGURE ABC
C
EQUIVALENT AIR SPACE
F
10'
63½°
D
E
THE CUBIC AIR SPACE SHOWN IN SECTION IKLM AND IN PLAN AT CDEF MUST AT LEAST EQUAL THE CUBIC CONTENTS OF THE TWO PORTIONS OF THE BUILDING SHOWN IN PLAN AT ABCD AND EFGH RESPECTIVLY AND IN SECTION AT IJK.
I
J
EQUIVALENT AIR SPACE
K
63½°
10'
M
L
PLAN
A
B
D
C
E
F
H
G
SECTION

twice the length of the smaller dimension complies with this provision if a square court of the same area would comply.

Unless the court is exceptionally narrow, the limit permitted by this provision will result in a greater height. Diagram XV taken

DIAGRAM XV

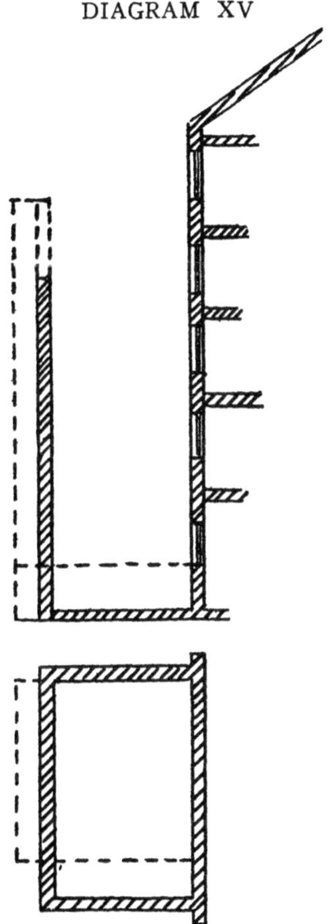

from Cubitt illustrates this. Cubitt, referring to this diagram, says (pages 91, 92):

"The wall hatched in black lines shows the maximum height to which it is possible, in the court in question and when complying with the original requirement, to carry a wall opposite to windows which light habitable rooms. The height of the wall—that is to say, measured from the dotted line at the level of the sill of the window on the ground story on the opposite side of the court—may not exceed the width of the court. The portion of the wall indicated in dotted lines shows the increased height to which it is possible to carry the wall by taking advantage of the proviso. This increased height is calculated as follows: A square court of similar area to the existing court is described as shown by the dotted lines on the plan. A dotted vertical line is drawn on the section to correspond with that side of the imaginary square court which is opposite to the window under consideration. Then the height of the wall, measured from the dotted line at the level of the sill of the window on the ground story, may be equal to twice the distance from the wall in which the windows occur to the dotted line in the section, or, in other words, equal to twice the width of the imaginary square court."

Habitable rooms in court open on one side

If the depth of a court exceeds twice its width, no habitable rooms above the ground story may be constructed, if lighted only from such court, unless the width of the court is equal to half the height of the wall on the opposite side measured from the level of the sill of the window which lights the habitable room.

Procedure and right of appeal [10]

This section provides for the service of notices in connection with an application for a greater height than that prescribed by the act, and an appeal from the council's decision in such a case, and the consents granted by the council.

The right of appeal can be exercised by all parties interested, both in the case of consent or in the case of refusal. The owner or lessee of any building or land within 100 yards of the intended building who may deem himself aggrieved by the grant of any consent, and also any applicant for consent which has been refused, may, respectively, within 21 days after the publication of the consent or of the refusal appeal to the Tribunal of Appeal.

PARIS [11]

The basic limitation on the height of buildings in Paris is the street width increased by an arbitrary unit of additional height. This arbitrary unit of additional height and the street width stand in inverse proportion: in the case of footpaths and very narrow streets, the arbitrary unit of additional height may even exceed the width of the street, but it diminishes gradually with each increment in the street width until in the case of very wide streets it disappears altogether.

Height below the cornice line

On streets 39.36 feet and less in width the maximum height below the cornice line may not exceed the width of the street plus 19.68 feet.

---

[10] London Building Act, sec. 48.

[11] References: Louis Bonnier, Les Reglements de Voirie; William Atkinson, The Orientation of Buildings, translation of the decree regulating the height of buildings in Paris, 128-136.

The following table shows the maximum height below the cornice line on streets less than 39.36 feet wide. Formula to ascertain maximum height: street width plus 19.68 feet.

Width of street (feet)	Constant factor (feet)	Maximum height below cornice (feet)
3.28	19.68	22.96
6.56	19.68	26.24
9.84	19.68	29.52
13.12	19.68	32.80
16.40	19.68	36.08
19.68	19.68	39.36
22.96	19.68	42.64
26.24	19.68	45.92
29.52	19.68	49.20
32.80	19.68	52.48
36.08	19.68	55.76
39.36	19.68	59.04

On streets over 39.36 feet wide the maximum height below the cornice line may not exceed 58.64 feet plus one-quarter of the amount by which the width of the street exceeds 39.36 feet.

The following table shows the maximum height below the cornice line on streets 39.36 feet wide and over. Formula to ascertain maximum height: 58.64 feet plus one-quarter of excess of street width over 39.36 feet.

Width of street (feet)	Variable factor* (feet)	Constant factor (58.54 feet) (feet)	Maximum height below cornice (feet)
39.36	.....	.....	59.04
42.64	.82	58.64	59.46
45.92	1.64	58.64	60.28
49.20	2.46	58.64	61.10
52.48	3.28	58.64	61.92
55.76	4.10	58.64	62.70
59.04	4.92	58.64	63.56
62.32	5.74	58.64	64.38
65.60	6.56	58.64	65.20
Over 65.60	....	.....	65.60

* One-quarter of excess of street width over 39.36 feet.

Height above the cornice line

The maximum height above the cornice line is determined by a mansard. The outline of this mansard depends on two planes, one of which is defined by a circular arc tangent to the highest point of the plane below the cornice, and the other by a line drawn at an angle of 45 degrees to the horizontal and tangent to this circular arc.

On streets 39.36 feet and less in width the radius of this arc may not exceed 19.68 feet. On streets over 39.36 feet in width the radius may not exceed one-half of the street width and a maximum of 32.80 feet.

A tangent to this circular arc drawn at an inclination of 45 degrees to the horizontal may be projected until it intersects either a vertical line bisecting the depth of the building at the ground floor level or a similar tangent of another such circular arc constructed in the same manner at the rear of the building. Diagram XVI illustrates the maximum height of the façade on streets of different widths and XVII the different ways in which the front tangent may intersect the rear tangent or the vertical bisecting the depth of the building. All of the diagrams in this paper are taken from the book by Louis Bonnier entitled "Les Reglements de Voirie."

Rear height

If adequate provision is made for the open court space required, the height below the cornice line may be the same in the rear as in the front of a building. The rear of the building may be built in the form of retreating stories to provide the necessary court space. An arc and tangent may be superimposed on the top of each section of wall set back to provide a rear mansard as shown in Diagram XVIII.

The length of the radius for the rear arc is identical with that for the front arc in the case of very low and very high buildings, but in the case of buildings with a height of between 40 and 60 feet below the cornice line it is greater.

Exceptions from height limit

In the case of private buildings of a monumental character, or in the case of buildings to be used for the purposes of art, science or industry, the prefect of the Seine may, with the approval of the "conseil general des batiments civils" and of the minister of the interior, authorize exceptions from the general height limit.

Definition of height

The height is measured through the middle of the façade from the level of the sidewalk or pavement at the foot of the façade. A fraction of a meter (3.28 feet) in the width of the street is taken as one meter. The façade of buildings on sloping streets must be di-

DIAGRAM XVI

ARC OF CIRCLE
TANGENT
22'-11⅝"
26'-3"
29'-6¾"
32'-9⅜"
32'-9⅜"
32'-9⅜" RAD.
HEIGHT TO CORNICE = 60'-8⅜"
62'-4"
63'-11¼"
65'-7⅜"
65'-7⅜"
65'-7⅜"
WIDTH OF STREET = 45'-11⅛"
52'-5⅞"
59'-0⅝"
65'-7⅜"
82'-0¼"
98'-5"

ARC OF CIRCLE
TANGENT
19'-8¼"
19'-8¼"
19'-8¼"
19'-8¼"
19'-8¼"
19'-8¼" RAD.
HEIGHT TO CORNICE = 26'-3"
32'-9¾"
39'-4½"
45'-11⅛"
52'-5⅞"
59'-0⅝"
WIDTH OF STREET = 6'-6¾"
13'-1½"
19'-8¼"
26'-3"
32'-9¾"
39'-4½"

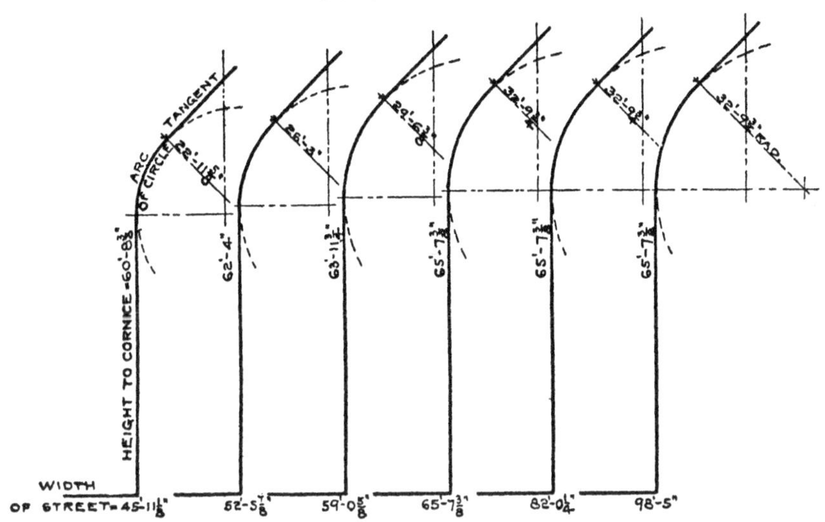

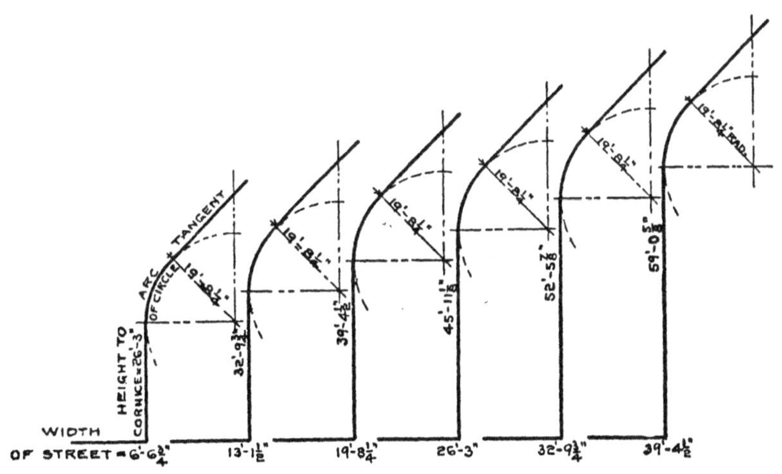

DIAGRAM XVII

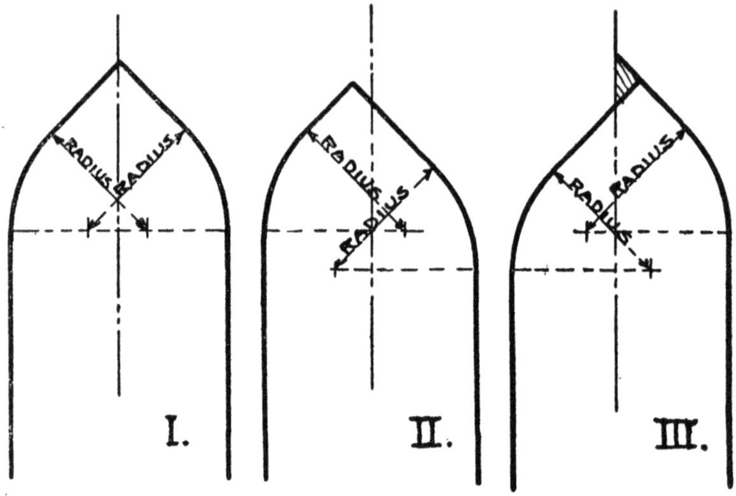

DIAGRAM XVIII

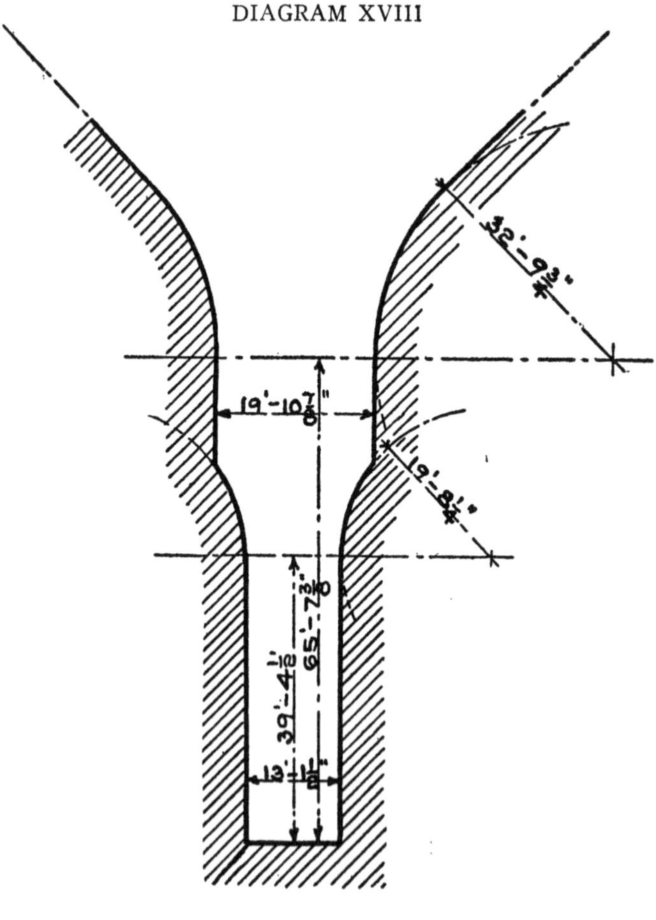

vided into sections not exceeding 98.40 feet in length; each section to have its height computed separately. The street width at a street intersection is considered as the width of the open space between the façades measured at right angles to each façade respectively. The additional height thus acquired by a building is, however, allowed only that portion of the building opposite the open space, as illustrated in Diagram XIX. This tends to make all the façades at a street intersection of a uniform height.

DIAGRAM XIX

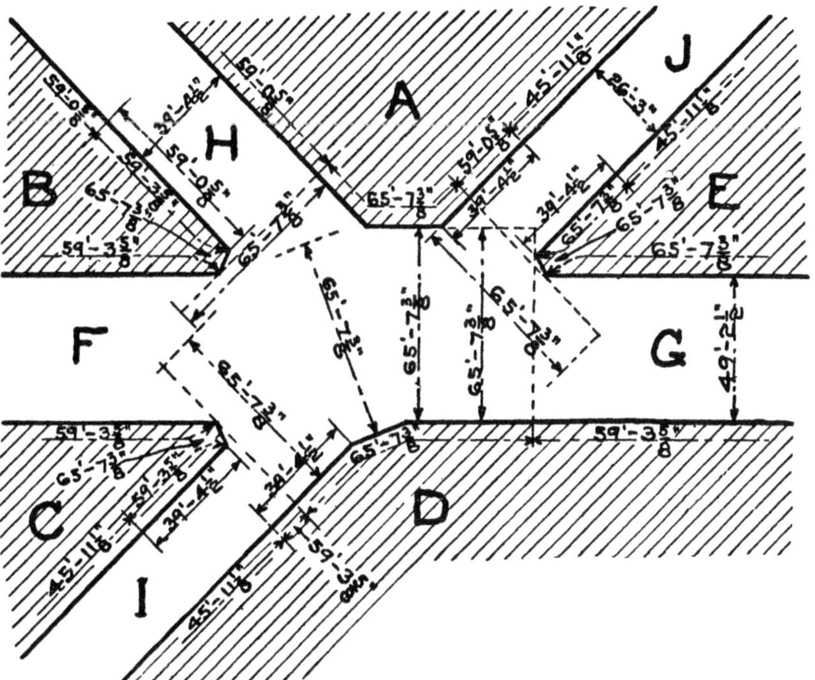

A building, however, upon a corner of two streets of unequal width and of any slope may have the same height on the narrow street as that accorded upon the wide street for a distance back from the wide street not exceding 1½ times the width of the narrow street. Where the intersecting streets are of equal width, but of different slopes, the height is taken as the average for the middle points of each frontage. Frontages on which the height is taken conformably to the level of the street on which such frontages face, as for separate buildings, need not be reckoned as in determining such middle point.

A building comprised between streets of different widths or of different levels has the height of each façade determined by the street upon which it faces except where the extreme distance between the two façades does not exceed 49.20 feet, when the façade upon the narrower or lower street may be built up to the same height as that allowed upon the wider or higher street.

Where portions of a building project beyond or are built back of the building line, the height is based upon a street width equal to the distance between the extreme projection of the façade and the street line opposite. A fraction of a meter (3.28 feet) is taken as a meter in calculating this distance. The set-back provision applies to the building or any section of the building, at the ground story or any other story, provided a solid and substantial wall one meter (3.28 feet) high is built on the street line.

Buildings not erected to the maximum height allowed below and above the cornice line may be constructed in all parts as the builder may desire, subject to the provision, however, that they do not project beyond the planes set down in the maximum limitations.

The height of the ground story and of the story above the ground story may not be less than 9.18 feet in the clear. The height of the other stories may not be less than 8.53 feet in the clear. For the top story of a building this height applies to the highest part of a sloping ceiling, but every room with a sloping ceiling must have at least 21.52 square feet of level ceiling.

The highest point of party walls and chimneys may not be more than 3.28 feet above a horizontal tangent to the circular arc. Chimneys must also be set back at least 3.28 feet behind the front line. Projections beyond the façade of buildings are regulated by the width of the street.

Court space

The least dimension and the minimum area are prescribed for all courts that furnish light and air to habitable rooms. In the case of kitchens these requirements are relaxed, the least dimension and the minimum area being only about half as stringent as those demanded for other habitable rooms.

Light shafts may be provided to light rooms that cannot be used for the purposes of habitation. These light shafts may, however, light the janitor's kitchen on the ground floor and the habitable rooms on the top story of a building. The minimum required area of a light shaft is 86.06 square feet; the least dimension 5.33 feet.

Owners of adjoining buildings may make an agreement to have courts and light shafts in common, the least dimension and minimum area of such courts and shafts to be the same as those required in the case of a single building. When two or more owners enter into such an agreement, they must notify the prefect of the Seine of their agreement, and execute with the city of Paris, before commencing the building, an agreement to maintain such courts and shafts for their common use.

The provisions relating to the height of buildings and court space are summarized in the following table:

				Courts			
				Dwelling Rooms		Kitchens	
Width of street (feet)	Height below cornice line (rear and front) (feet)	Length of front radius (feet)	Length of rear radius (feet)	Least dimension (feet)	Area (sq. ft.)	Least dimension (feet)	Area (sq. ft.)
3.28	22.96	19.68	19.68	13.12	322.80	6.56	161.40
6.56	26.24	19.68	19.68	13.12	322.80	6.56	161.40
9.84	29.52	19.68	19.68	13.12	322.80	6.56	161.40
13.12	32.80	19.68	19.68	13.12	322.80	6.56	161.40
16.40	36.08	19.68	19.68	13.12	322.80	6.56	161.40
19.68	39.36	19.68	19.68	13.12	322.80	6.56	161.40
22.96	42.64	19.68	21.32	14.21	358.91	7.08	179.26
26.24	45.92	19.68	22.96	15.30	394.47	7.64	197.23
29.52	49.20	19.68	24.60	16.40	430.34	8.20	215.20
32.80	52.48	19.68	26.24	17.49	466.50	8.76	233.06
36.08	55.76	19.68	27.88	18.58	502.06	9.28	251.03
39.36	59.04	19.68	29.52	19.68	537.92	9.84	269.00
42.64	59.46	21.32	29.52	19.68	537.92	9.84	269.00
45.92	60.28	22.96	29.52	19.68	537.92	9.84	269.00
49.20	61.10	24.60	29.52	19.68	537.92	9.84	269.00
52.48	61.92	26.24	31.16	20.77	574.08	10.36	286.86
55.76	62.70	27.88	31.16	20.77	574.08	10.36	286.86
59.04	63.56	29.52	31.16	20.77	574.08	10.36	286.86
62.32	64.38	31.16	31.16	20.77	574.08	10.36	286.86
65.60	65.20	32.80	32.80	21.86	609.64	10.92	304.83
Over 65.60	65.60	32.80	32.80	21.86	609.64	10.92	304.83

BOSTON

Boston has resorted to both the police power and the power of eminent domain in restricting the height of buildings.

The height of buildings has been limited under the police powers of the state and without compensation to the owners where the limitation on height has applied to the entire city or to some considerable area of the city.

The height of buildings has been limited under the power of eminent domain and with compensation to the owners where the buildings upon particular streets, limited areas, or individual estates have been subjected to special and more stringent limitations of height than those applicable to buildings in the territory outside these small restricted areas.

I—Restrictions Imposed on Height Under the Police Power

1. Special fire regulations

Under the provisions of the building law (stat. 1907, ch. 550) all first-class buildings have to be of fireproof construction. Buildings of the first class include all buildings adapted for habitation more than five stories in height and exceeding 65 feet above the basement or covering more than 5000 superficial square feet on the ground floor regardless of height. No building of the first class may be erected over 100 feet in height which is to be used above the first story for warehouses or stores or for the storage or sale of merchandise (stat. 1890, ch. 308). No wharves, sheds on wharves, market sheds or temporary sheds may be erected, if of wood, to a greater height than 27 feet. Outside the building limits the height of wooden buildings is restricted at 45 feet for dwelling houses and at 55 feet for other buildings. (Revised Ordinances, 1898, ch. 45, secs. 34 and 37.)

2. Height of buildings restricted to 125 feet

The height of buildings has been limited in Boston since 1891. In that year the state legislature passed a general act (ch. 355) applying to all cities in the commonwealth. This act forbids any building from being erected or increased to a greater height than 125 feet. The restriction applies, with minor exceptions, to all buildings without any reference to their location or use. At the time of its passage there were but two buildings in Boston that exceeded 125 feet in height.

3. Height limited to 2½ times the width of the abutting street

In 1892 the legislature imposed more stringent limitations on the height of buildings in Boston. Under the provisions of this act (ch. 419, sec. 25) the height of a building measured from the grade of the street may in no case exceed 2½ times the width of the widest street or square on which it fronts. The width of a street is defined as being the distance between the face of the building and the lawfully established line of the street on the other side. In case the widest street is of an uneven width, the average width opposite the building is taken. Where the effective width of a street has been increased by an area or set-back, the space between the face of the main building and the lawfully established line of the street may be built upon to the height of 20 feet.

The effect of these limitations may be best illustrated by quoting from the report submitted by the commission on the height of buildings, December 3, 1904:

"The situation created by the general laws permitting the erection of buildings in this city within certain limits to the height of 125 feet is that by 1904 such buildings have become very common in the down-town or business sections of the city; in fact, so common that the owners of real estate in that part of the city are, when rebuilding, quite generally compelled in self-defense to carry their buildings up to the 125-foot limit to which adjoining or neighboring buildings have already been erected. So far as the rest of the city is concerned, both the parts still exclusively residential in character and the parts (including such districts as the Back Bay) into which business is advancing, there have so far been but few high buildings erected; and these, at least all over 100 feet in height, have not, according to the best information that we have been able to secure, proved successful investments. The erection of half a dozen buildings of this character on the Back Bay indicates, however, a disposition on the part of some landowners to repeat in the residential districts of the city these conditions which have for some time obtained down-town."

4. Adoption of the districting system; Acts of 1904 and 1905

In 1904 an act (ch. 333) was passed by the legislature providing for the appointment of a height of building commission by the mayor of Boston. This commission consisted of three members, Messrs. Nathan Matthews, Jr., chairman, Joseph A. Conry, and Henry Parkman.

The commission was authorized to hold public hearings and to divide the city into two districts which were to be known respectively as District A and District B. The boundaries of these districts were to be fixed and recorded in the registry of deeds in Suffolk county by the commission within one month of its appointment. These boundaries were to remain unchanged for a period of fifteen years.

(a) *Appeals*—Persons aggrieved by the order establishing the boundaries of the two districts were given a period of thirty days within which to appeal to the commission for a revision. Appeals were to be acted upon by the commission within six months from the time of its appointment. If the hearing of an appeal resulted in a revision of the original order, the revision was to be entered with the registry of deeds as dating back to the date of the original record.

(b) *Boundaries of the districts*—The boundaries of District A were to be laid out in such a manner as to include those parts of the city in which all or the greater part of the buildings were used for business or commercial purposes; those of District B in such a manner as to include those parts of the city in which all or the greater part of the buildings were used for residential purposes, or for other purposes not business or commercial.

With a few minor exceptions the act restricted the height of buildings above the grade of the street to 125 feet in District A and to 80 feet in District B.

No restriction was placed on the height of coal hoists, grain elevators and sugar refineries in District A.

District A, as laid out by the commission in its orders of July 5, 1904, and December 3, 1904, comprised certain parts of East Boston, Charlestown and Boston proper, respectively. These parts were only separated from each other by certain arms of the harbor. District A included the down-town business section and practically the whole waterfront. District B included the South End, the West End, Beacon Hill, the Back Bay and the suburban parts of the city.

The waterfront was placed in District A because it was occupied to a large extent by coal hoists, grain elevators and sugar refineries—structures which were exempt by the act from any height limitation whatever in District A but restricted to 80 feet in District B. To serve their purpose such buildings have to exceed a height of 80 feet; for this reason the commission placed them in District A.

The commission refused to designate small business areas in

the residential section as District A or to designate small residential areas in the business section as District B.

The powers of the commission were construed as being too narrow to permit the designation of business streets in District B (and of the contiguous territory on either side for a distance of about 100 feet) as belonging to District A. Such a course also impressed the commission as being of very doubtful constitutionality under the police power of the state. The owners of property in the immediate rear of the property fronting in these streets, moreover, protested vigorously against gridironing the city with long lines of 125-foot buildings.

The commission, however, recognized a reasonable demand for buildings of a height between 80 and 100 feet on the main thoroughfare in the residential sections of the city and recommended that the law be amended to permit the erection of such buildings.

The commission said in making this recommendation in its report of December 3, 1904:

"We believe that the limit imposed on buildings in these districts by the acts of 1904 is too low for universal application, and that buildings higher than 80 feet should be allowed on the wider streets in these sections of the city. We are satisfied that there is a general and reasonable demand for buildings on these streets between 80 and 100 feet in height and that the erection of such buildings should be permitted under such restrictions as will secure the main purpose of the law of 1904. That purpose was, as we understand it, to prevent the erection of very high buildings in those parts of the city which, unlike the down-town section, are not yet condemned by the number of high buildings already erected to the perpetual toleration of this evil. On the other hand, an 80-foot building seems to us too low for many of the uses to which land abutting on the main thoroughfares of travel in this city is reasonably adapted, while, if the extreme limit of buildings throughout District B is kept at 80 feet, and the limit of second-class buildings kept at 70 feet, there will be no sufficient inducement to the erection of first-class or fireproof buildings in any section of the city outside of District A. Moreover, a height limit not exceeding 100 feet, if confined to the broader streets and to buildings of sufficient area or base, would be free from the objections which may forcibly be urged against buildings of that height on narrower streets, and so narrow themselves as to be a special menace to life and property in case of fire. We think that the conditions of the problem, as well as the reasonable demands of all reasonable property owners, can be fully met by permitting the erection of buildings in District B to a height not exceeding 100 feet in any case, not exceeding in any case the width between the front of buildings, and bearing some reasonable ratio to the frontage of the building itself. These provisions would permit the erection of 100-foot buildings on Boylston Street and Huntington Avenue, and of buildings between 80 and 100 feet on Massachusetts Avenue, provided the base or frontage of the building was so wide as to bear some reasonable relation to the height of the building.

"We are so much impressed with the undesirable conditions which have already resulted from the erection of high buildings in the down-town section of the city, and so thoroughly convinced that a general and uniform limitation to building to a reasonable height is neither an injury to real estate values nor a hindrance to the growth of the city, that if it were not for the considerations previously suggested, based on the great number of high buildings already erected in the down-town districts, we should recommend a maximum limit for the entire city of 100 feet.

"If the foregoing suggestions should be incorporated in our building laws, we believe that the limitations on the height of buildings should be permanent, and not subject to change at the end of fifteen years as provided in section 2 of the act of 1904.[11] If the limits adopted are satisfactory, we see no reason for holding out any definite expectation of a change. The legislature has, and will continue to have without express reservation, the power to modify the law, but the existence of a statute expressly providing for modifications at stated periods can only have an unsettling effect on real estate values."

(c) *The amendatory act of* 1905—In accordance with this recommendation, the legislature passed an amendatory act (ch. 383) in 1905 authorizing the erection of buildings to a height not exceeding 100 feet in such parts of District B and on such conditions as the commission might determine. The commission, moreover, was empowered to authorize construction of buildings 125 feet in height in that portion of District B lying within 50 feet of District A, provided the boundary line between the two districts as established by the commission divided adjoining premises owned by the same person. The commission's order of July 21, 1905, limits the construction of such buildings to that portion of District B which lies 50 feet westerly from the boundary line running from Columbus Avenue to the center of Boylston Street. The regulations laid down by the commission under this act were to be recorded with the registry of deeds in the same manner as those laid down under the act of 1904. The restrictions imposed were also to expire at the same time as those imposed under the original act. Persons aggrieved by the regulations of the commission were given 60 days within which they might appeal to the commission for a revision. The commission was obliged to act upon all appeals before its dissolution on the first day of January, 1906.

(d) *Provisions controlling the erection of buildings of an intermediate height in District B*—The conditions under which buildings may be erected to an intermediate height between 80 and 100 feet in District B are found in the commission's order of July 21, 1905, and November 20, 1905. These orders affect the whole of District B except those areas in which the height of buildings had been restricted under the power of eminent domain and which will be described elsewhere in this paper.

Buildings over 80 feet in height may be erected only on streets exceeding 64 feet in width. Buildings on streets exceeding this width have their particular height limit determined by two considerations: (1) the width of the adjoining street; and (2) the width of the building.

---

[11] The commission on building laws in its report of January, 1905, page 13, made a similar recommendation. "We recommend," said the commission, "the repeal of so much of chapter 333 of the acts of the year 1904 as fixed a time limit for the operation of its report. We make this recommendation because we believe that the discussion which the operation of that act has raised has thrown sufficient new light upon the subject to enable the city authorities to secure by ordinance, when necessary to adapt the law to changing situations, a more satisfactory result than can be accomplished by simply maintaining the present law for the period of fifteen years."

1. Buildings may be erected on streets exceeding 64 feet in width to a height equal to 1¼ times the width of the widest abutting street, but in no case may the height exceed 100 feet.

2. No building may be erected to a greater height than 80 feet unless the width of the building on each and every abutting public street is at least one-half of its height.

The effect of these requirements is to limit the erection of 100-foot buildings to plots with a minimum width of 50 feet fronting on streets with a minimum width of 80 feet. A building erected on a plot less than 50 feet in width on such a street could be raised only to a height equal to twice its width. The maximum height permitted a building on a 40-foot lot under these conditions would be the same as the general height limit for the whole of District B—that is, 80 feet. In permitting the erection of higher buildings on the wider frontages—a differential height was established which, under the most favorable circumstances, might equal 25 per cent of that allowed on the margin—this provision placed a great premium on plottage. The minimum frontage width required for the erection of buildings of different heights is indicated in the table given below:

Height of building (feet)	Minimum street width (feet)	Minimum frontage width (feet)
80	..	..
81	64⅔	40½
85	68	42½
90	72	45
95	76	47½
100	80	50

The fact that a building in order to get the benefit of additional height is required to possess this minimum frontage on each and every abutting public street materially adds to the stringency of this provision. In many cases it might result in buildings fronting on two or more streets being restricted to a lower height than that allowed adjoining buildings which front on only one street. The provision seems undesirable from an esthetic point of view as well—where the frontages are of an uneven width it militates against uniformity in sky-line.

The height of a building is to be measured from the mean grade of the curbs of all the abutting streets. The average width opposite the building is taken where the street is of an uneven width. The width of a street includes the width of any space on the same side of the street as the building and upon which no building can be lawfully erected by virtue of any building line established by the board of street commissioners, the board of park commissioners, the commonwealth or the city. All these streets, or portions of streets upon which buildings may lawfully be erected on one side only, are considered as of a width of 80 feet. In the case of irregular or triangular open spaces formed by the intersection of streets, the width of the streets is taken as the width of the widest street entering the space at its point of entrance.

By an act passed in 1907 (ch. 416) Rutherford Avenue, Charlestown, is considered as an 80-foot street in so far as the buildings on the westerly and southwesterly side are concerned, thus allowing them a maximum height of 100 feet.

(e) *Appeals from the commission's orders*—Only three appeals were made to the commission by property owners for a reconsideration of its orders. One of these appeals was acted upon favorably by the commission. Before the passage of the acts of 1904 and 1905 the city had acquired a site for schoolhouse purposes in the area later laid out by the commission as District B. The city had planned the erection of a 100-foot schoolhouse on this site. Districting the height of this building as 80 feet would have resulted in considerable expense and inconvenience to the city, and it appealed for a revision of the commission's order placing this plot in the 80-foot area of District B. The commission reconsidered its action and decreed that so long as this site was used for schoolhouse purposes a 100-foot building might be erected.

II—Restrictions Imposed on Height under the Power of Eminent Domain.

The limitations on the height of buildings described above apply to the entire city with the exception of three small areas:

1. An area contiguous to certain parkways, boulevards and public ways;
2. An area in the vicinity of Copley Square; and
3. An area in the vicinity of the State House.

The height of buildings in these three instances has been limited under the power of eminent domain. These areas have been subjected to more stringent restrictions than the surrounding territory, where the height of buildings has been limited under the police power, in order to provide superior light, air and view to adjacent streets or parks of a special character that have been created at considerable expense. Since these rights in the light, air and view over adjacent land have been treated in the nature of an easement over such land, the city, in acquiring them, has always done so, not under the police power, but under the power of eminent domain.

1. The area contiguous to certain parkways, boulevards and public ways

In 1896 a building known as Haddon Hall was erected on Commonwealth Avenue to a height of 125 feet. The public protest that followed the construction of this building induced the legislature immediately to pass an act (stat. 1896, ch. 313, amended by stat. 1897, ch. 379, and by stat. 1905, ch. 383) prohibiting any repetition of the offense. This act, which can be adopted by any city in the commonwealth at its own option, empowers the park commissioners to establish a building line at a distance not exceeding 25 feet from the exterior line of any parkway, boulevard or public way bordering on a park. When this building line is established by the park commissioners, the extreme height to which buildings may be erected on such streets shall be 70 feet or such other height as the city council or the inhabitants of the city may determine. The 70-foot limit authorized under this act does not apply to the buildings on those parkways, boulevards or public ways bordering on a park where no building line has been established by the park commissioners. (Williams *v.* Boston, 190 Mass. 541; March 1, 1906.)

The city council of Boston accepted the provisions of this act on May 18, 1896, and the park commissioners on August 3, 1896, imposed a building line of 20 feet along both sides of Commonwealth Avenue, between Arlington Street and Beacon Street. No suits were brought for damages due to this restriction of the height of buildings and the time for filing such suits has expired. That the restriction cost the city no damages is probably explained by the fact that the land was already subject to a similar servitude imposed by covenants in the deeds of the property conveyed by the original owners. The park commissioners have not imposed building lines on any other parkway, boulevard or public way bordering on a park under the provisions of this act.

2. The area in the vicinity of Copley Square

Considerable uncertainty seems to have existed in Boston as to just on what streets the height of buildings was limited by the parkway act of 1896. It was this uncertainty that caused the controversy that arose between the city and the owners of Westminster Chambers, a building erected on Copley Square during the winter of 1897–98. The public-spirited citizens that protested against the erection of this building were under the impression that this act restricted all buildings on any parkway, boulevard or public way bordering on a park to a maximum height of 70 feet. The owners of Westminster Chambers disputed this view, claiming that they had a right to erect a building of any height they chose on the plot so long as it did not exceed 125 feet in height.

In 1897 a trust company purchased certain estates in Copley Square on which it proposed to erect a 120-foot building. The building commissioner issued the permit for the building in July, 1897. The proposed building was opposite the Public Library between the Art Museum and Trinity Church. The public, supposing that the parkway act of 1896 protected the square against any invasion of high buildings, immediately offered vigorous protest against the construction of the building.

The greater part of the district adjoining Copley Square was at that time devoted to charitable, religious and educational purposes. Its total area is 1,128,868 square feet. Of this area, 557,164 square feet was occupied by the Public Library, the Museum of Fine Arts, the Institute of Technology, the Society of Natural History, the Horace Mann School, the Harvard Medical School, the Art Club, Trinity Church, Old South Church, and the South Congregational Church. Millions of dollars had been spent by the city, the commonwealth and benevolent persons to erect beautiful and artistic buildings on the square. The large land values in the district were primarily due to these expenditures.

In answer to public criticism the owners offered to erect a seven-story building instead of the ten-story 120-foot building which they proposed to erect, and then sell it to Trinity Church for the sum of $1,085,000. As an alternative to this proposition, the owners offered to limit the building at seven stories, if Trinity Church paid them $75,000 a story for each of the three stories omitted—that is, $225,000 for the three stories.

Trinity Church refused to accept this proposition. It chose to petition the legislature to pass a special act limiting the height of buildings on the square.

When the legislature met January 1, 1898, the foundations of the building had been completed. None of the iron work or of the other material was delivered until after the adjournment of the legislature.

A petition was promptly presented to the legislature praying for the enactment of a bill that would limit the height of all buildings within 500 feet of Copley Square to 80 feet. This petition was signed by 3000 persons from all parts of the state. The petitioners owned taxable property valued at $75,000,000. The real estate interests favoring the bill, including those in and about Copley Square which were exempt from taxation, amounted to about $100,000,000. The remonstrants attempted to obtain a bill that would permit a maximum height limit of 100 feet. Failing in this, they offered amendments both on the floor of the House and of the Senate making the limitation 92 feet. These, too, were defeated. A limit of 96 feet would have permitted the construction of Westminster Chambers as finally erected.

The petitioners maintained that the public had a right to control the land values which it itself had created, and that it was hardly decent of a private owner to erect a building which would destroy the value of those amenities in the neighborhood that had given his own property the greater share of its value. The fire hazard from a high building, they stated, would be a perpetual menace to the safety of the valuable collections of art and literature stored in the museums and libraries fronting on the square. They also claimed that a high building would impair, if not destroy, the light necessary for proper exhibition and use of these collections.

On January 29, 1898, the park commissioners wrote to the owners of the building calling their attention to the fact that St. James Avenue bordered on Copley Square and that their plans contemplated a violation of the 70-foot law. It seems that the owners paid no attention to this letter.

On March 29, 1898, the city of Boston filed a bill in equity in the supreme court to restrain the erection of the building beyond a height of 70 feet. Counsel for Westminster Chambers appeared, and, to prevent an application to the court for an injunction, orally agreed that pending final action by the legislature on the bill before it the building should not be erected to a greater height than 70 feet.

In spite of this agreement the owners proceeded with the erection of their building above a level of 70 feet. When this was called to the attention of the city, a written stipulation was filed in court signed by the counsel for Westminster Chambers that the building should not be erected above 70 feet. The expressed purpose of this agreement was to avoid the necessity for a temporary injunction.

On May 23, 1898, the legislature passed an act (ch. 452) that exempted Copley Square from the 70-foot law. This act restricted the height of buildings in the vicinity of Copley Square to 90 feet on land abutting on St. James Avenue, between Clarendon and Dartmouth Streets, and on the land occupied by the Pierce Building, the Public Library, and the Old South Church; and to 100 feet on land abutting on Boylston Street, between Clarendon and Dartmouth Streets. Such sculptural ornaments as were approved by the board of park commissioners might be erected above these limits.

The 90-foot limit applied to the east, south, and west sides, and the 100 foot limit to the north side of the square. In determining these limitations, consideration was paid to the shape of the square, which, owing to its configuration, allowed a greater height on Boylston Street than on other sides without injury to its appearance. A higher limit, moreover, could be permitted on this side than on the others without materially affecting the natural light of the park to the principal buildings fronting on it. Trinity Church, the Art Museum, and the Public Library are all on the three sides of the square restricted to 90-foot buildings. The fact that these buildings had need of greater fire protection than those on the north side was also an influential factor in deciding the legislature to restrict these buildings to a lower height.

At the time the act was passed the steel framework of the building was erected to a height of seven stories and the masonry walls were completed to a point between the third and fourth stories. Construction above the seventh story had been suspended in accordance with the agreement.

The owners now had to solve the problem of adapting their building to the limitations imposed by the statute. Their original plans had called for a ten-story building 120 feet in height. The act just passed permitted their building a height of only 90 feet.

The owners, however, on July 16, 1898, announced their intention of erecting an eight-story building 96 feet in height. On the two sides fronting on the abutting streets the brick walls of the building were to extend to a height of 90 feet. From this line upward to the roof the plans called for terra-cotta, partly in relief, to constitute the architrave, frieze and cornice of the building. The owners termed the six feet near the top of the building thus ornamented "sculptured ornaments." The two sides of the building not fronting on streets were to be of plain brick the entire height of the building.

These plans were submitted to the park commissioners, who on July 16, 1898, returned them without their approval.

The owners, however, proceeded with the erection of their building, according to these plans.

On October 31, 1898, after the completion of the building, which had been finished about the middle of August, the park commissioners passed a vote approving the "sculptured ornaments on the building." The owners claimed that the approval of the "sculptured ornaments" by the park commissioners was an authorization of that portion of the building back of the "ornaments."

The city law department refused to institute a suit against the owners to require them to remove that portion of their building above the 90 foot limit. The attorney-general, therefore, took the matter into the courts.

The owners of Westminster Chambers again did everything in their power to delay the decision of the court in the hope that they might persuade the legislature to pass a special act exempting their building from the height limit imposed on other buildings about Copley Square. Bills giving them this privilege were introduced in the legislature during the sessions of 1899, 1900, 1901, 1902 and 1903. The bill introduced in 1900 was passed by the legislature under circumstances that seem to have amounted to a scandal. A certain dinner given the night before the act was passed, it has been intimated, explained the vote of many representatives. Governor Crane vetoed this bill on the ground that he was unable "to give his sanction to a measure intended to relieve citizens of the commonwealth from the consequences of deliberate disregard of the provisions of a statute of the general court."

In March, 1901, the supreme court of Massachusetts in rendering its decision in the case of Attorney-General *v.* Williams (174 Mass. 476, 178 Mass. 330) ordered the offending portions of the building to be taken down and removed. The court held that no part of the main structure, not even the roof, could extend above the 90-foot limit set by the act. The authority of the park commissioners to approve sculptured ornaments surmounting a 90-foot building, the court held, did not empower them to approve the ornamentation of the architrave, frieze or cornice of a building exceeding that height. The order of the state court was sustained by the supreme court of the United States in the case of Williams *v.* Parker, 188 U. S. 491.

The owners and contractors of Westminster Chambers instituted a suit for damages against the city soon after the passage of the act of 1898. This suit, however, was not brought to trial until March, 1906. Although the court found that there had been a violation of the statute of 1898 by the owners in erecting the "sculptured ornaments" approved by the park commissioners to a height exceeding 90 feet, it found that they had acted in good faith on the advice of counsel in an attempt to make the best possible use of their unfinished building and were therefore entitled to damages. (Williams *v.* Boston, 190 Mass. 541.)

3. The area in the vicinity of the State House

In 1899 the legislature passed an act (ch. 457) limiting the height of buildings on three small blocks west of the State House to 70 feet.

The restricted area included the tract of land north of Beacon Street and south of Myrtle Street, between Joy Street on the west and Hancock Street and Hancock Avenue on the east. In 1901 an amendatory act (ch. 525) was passed restricting the height of buildings in a district east of the State House. By this act the height of buildings abutting on or within 42 feet of Bowdoin Street between Allston and Beacon Streets was limited at 100 feet and those within 95 feet of Beacon Street between the Claflin Building and Park Street at 70 feet.

At the time that the original act was passed no building west of the State House exceeded or equaled the prescribed limit of 70 feet in height. The Hotel Otis, at the northeast corner of Joy and Mount Vernon Streets, which was the highest building in the restricted area, had a height of 68 feet, exclusive of such projections as chimneys, etc., which were allowed under the statutes. There were several buildings, however, west of Joy Street, immediately opposite the restricted area, that exceeded 70 feet in height. The limitation east of the State House seems to have been set at 100 feet because it contained several buildings exceeding 70 feet in height.

Damages

The statutes limiting the height of buildings under the power of eminent domain have generally provided that a claim for damages has to be filed within a stipulated period. The courts have decided that it is within the power of the legislature to decree a limited period during which damages will be awarded for any injury suffered by private property owing to these restrictions and that a landowner's claim for damages is lost if he fails to take advantage of his right to compensation during this period (Raymond *v.* Commonwealth, 192 Mass. 486).

The statutes have also generally provided that damages are to be awarded in the same manner as prescribed by law for obtaining damages sustained by any person whose land is taken on the laying out of a highway. In other words, the damages to be awarded are the value of the property taken and of the resulting damages, if any, to the property not taken, less the amount of the special and peculiar benefit, if any, to the property not taken. If the special benefit equals or exceeds the amount of damages ascertained under this rule, the landowner is not entitled to any damages.

The Copley Square act (stat. 1898, ch. 452) is the only instance where the legislature provided compensation for the damages or loss sustained by the prevented use of materials bought or contracted for in the case of a building in the process of construction at the time the act was passed. The compensation that might be recovered was limited by the extent that the material bought or contracted for exceeded that which would have been necessary for a building not exceeding the height limit, less the value of such material not required on account of the limitation, and the actual cost or expense of any rearrangement of design or construction made necessary by the limitation. The amount recoverable under damages to real estate and under damages to material was each exclusive of anything that could be recovered under the other. Thus the court held in Williams *v.* Boston, 190 Mass. 541, that the extra foundations and the extra iron for a building 120 feet high not needed for a building 90 feet high, if incorporated in the building before the passage of the act, were an element of damages suffered by the real estate. In determining the difference in the value of the building as it was before and after the passage of the act, the loss on these materials, having become a part of the real estate, was not recoverable as damages suffered by material. The amount of compensation due, under the title of damages to real estate, was, therefore, the difference between the combined value of the unfinished structure and the land before and after the passage of the act.

In the case of Cole *v.* City of Boston, 181 Mass. 374, the court admitted testimony showing the price at which adjoining land had recently sold, but refused testimony stating that the price of such adjoining land had been adversely affected by the limitation of the height of buildings. The court held that such evidence might properly be excluded; for although the price of the adjoining land was competent, an inquiry into the considerations determining that price would open a collateral investigation.

The limitation imposed on the height of buildings in the vicinity of the State House was part of a general improvement which involved the laying out and grading of certain streets, the removal of buildings, the reconstruction and extension of the State House and the construction of a park between Bowdoin Street and the

State House. The original act restricting the height in this area (stat. 1899, ch. 457; stat. 1901, ch. 525) was amended by an act passed in 1902 so far as its provision for damages was concerned. This act (ch. 543) provided that only such persons whose property was damaged more than it was benefited by the improvement as a whole were to receive any compensation. The constitutionality of this act has never come squarely before the courts. In the case of the American Unitarian Association *v.* Commonwealth, 193 Mass. 470, the supreme court of Massachusetts, however, intimated that the constitutionality of limiting the compensation for a right of property taken to its value diminished by the value of the benefit received by the remaining estate from a general improvement to be a very grave question.

In only three instances has it been possible to ascertain the amount of damages recovered by the owners of property injuriously affected by these limitations. The owners of Westminster Chambers received $334,589; the owners of The Bristol $15,000; and the owners of a parcel on Dartmouth Street, $17,000.

Exemptions from Height Limit

The provisions affecting the projections above the roof line that were exempted from any height limit and which could therefore be erected to any height were in a most confused state before the act of 1905 was passed. Numerous acts had been passed by the legislature limiting the height of buildings. Each of these exempted different projections above the height limit than those exempted by the others. It was therefore very difficult to say just what projections might and what projections might not be erected above the height limit. The act of 1905 superseded all these conflicting provisions. It allows the following exemptions: churches, steeples, towers, domes, cupolas, belfries, or statuary not used for purposes of habitation, chimneys, gas holders, coal or grain elevators, open balustrades, skylights, ventilators, flagstaffs, railings, weather vanes, soil pipes, steam exhausts, signs, roof houses not exceeding 12 feet square and 12 feet high, and other similar constructions usually erected above the roof line of buildings.

Statistics of Building Operations, 1899–1910

The statistics of the building operations in Boston during the period from 1899 to 1910 are of such a character that, taken alone, they do not justify any conclusions as to the effect of these restrictions upon the building industry. During the five-year period of 1899–1903 immediately before the passage of the acts of 1904 and 1905 the value of the building operations totaled $78,631,451; in the five-year period of 1906–1910 after their passage the value of the building operations totaled $81,162,691. The value of the building operations in the five-year period after the passage of the acts consequently exceeded those of the five-year period before the passage of the acts by only $2,531,240. The acts are probably responsible for this small increase. The effect of the panicky conditions in 1907–1908 must, however, not be forgotten. Had it not been for this financial crisis, the building operations might have been considerably larger during the latter period.

ESTIMATED COST OF COMPLETED BUILDINGS—1899–1910

Year	Brick	Wood	Alterations	Total
1910..........	$10,950,390	$5,116,975	$4,808,306	$20,875,671
1909..........	7,285,550	6,148,395	3,322,486	16,756,431
1908..........	5,292,300	3,259,075	2,701,287	11,252,662
1907..........	10,607,367	4,464,052	4,151,807	19,223,226
1906..........	14,255,431	5,845,191	2,954,097	23,054,701
1905..........	7,510,325	1,349,695	3,504,727	12,364,747
1904..........	15,653,341	3,128,726	3,246,000	22,028,067
1903..........	9,199,700	2,531,922	3,533,318	15,264,940
1902..........	7,046,870	3,100,185	3,382,055	13,529,110
1901..........	10,844,801	3,064,410	3,950,500	17,859,711
1900..........	6,981,430	5,862,695	3,602,075	16,446,200
1899..........	5,799,467	4,191,010	5,541,013	15,531,490

NUMBER OF COMPLETED BUILDINGS—1899–1910

Year	Brick	Wood	Alterations	Total
1910........................	385	1,051	2,172	3,608
1909........................	390	1,154	2,158	3,702
1908........................	166	680	1,785	2,631
1907........................	355	865	2,326	3,546
1906........................	479	1,153	1,693	3,325
1905........................	156	222	1,871	2,249
1904........................	409	696	1,909	3,014
1903........................	287	549	2,071	2,907
1902........................	235	596	2,307	3,138
1901........................	413	610	2,239	3,262
1900........................	614	1,238	2,238	4,090
1899........................	317	990	2,234	3,541

BIBLIOGRAPHY

Commission on the Height of Buildings:

1. Order of July 5, 1904; Boston City Documents, 1904, No. 91. 6 p.
2. Report, December 3, 1904. Doc. No. 109. 18 p.

3. Order, July 21, 1905. Doc. No. 126. 3 p.
4. Order, November 20, 1905. Doc. No. 130. 3 p.
5. Final Report, December 22, 1905. Doc. No. 133. 30 p.

Myron E. Pierce. History of the Westminster Case, February 11, 1902. 7 p.

Petitioners for repeal of Chapter 333 of the Act of 1904. 9 p.

Samuel J. Elder. Limitation of Height of Buildings near Copley Square. Argument before Committee on Cities on behalf of the Museum of Fine Arts and Massachusetts Institute of Technology, February 17, 1898. 16 p.

Josiah Henry Benton, Jr. Argument for legislation to limit the height of buildings on and near Copley Square before Committee on Cities, February 17, 1898. 38 p.

Committee on Cities, Schedules to accompany petition for legislation to protect Copley Square, 1898. 13 p.

Shall Governor Crane's veto be upheld? Argument against Westminster Chambers Bill, March, 1901.

Albert E. Pillsbury. The Truth about the Westminster Chambers. Address to the Committee on Cities for the owners of the Westminster Chambers, April 4, 1901.

Woodbury & Leighton. The Westminster Chambers Bill circular appealing to the Massachusetts House of Representatives for fair treatment, 1900. 2 p.

E. A. Whitman. Change of Limitation in Height of buildings in Copley Square. Address before the Joint Committee on Cities in opening the case for the remonstrants against the bills for the change in the limitation in height of buildings in Copley Square, 1903. 16 p.

Report of the Commission on Building Laws (Massachusetts) Jan. 1905.

Cases:

Raymond *v.* Commonwealth, 192 Massachusetts 486.

American Unitarian Association *v.* Commonwealth, 193 Massachusetts 470.

Parker *v.* Commonwealth, 178 Massachusetts 199.

Attorney-General *v.* Williams, 174 Massachusetts 476; 178 Massachusetts 330. Sustained in Williams *v.* Parker, 188 U. S. 491.

Welch *v.* Swasey, 193 Massachusetts 364; 79 N. E. 745; 214 U. S. 91.

Williams *v.* Boston, 190 Massachusetts 541.

Cole *v.* Boston, 181 Massachusetts 374.

Statutes: Stat. 1892, C. 419; Stat. 1894, C. 443; Stat. 1891, C. 355; Stat. 1896, C. 313; Stat. 1897, C. 379; Stat. 1898, C. 452; Stat. 1899, C. 457; Stat. 1901, C. 525; Stat. 1902, C. 543; Stat. 1904, C. 333; Stat. 1905, C. 383; Stat. 1907, C. 416.

WASHINGTON

The height of buildings has been limited under act of Congress in the District of Columbia since 1899. The regulations, which have been amended from time to time, are more stringent than those of any other city in this country with the possible exception of Boston. The limitations in the business section in the District of Columbia are a trifle more lenient than those in Boston, but in the residence section they are more rigid.

The height of buildings is defined as the distance from the level of the sidewalk opposite the middle of the front of the building to the highest point of the roof. If a building has more than one front, the height is measured from the elevation of the sidewalk opposite the middle of the front that will permit the greater height.

No building may be erected to a greater height than the width of the street in its front increased by 20 feet. Buildings that face on a public space or reservation formed at the intersection of two or more streets, the course of which is not interrupted by such public space or reservation, have their height limit determined by the width of the widest street.

No building on a business street may exceed a maximum height of 130 feet except on the north side of Pennsylvania Avenue between First and Fifteenth Streets NW., where an extreme height of 160 feet is permitted.

On residence streets buildings may not exceed 80 feet in height to the top of the highest ceiling joints or 85 feet in height at the highest part of the roof or parapet. The height of the highest part of the roof or parapet, moreover, may not exceed the width of the street diminished by 10 feet on streets more than 70 feet wide; 60 feet on streets between 60 and 70 feet wide; and the width of the street on streets less than 60 feet wide.

On corner lots the height is determined by the width of the wider street.

On streets less than 90 feet wide where building lines have been established and recorded in the office of the surveyor that prevent the lawful erection of buildings in advance of such line, the width of the street, in so far as it controls the height of buildings, is held to be the distance between the building lines.

The Commissioners are also authorized to regulate the maximum height of buildings on such blocks as are immediately adjacent to public buildings or to the side of any public building. The height of several small areas has been regulated under this provision. The buildings fronting or abutting on the plaza in front of the new Union Station may not be more than 80 feet high.

The buildings on Pennsylvania Avenue NW. confronting the Treasury Building and the State, War and Navy Building and those on 14th Street SW., between B and D Streets, confronting the Bureau of Printing and Engraving, are limited to a maximum height of 80 feet. The buildings on G and F Streets NW., between 7th and 9th Streets, adjacent to the United States Patent Office, and those on North Capitol Street confronting the Post Office Building, are limited to a maximum height of 90 feet. The buildings adjacent to the Treasury Building, on 15th Street NW., between Pennsylvania Avenue and G Street, are limited to a height of 95 feet.

The Commissioners of the District are not only authorized but directed to denominate portions of streets as business streets. The Commissioners may from time to time denominate portions of streets as business streets subject to two conditions:

1. Where in a portion of a street not already denominated a business street a majority of a frontage not less than three blocks in length is occupied and used for business purposes; and

2. Where a portion of a street has already been denominated a business street and there exists adjoining such portion a block or more the frontage of which is occupied and used for business purposes.

All the streets in the District not designated as business streets are considered residence streets. The portions of streets denominated business streets number about seventy at present.

There is no statutory provision in the District that restricts the development of business streets to business purposes, or of residence streets to residence purposes. Every owner is free to develop his own property whether it is located on a business street or on a residence street as he sees fit.

LOS ANGELES

No city in this country has gone as far in the way of creating industrial and residential districts as Los Angeles. Baltimore regulates the location of certain industries. Minneapolis has established exclusive residential districts within a few of which only one-family residences may in the future be erected. Los Angeles has not done this. She has no exclusive residential districts. Certain industries are permitted in all of her residential district. But she has done what both Baltimore and Minneapolis or any other American city has refrained from doing: she has actually ejected obnoxious industries from the residential section and has been sustained by the courts in so doing.

The first districting ordinance in Los Angeles was passed in 1909. This ordinance has been amended more than seventy times. This paper, to avoid any confusion on the part of the reader, will state the general provisions of all these ordinances and amendments as in force to-day without any particular reference to the several ordinances.

The entire city of Los Angeles, with the exception of two suburbs, is divided into industrial and residential districts. These two suburbs, San Pedro and Wilmington, contain no residential district. Wilmington, however, has an industrial district.

That portion of Los Angeles which is districted is divided into twenty-five industrial districts and one residential district. The residential district comprises the whole districted territory exclusive of the areas within the several industrial districts. It therefore encircles and surrounds many of the industrial districts.

The so-called industrial districts do not fairly indicate the extent of the industrial area of the city. In addition to the industrial districts there are fifty-eight districts, known as " residence exceptions," in the residential district that are exempt from the regulations applicable to the residential district and in which business is permitted subject to certain conditions.

The industrial districts vary considerably in shape and size. The largest district has an area of several square miles. At its greatest dimensions, it measures five miles in length and two miles in width. The smallest district comprises one solitary lot. The combined area of the several industrial districts aggregates not more than one-tenth that of the residential district. The industrial districts are, on the whole, pretty well grouped in one part of the city.

The " residence exceptions " are all small. The largest is about a half mile square. With this exception no " residence exception " covers a greater area than two city blocks. In most instances these districts do not occupy more than one or two lots. The combined area of the fifty-eight " residence exceptions " is probably not more than 1 per cent of the residential district. The " residence exceptions" are, however, scattered more widely throughout the residential district than are the industrial districts.

In general the distinction between the industrial districts and the residential district is this: all kinds of business and manufacturing establishments are unrestrained in most of the industrial districts while certain specified businesses of an obnoxious character are excluded from the residential district. Those businesses not especially excluded are permitted in the residential district. All but the very lightest manufacturing is prohibited in the residential district. The less offensive business and manufacturing establishments excluded from the residential district may be carried on in the " residence exceptions." The owners of 60 per cent of the neighboring property frontage must give their consent to the creation of any " residence exception."

The industrial districts

Industry is unrestrained in most of the industrial districts. There are six industrial districts, however, that are very much in the nature of " residence exceptions." In districts 12, 13 and 14, it is unlawful to establish or maintain any works or factory, except a public hand laundry or wash house, where power other than animal power is used in its operation. In district 20, dye works, and in district 22, hay barns, feed, fuel and wood yards are included in the above exceptions.

In district 19 it is unlawful to establish, erect or construct any works or factory operated by any other power than animal power, or any winery, blacksmith shop, stone crusher, rolling mill, carpet-beating establishment, gas works, mattress factory, soap factory, fertilizer plant or factory, tallow-rendering establishment, tannery, glue factory, public laundry, wash house, brick yard or lumber yard.

After December 1, 1915, it will become unlawful to conduct, operate or maintain or to cause or permit to be conducted, operated or maintained in this district any blacksmith shop, planing mill, lumber yard, brick yard, hay barn, wood yard, public laundry, wash house stone crusher, or other works or factory operated by power other than animal power except as permitted in the residential district. In other words, after December 1, 1915, district 19 will become part of the residential district.

The residential district

Certain industries are absolutely prohibited in the residential district. Such industries, if established at the time the legislation was enacted, have been ejected from the district. The industries which it is unlawful to erect, establish, maintain or carry on in the residential district are: any works or factory using power other than animal power in its operation, or any stone crusher, rolling mill, machine shop, planing mill, carpet-beating establishment, hay barn, wood yard, lumber yard, public laundry, wash house, coal yard, briquette yard, riding academy, or any winery or place where wine or brandy is made or manufactured. Blacksmith shops already erected may be maintained in the residential district, but a ban is placed on the erection of new ones.

The installation and maintenance of one electric motor of a capacity not exceeding five horsepower is permitted on any lot or premises within the residential district. This motor may not, however, be operated in conjunction with any gas works, mattress factory, soap factory, fertilizer plant or factory, tallow-rendering establishment, tannery or glue factory.

The "residence exceptions"

A person desiring to erect, establish, maintain or carry on any works or factory using power other than animal power in its operation, or any hay barn, wood yard, winery, blacksmith shop or riding academy in the residential district may petition the council for the creation of a "residence exception."

The establishment, maintenance or carrying on of any stone crusher, rolling mill, carpet-beating establishment, gas works, mattress factory, soap factory, fertilizer plant or factory, tallow-rendering establishment, tannery, glue factory, public laundry, wash house, planing mill, brick yard, lumber yard, coal yard or briquette yard is expressly prohibited in all residence exceptions.

The petition for the creating of a residence exception must set forth the name of the person; the location and the nature of the establishment, works or factory desired to be erected, established, maintained or carried on; the record description of such property with its frontage and depth; the dimensions of each building proposed to be erected or maintained and the number of stories thereof, and if power is proposed to be used in the operation of such establishment, works or factory, the amount and character thereof. Each petition must be duly verified by the person making the application.

The council, however, grants no application for a "residence exception" unless it is accompanied by the signatures of the owners of 60 per cent of the property frontage in the immediate vicinity giving their consent to its creation. The area of such consent varies for different sites.

Where the proposed establishment, works or factory is to be situated on an inside lot in any block, the owners of 60 per cent of the property frontage in such block on both sides of the street must give their consent. The distance of such consent must be at least equal to the length of the side of the block where the proposed establishment, works or factory is to be situated.

Where the proposed establishment, works or factory is to be situated on a corner lot, the area of consent takes in the property frontage on both sides of each street within a 400-foot square having its sides parallel to the intersecting streets upon which such lot corners, the center of such square being the point of intersection of the center lines of such streets. Where such streets do not bisect each other, the center of such square is the point where the center lines of such intersecting streets would bisect each other if prolonged.

Where the proposed establishment, works or factory covers 60 per cent or more of any block, the area of consent embraces the property frontage on both sides of each street within a parallelogram surrounding such block, the sides of such parallelogram being 150 feet distant beyond the sides of such block.

A description of the property represented by each of these signatures must accompany this petition. This description must include the number of the lot, block, and the name of the tract wherein such lot is situated and the proper reference to the book and page of the recorded map showing such lot and tract.

The council refers all petitions to the board of fire commissioners for investigation and report. If the fire commissioners find the signatures adequate, and upon investigation recommend the granting of the petition, the council may adopt an ordinance excepting the territory from the residential district.

APPENDIX V

THE ENGLISH AND SWEDISH TOWN PLANNING ACTS

By Herbert S. Swan

THE ENGLISH TOWN PLANNING ACT OF 1909[1]

The English Town Planning Act of 1909 provides for a limited administrative control over the development and use of land in suburban areas. The act applies to England, Scotland and Wales.

The act makes no provision for the remodeling of a town as a whole. A city in inaugurating a town-planning scheme is as a rule limited to land in the course of development and to land likely to be used for building purposes. A scheme may include pieces of land already built upon or which are not likely to be used for building purposes provided their situation with respect to the land likely to be used for building purposes makes their inclusion desirable.

Land likely to be used for building purposes includes any land likely to be used for open spaces, roads, streets, parks and pleasure or recreation grounds.

Any land likely to be used for the purpose of executing any work upon or under the land incidental to a town-planning scheme may also be included. This work does not necessarily have to be of a building character.

The object of a town plan is to secure "proper sanitary conditions, amenity and convenience in connection with the laying out and use of the land and of any neighboring lands." The extent to which these objects may be dealt with is to be defined in a set of general provisions issued by the local government board in accordance with a schedule set forth in the act. This schedule mentions streets (including the stopping up and diversion of existing highways); buildings; open spaces (private and public); the preservation of objects of historical interest or natural beauty; sewerage, drainage, and sewage disposal; lighting; water supply; obstructive buildings, and any consequential works to the foregoing, as being within the scope of a town plan.

The local government board is to interpret what is meant by the three expressions: "proper sanitary conditions," "amenity," and "convenience."

[1] References: E. G. Bentley and S. Pointon Taylor, A Practical Guide in the Preparation of Town Planning Schemes (1911). J. B. Haldane, The Social Workers' Guide (1911), p. 417-420. Horace Cubitt, The London Building Law and the Development of Property. The Architect and Contract Reporter, Jan. 24, 1913. Transactions, Town Planning Conference, London, 1910. W. Thompson, Handbook to the Housing and Town Planning Act, 1909. Robert Donald, The Municipal Year Book of the United Kingdom for 1910, p. 596-597. Housing, Town Planning, etc., Act 1909, 9 Edw. VII, ch. 44.

Mr. Thompson explains the general meaning of these terms:

"Sunlight, fresh air, and vegetation are now recognized as the basis of all sound sanitary conditions.

"'Amenity' or pleasantness is a very elastic term, but may reasonably be held to cover the preservation, where at all practicable, of trees, hedges and other natural features which add to the beauty of the surroundings, by effecting deviations in the street lines, or judicious arrangement of gardens and other open spaces, while it may also include the protection of residential districts as far as possible from the smoke, noise, ugliness and other objectionable accompaniments of certain manufactures and other undertakings. It is of course necessary to protect the owner of one estate from another owner who for purposes of profit might desire to utilize his land in such a way as to lessen the amenities of residence, or unreasonably disfigure the district or spoil the view.

"'Convenience' mainly has regard to the streets and other means of communication between one part of a district and another, and would justify the local authority in varying their width, direction or construction, where so required, to meet the needs of pedestrian and vehicular traffic to and from adjacent estates and surrounding districts, as well as to suit the requirements of the residents."[1]

Authorities quite generally agree that the most important provision in the act is that which empowers a city to limit the number of buildings that may be erected per acre. This power over buildings extends not only to restricting the use of particular areas to specified purposes, but also to regulating the height and character of the buildings as well as fixing the minimum open space that must be left about the buildings in the several areas.

Property is not deemed to be injuriously affected by reason of the making of any provisions inserted in a scheme, which, with a view to securing the amenity of the area, or any part of the area, prescribe the space about buildings or limit the number of buildings to be erected, or prescribe the height or character of buildings. The local government board must, however, consider these provisions reasonable.

The local government board has to be consulted at nearly every stage of the preparation of a town-planning scheme.

A town-planning scheme prepared or adopted by a locality does not take effect unless approved by the local government board, which must be satisfied that there is a prima facie case for such scheme.

The local government board has power to compel a local authority to adopt any scheme proposed by the owners of land. The board may also, on satisfactory representation, order a local authority to prepare and carry out a scheme subject to its supervision and direction. The board in granting its approval to a scheme may impose such modifications and conditions as it sees fit. Schemes approved by the local government board unless opposed have the effect of a statute passed by Parliament. If a single owner, however, or any other person or authority interested opposes a scheme, it may be rejected by a resolution of either House in Parliament. Every

[1] Handbook to the Housing and Town Planning Act, 1909, p. 28.

town-planning scheme may include a provision suspending, so far as necessary for the proper carrying out of the scheme, any statutory enactments, by-laws, regulations or any other provisions in operation in the area included in the scheme. This clause to a large extent transfers the control over building operations from local to central control.

A city may purchase any or all land included in a scheme either through voluntary agreement with the owners or compulsorily—that is, by expropriation. In case a city does not purchase the land included in a scheme, it may claim one-half the increased value accruing to any property because of the scheme. The valuations now being fixed by the Finance Act of 1909–1910 will be of immense importance to a city in intercepting this increment.

By March 31, 1913, the local government board had already authorized the preparation or adoption of 33 schemes by 27 different local authorities, embracing a total area of more than 50,000 acres. Mr. John Burns, president of the board, estimates that 500,000 acres of rural land is urbanized every fifteen years in Great Britain.

THE SWEDISH TOWN PLANNING ACT[1]

The first national town-planning act enacted by any country was that passed by Sweden in 1874. Although the attention of this act with its amendments, including those of 1907 and 1910, is primarily directed to the development of new areas, it also enjoins every town to effect improvements in the plotting of its built-up area at every possible opportunity. Town plans may also be instituted in the case of burned areas.

The act makes the adoption of a town plan obligatory upon every town in the kingdom. About 600 plans have been made in accordance with the act.

The worst fault of the original act was that it favored the rectangular street and block system. In some instances, the gridiron plan was even forced on the old irregular inner parts of cities, thereby destroying many a picturesque street. The later amendments to the act have fortunately remedied this defect.

The law lays down the technical regulations for the building and planning of towns with reference to such requirements as traffic, health, comfort, beauty of arrangement and protection from fire.

The city council has the right to make a town-planning scheme for an area on its own initiative. It may initiate a plan without any demand on the part of the land owners. Land owners, as a matter of fact, have no power to plan their own areas. They must request the town council to do this for them. A town-planning scheme

[1] References: Byggnadsstadga för rikets städer den 8 maj 1874, med ändringar den 18 april 1884, den 30 nov. 1888, den 20 juni 1890, den 26 maj 1899; Stadsplan och tomtindeling, lag den 31 augusti 1907; Kommunal Författningshandbok för Stockholm 1910, p. 209, 246; Img. Lilienberg, Town Planning and Legislation in Sweden during the Last Fifty Years, Transactions, Town Planning Conference, London, 1910, p. 702-10.

adopted by the council must, with minor exceptions, have the approval of the king before becoming effective.

A town may exercise the power of eminent domain to purchase all or any of the land included in a scheme. This power prevents an owner from withholding his land from development to the detriment of the city. A town may also expropriate land in an unsanitary or overcrowded area.

Ample provision must be made for the convenience of traffic. The streets, which are to be wide, shall run in the directions most suited for traffic. Wide promenades and boulevards shall, if possible, traverse the town in various places and in different directions. Shrubbery is to be planted in the middle and on either side of these boulevards unless some other suitable arrangement is made for their ornamentation.

That the light, air and ventilation essential to the public health may be obtained, the law insists on the provision of as many open spaces as possible. This favors the creation of small residential districts and prevents the overcrowding of houses. It also reduces the fire hazard.

The building sites shall be of sufficient size to allow the erection of commodious dwellings and the provision of open and well-ventilated yards. All buildings must be adapted to the lots on which they are erected and their arrangement must be such as not to militate against the public health. No dwelling may be erected in an unhealthy location. Both the location and the arrangement of buildings are to be determined with reference to variety, good taste and beauty as well as to economy in construction and to a reduction of the fire hazard.

The zeal of the act to create a pleasing effect to the eye is illustrated by the provision that prohibits buildings from being painted with unmixed white paint—the paint must be tinted in such a manner that the reflection will not be harmful or disagreeable to the eye.

The town plan regulates the height of buildings in the district, but the height of no building may exceed the width of the street by more than 4 feet and 11 inches. A building erected on a plot situated at the intersection of a wider and a smaller street may base its height on the width of the wider street to a depth not exceeding 98 feet 5 inches. No dwelling-house may exceed five stories in height, including the ground floor. The garret is counted as a story provided it possesses a fireplace.

Industrial establishments may be prohibited in residential districts and vice versa. The maximum number of families which a house may accomodate may also be regulated.

In order to obviate any maladjustments that will have to be remedied in the future, the building department in granting a building permit has to determine:

1. The position of the building line;
2. The advisability of rearranging the lot's boundaries;

3. The street grades;

4. The height of the foundation with reference to the street grades; and

5. The lot level desirable to secure good drainage.

The plotting of a district shall be treated as a comprehensive scheme. It shall as far as possible be laid out at one time. Each district is to be developed in harmony with those surrounding it.

The building department has charge of the plotting. It determines the size of the proposed lots. The decision of the local authority in this matter is to be submitted to the king, who either approves the plan without any amendment or else rejects it in whole.

In the plotting of an area great care has to be taken that the lots laid out will be of such shape, size and general arrangement that they may be readily developed in accordance with the provisions of the act and the local building ordinances. The lot lines shall as far as possible be straight and form right angles not only with the street but also with the adjoining lot lines unless the plan established for the city demands otherwise. The integrity of the lot divisions must be preserved. No building may be erected in such a manner as to overlap the boundaries, or the proposed boundaries, of two or more lots. A lot which has once had its boundaries determined may not be subdivided into smaller lots or in any way diminished in area except under exceptional circumstances. A similar prohibition applies to the consolidation of lots or parts of lots.

It may happen in the plotting of an area that thé land included within the boundaries of one lot is owned by two or more persons. Where this occurs the lot may not be built upon until its ownership is merged in one person. The city, if it so chooses, may itself purchase and consolidate the several parts, and under certain conditions the owners may demand that it purchase them.

A city may prohibit all building operations within the area included in a scheme until the plans for its laying out are completed. The period of such suspension, however, may not exceed six months. Should the extension of a town into a district which is not included in the town plan become necessary or desirable, then a plan must forthwith be made for such district. No building may be erected that contravenes the town plan.

Lines of back gardens shall, where possible, be arranged in the residential districts of the town. Lines of front gardens shall also be laid out where this is found desirable and possible. Under no circumstances may either the back or the front gardens be built over or used for any other purpose than that of gardens. Owners are especially enjoined to maintain these gardens in a neat and painstaking manner.

An area equivalent to at least half that covered by the building must be devoted to garden purposes. In case of corner lots situated in those parts of the city where only houses of stone may be erected, the building department may, if the proper development of the lot so requires, relax this provision. The area of the garden in such cases must, however, be equal to at least one-third of that occupied by the building. The garden, moreover, must have a minimum area of 1936.8 square feet. The principal part of this open space must have a minimum width of at least 39.36 feet, and the minor parts a minimum width of at least 18.76 feet. No building may be erected nearer than 18.76 feet to the lot line.

An exception to these regulations is allowed where lots are developed in such a manner that the principal parts of their respective gardens lie side by side and form one continuous stretch. In such cases the local building ordinances may allow the gardens a minimum area of 1452.6 square feet, and a minimum width for their principal part of 37.52 feet.

Where the windows of a living-room are to overlook an adjoining lot, a space of 39.36 feet in width must be left between that part of the house and such adjoining lot. Each of the two owners may, however, agree to contribute a proportionate part of this space.

The stringency of the provisions with reference to open space does not apply in the case of "every-man-his-own-home" districts, such as Enskede near Stockholm.

APPENDIX VI

HEIGHT OF BUILDINGS IN MANHATTAN

There are 92,749 buildings in Manhattan. The average building height in Manhattan is 4.8 stories. Nine-tenths of these buildings do not exceed a height of 6 stories. The buildings over 10 stories in height constitute only a little over 1 per cent of the total. There are but 1048 buildings over 10 stories in height; 90 buildings over 17 stories in height; 51 buildings over 20 stories in height; and only 9 buildings over 30 stories in height.[1]

Manhattan has an area of 14,038 acres. The buildings over 10 stories high constitute 1.11 per cent of the total buildings. Allowing an average ground area of 10,000 square feet per building, these buildings cover an area of 240.58 acres. This is 1.71 per cent of the area of the borough.

The buildings over 17 stories high form 0.09 of 1 per cent of the total buildings. Allowing an average ground area of 15,000 square feet per building, these buildings cover an area of 31.33 acres. This is 0.22 of 1 per cent of the total area of the borough.

Even on Broadway, below Chambers Street, more than one-third of the frontage developed with private buildings has a height of not exceeding 6 stories. Only one-sixth of the frontage is developed with buildings exceeding 20 stories in height.

The average building height, excluding public buildings and churches, on Broadway, below Chambers Street, is 11 stories; on Nassau Street, from Wall to Frankfort, 8.56 stories; on Trinity Place and Church Street, from Morris to Chambers, 7.8 stories; on New Street 11.59 stories; on Exchange Place 14.1 stories; and on Fifth Avenue, from Washington Square to 59th Street, 6.4 stories.

The average frontage height, excluding public buildings and churches, on Broadway, below Chambers Street, is 13.92 stories; on Nassau Street, from Wall to Frankfort, 9.21 stories; on Trinity Place and Church Street, from Morris to Chambers, 9.18 stories; on New Street, 12.24 stories; on Exchange Place 14.9 stories; and on Fifth Avenue, from Washington Square to 59th Street, 7.5 stories.

The height of buildings in the district below Chambers Street, considered as a whole, is considerably lower than that on the abovementioned streets. The high buildings below Chambers Street are practically all grouped within the area bounded on the east by Pearl and Whitehall Streets and on the west by State, Greenwich and West Broadway. The average building height in this district, the area of which is a little more than half of the whole territory below Chambers Street, is 6.4 stories.

---

[1] See Table I—Height of Buildings in Manhattan, at page 15.

The average frontage height, however, is higher than 6.4 stories, as the average ground area covered by high buildings is very materially larger than that occupied by low ones. But even making allowance for this factor the average frontage height cannot be in excess of 8 stories. Remembering that the limited area under consideration is only about half of the total area below Chambers Street and also that the buildings outside of this area below Chambers Street have an average height of less than 5 stories, the average frontage height of all buildings below Chambers Street is well under 6.5 stories.

Taking the borough as a whole the discrepancy between the average frontage height and the average building height is much less than that indicated by the above streets. The really high buildings in the borough being but a tithe of the total buildings, the average frontage height is reduced to approximately the same level as the average building heights. If the agregate areas of the high and low buildings are not in the same ratio as their respective height, the average frontage height might even be lower than the average building height. The available data all indicate this to be the fact, but their insufficiency prevents our fixing the exact amount. Since the buildings not exceeding 6 stories in height constitute nine-tenths of the total, the amount can by no means be inconsiderable. If the whole street frontage of the borough were to be regarded as improved, the amount of this reduction would have to be very radically increased—1 out of every 12 real estate parcels being vacant. In view of these facts, the average frontage height in Manhattan, considering the entire street frontage as improved, is only a trifle, if at all, in excess of 4 stories.

The highest frame building in Manhattan is 6 stories; the highest non-fireproof building 14 stories. The great mass of the buildings are of non-fireproof construction. The number of frame buildings is more than double the number of fireproof buildings—1 out of every 13 buildings is a frame building; while only 1 out of every 29 buildings is a fireproof building. There are 6963 frame buildings; 82,544 buildings of ordinary construction; and 3242 fireproof buildings. The frame buildings are especially numerous about the waterfront. More than two-thirds of the fireproof buildings are less than 10 stories in height, one-third do not exceed 6 stories in height.

A classification of buildings according to use reveals the fact that hotels, and not office buildings, possess the greatest average building height. Hotels have an average height of 8 stories; department stores, 7.8 stories; and office buildings 7 stories. Factories have an average height of 5.9 stories; stores and dwellings 5.3 stories; dwellings 4.8 stories; stores 4 stories; and warehouses 3.9 stories.[2]

[2] See Table II—Height of Buildings by Classes in Manhattan, at page 16.

MAP XX—OFFICE BUILDINGS, HOTELS AND STORAGE LOFTS IN MANHATTAN.

Shading and numerals indicate buildings of six stories or more in height.

The following tables show the length of frontage in feet on certain streets in Manhattan below Chambers Street:

	Broadway	Nassau	New	Trinity Place and Church Street	Exchange Place
Subject to development:					
1. Built—					
Private buildings	5,344	3,410	1,831	5,209	1,666
Public buildings	190	198	....	....	....
2. Vacant	....	....	....	30	....
Total	5,534	3,608	1,831	5,239	1,666
Not subject to development:					
Parks, Public Spaces, Churches and Cemeteries	1,108	147	....	711	....
Street intersections	1,598	772	50	1,281	330
Total	2,706	919	50	1,992	330
Total	8,240	4,527	1,881	7,231	1,996

I. BROADWAY UP TO CHAMBERS STREET

Stories in height	No. of buildings	Per cent of total buildings	Frontage length in feet	Per cent of total frontage length
3	3	3.06	100	1.87
4	4	4.08	100	1.87
5	19	19.39	614	11.49
6	18	18.37	1,050	19.64
7	5	5.12	277	5.18
8	2	2.04	81	1.57
9	5	5.10	190	3.56
10	3	3.06	242	4.54
11	6	6.13	320	5.99
12	8	8.15	428	8.00
14	2	2.04	106	1.98
15	2	2.04	108	2.03
16	3	3.06	140	2.63
17	3	3.06	372	6.96
18	2	2.04	105	1.96
19	2	2.04	103	1.93
20	1	1.02	113	2.11
21	3	3.06	229	4.28
22	2	2.04	179	3.35
26	2	2.04	70	1.31
28	1	1.02	150	2.81
32	1	1.02	96	1.79
36	1	1.02	168	3.15
Total..	98	100.00	5,344	100.00

Considering Singer Building 11 stories and Woolworth Building 28 stories:
Average building height, 10.32 stories.
Average frontage height, 12.47 stories.
Considering Singer Building 41 stories and Woolworth Building 55 stories:
Average building height, 11.00 stories.
Average frontage height, 13.92 stories.

2. NASSAU STREET FROM WALL STREET TO FRANKFORT STREET

Stories in height	No. of buildings	Per cent of total buildings	Frontage length in feet	Per cent of total frontage length
1	1	1.79	15	0.42
2	1	1.79	198	5.49
3	3	5.35	103	2.86
4	9	16.06	289	8.02
5	16	28.57	768	21.29
6	6	10.71	273	7.58
8	3	5.35	317	8.79
9	1	1.79	61	1.66
10	3	5.35	320	8.88
11	1	1.79	93	2.59
12	2	3.57	130	3.61
14	1	1.79	85	2.37
15	1	1.79	76	2.07
16	2	3.57	142	3.94
19	2	3.57	211	5.85
21	1	1.79	98	2.71
23	1	1.79	101	2.83
30	1	1.79	98	2.71
31	1	1.79	76	2.07
36	1	1.79	154	4.27
Total..	57	100.00	3,608	100.00

Average building height, 8.56 stories.
Average frontage height, 9.21 stories.

3. TRINITY PLACE AND CHURCH STREET, FROM MORRIS STREET TO CHAMBERS STREET

Stories in height	No. of buildings	Per cent of total buildings	Frontage length in feet	Per cent of total frontage length
1	1	1.37	128	2.43
3	1	1.37	50	0.95
4	5	6.85	275	5.26
5	44	60.27	2,832	54.36
6	6	8.22	360	6.91
7	2	2.74	76	1.45
9	1	1.37	100	1.92
10	1	1.37	80	1.53
12	1	1.37	35	0.67
14	1	1.37	210	4.11
15	1	1.37	80	1.53
18	1	1.37	76	1.45
21	2	2.74	142	2.73
22	3	4.11	425	8.16
23	1	1.37	136	2.61
26	1	1.37	100	1.92
32	1	1.37	104	2.01
Total..	73	100.00	5,209	100.00

Average building height, 7.80 stories.
Average frontage height, 9.18 stories.

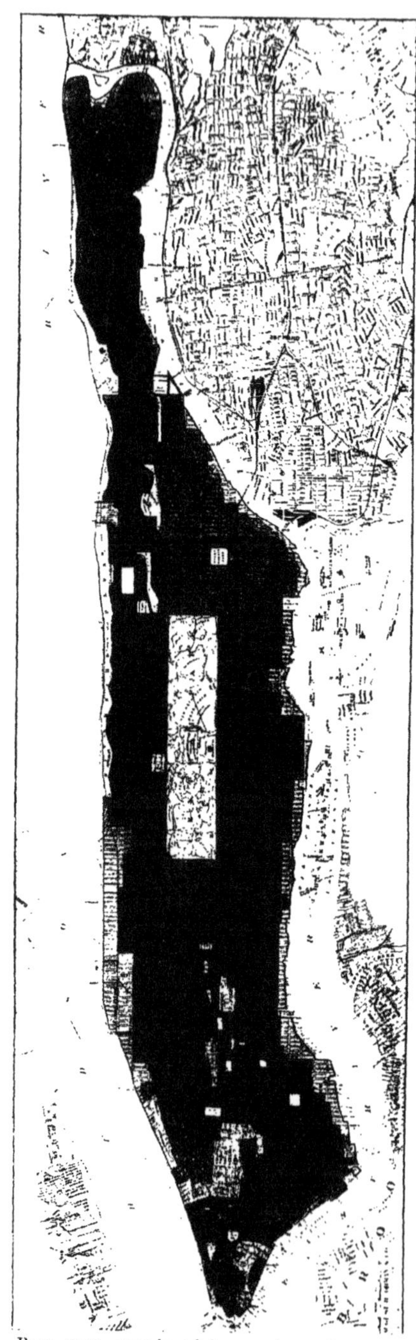

Base map reproduced by courtesy of Ohman Map Company.

MAP XXI—GENERAL CLASSIFICATION OF BUILDINGS IN MANHATTAN.

Shading from light to dark indicates: (1) factories; (2) residences; (3) business and offices.

4. NEW STREET

Stories in height	No. of buildings	Per cent of total buildings	Frontage length in feet	Per cent of total frontage length
4	4	14.82	155	8.46
5	2	7.41	99	5.42
6	1	3.70	58	3.19
7	2	7.41	165	9.04
8	1	3.70	62	3.38
9	2	7.41	211	11.54
11	3	11.11	172	9.48
12	2	7.41	192	10.48
16	3	11.11	196	10.47
17	2	7.41	175	9.63
19	1	3.70	41	2.24
20	2	7.41	153	8.36
21	1	3.70	58	3.19
22	1	3.70	93	5.12
Total..	27	100.00	1,831	100.00

Average building height, 11.59 stories.
Average frontage height, 12.24 stories.

5. EXCHANGE PLACE

Stories in height	No. of buildings	Per cent of total buildings	Frontage length in feet	Per cent of total frontage length
5	1	6.25	25	1.50
6	1	6.25	89	5.34
8	1	6.25	205	12.30
9	1	6.25	85	5.10
10	2	12.50	183	10.98
12	1	6.25	68	4.08
13	1	6.25	68	4.08
16	2	12.50	221	13.26
17	1	6.25	68	4.08
19	2	12.50	186	11.11
20	1	6.25	236	14.16
22	1	6.25	132	7.92
25	1	6.25	100	6.00
Total..	16	100.00	1,666	99.91

Average building height, 14.10 stories.
Average frontage height, 14.90 stories.

APPENDIX VII

THE RELATION OF HIGH BUILDINGS TO EXTRA INSURANCE PREMIUMS

No importance is attached to the height factor in the insurance of non-fireproof mercantile buildings unless they contain at least five stories. A 3-cent rate on the hundred dollars attaches to a 5-story building because of extra hazardous height. Above that height the rate increases very rapidly, each increase being progressive and cumulative. The rate, for instance, on a 6-story building is 8 cents, almost three times that for a 5-story building. For a 7-story building it is 20 cents. The highest non-fireproof mercantile building in the city is said to be 10 stories. The rate for a building of this height is 65 cents, about 22 times that for a 5-story building.

In the insurance of fireproof mercantile buildings the height element is ignored until the ninth story is reached. The extra charge for height on a 9-story building is 1 cent per hundred dollars. The charge increases very rapidly from that story upward. For a 10-story building it is 2 cents; for a 15-story building, 22 cents; and for a 20-story building 72 cents.

A very heavy surtax is imposed on the building in addition to these charges in the case of those buildings where merchandise is stored on or above the seventh story. Only sample stocks exempt the building from this charge. The less hazardous stocks subject it to a half-rate surtax. In case of lower buildings this surtax is many times larger than the height charge proper. In a 19-story building the two charges are about the same. This stock surtax on the building is 10 cents for a 7-story building; 19 cents for a 10-story building; 44 cents for a 15-story building; and 69 cents for a 20-story building. The onus of this tax no doubt operates in a very large degree to keep the storing of merchandise below the seventh story in the case of high buildings.

Fireproof office buildings 8 stories and under are free from any height charge. Above that height they are subject to one-fourth the height charge of fireproof mercantile buildings. For a 9-story building this charge is one-fourth of 1 cent; and for a 10-story building one-half of 1 cent. The charge leaps very rapidly above this point. For a 15-story building it is 5½ cents; for a 20-story building 18 cents; for a 25-story building 30½ cents; and for a 30-story building 43 cents. A 40-story building would have a charge of 68 cents and a 50-story building 93 cents.

No deductions have been allowed in the above computations for exclusive office occupancy or for coinsurance. These deductions are so considerable that the height charge is reduced considerably below that indicated in the above schedules. But even when these factors are taken into consideration, the height factor plays the most important rôle in determining the insurance rate for a very high building.

In the Woolworth Building, for instance, the height charge forms 62 per cent of the final rate on the unexposed building and 45 per cent of the final rate on the exposed building. The present unexposed rate on the Woolworth Building is 27 cents. If there were no height charge this rate would be reduced to 11 cents. In other words, an annual tax of 16 cents is imposed on account of height alone. The Woolworth Building, being valued at about $6,500,000, would therefore pay about $10,400 per year in height charges alone, assuming the building to be fully insured.

The height charge on a tower like that of the Woolworth Building is much smaller than that on a full building of the same height. The height of the tower is pro-rated over the base area of the entire building. The tower area in the Woolworth Building is only one-fourth that of the whole building. This levels the height of the whole building to 34 stories. If the whole Woolworth Building were erected to a height of 55 stories, the height charges would be twice those actually imposed.

The following schedule shows the charge made on account of height. The charges for the various kinds of buildings are not carried higher than the heights found in New York:

	Non-Fireproof Buildings			Fireproof Buildings				
Height stories	Mercantile buildings	Apartment houses	Hotels	Mercantile buildings	Mercantile buildings with merchandise above 7th floor	Apartment houses with unprotected floor openings	Hotels with unprotected floor openings	Office buildings
4	......	......	......	......	......	......	......	......
5	$0.03	......	......	......	......	......	......	......
6	.08	$0.02	$0.10	......	......	......	......	......
7	.20	.07	.20	......	$0.10	......	......	......
8	.35	.12	.30	......	.12	......	......	......
9	.50	.17	.40	$0.01	.14	......	......	$0.0025
10	.65	......	......	.02	.19	$0.0075	$0.01	.005
11	......	......	......	.03	.24	.015	.02	.0075
12	......	......	......	.06	.29	.0225	.03	.015
13	......	......	......	.09	.34	......	.04	.0225
14	......	......	......	.12	.39	......	.05	.03
15	......	......	......	.22	.44	......	.06	.055
16	......	......	......	.32	.49	......	......	.08
17	......	......	......	.42	.54	......	......	.105
18	......	......	......	.52	.59	......	......	.13
19	......	......	......	.62	.64	......	......	.155
20	......	......	......	.72	.69	......	......	.18
21	......	......	......	.82	.74	......	......	.205
22	......	......	......	.92	.79	......	......	.23

Height stories	Non-Fireproof Buildings: Mercantile buildings	Apartment houses	Hotels	Fireproof Buildings: Mercantile buildings	Mercantile buildings with merchandise above 7th floor	Apartment houses with unprotected floor openings	Hotels with unprotected floor openings	Office buildings
23	......	......	......	......	......	......	......	$0.255
24	......	......	......	......	......	......	......	.28
25	......	......	......	......	......	......	......	.305
26	......	......	......	......	......	......	......	.33
27	......	......	......	......	......	......	......	.355
28	......	......	......	......	......	......	......	.38
29	......	......	......	......	......	......	......	.405
30	......	......	......	......	......	......	......	.43
31	......	......	......	......	......	......	......	.455
32	......	......	......	......	......	......	......	.48
33	......	......	......	......	......	......	......	.505
34	......	......	......	......	......	......	......	.53
35	......	......	......	......	......	......	......	.555
36	......	......	......	......	......	......	......	.58
37	......	......	......	......	......	......	......	.605
38	......	......	......	......	......	......	......	.63
39	......	......	......	......	......	......	......	.655
40	......	......	......	......	......	......	......	.68
41	......	......	......	......	......	......	......	.705
42	......	......	......	......	......	......	......	.73
43	......	......	......	......	......	......	......	.755
44	......	......	......	......	......	......	......	.78
45	......	......	......	......	......	......	......	.805
46	......	......	......	......	......	......	......	.83
47	......	......	......	......	......	......	......	.855
48	......	......	......	......	......	......	......	.88
49	......	......	......	......	......	......	......	.905
50	......	......	......	......	......	......	......	.93
51	......	......	......	......	......	......	......	.955
52	......	......	......	......	......	......	......	.98
53	......	......	......	......	......	......	......	1.005
54	......	......	......	......	......	......	......	1.03
55	......	......	......	......	......	......	......	1.055

APPENDIX VIII

TABULATION OF VACANCIES IN THE HIGH-BUILDING DISTRICT

As illustrative of the effect of high buildings and dark offices on rentability, vacancies were tabulated for the high-building district below Chambers Street, east of Greenwich Street, west of Pearl and Gold Streets and north of the Custom House.

Floor	Net rentable floor area, sq. ft.	Vacant floor area, sq. ft.	Per cent vacant
1	3,153,467	313,441	10.1
2	3,152,881	472,368	15.0
3	3,115,030	491,624	15.8
4	3,015,789	515,811	17.1
5	2,650,232	421,115	15.9
6	1,501,601	240,758	16.0
7	1,186,065	138,074	11.6
8	1,086,685	104,431	9.6
9	943,212	72,225	7.7
10	850,954	73,299	8.6
11	767,458	54,022	7.1
12	667,572	60,407	9.1
13	538,041	43 698	8.1
14	495,640	28,601	5.8
15	463,416	22,230	4.8
16	371,812	25,830	7.0
17	269,675	19,415	7.2
18	252,872	27,537	10.9
19	212,940	16,745	7.9
20	197,940	13,128	6.7
21	165,607	7,884	4.8
22	121,335	16,570	13.7
23	86,855	1,734	2.0
24	71,075	1,470	2.1
25	54,675	1,258	2.3
26-41	134,616	7,363	5.5
	25,527,365	3,191,038	12.5

	Net rentable area, sq. ft.	Vacant area, sq. ft.	Per cent vacant
Above 1st floor	25,527,365	3,191,638	12.5
Above 5th floor	10,439,956	976,679	9.4
Above 10th floor	4,871,439	347 892	7.1
Above 15th floor	1,039,312	128,034	6.6
Above 20th floor	634,163	36,279	5.6
Above 25th floor	134,616	7,363	5.4

Floors	Net rentable area (5 floors), sq. ft.	Vacant area (5 floors), sq. ft.	Per cent vacant
1 to 5 inclusive	15,087,319	2,214,359	14.7
6 to 10 inclusive	5,568,517	628,787	11.1
11 to 15 inclusive	2,932,127	208,958	7.1
16 to 20 inclusive	1,305,239	102,655	7.1
21 to 25 inclusive	499,547	28,916	5.8
26 and over	134,616	7,363	5.5

APPENDIX IX

STATEMENTS SUBMITTED TO THE COMMISSION

STATEMENT BY MR. FREDERICK L. ACKERMAN, OF TROWBRIDGE & ACKERMAN, ARCHITECTS, NOVEMBER 3, 1913

Districting

I believe that it is absolutely impossible to frame proper laws governing the erection of buildings in a great city without first having determined upon a general plan for its future development based upon the principle of segregation of activities or a scheme of zoning.

This does not require us to readjust our conception of the rights and authority of the city to act in such matters, for at the present time we exercise upon a small scale and in an ineffectual way the same authority as do cities like Frankfort, Germany. We regulate the height of apartment houses and tenements upon side streets; we limit the area of all buildings in relation to the lot occupied, and this percentage varies for buildings of different class. We restrict the occupancy of factories and we prohibit offensive occupations within certain sections because the same would be detrimental to the land values of adjacent properties. In order to carry out an effective scheme of zoning, we have but to establish a standard wherein we fix in a more logical way the line marking the division between the rights of the community and the individual rights of the property owners.

Assuming that we have developed a general plan for the future development of the city, our first problem is that of devising a set of ordinances which will effect the scheme. We should divide these ordinances into two separate groups, the first dealing with the already congested districts of midtown and lower Manhattan, where the object to be attained is that of expediency and where the ordinances, in consequence, must be remedial in their nature. The second group should deal with the remaining areas of Greater New York, and we should so frame these ordinances that these areas will be conserved for a proper use. This is the vital part of our problem, for it is upon these undeveloped areas that the city must draw in its future development.

In both areas we should prohibit absolutely in all classes of buildings the vicious practice of borrowing or stealing light and air from abutting property by placing windows in the walls upon the party line. This practice has resulted in making values uncertain and temporary, and through speculative building has been the cause of the demoralization of certain sections which should logically have been used for other purposes. In both areas, also, we should prohibit the present manner of using the lot extending from street to street. Our present methods have seriously depreciated the values of adjacent property by reducing the amount of light and air within the center of the block.

Aside from the above two suggestions, little can be done in the districts already congested. We should restrict, however, the occupancy of buildings upon such a street as Fifth Avenue in order to insure the proper use of this street. We should also limit the heights of new buildings here to approximately 125 feet.

In the great area outside of the congested districts we should regulate the erection of buildings according to a scheme of zoning wherein the laws governing each zone should be related to the use and occupancy of that class of buildings desired in a particular zone. This is the only way whereby permanence of values can be maintained and the buildings of the city erected in a permanent manner.

In all of these zones, we should establish the height of façades in order to insure proper light for the buildings and for the streets. We should fix upon the multiple representing the number of times that an owner can repeat his original area without injury to adjacent property through the loss of light and also to provide against the congestion of the streets. We should also conserve to a greater degree the unoccupied area within the block to insure to all owners of property a proper return in rental for the lower stories of their buildings.

All of these regulations should vary in zones of different character, for it is obvious that the same law cannot be productive of the best results when applied to both office-building and residential districts. At the present moment I am not primarily concerned about the exact nature of these various regulations so long as we base these regulations upon the results of our own experience.

Districting versus restrictions

We should not confuse the term " zoning " with the ideas surrounding the present use of the word " restriction." It is true that restrictions upon property are a necessary part of any scheme of zoning, but there is a fundamental difference in the nature of the restrictions. When a group of individuals restrict a section of the city, it is done for the purpose of conserving that section for a particular use. In practice this object is rarely attained for the simple reason that there are parcels of property within that section which, for one reason or another, are withheld, with the result that sooner or later these pieces are used for a purpose detrimental to the adjacent property, causing the restricted property to depreciate in value. Oftentimes the restrictions made by individual owners hamper seriously the growth of a section, and in practice, instead of conserving the section to a better development of the particular activity for which it was intended, these restrictions simply serve as a check upon its development owing to the fact that owners know that sooner or later the restrictions will be removed, when other activities will enter and disintegrate the values. When the city places restrictions over a section, these apply to all properties, with the result that there immediately begins a more permanent development along the lines for which the section is to be used, and properties increase in value.

We have given too much weight to the ideas surrounding geographical location and have not considered seriously the idea that the value of property depends upon the degree to which a certain section is developed for a certain use. Values appreciate in sections where it is known that the development is to be maintained along definite and well-established lines. For instance, the values in office-building sections are dependent upon the degree of the development of that section for that particular use. This idea holds in loft, factory and residential sections, shopping districts, and the like, and experience has taught us that as soon as new elements are introduced into these sections of a nature tending to lower the standard of the section the values of the properties are correspondingly reduced. There is no economy in the present method of continually shifting geographically the various interests of the city. We should rather foster the idea of developing various sections for a particular use and place a premium upon the erection of permanent, well-designed structures within that section, to be used for that particular purpose for which the section is restricted.

In other words, we should consider community interest as dominating individual interest, for it is alone through such a conception of the problem that we can produce laws which will protect the individual owners of property against serious loss through the acts of other property owners.

Limitation of height

I do not believe that we can properly provide light and air for the interior of the block or for the streets, or insure our streets from being intolerably congested, unless we so frame our ordinances in office-building sections that the total volume of the buildings upon a block shall not exceed the volume of the present 12-story structure built under the present laws and ordinances.

In apartment and tenement-house districts we should allow no part of a structure to exceed 12 stories in height, and we should materially increase the area of the unoccupied space within the block. In sections given over to the use of lofts and factories we should limit the maximum height to 12 stories, materially increasing the area of open spaces, and we should limit the occupancy by a coefficient in such a manner as to make it highly advantageous for owners either to improve their property or to erect a better class of buildings than is now provided under our laws.

The limit of height of façade upon the street may well vary in these different zones, but in all cases it should be related to the width of street and in no case should it exceed twice the width of the street.

Reflective walls

In all new structures in the office-building section we should demand a white, reflecting wall surface for the exterior, and we should require that the walls of all yards, courts and open spaces within the block be made and maintained white.

STATEMENT BY MR. D. AUSTIN, ARCHITECT, BOSTON, MASS., OCTOBER 3, 1913

Mr. Austin said he was glad that the high buildings were in New York and not in Boston.

STATEMENT BY MR. F. R. BANGS, TRUSTEE AND REAL ESTATE OPERATOR, BOSTON, MASS., OCTOBER 4, 1913

Height limit a benefit to real estate values

Mr. Bangs said that no prudent investor would care to erect buildings above the height limit in Boston. If all buildings were built up to the extreme height allowed, the lower stories would be less valuable than at present. The lower stories would produce a smaller return. This being the case, he thought it uneconomical to build high structures. He would be sorry to see the height limit removed in Boston. The net return from buildings has not been diminished by the height limit in Boston. Land values have not been depreciated. The height limit has not retarded the improvement of property or prevented advance building. If all buildings in District A were raised to a height of 125 feet, tenants could not be found for the increased floor space. Office rents in Boston vary between $1 and $2.50 per square foot of floor space, with $1.50 about the average.

STATEMENT BY MR. WILLIAM P. BANNISTER, PRESIDENT OF THE BROOKLYN CHAPTER OF THE AMERICAN INSTITUTE OF ARCHITECTS, OCTOBER 10, 1913

Suggestions have been made to you by Mr. Flagg and others which if put into effect would regulate the height of buildings relative to their surroundings without trespassing upon the right to light and air of the holders of adjacent property, yet admitting of a latitude regulated only by the existing conditions; this is the true solution to the problem.

The following reasons for the regulation of the height of buildings not only justify such regulation, but should make it imperative:

1. The preservation of the right to light and air to all those who own or occupy adjacent property.

2. As a health provision, the existing lack of regulation ultimately leading to injury to health of thousands employed to work under intolerable conditions of artificial light and lack of wholesome ventilation.

3. The concentration of property values to the detriment of an average development of the city as relates to building.

In the passing of any rule regulating the height of buildings the first question to be answered is, can it be lawfully done; the answer is that such a law has been enacted and undisputed in the Tenement House Act, and that the regulation of ground occupancy by city ordinance, a restrictive measure, has never been declared unlawful.

The next question is whether the owner of any property has any property right to a reasonable amount of light and air of which he may not be deprived without compensation; elevated railroad litigation would indicate that he has such a right.

Under such a rule as laid down by Mr. Flagg it appears to me that the owner of a piece of property is restricted as to the height of his building only to the extent that such development would deprive the citizen and owner of adjoining property of an unquestionable right to light and air.

Statement by Mr. Alfred D. Bernard, Real Estate Officer, United States Fidelity and Guarantee Company, Baltimore, Md., December 11, 1913

Light and air

All the larger cities of the country are experiencing a terrible depression in what is known as inside residence real estate. Why? Because changes in the mode of living, the improvement in rapid transit conditions, the call of the suburbs has created a new outside residence district where sunshine, light and air are possible. The advantages of sunshine, light and air are self-evident, and are extending to the office, the factory, the store building and to-day these conditions must be met. Therefore, before we consider the regulation of the height of buildings, we must consider the radiation of light and reasonable ventilation, and pass some laws regulating light courts, vent shafts, and light larceny.

A number of the larger cities have passed laws affecting outside light in various buildings, principally tenements, which are held valid exercises of police power, and in a number of the cities where height regulations are in force the sky limit bears a proportion to the width of the street.

Construction engineers have found that floor space is undesirable over 25 feet from outside light, so that a building 50 feet wide must be served with light on at least two sides. Therefore modern sky-scraper construction must reckon with the light problem, and in our observation all the tall buildings which give reasonable returns are located on corners, and either have their side light protected by ownership of the adjoining property or steal their light over the adjoining holding.

We would therefore advocate the passage of a law requiring all construction to be used for homes, tenements, apartments, hotels, offices and factories to have at least 1 square foot of window space to every 100 feet of cubic contents. This, however, is not to apply to shops, stores or warehouses. No radiation of light through a light court or skylight should be permitted further than one-tenth of the area of the court or skylight. That is to say, each room in an office building, apartment or tenement would require a window approximately 3½ by 7 feet for every 250 square feet of floor space 10 feet high, if the window is located on a street; and no room could be located on a light court larger than the area of such court, and no room could be lit by a skylight 10 x 10 which would be farther than 10 feet from a point 25 feet from street light, with the same exceptions in favor of shops, stores and warehouses for storage.

Fire

The modern sky-scraper is advertised as fireproof. Baltimore and San Francisco have demonstrated that this is not true, and while we might safely assume that under ordinary conditions a fire in a modern steel-cage building would not make any considerable headway if its contents were not a special hazard, still we must reckon with the conflagration, which when well started will burn out if not burn down the most approved steel and concrete construction. It is therefore apparent that if we must have the sky-scraper we must safeguard its occupants so that reasonable fire protection may be had.

To this end we would recommend that every building above 5 stories in height be provided with adequate fire apparatus, and if the city water pressure is not sufficient to furnish water to the top, that a sprinkler or water tower be provided.

That all factories and lofts over three stories in height have the first floor fireproof.

That all factories, warehouses or lofts having their own heating plant have a fireproof ceiling over the basement.

That all factories and lofts or warehouses used for light manufacturing above 4 stories above cellar have fireproof elevator shafts with automatic wire-glass doors, so that in case of fire they will not act as flues to carry the fire.

That every factory, loft or warehouse used for light manufacturing be provided with one fireproof stairway for every 25,000 square feet of floor space in the building, and that the stairway shall not be located adjoining an open elevator shaft, and must go to the street level.

Additional outside fire-escapes should also be provided, and monthly fire drills be held in all factories where employees work above the third floor.

These ideas are merely suggestive, but where lives are lost in fires the conditions usually show that the fire shot up the elevator shaft, or the stairway was cut off, or the loss the result of panic. There is no such thing as reasoning with a panicky crowd. The writer was in one, and he thinks he has a fair share of nerve, but he lost his head and ran with the others.

Esthetic considerations

Building heights should not and in our judgment cannot be limited by esthetic considerations. If the owner of a lot cannot improve it as he desires, it must be because the improvement transcends the police power in the absence of land restriction, and the only practical way to preserve neighborhood building harmony is to impose mutual building restrictions on acreage tracts before development, which restrictions will operate as covenants running with the land. Reasonable mutual restrictions of this kind have been generally upheld by the courts throughout the country.

Congestion

It is an axiom that the shortest distance between two points is a straight line, therefore congestion of thoroughfare is not necessarily on the best business streets. Traffic follows the straight line of least resistance, so that in the larger cities of the North, South, East and West thoroughfares have some objective points; but are naturally augmented by the character of the streets and the topography of the city.

New York has been badly developed. The shape of Manhattan should have suggested to the city solons of one hundred years ago that the north and south streets should be 200 feet apart instead of the east and west streets. The congestion on Fourth, Fifth and Sixth Avenues and Broadway is natural. It is intensified by the added height of buildings, but if we were to adopt a 150-foot or even 100-foot skyline for any of these streets the congestion would still be apparent. To my mind the congestion of thoroughfare follows naturally the growth of the city. Broadway is no wider to-day than the first day the writer saw it, while the population of the city has doubled.

Prevention of wider area of development

Able engineers and real estate experts have argued that the unlimited skyline has restricted the growth of the business areas of large cities. and, given a sane building height, the natural growth of cities would increase the usable area of high valued land, which would hold the taxable basis up to present levels by increasing the territory available for business. Whereas the sky-scraper has created abnormal land values in limited areas, and depressed the adjoining real estate by curtailing its utility.

At first blush this proposition would appear unanswerable, but with great deference to the exponents of this line of thought, we would say it is almost analogous to the argument in favor of free silver.

It was possible for the United States to keep silver at a parity with gold so long as we could persuade other countries that it was as good as gold; and in real estate you can create a business area wherever you can convince the people business can be successfully conducted, and you can enlarge that area as far as people will circulate.

Let us illustrate. The great mass of buyers reach the shopping district by the cars. If you are not able to answer the question yourself, ask your wife if she went to Wanamaker's for a piece of ribbon of a particular shade, and Wanamaker did not have the exact shade but something that would answer, would she go to Macy's for it? Each large city has its financial district, and it must be bounded by an ordinary walk. It is quite true that a small bank could do a good business in Harlem, but the business would be neighborhood. It is equally true of the shopping district. If the landlords on 23d Street lost their heads and by extortionate rents drove the retail business a mile farther north, why did values ease off if a retail district has no limit in area? The exclusive shopping district once centered around Madison Square is pushing up to 40th Street; so is the shopping district for the masses. They tell us that Fifth Avenue values are coming off. Did they ever exist? They tell us that the exclusive shopping district is working into the cross streets because of undesirable congestion due to pouring a non-buying working class on the street during shopping hours. This is only qualifiedly true, in the writer's judgment, but the principal reason is that the exclusive shop is passing, just as the row of brownstone fronts is passing. The multiplicity of the high-grade department stores has hit the exclusive shopkeeper harder than the loft building, and the shifting to the cross streets is largely due to falling off of business and inability to pay the rents demanded.

The location of the retail business district in a given city is often capricious. In Baltimore the best retail business street is narrow, crooked, practically blind at one end and has a steep grade at the other. It has no inherent thoroughfare conditions whatever, and was started by the removal of a milliner from the then leading street because she could not pay the rent demanded by her landlord, and to-day values on the then leading street are about one-half the values on the street this enterprising woman changed from a second-class boarding-house district.

In Washington what was designed to be the business thoroughfare has been a failure, while the business is largely conducted on two ordinary width streets, one of which is not a natural thoroughfare.

In Philadelphia the best retail street until recently was narrow and congested till values got too high for ordinary business, which broke into the next street.

Take another illustration. Let us assume that ten merchants would build as many large first-class department stores within three blocks of Broadway and 44th street, and each of these merchants would agree to run half-page ads. in four leading daily newspapers at least four days a week. How long would it be till the retail shopping district was at Broadway and 44th street? Take the same ten merchants with the same size stores and the same amount of advertising and locate the ten on Fifth Avenue between Union Square and Central Park. Is it not common sense that all would suffer, and the small shops all along this 2½ miles of street reap to a large extent the advantages of their advertising?

In the writer's judgment, taking his observations of cities, the advertising features of the large department stores are more potent in fixing shopping-district values than any other factor except general location and utility.

Necessity for high buildings

Now let us point out three arguments in favor of the sky-scraper: No building may be successfully rented higher than three stories above the cellar without an elevator. This elevator with the entrance and service stairway must of necessity diminish the usable ground-floor space a minimum of 140 square feet. If an elevator is a necessity, it will furnish service for loft purposes to three additional floors, making six; therefore the lowest serviceable elevator building would be six stories above the cellar. Now a building depending on the service of one elevator is necessarily unattractive, as every prospective tenant above the second floor will want to discount the danger of breakdown. Two elevators would deduct only 40 feet additional from the usable ground-floor space, and the two elevators serve an ordinary building, say 50 by 100, 10 stories high. If this is true, the most economical elevator building is 10 stories above the cellar, which indicates an extreme skyline 125 feet above curb, allowing 18 feet for main floor, 10 feet net for 9 stories, 10 feet for floors and 7 feet for roof pitch. The first floor might be cut to 16 feet and the second increased to 12 feet, under a 125-foot skyline.

If the skyline is restricted, the first argument is the argument of the tax-payer, that because of economies of operation and management, a tall building will produce a greater net revenue, and there being no happy medium, the average improvement must be at least 10 stories in height or cut to a maximum of 3 stories; that the basis for taxation would suffer because the real estate owner must for economy of construction choose between a 3-story and 10-story building.

We will refer to this proposition again to prove that it is sound, but assuming for the time being its truth, we produce for your consideration as our first main proposition that it is not practical to reduce the skyline below a point 125 feet above curb level unless you propose to eliminate entirely the tall building.

The second argument in favor of the sky-scraper is the increased demand for office space. The writer remembers when the majority of physicians, surgeons, dentists, dressmakers, and not a few lawyers had their offices in their homes. To-day in the average large city the majority may be found in office buildings. Twenty-five years ago the high-grade tailors occupied large ground-floor spaces. To-day a large number are found on upper floors. This indicates that certain classes of business may be conducted above the ground floor, and this fact has gone to increase the value of the land, so that to-day land in many of the large cities will not earn on a ground-floor rent, interest and taxes on the cost of land plus the cost of a 1-story structure. Therefore if building heights are restricted, the tendency is to decrease the utility of the land and curtail improvement to the lowest type, increasing the fire risk, spreading out the area of the business district, thus increasing the cost of government without any compensating returns, for it is notorious that the burden of the cost of government is more evenly distributed over a compact than a spread-out city, which leads me to observe, in parenthesis, that Manhattan is suffering from too much annexation.

The third argument in favor of a restricted skyline is that it is a prohibition of legislative action, which is liable to repeal, and while if uniformly enforced and continued in force, it would in time have a tendency to equalize some land values, but if subject to enlargement or possible repeal would work hardship in places where it was followed.

Statement by Reginald Pelham Bolton, President R. P. Bolton Co., Consulting Engineers, September 22, 1913

High buildings uneconomical

Some limitation of the present excessive height of building construction would be a benefit to the general value of real estate, and would not injure values.

The construction of very tall buildings has been supposed to bring about an increased return, commensurate with the value of the site. It has been commonly assumed to be a necessity, in order to establish such values. But many disappointments have resulted in Manhattan and elsewhere, because the fundamental facts have been lost sight of by those responsible for proportioning and planning such buildings. These facts are:

1. Increased height involves increased cost of construction *per cubic foot of building.*

2. Increase of height involves increase of cost of operation and maintenance of *all tenantable space.*

3. Excessive height injures neighboring properties and reduces local rentals by creating excessive rentable space.

4. Rentals must be raised in proportion to height of a building.

5. Less rentable space per floor is available as height increases.

Sky-scrapers create blighted districts

The facilities for vertical construction, afforded by the steel cage, have unduly hastened the increase of certain properties and sites, to the disadvantage of others. The logical growth of Manhattan caused the general average of height to be raised about one story every thirty-five years, or one generation, until the advent of steel framing about twenty years ago disturbed the process. The general height of all buildings in lower Manhattan would, without this disturbance, have been at the present time 8 stories. As it is, the majority of the older buildings remain unimproved at low levels, their share of available tenants having been absorbed by steel-cage buildings. The vicinity of most sky-scrapers has remained stagnated, and in close proximity to such buildings as the Whitehall, West Street, Liberty Tower, 60 Wall Street, and numerous others, will be found old unimproved properties, abandoned residences, the poorest foreign tenements, cheap lofts and stores and warehouses, almost if not quite equally as well located, which no one would venture to improve.

This condition cannot be to the advantage of real estate in general, however much a few may benefit. Usually the process is a general loss. The construction of a sky-scraper amid poor surroundings sets a forced taxable value on its site. This is promptly used as a basis of comparison for the values of contiguous sites, on the assumption that they, too, can be improved to equal extent.

But, as has been shown by experience, they are really of less value than before, because their possible improvement is discounted by the large access of rentable area in their vicinity. They may make some small gain by reason of the introduction of the larger body of tenants into the district, but as often as not the latter are of different character to the prior class of occupants, and have little or no relation to the business or purposes of the locality.

The unlimited liberty to construct to any extent, without regard to the needs or desires of neighbors, and often to their direct detriment in deprivation of light and air, as well as reduction in rentable values, does not appear to me to be a constitutional right of a property owner. Ownership of real estate carries with it obligations of various kinds, imposed on all properties as common sharers in the public weal. The mere limitation of height only does not therefore fully meet the rights of all property. It would be met by the limitation of multiplication of the site or lot area.

The effect of the introduction of a sky-scraper into a city block is to increase the area of the block. If one plot owner builds a sky-scraper, he may double the tenantable area of the block and drain away every tenant from the rest. It would seem that the injured neighbors would have some recourse. The assumed conditions are not fanciful. The agents for new buildings habitually seek out neighboring tenants and offer all kinds of inducements to them to abandon their tenancies. Such buildings as the Hudson Terminal by these tactics did irreparable injury to other property owners in the vicinity.

Nor is the multiplication of plot by sky-scrapers less striking. The Liberty Tower, constructed over the whole plot area of 5197 square feet, with thirty floors above the ground level and two below, has added twenty-three times the plot in occupiable space, and thirty-two times the plot in gross building area. The Woolworth Building, occupying a plot of 29,640 square feet, has increased the area eighteen times in net occupiable space, and thirty-one times in gross floor areas.

Restriction of floor area as a height limitation

A limitation of the amount of increase of plot area would, in my judgment, be the best basis for limitation of excessive heights, as it would combine with the financial and physical considerations to bring about limitations of the shape of the building, to the advantage of neighbors.

Such a limitation as, for instance, to ten times the plot area would have permitted the construction of the Woolworth Building to a height of 12 stories, and its tower to 40 stories. If there were suitable restrictions as to building frontages on streets, the form of the building would have been somewhat changed by the tower being located near the center of the plot, to the advantage of neighboring properties.

The limitation which appears justifiable in the public interest at this date is nine times the gross plot area in gross interior floor areas. Coupled with a restriction as to cornice heights, and permission to build higher only by recession from all sides of the property lines, the access of light and air to streets and neighbors would be secured.

The result is that advocated by Mr. Ernest Flagg, and demonstrated by his design of the Singer Tower.

The financial cost of excessive height would limit the construction of unduly high towers. The cost of such towers as we now have in this city is from 40 to 80 per cent more than the body of the building *per cubic foot.*

The rentable area is relatively less per cubic foot, and it therefore follows that the rentals must be excessively high if a proper return is to be secured. When the cost has been so excessive, the rentals obtainable cannot pay a fair return on the investment. Consequently the lower portion of such buildings must make up the deficiency by increased rentals therein; but it is a fact that the mere height of buildings does not bring in commensurate rentals. There are actually instances in lower Manhattan where the lower floors of some sky-scrapers are unrentable as office space, and are rented for storage purposes, on account of the insufficient light and air they afford.

This has come about in part by the construction of the building itself, which has not only robbed its neighboring properties of their share of light, but has robbed itself of its own share of reflected light. The same remarks apply to access of air for ventilation.

If such buildings had been constructed with due regard to these two features, a much less height of building would have been found to produce equal if not better returns.

Advantage of light and air

As I have shown conclusively in my book—"Building for Profit"—the economic principle of building construction is to build the least possible amount producing the highest possible rental. The construction of buildings over an entire plot, even if it be a corner plot such as the Liberty Tower occupies, is not an economic financial undertaking. The mere financial value of direct sunlight in a building is worth consideration. Apart from its pathogenic value, it has a distinct effect upon the heating cost of a building. As laid down by the Smithsonian Institution, the average value of direct sunlight in this region is 274 heat units per square foot per hour, which will raise the temperature of 214 cubic feet of air from zero to 70 degrees per hour.

The admitted sunlight in windows constructed in unduly thick walls is extremely limited. In a window 3 feet 6 inches wide, in a wall only 12 inches thick, the total entrance of sunlight is limited to 145 degrees. In the lower floors of buildings of great height this supply is in increasing ratio to the height of the building.

The tower form of building is the most advantageous, because it admits of the passage of light and air past the sides of the building on the street frontage, and admits sunlight and reflected light, as well as air to the lower parts of the contiguous properties.

Cornice line

The limitation of the cornice height of buildings on street frontages is important, but it cannot be made, in my opinion, uniform. The height which would desirably admit light to opposite properties upon a 60-foot street is different in the case of a north and south and east and west direction. If a system, therefore, can be evolved by which an inducement will be offered to a property owner whereby for all reductions in the shape of the building above a certain limited height he will be permitted to add to the total area to be constructed, then we might have buildings which would not occupy the whole of their street frontage above the ground floor, and would set back from a moderate height toward the rear of the lot into the tower shape. The probabilities of excessive construction of the tower would, as I have pointed out, be limited by the financial cost of construction.

Corner lots should not be favored

I am convinced that the limits of construction should apply equally to corner lots as to interior lots, because I do not see any inherent right in the ownership of a corner plot over the rights of the ownership of interior lots. The effect of excessive construction on corner lots is pronouncedly to the disadvantage of the general public in the matter of light and air upon the public streets. I do not believe, in view of the variations in the width of our streets, that this element can be made the basis of the limitation of the height of a building. If it were done, it would have extraordinarily irregular effects in the narrow side streets down-town; but where a standard is set, as in the upper portion of our city, of cross streets 60 feet and others 100 feet in width, I believe the height of cornice should not be higher than 1¼ times the width of the street for all streets east and west, and for avenues, 1½ times the width of the street. The difference is due to consideration of the orientation of the street system of Manhattan, the avenues of which lie five degrees east of north-northeast.

Districting

I am further convinced that a general regulation cannot be equitably applied to all parts of the city, but that variations of conditions can properly be made upon a careful study of each location. This is due to numerous conditions rendering a height justifiable in one place, or even on one site, where it would be entirely unjustifiable on another.

Restriction on floor area most desirable height limitation

I consider that the most desirable solution of the problem would be found, first, in the general regulation of the reproduction of lot area, and inducements toward the construction of less building above the street level. The administration and application of this general principle should be placed in the hands of a standing commission, with power to determine upon the suitability of every plan submitted by a property owner. This is practically the process now in successful operation in the city of Paris, and unless some such body is placed in control of the situation in New York we cannot expect that the growth of the city will proceed on any better lines than it has in the past, which must be admitted to be the most haphazard, irregular and heterogeneous combination that has ever afflicted the growth of a metropolis.

Advantage to buildings already constructed

One of the points which has generally been raised in opposition to any process by which the restriction of building heights is contemplated is that those who have already constructed buildings will possess a superiority of advantage, of which their neighbors are deprived. The answer to this suggestion is twofold: In the first place, excessive construction carries with it an increasing burden as time proceeds, due to excessive depreciation, and so soon as other buildings are constructed, relative possibilities of reduction of income. The possession of an already constructed sky-scraper is by no means to be regarded as unmitigated advantage, but in any case, if the limitation goes into effect, it must have the eventual result of limiting the taxable liabilities of property improvement in their vicinity while it leaves the existing excessive construction liable to an increased share of the burden of taxation. If, for instance, a single building has been constructed, reproducing the area of the lot twenty times, while the contiguous properties are permitted in future only to increase the plot ten times, then in the general adjustment of taxation it will inevitably come about that the high building will be taxed in proportion to its total available area.

High buildings and congestion

Finally, in the matter of safety, the interests of the general public, of the tenants and their employees, as well as of the property owners themselves, all combine in requiring limitations which will preclude some of the very dangerous and inconvenient conditions resulting from excessively high building construction. The congestion in streets has been frequently referred to, and is increasingly apparent where undue amounts of tenantable area are crowded upon a single thoroughfare. The limitations of the movement of foot passengers are fixed by physical laws. I have made extensive observations upon the movements of crowds in Manhattan, and have determined the average speed of movement of individual and numbers of pedestrians.

The speed of individual women on level sidewalks is 270 feet per minute; that of men, 320 feet per minute; but these speeds are reduced as soon as the individuals merge in the crowd to an average rate of only 224 feet per minute.

High buildings dangerous in case of fire

The element of safety in panic and fire, by prompt removal of the occupants of a building, is one which occupies a prominent place in the public mind at present, with the lessons of the recent disasters before us. Unless some system such as the fire-dividing wall, devised and advocated by Mr. H. F. J. Porter, which to my mind is the only thoroughly satisfactory provision to be adopted, then the limitation of occupancy of the floors of high buildings should be rigidly defined and enforced.

Some years ago I made inquiry of Chief Croker as to his ideas of the maximum time allowable in securing the exit of the occupants of office buildings. In view of the fact that in these sky-scraper buildings the stairway is practically impracticable as a means of egress from the upper floors, the determination of safety of the occupants under present conditions is found in the limitation of elevator capacity. Mr. Croker expressed the view that the elevators should be able to take the entire occupants of a building to the street level certainly within a period of time not exceeding twenty minutes.

It will suffice for me to say that there are buildings in Manhattan the occupants of which could not be removed by the elevators in half an hour, although the number of persons occupying the space is less than one-fourth of what is permissible in loft buildings under the factory law.

In the latter class of buildings now so prevalent in heights of 12 stories and upward, it is possible to crowd employees into a space allowing only 25 square feet to each person. If these occupants are expected to make their exit by the stairways such as are now commonly in use, then such occupancy should be prohibited, and the number of occupants reduced to that which can readily find an exit within a very few minutes' time.

Mr. Porter has made the most enlightening investigations and tests upon this subject, and from his figures I have derived the fact that, if such buildings as I have referred to should be crowded to their maximum presumable occupancy, while the occupants of the lower floors could make their exit within two minutes, yet the occupants of the upper floors could not make any exit at all until the lower floors have been progressively emptied, and therefore the occupants of the top floor would not be able, under the best circumstances, to secure an exit under about fifteen minutes.

If security to the occupants of tall buildings is an object, then the methods of construction should require the provision of a zone of safety in the form of a division of the building by a fire-wall, each portion having separate means of exit by elevator and stairway. If this provision were established as a condition of high construction of any type of building, it would have a distinctly limiting effect upon the height. Summarizing my suggestions, therefore, I should recommend:

1. The establishment of a standing commission of examination on plans of all buildings, empowered to pass upon the general questions of suitability to locality and influence upon contiguous properties.

2. The restriction of the allowable increase of the area of a site to an extent variable with the locality, but not exceeding that which can be profitably applied not only to the property for which a plan is proposed, but to contiguous property.

3. The restriction of allowable height of vertical construction on street frontage, the height being varied by permission to increase in proportion to the amount of frontage construction omitted, admitting air and light to the street.

4. The prohibition of dependence for interior light and ventilation upon borrowed openings on abutting properties.

5. The application of assessed valuations of buildings upon the proportionate extent of reproduction of lot areas.

Statement by Mr. David Knickerbacker Boyd, Architect, Philadelphia, June 27, 1913

Elevator service and high buildings

It is satisfactory for the rest of the world that New York should proceed as fast as it can to the logical extreme in high buildings. What the rest of the world wants to know is: What will it come to? What is the limit, and what are going to be the consequences of building up to the limit?

The limit in height is practically in sight, says Mr. W. A. Langton in the "Canadian Architect." Passenger elevators, which were the generating factor in these buildings, are also fixing their limitations. Accessibility to the street level is what is required for an office; and when buildings are so high that time is wasted in going and coming in the elevator the offices in the highest floors will not rent sufficiently well. The device of express elevators gets over the difficulty to some extent, but in the first place there is a limit to the percentage of floor space that can be given up to the elevator shafts if the building is to pay, and in the second place there is a speed limit to elevators. What is known as a "nausea limit" is recognized; anything above this rate of speed is found to be uncomfortable, at least for landsmen. For men this rate is said to be 720 feet a minute; for women not more than 600 feet, and the descent must be much less rapid than this. Anything faster than 400 feet a minute going down is distressing; so that about 600 feet per minute up and 400 feet per minute down is the maximum for an express elevator. The floor-to-floor elevator is still further reduced in speed to enable the operator to make a prompt stop. If with higher speed he bobs up and down at every floor, a consequence partly of human weakness and partly of elasticity of steel rope, there is no ultimate gain in speed and considerable waste of power. Limiting calculations are often upset by new inventions; but where the human body is the measure there is a standard which may be relied on not to change. It is difficult to conceive a more rapid motion up or down for human beings than the present nausea limit, or of more abrupt stops at this rate of speed without great discomfort to the occupants of the car; and we may therefore accept as a scientific datum the present opinion of engineers in New York that the limit of business buildings due to the limited speed of elevators is between 25 and 30 stories.

Air and ventilation

This may be the limit of height, but how to fix the limit of continuity? A sky-scraper at intervals is a gain in every way; it gives well lighted, airy and quiet offices, and it makes the street picturesque. A row of sky-scrapers converts the street into a box canyon of unwholesome gloom; but it is not to be compared to the gloom and unwholesomeness within the buildings themselves. This condition of affairs is rapidly approaching in New York. There is what almost amounts to a sky-scraper war going on. The early tall buildings in which, with more confidence than judgment, the party-walls were filled with windows, are now in an awkward position. Sky-scrapers are rising beside sky-scrapers and blocking up whole walls of windows. Rooms which, when the buildings were erected, had the winter sun and the summer breeze, are now sealed up in darkness forever, and the sanitary consequences are beginning to cause alarm. In the lower rooms, in a street of continuous sky-scrapers, there is no light anyway, and if darkness is to invade the upper stories too the unwholesomeness of the overcrowding in these expensive offices is going to be as bad as that in the poor tenements, which so much effort has been made to stop. At a recent meeting of the Municipal Art Society a prominent speaker said:

"I read in my newspaper to-day of the benevolent project to build a great hospital for consumptives, the victims of tuberculosis, where they may have air and sunlight. And in the same paper I read of plans for a 30-story building. What are we trying to do? What do we mean by putting up these horrible structures, to the lower floors of which no light can ever penetrate? We build hospitals for the poor consumptive, and then we turn around and erect sky-scraping structures where consumption may breed, so that we shall not lack for patients."

Congestion

It is not merely the darkness, but the crowding of the streets and buildings which is a menace to health and safety. This same speaker calculates that "when Broadway is lined with these structures there won't be room for the tenants, unless they are packed horizontally 30 feet thick." It is not hard to believe that this calculation, if checked, will be found to be not far from the truth. It was calculated at the beginning of the year that the buildings of 9 stories or more in the lower part of Manhattan Island, below Leonard Street—that is to say, only in the tall-building district proper—have added in the floor area above their fifth stories 180 acres of area to the island. The estimated cost of these buildings was $33,000,000. There is said to be $10,000,000 worth of buildings of the same sort in process of erection now, so that, as area may be presumed to compare consistently with prices, when these are completed, which will not be long at the rate these buildings go up now, there will be added to this small district 240 acres of standing room above the streets; but there will be only the same old streets to walk in, and these more than ever filled with vehicles from other parts. The Broad Exchange Building has a floor area of 12½ acres and a normal population of 4,000 persons. Apply this rate of population to the 60 acres or so of floor area (above the fifth story) which are now being constructed, and it will appear that this portion of New York is about to receive an increase in daily population of at least 20,000 souls. If they only were souls, if "in going from place to place" they need not "pass through the intermediate space," it would be all right, but 20,000 hustling bodies in streets where one has already, in going to keep an appointment, to allow time for hindered progress, is nearing the limit.

Method of limiting height

The cure is exhibited in a trio of buildings on Broadway: a two-story bank between two sky-scrapers. This is, at any rate, the solution of the light and air problem. It would also solve the problem in design. The two stories of the bank run with the two stories which constitute the base of the tall buildings; the bank's cornice with the top member of this base; their columns and arcades are fairly comparable. Here is dignity without monotony, picturesqueness without extravagance, height without gloom, every gain without any loss except loss of space, and loss of space is gain in this case.

What other cities have to learn from New York is to put the limit out of the question by taking precautions in time. The limit is not practical. It is not worth while to shut numbers of people in darkness for the sake of getting them all together, only to find that it would be better if there were not quite so many together. The limit of elevators and the limit of traffic and transit in the streets seem to point to the same moderation in close building which is indicated by the requirements of planning for light. It is not extreme to advocate the attainment of this moderation by municipal regulation requiring that every tall building should be isolated above such height as usually forms the base stories of a sky-scraper. This allows for such an arrangement as is suggested by the bank on Broadway between two such buildings. It would make a satisfactory street effect if the cornice at this height were continuous and the skyline above broken at intervals, more or less regular, by buildings more or less tall.

A way to bring this about would be to require every high builder to isolate his upper stories by the purchase of land sufficient for the purpose. This would not be tyrannical legislation. If any criticism is to be made of it, it might be called grandmotherly legislation, for it is looking after the interests of the high builder himself to compel him to guard the value of his building in this way. It is not, however, entirely grandmotherly, for the interests of the public are also guarded in matters for which it is certainly within the province of the city fathers to care, viz, light and air and reasonable density of population. There is also plenty of precedent in cities which owe part of their success to regulations of this kind for requiring that the low part of the building shall have for esthetic considerations a cornice line or a fixed height.

STATEMENT BY MR. EDWARD B. BOYNTON, PRESIDENT AMERICAN REAL ESTATE CO., SEPTEMBER 26, 1913

Argument in favor of height limit

Mr. Boynton said he thought the time had come for New York to limit buildings at a reasonable height. Restricting the height of buildings is both sanitary and equitable. If all of Manhattan Island was covered with tall buildings, a wholly insufferable situation would be created. Resulting congestion and lack of light and air would be intolerable. In limiting the height real estate values should be carefully considered. He feared that any limitation would temporarily harm real estate values. He would oppose any limitation that would cause a serious break in values.

Mr. Boynton said that a height limit was desirable since it would spread the population of the city over a larger area and would tend to diminish congestion. Tall buildings naturally concentrate business in a restricted area instead of distributing it over a wide area. Street congestion is also greatly increased by the construction of too many tall buildings.

Rules for height limit

Mr. Boynton said that, broadly speaking, the street width should regulate the height. The height might be controlled by the percentage of lot area covered by buildings. Consideration should also be given to the uses to which the buildings are put. In his judgment fireproof apartment houses should not exceed 12 stories in height, no matter what material is used in their construction. He would favor a height limit of 125 feet and two stories in a mansard on Fifth Avenue.

Zoning

Mr. Boynton said that the so-called zone system is not altogether feasible because new sections are growing up in the city constantly. Sometimes these new centers are in the older parts of the city and sometimes they develop in the newer sections. As the city becomes larger and larger, these new centers are a logical feature of the city's development.

STATEMENT BY MR. W. H. BRAINERD, BOSTON, MASS., OCTOBER 3, 1913

Mr. Brainerd said that the 2½ times the street width limit was a very real limitation on the height of buildings in down-town Boston. The application of this rule makes the maximum height considerably less than 125 feet in the case of much property.

Statement by Mr. Simon Brentano, Representing the Fifth Avenue Association, June 19, 1913

Fifth Avenue

The regulation of the heights of buildings in the city of New York is a question that necessarily arouses serious discussion, and which admits of no solution unless the subject is considered in its bearing upon all the great disadvantages that come from no restriction in height as compared with the advantages that come from such restriction or limitation in height.

The question of building heights limitation cannot be argued or advanced except in connection with the best and highest interests of the community, and it involves also the consideration and almost the necessity of adopting, as a first measure, a permanent city-plan commission; a study and knowledge of the economic effects through greater or lessened taxation if such height is restricted; the safety of the city through the fire hazard created and maintained by reason of buildings of unrestricted height, and the health, comfort and general welfare of the city, whether promoted or menaced by reason of buildings of unrestricted height.

One thing this inquiry has already established, it seems fair to say, namely, that it is no longer a universal opinion that a building of unrestricted height is necessarily the final form of construction in the city of New York for the purpose of conveniencing the needs of modern life, or business, or that its relation to the economy of the city is such as it was but a short time ago believed to be by almost every one.

Statement by Mr. Charles S. Brown, of Douglas Robinson-Charles S. Brown Co., October 17, 1913

Limit at which height should be fixed

Mr. Brown said that high buildings interfere with the healthy growth of the city and of the inhabitants. They are a menace to life and property. The whole city should be subject to a limit in height of all buildings to 125 feet. This limit would not harm real estate values. The width of the lot automatically acts as a limit in height. Mr. Brown prefers to see 10-story buildings on 50-foot lots rather than on 25-foot lots. He would not, however, favor preventing the erection of a building 125 feet high on a 25-foot lot.

The net return on real estate does not increase with the height of buildings. The depreciation is larger in the case of a high building than in the case of a low building. He knew of only one building where the owners maintained an exact and elaborate sinking fund of the structural loss. In his opinion, the loft buildings of, say, 9 and 10 stories produce the best return. None of the very high buildings in New York pay a good return, when structural depreciation, etc., is considered; they are also extremely difficult to sell.

Light and ventilation

High buildings are a danger to health because of the absence of sunlight and air; because they are bad for the eyesight; because they make streets like canyons (see Exchange Pl.), casting long shadows, and putting far off property in the shade. When built to the south of a certain piece of property they take away from the latter the sun and the southerly winds in the summer. High buildings interfere with the natural rights of adjoining land by taking away its view, air, sun, etc., and they encroach on it with windows.

High buildings and congestion

The streets of New York were made for buildings of from 4 to 6 stories high, and have no sewer capacity or sidewalk capacity for the great mass of tenants housed in very high buildings. These high buildings, owing to their size, make very serious congestion in times of excitement, and are therefore dangerous. In the cases of mercantile buildings the streets are crowded with trucks, and unless the building is very broad the trucks take up more space than the frontage and overlap adjoining buildings, which they have no right to do, and fill up the street, and, because of the crowd, interfere with their own traffic and cause great delay and expense.

Fire hazard of high buildings

Smoke alone would cause a great panic in a high building as it rises through the stairs and elevators. The stairs are generally near the elevators and are never very broad and are usually crooked, and do not act as fire-escapes in times of distress. If the fire is high up, the Fire Department cannot get to it for a long time, and then only after great trouble. In case of a conflagration, the high fireproof buildings would crumble (see San Francisco and Baltimore). If an earthquake should come, the danger is incalculable.

High buildings uneconomical

High buildings do not pay. Almost every one who is familiar with them realizes this fact and knows that the net return is very small, and, in addition, no one knows what deterioration a high structure suffers, but every one does know that every year the amount of the upkeep increases; and, now that real estate values have fallen in New York, those who have invested in these high buildings have made serious losses, much greater than if they had improved their land with comparatively low buildings. It is also known that in the case of tall buildings the structural depreciation is large, owing to the great amount of machinery and metal in them, and owing to the possible changes of style in construction and arrangement which are continually being made.

Extra insurance charges because of height

In high mercantile buildings it is often difficult to get the full amount of insurance required, and it is believed that in some of the new concentrated districts in New York it is almost impossible to obtain full insurance on valuable stocks, such as silk, laces, etc. The fire insurance companies, as a whole, are uneasy over the general situation, and feel that their business, owing to the congestion and concentration of great masses of goods and buildings, is liable to large and sudden losses, which, in New York City, in case of a conflagration, would be many times greater than in San Francisco and in Baltimore.

The appearance of the city

The city can be much improved in appearance if a limit of height is put on buildings. (See Paris, London, Berlin, etc.) The city will develop on an artificial basis if continued on its present lines, and the net result will be an injury to the health of the citizens. This general question has reached such a pass that the large lending institutions are not willing to loan on high buildings, realizing that these buildings, in case of foreclosure, are almost impossible to sell.

Injury to real estate in general

Real estate would be stronger as a whole if a height limit was put on. Then the new buildings would spread over a large area; this would increase the land value of outlying land; increase building operations, and give the city much greater taxes. (See the property west of Broadway below Chambers Street and east of William Street, which should logically be improved.)

It seems to be, without doubt, true that a city which is built in a normal way, with buildings of moderate height spread over a large district according to the demand, is stronger financially and morally than one which has intense congestion in its buildings, with consequent absence of improvements near the congested parts.

High buildings depreciate land values

High buildings lower values of land near them. In theory they should not; practically they do, partly because they cause an oversupply of renting space which, to be filled, must be let at such low prices that it takes tenants from other buildings near by. If the supply of tenants kept pace with the supply of space, this would not occur, but, in the case of New York, the growth of the city has in no sense been equal to the increase of high buildings.

It would seem to be the duty of the city of New York to protect its citizens and limit the height of buildings, so that a man who either cannot or does not improve his property with a modern building may not be injured by his neighbor who does.

One of the objections to limiting the height of buildings is that it takes away the right of a man to do what he pleases with his property. This is not well founded. Under the present laws an owner is restricted greatly as to improvements (see Building Code and Tenement House Laws as to height, size of court yards, size of rooms, sanitation, etc.), and in a great question like this the general welfare of the city must first be considered and the lesser rights must give way to the greater rights.

The erection of high buildings should be stopped on the ground of danger to life and health, and because these buildings interfere with the general growth of the city along healthy lines.

This subject has evidently been very seriously considered by the fire and building departments of the city of New York and by the state factory inspection departments and by the Board of Fire Underwriters, because many stringent and special rules applicable to high buildings have been made regarding fire-escapes, staircases, halls, quality of occupation and rates of insurance on structures and contents, and it is well known that many papers on fire danger caused by high buildings have been read and discussed.

Statement by Mr. William H. Browning, President Browning, King & Co., September 25, 1913

I do not think any one who has seriously considered the welfare of the city doubts that the height of the buildings should be limited. The points of issue are, how low shall this limitation be made, and shall it be the same all over the city without regard to the uses to which the buildings are put, and the width of the streets or squares they front on. And should there be some charge or tax on existing buildings already erected above the agreed-upon height.

Argument for flat height limitation

Personally, I think a limitation of 8 stories would be as high as we should allow, for if the whole city was built up to that height it would be livable. If it was built to 12 stories it would be unlivable, and we ought to consider the future possibility of this. The proposition would be much simpler to make a general restriction covering the entire city to that height rather than to allow certain sections to build higher. A building of 12 stories on Canal Street might not be as objectionable as a building of 4 stories on Nassau Street, but the 12-story building may extend back to a narrow street injuring a neighboring property that could not be similarly improved. While personally I would much prefer a restriction that was governed by the width of the street on which the property happened to face, looking at the proposition unselfishly, I can see that such a restriction would benefit a few people to the injury of a much larger number and also greatly complicate its application.

The assessed value of the city as a whole would not be injured by such a restriction, but values would in time be more evenly distributed. Unwise or unduly severe laws regulating manufacture would in time tend to drive it out of the city and injure values, but a restriction in height would not.

Tax on buildings in excess of prescribed height

Now supposing the height be fixed, I cannot see any great injustice in a small tax on existing buildings already erected higher than the agreed-upon height. It should not be by any means confiscatory, but it should be a tax proportioned according to the rentable space they contain above the agreed-upon height to that below in the form of a certain percentage added to the assessed value of the building. I think it can be shown that in addition to the obstruction of light and air, these excessively high buildings cost the people more in their demands on the public service that the people pay for than they render in return by taxes on their assessed valuation.

They have burst many sewers with the high pressure from their mains. They have forced the city to install a high-pressure system as a preventative against fire. It surely costs more to provide service for say 10,000 housed in one building than it does say for 500, and the building housing 10,000 does not begin to pay in taxes the amount that low buildings housing a like number would if spread out over four or five lots.

They have been quite largely erected for the sake of advertising, and if the committee passes a resolution restricting the height of buildings, as it seems they surely will do, they prevent neighboring property from building up in a like manner, consequently assuring to the owner of the present high building an advertisement for which he ought to be willing to give something to the public in return.

Statement by Mr. Arnold W. Brunner, Chairman Fifth Avenue Commission, June 19, 1913

Fifth Avenue

The Fifth Avenue Commission, of which I have the honor to be chairman, has devoted much time and thought to its endeavors to suggest measures to save Fifth Avenue from ruin.

In our preliminary report, which was submitted to the Hon. George McAneny, President of the Borough of Manhattan, in March, 1912, we made numerous suggestions, but the principal recommendation was a proposed limitation of the height of buildings, as this seemed to us by far the most important step to be taken.

We believe that a limitation of the height of the abutting buildings would prevent Fifth Avenue from becoming a canyon, as it were, and we presented drawings indicating the difference in expression of the old Fifth Avenue with the new conditions, showing how the continued erection of high buildings on both sides of the street would be clearly disastrous. We selected for comparison the Rue de La Paix, of Paris, as it was not one of the *Grands Boulevards,* but a noted shopping street familiar to every one. It is bright and sunny and might well be taken as a successful model. We suggested that the maximum height of cornice be placed at 125 feet above the curb, with an allowance of two extra stories in a mansard, and this regulation was to apply to all buildings on side streets within such distance east and west of Fifth Avenue as might on further investigation be found to be just and adequate.

Our report states that "while this may seem to be too slight a restriction of height, yet in view of the situation as it exists it is regarded as a satisfactory and practical compromise between what would be absolutely desirable and what relatively seems fair and judicious for the interests of the property owners and of the city. . . . In our opinion, the plan proposed is justified, not as a matter having to do with esthetic considerations, but as a business measure, favorably affecting the value of land abutting on Fifth Avenue and adjacent to it for the ultimate benefit of the private owners, and favorably affecting as well the interests of the city by preserving and increasing the taxable value of property for the public revenues."

The validity of legislation affecting the height of buildings has been questioned; but Boston has solved this problem, and the highest court in the State of Massachusetts has confirmed its right to set a limit of height—in fact, different limits in different sections of the city.

Congestion

The increased congestion of our streets has reached a point when some action must be taken. It seems obvious that the heights of buildings should be proportioned to the width of the streets on which they are built. The roadways will accommodate a certain amount of traffic and the sidewalks will take care of a certain number of pedestrians, but as the population of the abutting buildings becomes greater the streets are inadequate. Mr. McAneny has done whatever was possible to increase the capacity of the streets by removing the illegal projections, but there are no more projections to be removed and the streets cannot be widened, but the height of the buildings can be restrained.

Height limit a benefit to real estate values

We are told that the owner of a piece of property should not have his rights abridged, but his neighbors have rights and the public has rights. We believe that the good of the entire city is more important than the desires of the individual. We believe that a reasonable limitation of the height of buildings would be in the interest of real estate investors. Some real estate speculators may object, but the investor is of more importance.

After conferences with many owners of real estate it is gratifying to find that they would welcome a law limiting the height of buildings. It would steady the value of real estate, make it a more permanent investment and less of a speculation.

From an esthetic point of view the advantage is obvious. Bright, sunny streets are desirable and necessary. The Nassau Street type is highly undesirable. Sky-scrapers themselves may be beautiful and not work a hardship to their neighbors if they are sufficiently well distributed and far enough apart, but it seems difficult to formulate a law that will permit sky-scrapers that will be equitable to all.

When property is restricted in a sensible manner it becomes more valuable and the remarkable increase of population of certain German cities, where not only the height of buildings but their architectural character, quality and proportion of ground covered are absolutely regulated, prove that restrictions of this kind do not discourage building, but on the contrary stimulate it.

We believe that the city must preserve its principal thoroughfares from mistaken or selfish activities of individuals, and I strongly urge your Commission to recommend legislation limiting the height of buildings.

Statement by Mr. Irving T. Bush, President Bush Terminal Company, June 26, 1913

Location of industries

Mr. Bush said that the labor market controlled the location of industries only in certain cases. He cited the shirt-waist industry as an instance of an industry being located with reference to the labor supply. Mr. Bush thought that shipping facilities controlled the location of industry to a greater extent, on the whole, than the labor market. The cost of carrying freight to and from the railway is a very important consideration in the location of factories. Labor can be supplied anywhere in Manhattan or Brooklyn, but shipping facilities cannot. After the industry has been established a year or two it draws its labor supply from within a radius of about a mile.

It is impossible for the city to lay railway tracks to afford shipping facilities for factories in all districts. The area that can be opened up by the laying of railway tracks for factory purposes is limited, and the tracks that are laid down should be planned in such a manner as to utilize space to its maximum advantage.

The Bush Terminal Buildings at their widest part are only 75 feet. They vary in height from 6 to 8 stories. The 8-story building has a 210-foot court. Some of the stories are 14 feet in height; others 12½ feet. A space of 55 feet is left between the buildings.

In the way of fire protection, these buildings possess fire walls, sprinkling apparatus and a supply of city and salt water. The fire risk has been reduced to a minimum. A space of 55 feet in width would be sufficient for the purpose of lighting buildings 75 feet in width and 8 stories high. Buildings with a width of 75 feet are very desirable for most factory purposes. Buildings of a narrower width than this increase the cost per square foot area.

The city's competitive position with other cities is greatly improved by reducing the cost per square foot of its industrial area.

Height fixed by contributory vacant area

Mr. Bush said that the space devoted to streets and courts should be very carefully considered in limiting the height of buildings. Ordinary avenues in Brooklyn are 80 feet in width. Streets of this width would support 12-story buildings. In the Bush Terminal area it would be a mistake to limit buildings at a lesser height than 12 stories. He said that 160 to 170 cubic feet of building space would be about proper for every square foot of vacant area contributory to the building.

Horizontal exits

The Bush Terminal factories are divided every few hundred feet by double fire walls across the building and from cellar to roof. Between these double fire walls are the corridors and stairs.

Statement by Mr. F. E. Cabot, Secretary Board of Fire Underwriters, Boston, Mass., October 3, 1913

Mr. Cabot stated that he was not aware that there existed any data for calculating the comparative fire losses in the city of Boston before and after the enactment of the height limit. There are only two or three buildings in the city which exceed the heights set down in the present law. Up to the present time these have not been affected by fire.

He also stated that fire cannot be fought by the portable apparatus used by fire departments at a greater height than 125 feet. Standpipes, where properly constructed and used by the fire department, probably add to the protection of a building. When only used by the occupants of the building, they do not materially add to its protection. In most cases the occupants of a building are not trained to use a hose.

Automatic sprinklers with an adequate water supply are the surest means of extinguishing fire under any conditions, except that of explosion. All mercantile or loft buildings over 100 feet in height should be equipped with automatic sprinklers and supplied with an adequate amount of water, according to the rules now accepted in most of the large cities of the country. All loft buildings more than 6 stories in height, or having more than 8000 square feet of area on any floor, not broken by fire walls, should be equipped with automatic sprinklers.

STATEMENT BY MR. SAMUEL CARR, TRUSTEE AMES ESTATE, BOSTON, MASS., OCTOBER 3, 1913

Mr. Carr said that on the whole he thought well of the height limits in Boston. However, he was very glad that the Ames Estate, which he represented as trustee, owned the highest building in Boston, the Ames Building, 189 feet high. The offices on the higher floors in this building rent more easily than those on the lower floors. If adjoining buildings were erected to an equal height his building would lose this advantage. He did not know how the height limit in Boston could be improved upon. He only knew of three buildings in Boston that were over 125 feet in height: the Ames Building, the Fiske Building and the Exchange Building, although the Massachusetts Life Insurance Building on State Street, built a short time before the Ames Building and previous to the height regulation, may possibly exceed 125 feet in height.

STATEMENT BY MR. FRANK R. CHAMBERS, REPRESENTING THE INDUSTRIAL COMMITTEE OF THE MERCHANTS ASSOCIATION, JUNE 12, 1913

Enclosed stairways

Mr. Chambers said that the fire hazard would be greatly reduced by requiring that all factory and loft buildings should be provided with enclosed stairways and openings. A requirement that all stairways be made fireproof would not only work a hardship to property owners, but is unnecessary if the stairways are boxed or enclosed with a fire-resisting material. As showing that such work is not excessively costly, he submitted the following bids from a company for the installation of stairway enclosures in an old building:

"We herewith submit our estimate to furnish material and labor to make the following improvements:

"1. Box stairways from basement to top floor, inclusive, with 1-inch boarding and self-closing doors, for the sum of $60 per floor.

"2. Enclose stair as above and cover inside and outside of partitions with heavy metal for the sum of $100 per floor.

"3. Enclose stairway from basement to roof, with angle-iron frame and terra-cotta block, with self-closing fireproof doors, for the sum of $225 per floor.

"We propose doing the above work in accordance with the requirements of the Building Department and the New York Fire Insurance Exchange and subject to their approval on completion."

Mr. Chambers expressed the opinion that for the ordinary four or five story building, a wooden box stair enclosure covered with heavy metal, as per item 2 in the foregoing bid, would be sufficient;

also that such enclosure should be required even in buildings equipped with automatic sprinklers because the efficiency of automatic sprinklers is greatly reduced by open well holes and elevator shafts, as these lead off the heat from the room on fire and retard the opening of the sprinklers, thus permitting a greater spread of the fire before the sprinklers operate.

Automatic sprinklers

Mr. Chambers believed that every building used as a factory, warehouse or shop should be equipped with sprinklers, especially in view of the fact that on the completion of the new Catskill water supply the city mains will provide a pressure sufficient to operate sprinklers independent of gravity or pressure tanks as now required up to a height of all except tallest office buildings. The cost of such installation would thereby be greatly reduced and would be returned to the owners in a comparatively short time in the reduction of insurance rates.

From an underwriting standpoint Mr. Chambers said that a non-fireproof building equipped with automatic sprinklers is a better risk than a so-called fireproof structure filled with inflammable material. As proof of this insurance companies are writing sprinklered risks at extremely low rates; and a general use of automatic sprinklers even in small shops, the ground floor and basement of which are used for business and the upper floors for dwellings, would practically eliminate what is known to underwriters as the "conflagration hazard." It is highly important that the city authorities take this feature of municipal development into their plans for water distribution in the future.

Statement by Mr. J. Randolph Coolidge, Jr., President Boston Society of Architects, October 3, 1913

Height of buildings in Paris

Paris with a height limit of 80 feet is more densely built up than Manhattan. Most of the buildings in Paris are up to the maximum limit. Buildings of the capacity allowed by law in Paris house as large a population as the streets can care for. Owners in Paris are finding it profitable to replace old buildings with new ones even though they cannot be reerected to a greater height.

Boston height limits

Mr. Coolidge said that the height limit in Boston should be permanent. Less than half of the buildings in District A (Boston) are erected to the maximum height allowed by law. The principal down-town streets, which are already overcrowded, will probably have to be arcaded when all buildings are erected to the maximum height (125 feet). The limit in Boston is too high for residences; it might be all right, however, for offices.

The practice of basing the height of buildings on the widest abutting street seriously affects the lower buildings on the opposite side of the narrower street, and sometimes causes a great loss of sunlight in such narrower streets.

Districting

A height limit restricts the maximum land values, and stimulates *extensive* rather than *intensive* development of real estate. Height limitation should be districted. Districting should be adopted in order to preserve residential districts. Brookline is at present considering three classes of streets: urban, suburban and rural. The height limit on the first is 80 feet. He hoped to see the height on the second restricted to 60 feet and on the third to 40 feet. These height limits will preserve the present character of each neighborhood and make its growth steady and rational.

Building lines

Mr. Coolidge said that building lines requiring a set-back of not over 40 feet may be laid down in Massachusetts towns and cities. These are usually laid down long before abutters desire to build out to the street line and consequently cost the city very little money. They greatly improve the appearance of the highways, besides making it easy to widen the streets to accommodate increasing traffic.

Statement by Mr. Richard Deeves, of Richard Deeves & Son, Inc., Representing the New York Board of Trade and Transportation, September 23, 1913

I am fully convinced as a builder, a real estate owner and as a citizen that the interests and esthetics of this great city would be best conserved by the limitation of the heights of buildings to 12 stories.

Different interests, chiefly for advertising, are erecting monstrosities in the shape of very tall buildings, and other people are erecting manufacturing buildings of such a height that they are a menace to the working people, and glutting the streets with trucks so that the streets are hourly congested.

As a member of the Board of Trade and Transportation and as one of the committee having Mr. Simon Stern for the chairman fifteen years past, our committee brought in their report virtually prohibiting buildings over 12 stories in height.

We trust before any more monstrosities are built your Commission will restrict the heights of buildings in this city to a reasonable limit.

STATEMENT BY MR. ROBERT W. DE FOREST, PRESIDENT CHARITY ORGANIZATION SOCIETY, EX-PRESIDENT MUNICIPAL ART COMMISSION, JUNE 30, 1913

Height of buildings should be limited

I am deeply interested in the subject of limiting the height of buildings in New York. I think the future welfare of the city, from many points of view, depends upon adopting limitations of height. It should have been done long ago. It is too late to do it now, probably, in lower Manhattan. It is not too late to do it in other sections.

Under the Tenement House Law of 1901 limitations have been placed upon the height of all tenements, these limitations in the case of fireproof tenements being based on 1½ times the width of the street on which they are built and in the case of non-fireproof tenements, so-called, being 6 stories. So far as I am aware this limitation has worked no hardship on property interests, and if it has, these hardships are far more than offset by thus safeguarding living conditions.

Streets not sufficiently wide for high buildings

When our city was laid out and its width of streets and size of sewers were determined, the power elevator had not been invented. These streets were laid out, as had been the case in all cities at home and abroad, in reference to buildings the height of which had the natural limitation of human endurance in walking up and down stairs. Four-story buildings were the exception, and five or probably six story buildings, the extreme limit of height. Consequently our streets and sewers were not designed for buildings of greater height, nor was greater height conceived of as a future possibility. The power elevator has absolutely revolutionized these limitations and made expansion upward quite as practicable as extension laterally.

To meet these new conditions we must do one of two things—either reconstruct our city plan and widen our streets to adapt them to elevator-served buildings (which is impossible) or limit the height of buildings, with some regard to the width of streets (which is still possible outside of lower Manhattan).

Districting

If it were possible to begin to build New York from the ground up, it would be desirable to have the same regulations of height apply universally. This method is not possible. The different parts of the city are being used for different purposes. Even in the residential parts of the city social needs are so varied in different sections as to produce in some five or six story dwellings and in others two or three story dwellings.

Practically, in limiting height, we must recognize existing conditions, and we must divide the city into zones or districts, which might vary much in shape and area, and in which the limitations of height might be different. Hence, bearing in mind the proposition that our streets are what they are, the greatest limitation of height practically possible should be secured. Nor should the limitations of height in such zones be necessarily merely proportionate to the width of the streets. Other open spaces at the rear or the sides should be considered. Indeed, open space around the buildings, be it street or court or anything else—that is, space which will give light and air to the different stories of the building—is the true basis of height regulation; and there need be no valid objection to the tower building if only sufficient open space all around it be perpetually maintained. And the necessity of maintaining open space, if legal requirements to this effect exist, will put a natural limit on the height of buildings.

Statement by Mr. Edward I. Devlin, Superintendent New York Life Insurance Co., June 19, 1913

Argument for height limitations

I am in thorough accord with the movement for restriction of the height of buildings. It seems to me that no more convincing argument should be necessary than existing conditions on the lower end of Manhattan Island and in the active sections of Fifth Avenue. In the former zone the streets are fast becoming veritable canyons, excluding sunlight and fresh air, which are so necessary to health. On Fifth Avenue the outpouring of people engaged in the various industries housed in the adjoining streets is threatening to injure seriously the finest thoroughfare in our great city.

Fire hazard of high buildings

Apart from these considerations of public health and convenience, we know from experience that the so-called sky-scrapers are not really fireproof in case of serious conflagration. The insurance companies also recognize the additional hazard by increasing their rates with progressive stories. The protection of human life from the fire hazard appeals strongly for limitation of height.

Districting

In my judgment it is desirable to map out a system of zones on the general lines used with success in some of the foreign cities. While this may not accomplish results rapidly, it will constantly tend in the right direction and in time we will have buildings conforming to the neighborhood uses and interests. I further believe in restriction based on the width of the street with modifications, perhaps, in relation to the portion of the plot occupied.

Height limit a benefit to real estate values

Any general measure of restriction will naturally result in some readjustment of values. It may in particular instances work hardship, but I believe that, with the wider use of land, benefit to the many will come from a broader distribution of values. We can hope for no reform worth the while without some attending inconvenience and possible injury, but where the public safety, health and comfort are so much concerned there should no longer be hesitation. Indeed it is to be regretted that reasonable regulation was not made effective some years ago, thus avoiding results which may no longer be eradicated, but can only be relieved at this late day.

STATEMENT BY MISS EMILY W. DINWIDDIE, REPRESENTING THE NEIGHBORHOOD WORKERS ASSOCIATION OF NEW YORK (CHAIRMAN OF TENEMENT HOUSE COMMITTEE), ALSO THE AGENT FOR THE TRINITY CORPORATION, JUNE 30, 1913

Congestion

Miss Dinwiddie said that further restriction of the height of buildings is urgently needed. The existing limitation of the height of new tenement buildings to 1½ times the width of the widest street on which they stand is far from an ideal standard. The requirement that tenements seven stories high or more must be fireproof, having the practical effect of limiting most new buildings of this character to six stories, still allows a height that is most undesirable and that should not be permitted in the outlying districts. Inadequate regulation up to the present time has allowed the growth of blocks in the city with a population of 3000 and more persons to the single block. Such a state of affairs is intolerable and ought to be prevented in the newer areas. Where there is so great a density of population a park and playground are almost needed for each block. Much juvenile delinquency is due to the fact that children have no place for play.

Miss Dinwiddie said that it would not be possible for certain streets on the East Side to hold all the people living in the adjoining buildings if they wished to come out at the same time. Street congestion delays the firemen in reaching fires and the evils of traffic congestion are too familiar to need comment.

Miss Dinwiddie expressed herself as strongly in favor of the district system of regulating the height of buildings.

She thought race cohesiveness an important factor in producing congestion of the sections in which immigrants live, the Italians tending to crowd into the Italian quarter, the newly arrived Russian Jews into the Jewish districts, and so on. She cited a case of Italian laborers working in the suburban part of Philadelphia where rents are cheap, but living in crowded tenements in the center of the city because their countrymen were there. She called attention to the fact that existing labor conditions necessitate the living of many working people near their places of employment. She thought that proper distribution of immigrants and removal of factories from congested areas would relieve some existing evils. She said that temporary congestion in a given locality was brought about at times by improvements involving dishousing. For example, a large percentage of the families which the Pennsylvania Railroad Company dislodged in building its terminal on 33d Street moved into houses in the immediate neighborhood, thus increasing overcrowding in that part of the city. Cheap, adequate rapid transit, however greatly needed, Miss Dinwiddie thought, would not alone solve the city's congestion problems.

Statement by Mr. Edmund Dwight, President Casualty Insurance Co., July 10, 1913

Elevators as means of exit

In considering the matter of elevator service in buildings of great height, attention should first be paid to the matter of safety of tenants. There is nothing in the record of elevators in very high buildings to indicate that accidents are more likely to occur in the elevators of such buildings than in the elevators of lower buildings, but there is an element of risk in such buildings which is necessarily related to the elevator service. This element of risk is due to the fact that in high buildings the tenants on all of the upper floors are virtually dependent upon the elevators as a primary means of exit in case of fire or in case of any condition which might produce panic, resulting in a rush to escape.

Irrespective of the length of time which it would take to reach the street by the stairs from a floor above a twentieth floor, the stairs in a fully occupied high building would be quickly congested (even if the stair well were not so filled with smoke as to render the stairs an impracticable means of exit), and dependence would necessarily have to be upon the elevators for at least a considerable percentage of tenants and for all who were in any way infirm.

Time consumed in emptying high buildings

There is at least one high building in New York which, if fully occupied, would require more than a half hour to empty its occupants on the street by means of the elevators.

Elevator service in case of fire

Well-organized buildings of great height have special rules for the elevator service in the event of fire. Under such circumstances the elevators would run free from schedule under the direction of the superintendent, discharging their passengers at a floor below the fire. From such floor tenants would be expected to proceed by stairway to the street.

Elevator shafts as fire flues

Elevator shafts are flues admirably designed to increase draft and to carry smoke and flame. Even in shafts in which there is not a particle of wood there is of necessity much grease or other lubricants upon the guides and on the hoisting and other cables which can be set to burning if fire reaches the lower part of the shaft. Such a fire might of itself not greatly endanger the life of tenants above, particularly of those who remained in closed rooms, but it might easily produce violent panic in the upper floors. I think that fire or an alarm of fire or an explosion or some other violently disturbing cause might easily produce such a panic and that it is a peril to be constantly apprehended in very high buildings.

High buildings not productive of efficiency in business

Another matter in connection with the elevator service in high buildings which is connected with the question of convenience rather than of safety is the great loss of time to tenants on the upper floors. The time involved in reaching say a thirtieth floor from the sidewalk, and involving the average period of waiting for an elevator, is substantially equal to that which is involved in going to the subway, waiting for an express train, and traveling a distance of at least a mile thereon, so that a tenant located on a thirtieth floor or above is as remote from customers or clients in other buildings in the near vicinity of his office as if he had moved his office to a comparatively distant point and become a tenant of a low building.

The most important purpose of occupying an upper floor in a very high building must be the getting of light and air. This can be achieved by moving out of the congested district and, in the matter of quickness of approach by a tenant, his employees and his customers, no greater time would need to be involved.

Inaccessibility of intermediate floors in high buildings

This matter of inaccessibility and inconvenience becomes very pronounced at certain hours of the day. Elevators are unlike surface cars which follow each other on the same tracks in a continuous stream. Only one elevator can run in one shaft; it has to complete each journey and return. At those periods of the day when there is a great movement in one direction, elevators in very high buildings become congested and passengers are compelled to wait on upper floors, sometimes permitting one or two or more cars to pass them before they can get on board. The tenants located at the extreme top may be invariably able to use the first elevator which comes. Those who are located on lower floors or at any point near the middle of the run of the elevator which serves their floor must constantly be subjected to great inconvenience in this respect. The result of this is shown in the demand of tenants for floors at or near the end of the run of any set of elevators; the intermediate floors being regarded as undesirable.

Elevator space in high buildings disproportionate to increased height

Still another matter which must affect the income value of buildings of great height is the disproportionate amount of space which has to be given up to elevators. The number of elevators made available for service increases in a greater proportion than the height of the building. If a building of 12 stories requires 5 elevators, a building of 36 stories, of the same area, could not be served with 15 elevators, but would require at least 20.

Assuming that the additional 15 elevators serve the floors above the twelfth floor, it will be observed that the space required by these additional 15 elevators is not only taken from the 24 upper stories, but is also taken from the 12 lower stories, including the ground floor. Therefore, in order to provide space for tenants above the twelfth floor there must be a sacrifice of room on each lower floor. This becomes particularly important as to the grade floor itself, the rental value of which must be regarded as approximately six times the rental value of space in the floors above it. It is conceivable that a building could be built of such area and of such height that the mere requirements of the elevator service would of itself destroy any possibility of income on the entire investment.

Height of buildings should be limited

In making the above comments I have confined myself to questions in relation to the matter of elevators in high buildings, and have expressed no thoughts regarding high buildings from any other point of view. I desire however to put myself on record as believing that the time has come in New York when there should be a most rigid limitation of the height of buildings. I believe that it has been demonstrated that an owner of a plot of ground who builds a high building thereon is robbing other owners of light and air to which they are equally entitled, and is robbing every person on the streets of light and air to which such persons are entitled. I believe that it is susceptible of demonstration that upon the whole there is neither an advantage to the community in the existence of very high buildings nor an advantage to the tenants on the upper floors of such buildings which could not be better achieved in other ways. I believe that the effect of very high buildings will ultimately be destructive of real estate values instead of beneficial to them and that they will be a failure from an income point of view to the owners, and, finally, from the point of view of safety both of their own occupants and that of people in their vicinity, I believe that very high buildings constitute a greatly added menace and peril to the community.

Statement by Mr. Amory Eliot, Lawyer and Trustee, Boston, Mass., October 3, 1913

Height limit a benefit to land values

Mr. Eliot said that the height limits in Boston helped the city as a whole. The desire of any owner to erect higher buildings arose purely from selfish motives and would injure the city. The height limit diffuses land values.

Effect of height limit on capital

Mr. Eliot said that the height limit had had no effect on values in District A. Buildings could be erected with a fair return even if limited to a height of 125 feet. Eleven and twelve story buildings can be operated profitably if they cover a sufficient area. The average return in Boston is about 4 per cent net. Some buildings produce more than this. This profit makes allowance for depreciation and upkeep. The capital value of fully developed real estate is about 25 times the net return. Mr. Eliot said that the amount that should be set aside for the amortization of a steel frame building was uncertain because the experience with such buildings was as yet insufficient to determine the extent of their depreciation.

Statement by Mr. Lawrence B. Elliman, Representing the Real Estate Board of Brokers, June 12, 1913

Districting

Mr. Elliman said that the chief trouble with the zone system was in the possible hardship it would work under certain conditions a number of years hence.

Fifth Avenue limitations

Mr. Elliman said that one of the largest builders along Fifth Avenue said that a number of people agreed with him in wanting to have 25 per cent of the area of buildings along Fifth Avenue left free with the idea that 20 per cent of this could be in a rear yard and the other 5 per cent in light shafts, etc. This 20 per cent free area at the rear would mean that there would be 40 feet back to back between buildings. This would undoubtedly increase the total net rentability.

The limitation of the heights of buildings in a section where values have been established because of the fact that there was no limit should be very carefully considered before a limit is fixed. In the outlying districts a limit of height would seem to me to be most desirable and would work no injustice, but in the Fifth Avenue section and in other places where the land values have increased enormously because of no restriction being placed on them, I sincerely hope that your Commission will act very cautiously and only after a very careful consideration of all the facts which have been submitted, as I personally feel that while from an artistic standpoint and perhaps from a health standpoint a limit is most desirable, it is a question whether it is a just action on the part of the government in depriving a citizen of some of his rights without due process of law.

STATEMENT BY MR. ARTHUR G. EVERETT, BUILDING COMMISSIONER, BOSTON, MASS., NOVEMBER 7, 1913

Boston height limits

What may have been learned from the visit of your Commission to Boston is that there is little if any expression of dissatisfaction with the conditions resulting from the limitation of heights of buildings. The objections raised against arbitrarily limiting the height of buildings in one part of the city to less than that allowed in the business section seems not to have been well founded, as the opportunity to build to a height of 100 feet in the district generally limited to 80 feet has seldom been availed of, showing, it seems to me, that there is no demand, at the present time at least, for buildings exceeding a height of 75 feet allowable in "second class" construction.

I am not aware of any building enterprise which has been abandoned because of the restrictions imposed upon the height of buildings in Boston, nor should I consider any such case as weighing against the enactment of regulations intended for the health and safety of the community.

Height of parapet walls

If as one reason for placing a limit of height upon buildings the preservation of light, air and sunshine is to be considered, then the height of parapet walls should also be limited in the height to which they may extend above the roof, as the interference with light, air and sunshine is as great from such structures as if the buildings themselves extended to the top of such walls.

Traffic

One of the principal considerations in determining the height of buildings should be the capacity of the street upon which buildings abut to provide for the occupants during the hours when most persons are going to or leaving the buildings. Another matter of serious moment is the possibility of emptying the building itself in case of emergency or during regular use when most or all of the occupants are leaving.

Exits

Panic conditions cannot be provided for, but reasonable means of egress from a building means more ample provision than is generally supposed, and to adequately provide for the large number of persons in a tall building would, in an extreme case, mean that the lower stories should be almost entirely occupied by stairways.

The main considerations seem to me to be, provisions for light, air and sunshine and adequate provisions for the travel of numbers of persons.

Statement by Mr. William Ewing, Engineer, Boston, Mass., October 4, 1913

Mr. Ewing said that a set-back did not permit of very much increased height in the case of shallow lots. A set-back would tend toward the erection of high buildings on large lots. Some competent authority should pass upon the front of every building before it is erected.

Statement by Mr. Bruce M. Falconer, Attorney for the Fifth Avenue Association, June 19, 1913

Fifth Avenue

There is probably no street or avenue in this great city to which the question of height limitation is of as much importance as Fifth Avenue, no district whose interests and character are as much affected by it as the Fifth Avenue district. It is now, and for some years to come will be, in a constant, seething turmoil of tearing down and rebuilding, and it is safe to say that a few years from now, with perhaps a few exceptional houses, the busy section of Fifth Avenue will be composed entirely of new buildings.

There are already at least 15 buildings on the avenue itself that are over 12 stories in height, quite a number of them being of the loft variety. Of these buildings there are two of 20 stories, one of 19 stories, seven of 18 stories, one of 16, three of 15 and one of 14 stories. In the side streets adjacent to the avenue there are also a large number of tall buildings. The records of the bureau of buildings show that in the past few years one-third of the number of fireproof buildings erected in Manhattan were within that section of the city lying between 14th and 40th Streets and one-fifth of all the new buildings of any character of construction were within that district. The same proportion holds true of alterations.

The movement to restrict the height of buildings on Fifth Avenue began about two years ago, with the Fifth Avenue Association. In the winter of 1911–1912 Borough President McAneny, after consultation with the President of the Fifth Avenue Association, appointed the Fifth Avenue Commission, a body of seven members, to investigate and advise upon all matters concerning the improvement and development of Fifth Avenue. The President of the Fifth Avenue Association, Mr. Robert Grier Cooke, was appointed a member of this commission, and became its secretary. In March,

1912, the commission submitted a report to the Borough President containing, among other things, the recommendation of the passage of legislation limiting the height of buildings on Fifth Avenue and within a prescribed distance east and west to 125 feet, with two mansard roof stories. In May, 1912, the Borough President introduced a resolution in the Board of Estimate and Apportionment requesting the Board of Aldermen to consider the adoption of the legislation recommended, the distance east and west being specified as 100 feet from the avenue. The resolution was referred to a special committee. Some few days later the executive committee of the Fifth Avenue Association passed a resolution approving of the proposed legislation and recommending that the prescribed distance east and west of the avenue be changed from 100 to 300 feet. On March 6, 1913, the Board of Estimate and Apportionment adopted a resolution providing for the appointment of the present Commission on the Height, Size and Arrangement of Buildings.

During the past winter letters were sent by the Fifth Avenue Association to owners of property on and near the avenue from Washington Square up to the Nineties. The replies received indicated that only one or two property owners opposed the movement, the rest of those replying being unanimously in favor of some height restriction.

Arguments for limitation

There are many arguments which have been and can be adduced in favor of a general limitation upon the height of buildings, some of them much more important than others, and there are in addition certain other arguments which apply specially or solely to Fifth Avenue because of special conditions existing there. All of these arguments save one have more or less direct relation to the public health, safety, comfort or convenience, and to the welfare of property owners and the public generally. This one exception relates to the argument of beauty and esthetic taste, which, though it may have little or no weight with the courts, is not out of place before a commission unhampered by precedent and closely in touch with public sentiment. These various arguments may be briefly summed up as having relation to sunshine, light, air, wind currents, fire, congestion in traffic and in living conditions, the prevention of a wider area of improvements, beauty, the loft-building menace, and the unique character of Fifth Avenue.

Sunshine and light

Nothing is more desirable in the planning of the future of the city than to see to it that as much sunshine and light as possible shall fall upon the streets and enter the windows of homes and offices. The right to the enjoyment of these priceless gifts of nature is common to all and supposedly inalienable. Yet there are streets and parts of streets in the lower end of the city to which the sunshine has access for only a limited period during the day, reminding those who have traveled of conditions as they exist in some of the deep narrow valleys in Switzerland. The Woolworth Building cuts off the sunshine from City Hall Park during a large part of the afternoon, where formerly the park was bathed in sunshine, and it stands there like a great mountain against the sky. The sky-scraper has turned lower Broadway, Wall Street, Exchange Place, William Street, Nassau, Cedar, Pine, Liberty and other down-town streets into what resemble hemmed-in gorges, dark, gloomy and cheerless. Here thousands of men and women are working day after day in rooms that have never been and never will be lighted by a ray of sunshine, while other thousands, still worse off, spend their working hours in rooms where even on sunniest summer days it is too dark to work without the continuous use of electric light. It needs no oculist to tell us that continuous daily work under electric light is injurious to the eyes, and no physician but our own experience and feelings to tell us what effect such work has upon the nerves, disposition and general health of those who are subjected to these abnormal living conditions.

We have heard much in this country and city about the high cost of living, but very little about the high pressure of living. We in this city, especially, are living under tremendously high pressure. We often fail to realize this fact until we go away for a vacation and return again, and at such times during the first few days and hours of our return many of us are probably keenly cognizant of a strong sense of tension and pressure. We are a people of extremists, we want the finest, the fastest, the best or the biggest of everything, as the case may be, and nothing less seems to satisfy us. The sky-scraper has greatly increased this high pressure of living, and it is likewise the best possible example of the American love of superlative material achievements and results. But while the awe-struck foreigner gazes up at the sun-crowned tower of some dazzling monument of this kind, it may be that scores of men and women hemmed in on the lower floors of the same buildings are longing for a glimpse of sunshine or daylight and some other outlook from their windows than that of a near-by blank wall. So it is that we Americans, being a nation of star-gazers, stumble sometimes because we fail to see the things at our feet.

The high building is a menace to health in other ways. Not only are eyes and nerves endangered, but communicable diseases are more easily fostered in the dark and gloomy conditions which tall buildings tend to create. The Fifth Avenue Association has in its possession a letter from a physician, who is also a representative of owners of property on the avenue, stating that high buildings by shutting out light and sunshine add to the danger of tuberculosis which of course is in line with the common knowledge we all have of the conditions under which the possibility of that disease is increased. The cleanliness of the streets in their relation to health is also affected by dark conditions. It goes without saying that on streets with but little sunlight conditions are far worse in winter after a snow-fall than they are on sunny streets, that the snow melts less quickly and increases the length of time and the amount of work spent in cleaning, and that heaps of snow soon become masses of dirt, mud and refuse which increase materially the amount of flying dust.

In guarding the future of Fifth Avenue as well as that of the entire city, all these conditions so directly affecting health and comfort should be borne in mind. But it should be also particularly remembered that Fifth Avenue is the chief promenading avenue of the city, and that thousands of people are attracted to it daily because of this fact. There is added reason, therefore, for keeping the avenue as cheerful and sunny as possible, and for preventing it from being walled up into a street of shadows. It might be said of Wall Street and the other canyons of lower New York that the people who walk on these streets are too busy to think of sunshine, but of Fifth Avenue, at least in the afternoons and on Sundays, this cannot be said, for thousands delight to spend a leisure hour or so there, while even shopping along the avenue is a pleasure rather than a task. In view of these conditions can it not be said that the uninterrupted access of light and sunshine to Fifth Avenue becomes of even more pressing importance than in the case of other streets and avenues? Unfortunately there are already certain points, as at the St. Regis and Gotham, where sunshine is already at a premium, and many of those who give the matter thought are fearful of the possibilities that may be contained in every new building contract, and are longing for the day which shall see the passage of a law that will perpetuate for all time the general welfare of our principal thoroughfares.

Air

Although the inner court is not to be feared in the modern building to the extent that it has been in the past, nevertheless if unrestricted building heights are permitted conditions will continue to exist where the lower windows of neighboring buildings are deprived of proper air and well-shaped or shaft-like areas left remaining in between building walls.

Wind currents

The sky-scraper has created conditions in regard to the force and variability of wind currents which are possibly unique. Particular attention is called to the neighborhood of the Flatiron Building, Times Square, and Broad Street, the Woolworth Building, lower Broadway and to the junction of 59th Street and Plaza Square near the Savoy and Netherland Hotels. At these points particularly, as well as at many others, the force of the wind on gusty days appears to be greatly intensified and the air currents deflected and twisted into a veritable maelstrom, which make conditions uncomfortable and inconvenient for men and particularly unpleasant and disagreeable for women. Conditions in the Flatiron district on windy days constitute, if not in legal phraseology, at least in common parlance, a nuisance. On Broad Street crowds sometimes collect to watch the sport of throwing out ticker-tapes that float up and over the roof-tops, and to cheer the owners of flying hats that are caught and blown up many stories high. Cases are not infrequent where accident or death results from the strong wind currents prevalent in the neighborhood of high buildings. We cite one case that occurred not long ago, and quote from the New York "Herald" of March 7th:

"Fighting against the strong wind which carried him toward an approaching street-car, an unidentified man, sixty years old, was struck while trying to cross West 42d Street west of Seventh Avenue. Although the motorman tried to check the car's speed, the man was hurled 20 feet. The man was carried into a store and before an ambulance arrived from the Polyclinic Hospital he died."

If Fifth Avenue were permitted to become lined with many more buildings as high as the Gotham and St. Regis, conditions on windy days would become highly disagreeable, if not almost intolerable. There is no desire to exaggerate the importance of this particular argument, nevertheless it seems to be quite important enough to merit serious consideration, or at least to be weighed in the scales along with other arguments.

Fire

The last but not the least of the elements that must have its day in court on this question is the most terrible of them all, still as always our master when we most think we have conquered it, or at least robbed it of its strength and its possibilities. Baltimore and San Francisco answer the man that tells us we have fireproof or at least slow-burning buildings. Even if it be admitted that there are fireproof buildings, it must still be remembered that the contents of buildings are not fireproof, but that no building is slow-burning or fireproof in the face of terribly intense heat or an unusual mass of flame has been proved to us so many sickening times, with its terrible corroborative evidence of loss of human life, that it is surprising to hear it restated so positively. The theory should fall before the facts just as it did in the case of "the unsinkable Titanic." It is a significant fact that in 1904 after the great fire in Baltimore, which literally melted innumerable high buildings in its path, the height of buildings in that city was limited to 175 feet.

There is perhaps no man in New York more alive to the fire danger in connection with the sky-scraper than the man whose official duty it is to know all about them—Mr. Adolph Ludwig, the chief inspector of buildings in Manhattan. We quote as follows from a letter written by him to Borough President McAneny, published in the "Evening Post" of March 6, 1913:

"In view of the abnormal height to which buildings are being erected, especially in the Borough of Manhattan, the tendency being to erect buildings of greater and greater height, it seems that ordinary prudence would dictate that a halt be called and steps be taken to prevent a great disaster or calamity in the future.

"It may be stated as a general proposition that the danger to life increases almost in direct proportion to the height of the building. The nearer to the ground the greater the chance to escape in case of fire or panic, and every story added to a building diminishes the chances of escape, and the higher the building the greater the ultimate loss of life is liable to be in case of fire or panic. It is argued by some that in as much as the buildings are of fireproof construction the danger from fire is remote, sight being lost of the fact that neither the human inmates nor the contents of these buildings are fireproof and can burn as readily in a fireproof as in a non-fireproof building.

"A stove is fireproof or of incombustible material, but this does not prevent the fuel from being consumed. As a matter of fact, many of the fireproof sky-scrapers, as existing in New York to-day, with their open stairways and elevator shafts, present many similarities to huge stoves or furnaces, the stairways and elevator shafts being the flues and the contents the fuel. The only thing needed is the striking of a match. To call the sky-scraper, as being erected in New York at the present time, fireproof is a misnomer and creates a false sense of security in the mind of the public.

"In fighting fires in buildings of great height, the fire department is seriously handicapped, in as much as its apparatus is effective only for buildings about 100 feet, or 8 stories, in height. Beyond this limit reliance or dependence must be placed upon the internal fire equipment of the building itself, such as standpipes and sprinklers, which may or may not be in efficient condition. In buildings under 100 feet in height, in case of fire or panic, many of the inmates can be rescued by the firemen by raising ladders to the windows, should the stairways and other means of escape be cut off, but beyond this height rescue by this means is well-nigh impossible, and those who happen to be trapped must be left to their fate.

"That more serious mishaps have not occurred in our great towering buildings is due more to good luck than to any precautions that have been taken. In fact, it may almost be said that in rearing these gigantic buildings little or no thought has been given to the safety of the inmates, the main consideration being the maximum revenue that can be derived from the money invested."

It is unnecessary to picture what would happen should a fire in the lower part of a tall building get beyond control or gain serious hold in, say, the tenth story or so, out of reach of the firemen. Nothing we can say in respect to the question of fire can possibly have the force of the following quotation from the opinion of Judge Worthington in a case decided in the Maryland Court of Appeals some four years after the Baltimore fire, when the constitutionality of a law limiting the height of buildings in a certain part of Baltimore was being tested:

"Extracts from an account of the fire will demonstrate some of the dangers to be apprehended from this devouring element. The account says: 'The fire spread to the north and east, rapidly devouring block after block of buildings. Landmark after landmark went down. Nothing but burnt clay, bricks and cement could stand against a conflagration which developed 2500 degrees of heat, and was carrying itself along by its own volume, against which no water supply, no human effort could be effective. The lofty sky-scrapers on Charles, St. Paul, Calvert and Baltimore Streets burned like great torches up to the sky. . . . Shortly after midnight the American newspaper office was enveloped in flames, which quickly spread across to the

Sun Iron Building, involving all in common ruin. Devastation was carried down Calvert Street, down South Street and Holliday Street and Gay Street, wiping out hotels, newspaper offices, bank buildings, warehouses, and nearly everything in the way clear to the waterfront of the inner harbor.' Among the buildings destroyed were many so-called fireproof structures. After the fire these loft buildings stood amidst the ruins of lesser buildings, like gaunt skeletons, burned out interiorally, but still structurally fireproof, with from 40 to 60 per cent salvage credited to their construction. Great impetus is given to such a fire by very tall buildings. They serve as so many large funnels furnishing draft for the flames, thereby intensifying the heat, and outreaching the efforts of the firemen. Already some very tall buildings have been erected in this locality: the Hotel Stafford being 132 feet high, and the apartment houses known as The Severn being 115 feet above the pavement of the base line of Washington Monument. It was to prevent the multiplication of such buildings in this neighborhood, and the increased danger from fire attendant thereon, that this statute was no doubt passed. We consider such an object entirely legitimate, and the statute valid as far as its purpose is concerned."

Congestion

It is a fact which becomes evident after slight investigation or thought that high buildings increase the congestion of the streets and sidewalks. Conditions in the streets and sidewalks in the down-town sky-scraper district in the morning when the buildings are being filled, in the afternoon when they are being emptied, and particularly at lunch hour, are familiar alike to all, and the experience of being forced off the sidewalk, dodging between trucks or pushing aside a horse's nose at crossings is a common one. If high buildings had not been permitted in that district the hundreds of thousands who are now making daily use of an abnormally small area would have been spread over a larger area and street conditions would never have become what they are at the present time.

Fifth Avenue has what is probably the heaviest vehicular traffic of any street in the New World, and with the exception of a few streets in London probably of any important street or avenue in Europe. Its foot traffic is also very heavy in certain sections. In addition to its normal traffic, peculiar conditions of congestion have arisen at certain hours of the day owing to the presence of high loft buildings containing large masses of workers and operators, especially at the noon hour, between 14th and 23d Streets. Particular reference will be made to these conditions later. Fifth Avenue traffic, both foot and vehicular, has vastly increased during the last few years owing to the increase in the number of high buildings on or near the avenue, the fact that the avenue has become the great shopping street, and for other reasons. The question of laying out another avenue between Fifth and Sixth has been seriously agitated as a means of relieving this congestion. The police department is using all the ingenuity and experience at its disposal to devise all rules for the lessening of this congestion. Commercial traffic except on the very blocks where the goods are to be delivered or received is now prohibited between 2 and 6 P. M. Other rules have been devised and an ordinance has been suggested forbidding all hackmen from cruising along the avenue without passengers between 2 and 6 P. M. These remedies are, however, as a drop in the bucket, and the vast stream of vehicles and pedestrians seems slowly and steadily to increase in volume.

The objections to overcongestion are quite obvious. Any one who has ridden up and down Fifth Avenue during the afternoon hours is aware of the long, vexatious delays. Freedom of movement on the street, both for persons and vehicles, is a thing instinctively desired. The particular conditions in the loft district are such that walking on the sidewalks during the lunch hour is in reality making one's way through a crowd. It is needless to add that discomfort and inconvenience are not the only results, but that the dangers to life and limb are increased. As is commonly known, so pressing have conditions of congestion become along Fifth Avenue, as well as in other parts of the city, that the Borough President has been engaged in a campaign for the widening of streets, Fifth Avenue in particular, to the limit authorized by law.

It is axiomatic that the higher the building the greater will be the street congestion. If conditions are what they are at present on Fifth Avenue, *i. e.*, close to intolerable, it is unpleasant to think what they would be if building heights along and near the avenue were to remain unchecked and a considerable additional number of high buildings were erected, bringing their added hundreds and thousands of people. Attention is also called to the fact that high hotels naturally increase the number of motors and carriages and high commercial buildings the number of commercial vehicles. If the facts are looked squarely in the face, it must be admitted that should the ratio of street congestion on Fifth Avenue increase during the next ten years at it has during the past ten years, the new north and south avenue with its untold expense to the city and its many drawbacks might become a thing of necessity. In conclusion upon this point, it is hardly necessary to state that everything that has been said about congestion upon the avenue itself applies with equal force to many of the side streets for some distance east and west, where conditions are much the same as upon the main artery of traffic itself.

Prevention of wider area of improvement

To those who have studied the sky-scraper problem it is obvious that the erection of tall buildings is distinctly disadvantageous in its relation to the making of other possible improvements. Experience has shown us that tall buildings mean limited areas of improvement and apparently the making of a lesser number of improvements. For the sake of making the proposition very clear let us suppose that a building 50 stories high is the equivalent in floor space and in number of occupants to five buildings of 10 stories each. The erection of such a building on one lot would then take the place of four other possible improvements on four other lots.

Instead of tearing down five old and antiquated structures, and instead of having five modern buildings of up-to-date requirements and handsome architecture, only one is demolished and one new one erected. Instead of spreading the area of improvements and lessening the congestion of street and living conditions, the improvements tend naturally to confine themselves to a more narrow and prescribed area, and the occupants of buildings to be centered in a particular district.

That there has been an overproduction of tall buildings in the lower end of the city is almost a matter of common knowledge. Floor space is thrown upon the market for which there is not sufficient demand. Tenants are lured from other buildings by the ensuing low rentals, leaving empty floor space behind them. It is understood that in some cases agents have been sent about to canvass for new tenants. In some instances high buildings are erected by wealthy men, it is believed for the primary purpose of advertising a particular name or business, or perhaps leaving behind a monument, and without hope of any return on the building as an investment. Legitimate building operations for investment purposes are thus discouraged, rents are greatly affected and the real estate market is drugged and put to sleep, where normally it would be active and healthy. The general welfare of the district is thus subordinated to the private interests and ambitions of a few wealthy men or corporations. The Woolworth Building is from certain points of view "a thing of beauty and a joy forever," but there are scores upon scores of unsightly, disreputable-looking old buildings in its immediate neighborhood which might otherwise have been improved, which will now in all likelihood continue to remain as they are for years.

It is to be hoped that such a condition of affairs will not be permitted to exist in the Fifth Avenue district. It is certain that eventually the avenue itself will be almost entirely rebuilt; but if tall buildings are permitted to be erected along the avenue and become grouped there, and everything at present indicates that this is the trend, the neighboring districts will suffer in consequence and hundreds of the ugly old brownstone houses will long continue to exist which might otherwise be replaced by attractive modern buildings of moderate height and graceful architecture.

The discussion of this topic may be fittingly concluded by the following quotation from an article in the "Real Estate Record and Guide" of February 22, 1913, by Mr. Lawson Purdy, president of the board of tax commissioners:

"If thirty years ago suitable restrictions had been placed upon the height of buildings, there would not to-day be one dollar's worth less of land value south of Chambers Street; but the high points would not be so high and the low points would not be so low. The value would be more evenly distributed throughout the territory. The streets would not be so congested; so many men and women would not be working by artificial light; there would be more health and comfort for every one in the down-town district, to say nothing of more beauty and less waste of capital invested in business."

Esthetic considerations

Fifth Avenue has particular reason, as will be pointed out, for demanding some consideration for its appearance. Filled as it is with noble public buildings, churches, handsome residences, magnificent hotels and beautiful store buildings, everything possible should be done to maintain its dignity and beauty. There need be but little argument to show that if the avenue were lined in great part by tall buildings it would, as has been often stated, take on the resemblance of a canyon, and lose forever the charm and distinction that it has always possessed, and which unfortunately in certain sections, as between 23d and 14th Streets, has already been sacrificed on the altar of high buildings and low standards. Surely Fifth Avenue of all the highways in this city is entitled to ask for low buildings and high standards, and that those elements and principles of beauty it now cherishes may not only be retained, but, if possible, improved upon.

Loft buildings

Mention has been made of the increasing presence of loft buildings in certain parts of the Fifth Avenue district. These buildings have practically ruined that part of the avenue which lies between 14th and 23d Streets, have utterly changed its former high-class character, and have had a derogatory effect upon the entire neighborhood. Many of them are cheap in construction and appearance and are at the same time of considerable height, the highest reaching to about 18 stories. It is anticipated that a height restriction will at least keep down the number of such structures, and if nothing else it would cut down the number of floors and greatly aid the problem of congestion. These buildings are crowded with their hundreds and thousands of garment workers and operators who swarm down upon the avenue for the lunch hour between twelve and one o'clock. They stand upon or move slowly along the sidewalks and choke them up. Pedestrians thread their way through the crowds as best they may. Women shoppers tend to avoid the section in question at this hour. Ordinary business is practically at a standstill until one o'clock, and shopkeepers complain bitterly of financial losses.

Aside from the obvious discomfort and undesirability of these conditions in themselves, the result of them has been that high-class shops and stores have been driven away from this part of the avenue, property values and rentals have fallen, and the avenue has undergone many changes. But the worst of the matter is that this condition of affairs, at first confined to below 23d Street, has in the last two years been breaking out in the avenue district all the way up to 50th Street, and as work ends at the close of the day thousands of these operators pour out upon the sidewalks within a short space of time and congest the side streets with a steady stream of humanity that moves its way to the East Side.

This condition of affairs is well summed up in an interview given out some time ago by Mr. Robert Grier Cooke, president of the Fifth Avenue Association:

"The situation confronting Fifth Avenue to-day is most serious. It is not too much to say that the very existence of the avenue, as New York residents have known it for many years, is threatened. The merchants and property owners who come into actual contact with the abuses every day and are directly suffering therefrom have naturally been the first to realize the seriousness of the menace. They have been the first to make vigorous protest against the destructive tendencies now at work, but the matter is one of vital moment as well to every New Yorker who has a spark of civic pride in his system.

"There is a place for everything and everything ought to be in its place in a great city, just as much as in a man's office or in his home. Obviously the high-class shopping district and residential district of New York is not the place for its factories. The two things simply will not mix any more than will oil and water. The logical results from the continued encroachment of the factory will be to take from the avenue those characteristics which have given it its greatest charm, to depreciate its property values and to make certain its rapid deterioration."

The Fifth Avenue Association believes that a limitation upon the height of buildings upon and near Fifth Avenue, though it cannot prevent entirely the increase of such conditions, yet, in conjunction with the recent passage of certain salutary factory laws preventing crowding in buildings of this character, etc., cannot but have effect not only in preventing the rapid increase in the number of workers employed in these buildings and thus reduce increase of congestion, but in discouraging the erection of many of the buildings themselves.

Special claims of Fifth Avenue

When the present Commission was appointed to investigate the question of height limitation throughout the whole city, the pressing necessity for legislation on Fifth Avenue in particular was recognized in the resolution authorizing the appointment of the Commission, and an early report was specifically requested upon the subject of height limitation on and near Fifth Avenue. The claims of Fifth Avenue upon this subject have thus been officially recognized by the city.

Fifth Avenue is probably the most important thoroughfare in this city, perhaps in any city in the New World, and its reputation is world-wide, its history and associations rich in memories. It is unique in character as well as in appearance. Filled with many beautiful and important buildings, it is an avenue of dignity and, in parts at least, of considerable beauty and nobility of appearance. It is not only the common property, but the common pride, of all citizens, rich and poor alike, their chief promenading avenue, and their principal shopping thoroughfare. Thus all alike are interested in maintaining the unique place that the avenue holds not only in the traditions of this city and in the imagination of its citizens, but in the minds of the countless thousands and hundreds of thousands from other cities and countries who have at some time or other enjoyed the delights of this unique street. Furthermore, the avenue is also in a class by itself in its relation to the question of height limitation. The lower part of the city has already been given over to the grip of the giant sky-scraper. The uppermost part of the city is not seriously threatened with the menace of tall buildings. But the Fifth Avenue district, at the heart of the city, is in a crucial stage and at the parting of the ways. Its location is such that it has been subjected to an abnormal activity, and though this activity has not resulted in giving the avenue over entirely to high buildings, nevertheless it has already a far greater number of such buildings than is desirable, and everything now points to the probability that many more high buildings will sooner or later be erected upon it if no height limitation is fixed. Now, therefore, is the critical moment to decide what shall be the future character of the avenue, which is thus peculiarly related to the problem of height restriction.

Unique in the situation which it is facing, unique in its importance, its character, its charm, its associations, and in the place it holds in the hearts and minds of the people, is it too much to assert that Fifth Avenue is indeed entitled to special consideration? If not, it is suggested that legislation be enacted limiting the height of buildings in the Fifth Avenue district, regardless of whether the city-wide restriction is recommended or not. Even if it should be decided that the city in general needs no restriction, there still remains peculiar and important reasons, as we have endeavored to show, why Fifth Avenue should, nevertheless, have the particular legislation it has for some time been seeking.

Recommendations

The Fifth Avenue Association has gone on record, through its executive committee, as approving of legislation which would restrict the height of buildings on Fifth Avenue and within an area 300 feet east and west of the avenue to 125 feet to the cornice line, with not more than two mansard roof stories additional, the restriction not to apply to steeples, domes, towers, or cupolas of fireproof material erected for ornamental purposes.

The position already taken by the association is here again reaffirmed and a most urgent appeal made for the recommendation and enacting of the desired legislation at the earliest possible date, to the end that the making of further contracts for the erection of tall buildings may be at once terminated. Time is most precious to the avenue, and further delay would be most unfortunate in view of the extreme activity of the Fifth Avenue real estate market.

To ruin finally the beauty and charm of Fifth Avenue, to take away its light and its sunshine and turn it into a dark and gloomy canyon, to allow its conditions of congestion and its cheap loft buildings to increase, is forever to spoil the avenue as the people of New York have known and loved it. That this will be the result, if the present tendency to the erection of high buildings is permitted to continue to exist, there cannot be any serious doubt.

Statement by Mr. Ernest Flagg, Representing the New York Chapter of the American Institute of Architects, May 29, 1913

Disadvantages of high buildings

It seems now to be generally conceded that something must be done to limit the height or area of buildings. We are learning by experience that streets designed for a city four or five stories high cannot be made to serve properly for one, two or three times that height. We find that these high buildings produce certain inconveniences, among them the following:

1. Too great congestion of the streets;
2. The shutting out of sun and light from streets and buildings;
3. Increase in the fire risk owing to the danger of the spread of flames from one high building to another;
4. Injustice as between adjoining property owners through the preemption of light;
5. The inflation of values within certain favored districts at the expense of the surrounding land;
6. The obligation which those inflated values imposes on owners to build high to escape ruin by taxation;
7. The disfigurement of the city by giving to the streets a wild, western, ragged air, incompatible with dignity, order or sobriety of appearance.

Advantages of high buildings

On the other hand that there are certain advantages attached to these high buildings is evident enough from the fact that we have built so many of them, and those advantages ought not to be lost sight of. They are as follows:

1. When not too close together they afford most agreeable, healthy and desirable quarters;
2. They increase the available floor area—a very desirable feature, especially on Manhattan Island;
3. They increase the value of land by permitting greater use to be made of it;
4. They swell the city's tax roll because they do make land more valuable;
5. Some of them are very good looking and they have come to be regarded as distinctive of our type of architecture;
6. We are used to them and a large part of the community do not want to give them up.

Is it not evident, therefore, that a plan for regulating high buildings which will remove their bad features while retaining their good ones should be the best one to adopt?

Argument for height limitation

Of course the first plan to suggest itself is a simple limitation of height, such as is found in almost all European cities. This expedient is, undoubtedly, the best from the esthetic standpoint for places where high buildings do not already exist.

To me it is absolutely incomprehensible how any one can prefer the wild disorder of the American city to the dignified, restrained and artistic arrangement of the European one, where the uniform sky lines of the ordinary buildings give an appearance of refinement and civilization to the streets and afford a suitable setting and a proper background for the public buildings, churches and monuments which rise above them.

Recently the encroachments of private owners on the streets of Manhattan, in the form of stoops, porches, areaways, etc., have been removed from some of the more important thoroughfares, and few people can be found who do not admit that the improvement in appearance is great. The streets have lost somewhat of their ragged provincial aspect and have assumed more of a metropolitan air, but this improvement, though great, would appear slight in comparison with the improvement which would accrue if the sky-line could be regulated. Unfortunately, that cannot be done on Manhattan Island. We have the high buildings and we cannot get rid of them.

Methods of limiting height

While it must be admitted that a flat limitation of height is the best expedient to adopt in places where high buildings do not exist, we should not lose sight of the fact that such a measure even then is not entirely without its disadvantages. Regulations of that sort serve to reduce both story heights and areas which should be left vacant for light. We have here in New York a limitation on the height of apartment houses, and the result has been that most buildings of the sort which have been built since it has been in force have ceilings as low as the law will allow and courts as small as it is possible to make them. Moreover, limitations of height, if low enough to insure light for buildings and streets, place a check on congestion, reduce the fire risk, insure justice as between adjoining property owners and correct the other evils which threaten us through the indiscriminate building of high buildings, would seriously affect the value of property and greatly reduce the city's income from taxation or else correspondingly raise the tax rate.

No limitation of height can have much effect in improving the appearance of that part of the city which is on Manhattan Island, because the high buildings which now exist will continue to exist much longer than we will, so the benefits which might accrue from such a limitation under other conditions cannot be reckoned upon here. Esthetic considerations, therefore, which under other circumstances ought to have chief place in the determination of a matter of this sort, unfortunately do not form so important a part of our problem as they otherwise would. The damage has been done and it can serve little purpose to shut the barn door after the horse has left. Let us then consider the benefits other than esthetic which are to be hoped for through a regulation of the height or area of buildings. In my judgment, a simple limitation of height for Manhattan Island would be entirely ineffectual in securing them, because no limit of the kind sufficiently low to accomplish the desired objects will be agreed to here.

American municipalities have a great faculty for making mistakes in matters of this kind; they will not learn from European experience, but only through their own mistakes.

The appointment of this Commission shows that it is now beginning to be realized that a mistake was made in permitting the indiscriminate erection of high buildings; but twenty years ago no one would listen to warnings of that kind as I learned by experience.

Now unless I am a very bad prophet, another mistake of the same kind is likely to be made in spite of warning—that is to say, a limit of height placed on buildings far above the level at which it can be effective in securing the objects sought for. We have not yet made enough mistakes to insure the adoption of a remedy for those we have made. That will come later.

Let us consider what this effective height is. The most abundant evidence is available on that score, viz., the experience and practice of all that part of the civilized world where municipal affairs are admittedly well regulated. It is a thing which is perfectly well understood in all the great cities of Europe, and neither the introduction of the steel-frame method of construction nor the elevator, those two factors which have wrought such a change in our method of building, have been able, so far as I know, in a single instance to induce a city of the Old World to depart from its standard of height. Their experience has taught them that the necessary limit of height for buildings is equal to about once the width of the street and that it would be folly to exceed it.

If a demonstration is wanted to show that about this same limit is necessary here, a very interesting one can be found right at hand. The City and Suburban Homes Company have built some large blocks of model tenements. The height of these buildings is 60 feet, and the area left vacant 30 per cent of the area of the land, yet the buildings are only fairly well lighted. This illustration is important because rare in America. A very small part of this or any other city in the United States is solidly built up to a given height after the fashion of European cities. Some of our buildings are high and some are low, but the low ones greatly predominate, and it is not easy to find examples covering a considerable area illustrative of what will happen after a definite limit of height has been established and buildings built up to it. Of course, if such examples were common, there would be no more doubt among our people than there is in Europe as to what is the necessary limit of height.

I think few people realize how small a percentage of the area of this city is occupied by tall buildings. Those which we have are so much in evidence that they appear to occupy a much greater area than they do. Heretofore they have stood isolated in the midst of open surroundings enjoying the benefit of the light which legitimately belonged to the neighboring land, and it is only recently that they have begun to interfere with each other's light.

The time has certainly come when we should understand that the open surroundings which have heretofore made our high buildings desirable cannot continue, and regulations should be made accordingly.

If we consider the list of evils, as enumerated, which have resulted or which seem likely to result from the unrestricted erection of high buildings and also the list of admittedly good points which these buildings possess, we find that all the evils, with the exception of ugliness, are due to overcrowding, and that all the good qualities are dependent upon not overcrowding. Therefore we can safely conclude that a plan which will prevent overcrowding while still permitting the erecting of high buildings is the best one to adopt. If such a plan can be found, why is not the problem solved, for what more can be desired than to avoid the evils while retaining the benefits of high buildings?

Plan recommended

I wish I could feel as confident that the plan I have suggested would be adopted at this time as I am that it would accomplish these results. It is very simple and entirely practical. Stated broadly, it is as follows:

I would establish a general level of height for all buildings low enough to be effective in accomplishing the objects already enumerated—that is to say, equal to about once the width of the street on which the building faces; without other restrictions as to area than that the least horizontal dimensions of any court or areas left vacant for light should equal a certain proportion, say, one-tenth of the height of the wall or walls of the building to which it belongs and which enclose or partly enclose said court or open space. Then on an area sufficiently restricted, say, one-quarter of the area of the plot on which the building stands, I would allow the building to any height without other restrictions than that this part of the building be set back somewhat from the street so as not to darken it. For corner plots and plots facing on open spaces more liberal rules might be made than for inside plots. I would also allow an owner to dispose of his right to build high in favor of any adjoining plot.

Effect

The effect of such a law would be as follows:

1. It would act as an efficient check on the building of high buildings and consequently a check on congestion; for not every one would exercise the right to build above the general level if that part of the building was restricted to so small a percentage of the area of the plot, and it would not generally pay to do so at all on small plots; if the right was exercised in such cases the height would then be sufficiently restricted by the practical requirements for elevator service and staircases; but even if the owner of a small plot was debarred by these considerations from building high he would not necessarily lose the value of his privilege to do so because he would have the right to dispose of it in favor of adjoining land.

2. Every owner would be protected in his right to a fair share of the light of day because, if adjoining owners could build above the general level only on one-quarter of the area of their plots no great damage could be done him however the buildings might be disposed. If an owner sought to acquire his neighbor's right to build high so that he could cover a greater percentage of his plot than he otherwise could, he would have to pay what it was worth and the person selling would thus receive compensation for damage done him.

3. Sufficient light for the streets would be assured because the high parts of buildings would be set back from the street line and because they would occupy so small a percentage of the area of the land.

4. The plan would assure to every owner of land the right to build high on an area as large as can be built on without injury to the rights of his neighbors and the right of the public to light for the streets, and this is all the liberty he ought to have, for it is all he can exercise without injury to others.

5. Although the value of land might be decreased by this plan in certain cases, the general average of value would undoubtedly be increased, because every one would be assured that his light could not be seriously obstructed, and that this is a most valuable asset is being more and more realized as we find our land shut in and darkened by the greed of neighbors.

6. Under this rule, land values would be more evenly distributed, for by just so much as the plan would serve as a check on the erection of high buildings it would serve to spread the area of business centers. The area of the financial district, for instance, has scarcely increased at all during the last 40 years, while the floor area in that district (much of which is most insufficiently lighted) has increased tenfold during that time.

7. The separation of high buildings which the plan would effect would greatly lessen the fire risk because there would be less danger of fire leaping from one high building to another, and this might

very properly be further reduced by requiring that all structures which exceed the general level of height should be made entirely without the use of inflammable material.

8. While it must be admitted that a flat limitation of height would be the best plan from the esthetic standpoint, provided we had no high buildings, that condition does not exist; and accepting the case as we find it, this plan seems much better. Under it some degree of order would be secured by the establishment of a uniform cornice line for the street façades, at the general level, and this is all that any flat limitation of height could do.

The one redeeming feature of our high buildings from the esthetic standpoint is that they are picturesque when seen from a distance. The plan which I propose would certainly add to that quality. The high parts of the buildings as they would be exposed to view from all sides would be treated architecturally on all sides. The most characteristic, interesting and beautiful of our high buildings are undoubtedly those which have been treated as towers, and this plan would certainly encourage that treatment.

9. The plan while placing a check on the erection of high buildings would deny to no landowner the right to build one.

10. It would not hinder the construction of more of that kind of floor space which all who have occupied the upper floors of high buildings know to be the most desirable, healthy, and agreeable quarters which it is possible to get. On the contrary, it would permit of the building of just as much of it as can be lighted without doing injustice to adjoining owners and to the public.

11. It would therefore permit of the utilization of the land to the greatest practicable extent.

12. The plan would be applicable to and advantageous for all classes of buildings.

13. Unlike the flat limitation of height, it would tend to supply air, not shut it out; it would contain no inducement to limit story heights, and the permissible area which could be occupied above the general limit would be fixed at a point where no improper shutting out of light could occur.

14. This plan would secure to us all the advantages of high buildings while avoiding their disadvantages. What more is there to desire? Moreover, it is the only plan which has been suggested, as far as I know, which would do these things.

STATEMENT BY MR. JAMES L. GERNON, MERCANTILE INSPECTOR OF THE STATE DEPARTMENT OF LABOR, JUNE 26, 1913

Loft buildings

Mr. Gernon said it was very hard to tell whether the modern loft building was used for the purpose of factories, mercantile establishments or business offices. The buildings erected in the city during the past three years that are nominally called loft buildings are practically factories. There are manufacturing, mercantile and office work all together in many of these buildings; many of them do not afford sufficient toilet facilities for the number of employees. Many of the firms in offices and mail-order houses have regular recess periods, during which the employees must use the toilets. All the elements injurious to factory employees exist in many of the office buildings, such as overcrowding, poor ventilation, inadequate light and insufficient exits in case of fire. The placing of partitions in stores and offices should be prohibited or regulated, as they destroy ventilation and light in many of the buildings.

Fire hazards in department stores

Mr. Gernon said that during the holiday season 30,000 persons congregated at one time in a certain department store in New York City. This store has about 7500 employees; there are many other department stores in the city having between 3000 and 4000 employees. There is a very great fire hazard in department stores; the existing stairways are not adequate for the holiday crowds. Panic is even a greater hazard than fire. In recent years panics have occurred in department stores in Paris and London. Certain department stores do not have their exits on the main floor opening at the street level.

Statement by Mr. William M. Greve, Second Vice-President, Realty Associates, Brooklyn, September 26, 1913

Height limit a benefit to real estate values

The highest office building in the Borough of Brooklyn is 12 stories and the highest factory 10 stories. I do not believe at the present time that a limit as to the height of a building to be erected in the Borough of Brooklyn would in any way reduce values. Of course I have in mind that the limit shall be reasonable and that it would be taken up by streets and that the different localities be given consideration.

If it were possible for your Commission to make recommendations as to restricting of centers and localities, it would be a good thing. In many sections of the Borough of Brooklyn values have been reduced by the expiration of restrictions. In other places values have been largely fictitious owing to their proximity to restricted areas. These values as a rule decline as soon as the restrictions on the restricted area expire, throwing on the market large areas unrestricted. When this has happened the values of private residences within the formerly restricted areas have declined. This is, of course, considering the land and the building as one.

Statement by Mr. William Guerin, Acting Chief Bureau of Fire Prevention, June 26, 1913

Elevator congestion

Chief Guerin said that tenants in high loft buildings had considerable difficulty in receiving their freight. The drayman in taking it to and from the building at times had to wait from two hours to half a day before getting an opportunity to use the elevators.

Fire fighting

Chief Guerin said that the fire department could not readily remove people from burning buildings at a greater height than six stories. Buildings above that height should be constructed as if the fire department were unable to remove marooned persons. Above the tenth floor the apparatus of the fire department cannot be considered the primary means of extinguishing fires. The standpipes in the building itself will have to be depended upon almost exclusively. The water towers are very ineffective above the seventh floor—that is, about 85 feet above the ground. Standpipes in buildings have three sources of supply: house pumps, the gravity or pressure tanks and fire department steamer connections. An automatic sprinkler apparatus is an absolute necessity in buildings over six stories high. Standpipes cannot be connected with the city's high pressure water system, because this would tempt the owners to use the water for private purposes.

Fire drills

Chief Guerin said that some of the best fire drills in New York City are held in the department stores. Chief Guerin also stated that school drills were ideal. The time consumed in emptying a school building of a certain number of pupils would have to be discounted between 40 and 50 per cent for the same number of occupants of any other building.

Conflagration hazard

Chief Guerin said that the heat wave in the Wicke Cigar Box Factory fire which occurred on January 31, 1901, leaped a distance of 65 or 70 feet, consuming everything in its path within a moment. As a rule, a fire will leap any distance less than 50 feet. The tendency of a fire is to pass over the low buildings and set fire to the higher buildings beyond. In the case of high buildings, a limit of 150 feet could be supported by argument as being a reasonable regulation under the police power of the state. In the case of one-family two-and-a-half-story wooden houses an open space of 20 feet between buildings could be shown to be a reasonable minimum. A fire in a neighboring building nearer than 20 feet would constitute a hazard. If frame buildings are to be erected nearer than 15 or 20 feet to each other, a brick wall ought to be required.

Exits, stairways and fire-escapes

Chief Guerin said that the exit facilities have not been increased with the increased height of buildings. Elevators cannot properly be called a means of exit. This has been proven time and again by experience.

The fire department has not worked out the graduated stairway —that is, one which increases in width in the lower stories. Chief Guerin thought that an increased number of inside stairways would be more desirable than a graduated stairway. The law at present bases the number of stairs on the square feet area of the building. The present factory and building laws are not adequate and do not afford sufficient exit facilities in many cases.

Chief Guerin said that if a department store should have ten stairways, each alternate floor should have an entrance to five of these stairways. This would obviate stairway congestion in case of panic. Every stairway should have its exit directly on the street. At present only a few of the department stores have stair line exits emptying directly into the street.

Chief Guerin also said that all persons should be able to get into a zone of safety in a building within three to five minutes. Any person that cannot get into a zone of safety in that time is in an extremely hazardous position. Descent can be made from a 12-story building in three minutes. Between 380 and 400 operatives can walk down a stairway in a 12-story building in five minutes.

A person suffocated by smoke can be revived if properly treated within ten or fifteen minutes.

Fire walls

Chief Guerin said that the fire doors in fire walls should be eliminated and exterior fire balconies substituted. Keeping the doors closed in fire walls is most important. Even the most carefully managed buildings at present do not close the doors in their walls, and the doors are frequently obstructed so that they would not close in case of fire. Fire walls should possess exterior exits. The fire wall is of no use when the doors are open. The New York department stores would be unwilling to follow the Philadelphia Wanamaker method of dividing their buildings into fire sections, as the spirit of the department store is a large unbroken area.

Statement by Mr. Edward R. Hardy, Representing the New York Fire Insurance Exchange, June 19, 1913

Factories

Mr. Hardy said that 7 and 8 story non-fireproof lofts on the East Side of Manhattan were always full, because they were within easy walking distance of the labor market. He believes in the segregation of manufacturing into districts.

Fire fighting and insurance rates

Mr. Hardy said that the fire insurance companies avoided stock risks even in fireproof buildings above the fifth story, as the difficulty of fighting a fire above the fifth floor was very great. Even the fire tower could not effectively reach above the sixth or seventh floor. There are two non-fireproof 10-story buildings in New York.

Mr. Hardy said that even in fireproof buildings there is a very rapid increase in the insurance rate on the stock carried and on the building itself for the upper floors. On the Woolworth Building the rate due to excessive height is 25 cents on $100. The contents of the upper floors pay $2 to $3 per $100.

Mr. Hardy said that the use of sprinkler equipment has grown very rapidly since the Asch Building fire, so that now they are put in all new lofts as a matter of course, principally because of the much lower insurance rate which they bring. Sprinklers put out two or three fires a day in New York, usually by the opening of only one or two heads. Sprinklers level all hazards regardless of height in manufacturing lofts, and the rates are as low on the fortieth floor as on the lower stories. No allowance is made for the failure of a sprinkler system, as they are inspected monthly and there have been practically no failures.

Mr. Hardy said that the Senior Mutuals of Boston insure for 6 cents on $100, even on the heaviest risk, if the building is sprinklered and otherwise built according to their standards. He said that the average rate throughout the United States for everything was $1.15 on $100.

Mr. Hardy said that the Hardman-Peck Building, a frame building 8 stories high and 40 years old, which was sprinklered, had withstood several severe exposure fires by sprinkling alone. A fire has been confined to the 26th floor of the Singer Building and to individual rooms in the Hotel Plaza. The great trouble is in exposure hazards.

Mr. Hardy believes that a limit of 125 feet is satisfactory for every one, and personally he prefers an even cornice line. He does not like towers.

Mr. Hardy considers water storage tanks on upper floors to be of no particular advantage. We have had no test of the value of standpipes in tall fireproof buildings. The difficulty is that no human being could withstand the heat, which often rises to 1800 degrees.

Mr. Hardy submitted the following memorandum showing the charge for height in different classes of risks:

1. The non-fireproof building of ordinary construction: No charge up to and including the fourth story; fifth story, 3 cents; sixth story, 5 cents; seventh story, 12 cents; eighth story and each story over eight, 15 cents. These charges are cumulative. Thus a 7-story building would have a total charge of 20 cents.

2. The schedule at present in use for apartment houses of non-fireproof construction makes no charge for height up to and including the fifth story.

The charges then are as follows: sixth story, 10 cents; seventh story, 20 cents; eighth and any above, 30 cents.

4. The present schedule recently adopted for rating fireproof apartment houses makes no charge up to and including the ninth floor.

This would make a charge of three-fourths of 1 cent for the tenth floor and 1½ cents for the eleventh floor.

The fireproof hotel schedule, which the Commission may be interested in, is what is known as the New York Fire Insurance Exchange for Fireproof Buildings. It is this schedule which is used in rating the office buildings of fireproof construction and most of the loft buildings of the same construction. The charges for height on this schedule are as follows:

No charge up to and including the eighth story.

From the eighth floor to the eleventh inclusive, 1 cent for each story.

For the twelfth floor up to and including the fourteenth, 3 cents for each story.

For the fifteenth and for each story over, 10 cents.

For an office building, one-fourth of these charges would apply.

These charges are subject to a large reduction under the location rule for insurance to be carried equal to 80 per cent of the value. To illustrate: In a building of 11 stories in height the gross charges for height would be 3 cents. The net charge would be 1 cent. In a building of 14 stories the gross charge would be 12 cents and the net charge 4 cents. In a building of 20 stories, the gross charge would be 72 cents and the net charge 24 cents, assuming there are no special reductions to be made on account of fire appliances, etc. If there were, these would operate to reduce the charge to a greater extent.

It perhaps should be pointed out to the Commission that experience and the best judgment of underwriters generally concede that the installation of a high-grade sprinkler equipment operates to nullify to a great extent unusual area and unusual height.

Statement by Mr. William E. Harmon, President of Wood, Harmon & Company, June 12, 1913

Do sky-scrapers pay?

Mr. Harmon said that throughout the country the so-called sky-scraper probably does not on the average produce a net income of over 3½ per cent after a proper provision for depreciation has been made. He further stated that the space above the third floor in such buildings rarely brings in a net return over the current interest rate on the cost of the building alone, without giving any consideration to the site value. He doubted if 1 per cent of the sky-scrapers in America pay 7 per cent net over a series of years when a proper charge has been made for depreciation and repairs.

Towers and pyramidal limitations

Mr. Harmon considered a flat limitation proportionate to the width of the street to be wrong in principle, and from an artistic point of view bad in practice. He preferred a pyramidal limitation with modifications to meet the difference in the strategic importance of different locations.

Boston height limitation

Mr. Harmon testified that while the Boston height limitation met the utilitarian requirement of light and air, it produced monotonous and inartistic uniformity. He claimed that we can do better by allowing individual expression as far as the requirements of light and air will permit.

Zoning

Mr. Harmon said that owing to the constant physical changes taking place in New York City and the tremendous movement in population any system of zoning would be not only very difficult, but, in all likelihood, would be injurious in its effect on certain superior land values, without correspondingly benefiting inferior property.

Fifth Avenue limitations

Mr. Harmon considered that Fifth Avenue heights should be so limited as to make the street particularly valuable for shopping and for show places of unusual artistic quality.

STATEMENT BY MR. THOMAS HASTINGS, OF CARRERE & HASTINGS, ARCHITECTS, AUGUST 4, 1913

Unlimited height a calamity

Without exaggeration, I believe that the greatest calamity that has ever come to any municipality has been due to the fact that there have never been laws limiting the height of buildings. Since the total destruction of Pompeii, whenever a great earthquake or fire has visited a city—as at San Francisco—there has always been the possibility of again putting up the wrecked buildings; but there seems to be no hope of ever taking down buildings that have been put up without restriction.

Esthetics

Where I believe we American architects so often make a mistake is that we present our case as an appeal for esthetic consideration and for the general appearance of a city. In my opinion it is not a question of art, but of sanitation and of justice and of law. Should we not consider seriously the past experiences of the great cities of Europe? Why have they restricted the height of their buildings and why do they continue their restrictions? In Paris there are several formulas to govern the height of buildings, as, for example, for all buildings on a street under 12 meters wide the front wall must not exceed the width of the street plus 6 meters, and the roof must be contained within the half circle drawn tangent at this highest point with a radius equal to one-half the width of the street.

I do not believe that the esthetic argument will do any good. A city will look well if the conditions imposed upon architects are reasonable. I do not believe in the idea that for the sake of beauty we should look for any uniformity of belt courses or cornices on buildings. In European cities this uniformity has been brought about because there has been a general restriction as regards the minimum height of the first and all other stories of buildings erected within a limit of height.

Height limit a benefit to real estate values

If I own property near by a main circulation or city thoroughfare, I should benefit proportionately by the increased demand for property on that thoroughfare or adjacent to it. I know a man who leased the northern corner of one of our side streets at a considerable loss because a 25-story building was erected south of him which shut out the sun from his building. What cannot be universal should not be allowed—and what is going to happen when all buildings are over 25 stories high on our narrow streets? How will people travel up and down town? If I own a lot 25 feet wide, and my neighbors build without limit in height all around my property, this property becomes practically worthless. Already in the lower part of the city the people are living and working through the day with artificial light. The argument that New York is on a narrow island is without effect when we realize that the lower and narrow part of New York, within a stone's throw of Broadway, is not rebuilt, and much of the property is only three or four stories high.

The argument of easy access and saving of time to do business because of high buildings is not a good argument, because reasonable restriction through natural laws will bring about an equally good solution of this problem.

Surtax on high buildings

I heartily believe that there should be a progressive tax on every building now erected above a certain height for each story in addition to an established limit. If 10 stories is a reasonable number to be placed upon a lot of a given size, that same lot should be taxed on double its valuation when a man has built 20 stories upon it; or an equal fractionally increased taxation when over 10 and under 20 stories. Such a law as this would be beneficial to property owners who may have built within reason as to height, in that the city could afford to diminish the tax on their property while increasing the tax on the tall buildings.

Statement by Mr. George L. Hoxie, June, 23, 1913

Special tax on high buildings

It strikes me that the best way to control the matter is through the taxing power. A control of this sort may also be made to compensate, in part, owners of property adjoining sky-scrapers for their present sacrifice of light and air and their possible prevention by new regulations from appropriating in their turn light and air of their neighbors.

Let it be decided that some proportion between land area and cubical contents of building is the most desirable one. Then let a building that has a cubical content greater than this for say each square foot of ground area owned in the same lot carry a surtax on the value of the excess. The surtax might be graduated in proportion to excess of cubical content over the desired limit.

If then an owner desired to build a sky-scraper in the center of a private park, he would suffer no penalty; but the evils of the present situation would be corrected for the future, while existing sky-scrapers would compensate for their presence by an addition to the revenue.

If desired, this scheme could be combined with the plan of taxing land at one rate and improvements at another. Say that the land carries a given tax rate, that a building up to the most desirable content for area carry half that tax rate, that an excess content up to twice that most desirable carry the same tax rate as the land, and that a still further excess of building carry twice the tax rate of the land. In other words, make it to the owners' interest to put up the sort of building most desirable to the community, rather than to try to make laws compelling this.

Statement by Mr. Raymond V. Ingersoll, Chairman New York Congestion Committee, June 30, 1913

While it is not feasible for us to suggest the details of limitations upon the height or size of buildings in New York City, we suggest that the following principles should obtain:

Districting

Varying regulations should be enacted for different sections of the city, and usually for different kinds of buildings within the same district. It is not practical to apply the same rules to a rolling mill as to a tenement. We believe that tenements and dwellings should be limited to a certain number of stories, not exceeding in height a designated number of feet, but that all other buildings for ordinary use, such as factories and office buildings, should be limited as to ratio of volume to lot area. Not only should tenements and dwellings in outlying sections of the city be limited to three stories, but the proportion of the lot area which they may occupy should be reduced below that permitted in sections of the city where present land values of capitalized congestion may prevent the enforcement of even a healthy standard of housing. Variety in arrangement of tenements might be secured by permitting one additional story above the number permitted in any zone or district for the minimum required for such district. Certain sections of the city, where land has now only an acreage value, or is, at most, worth only a few hundred dollars per lot, should be restricted to detached dwellings.

Limitation of cubage

We would suggest that a limit of about 174 times the area of the lot as recommended by the first Mayor's Building Code Revision Commission should be placed upon the volume or cubage of all sky-scrapers even in lower Manhattan, and a lower limit in other and new sections of the city.

Distribution of factories

The distribution of factories can be indirectly effected to some extent at least, although it may not be constitutional explicitly to prohibit their location in any particular locality. We suggest that factories should be set back some distance from party lines, so as to provide for better ventilation, not only of factories, but of tenements on adjoining lots, and also that an unoccupied area be left at the rear of all factory buildings extending the entire width of the lot. If within the scope of the Commission's functions, the planning of lines for carrying freight should be considered. The distribution of factories is of importance in its relation to the width of streets. Fewer wide streets will be required for surface tracks if the volume of passenger traffic be reduced by such distribution of places of work.

Width of streets

The width of streets should be carefully considered. Mr. Thomas Adams, of the town planning department of the Local Government Board of England, has stated that the system of high tenement blocks of Germany and Sweden is as much the result of wide roads as wide roads have been the result of the tenement system. Alderman W. Thompson, chairman of the National Housing Council of England, states that the English by-law requirement that streets have a paved or macadamized road surface of about 40 feet has made the cost of thoroughfares in newly developed estates on the outskirts of towns "more than the land itself." Mr. Raymond Unwin, one of the best qualified of English town planners, has demonstrated the same saving by the use of narrow roads.

Not only is the initial cost of wide roads saved by adapting the width of the street to the neighborhood, but the cost of upkeep or maintenance is similarly reduced. The result in reducing rents or the cost of small houses is apparent. Where the subsequent use of a district cannot be foreseen, or until such time as the city can definitely determine what it will be, houses might be set back from the front line 10 or 15 feet, so as to permit the widening of the street at a minimum expense later, or a grass plot might be left in the middle of the street.

STATEMENT BY MR. CLARENCE H. KELSEY, PRESIDENT TITLE GUARANTEE AND TRUST COMPANY, SEPTEMBER 24, 1913

City hurt by high buildings

Mr. Kelsey feared that the high buildings had irreparably damaged the residential districts in Manhattan. He did not know how the situation could be remedied. No loft building should ever have been allowed betwen 14th and 59th Streets between Fourth and Sixth Avenues. He considered it a great pity that buildings over 12 stories down-town and 8 stories up-town had ever been erected.

He thought, however, that what was left of the city should be protected. Property owners should be protected against themselves. He said that the Commission should err on the side of strictness in protecting what is left of the city. A limitation of height would not destroy values so seriously that one should not be adopted. He considered it the duty of the Commission to recommend one and run the criticism that such action would involve.

Mr. Kelsey said he did not believe in unrestricted personal liberty. Every one should not be permitted to do as he pleased. The erection of high buildings should be stopped and the burden ought to fall on those who would have to bear it. Although Mr. Kelsey thought that no height limit could be imposed without injury to real estate values, he said present real estate values were higher than they ought to be because there was no restriction on height, and those who built the high buildings first got more than the normal value for their land. A proper limitation now would stop this robbing of neighbors for the future, and all had better share what depreciation resulted from stopping the practice than delay and let a few more agile ones rob the rest of still more and cause them to suffer a still greater depreciation.

Arguments advanced in favor of height limit

Mr. Kelsey advanced the following arguments in favor of a height limit:

1. High buildings will make present streets and sidewalks inadequate for traffic.

2. The present sewer system was not constructed to serve high buildings. If the city is to be developed with 12 and 14 story buildings, its entire subsurface will have to be rebuilt.

3. High buildings make it impossible to forecast real estate values. They have brought the business section into the residence section. Mr. Kelsey didn't know where a high-class retail section could be developed.

4. It is becoming increasingly more difficult to borrow money with which to erect high buildings. There has been a decided

change in the attitude of the insurance companies and the savings banks in granting mortgages on sky-scrapers.

5. High buildings encourage the wrong kind of speculation. Mr. Kelsey thought it better to have 12 low buildings owned by 12 men than 4 high buildings owned by 4 men. It is not well to force land into large ownerships.

6. High buildings depreciate other land values. The land values south of 23d Street have lost every bit as much as those north of 23d Street have gained by the erection of high buildings. The sweatshops have destroyed the Fifth Avenue section. A height limit will make real estate values more stable by diffusing them.

7. High buildings rob their neighbors of light.

Rule for height limit

Mr. Kelsey said that the height limit should bear some relation to street width. He said that a flat height limit should be established in certain districts regardless of the width of the building. He said he preferred a uniform height on the cross streets. On side streets a 12-story limit would be too high. A series of 12-story buildings should never be allowed on 25-foot lots. They might, however, be permitted on 50-foot or 100-foot lots. An 18-story building is too high for a 60-foot street. He said he prefered a uniform skyline.

Districting

He said that the migration of factories into residential sections should be stopped. Side streets afford no shipping facilities. He said he did not know why further manufacturing could not be prohibited on the side streets south of 59th Street and north of 14th Street and between Fourth and Sixth Avenues.

Statement by Mr. John Kenlon, Chief of the New York Fire Department, September 12, 1913

Height should be limited

Mr. Kenlon said that there were many coordinate phases involved in the question of limiting the height of buildings. Fire-fighting is only one of them. This is an auspicious time for limiting the height of buildings. The old part of the city is being rebuilt and it will be reconstructed in 25 years.

Fire loss

Mr. Kenlon said that the fire loss in the city was $12,000,000 in 1911 and $9,000,000 in 1912. The fire premiums collected by the insurance companies are about four times as large as the fire loss. New York pays for the rest of the country.

Safety of high buildings

Mr. Kenlon said that high buildings were not absolutely safe from a fire-fighting standpoint. The office buildings down-town are fairly safe, but they may at any time be made very unsafe by a change of occupancy. The safety of a building depends not so much upon the building itself as upon its contents. Office buildings are therefore safer than loft buildings. Libraries filled with books are dangerous, but not as dangerous as shirt-waist factories.

The inside fire protection of a high building can be made quite satisfactory. A limitation on height is, however, desirable if the time of emptying a building is to be considered. The streets, moreover, are not wide enough to hold the people in high buildings if they were all to be emptied at one time. Fire can break out of windows and set the upper stories on fire from the outside.

Mr. Kenlon said that a fire must be controlled in one of two ways: either by water or by isolation. If the firemen can get on the same floor as the fire and to the floors above, the persons in the building are fairly safe; if the firemen are unable to get on the same floor as the fire and to the floors above them, persons above the fire are in great danger; the persons on the other floors in the building are safe unless the floors collapse.

Mr. Kenlon said that he was not afraid of high buildings so long as the city did right by the fire department. He said that he had no fear of a conflagration. It is impossible to control a panic; panic might occur in any building. If people get panic-stricken and jump, they might just as well jump from the forty-ninth floor as from the tenth. Death would be certain in either case.

Mr. Kenlon said that fire protection cannot be afforded buildings from the street level to a greater height than between 100 and 130 feet. A higher nozzle pressure than that required to force water to this level is impracticable. Buildings higher than 85 feet should therefore have standpipes, automatic sprinklers, etc. A building need not necessarily be touched by a flame to be set on fire: the heat wave, which is greatest from 100 to 150 feet above the fire, may set it on fire. If the height of buildings is limited with reference to the fire protection that can be afforded from the street level, the limit should be placed at a maximum of 100 feet. When a flame strikes a cloud of gas and smoke in an enclosed shaft, the whole building is instantaneously set on fire.

Mr. Kenlon said that he considered 85 feet to be the ideal limitation on height. It is very difficult to say what time limit should be required for the occupants to vacate a building; a quick-burning building should be vacated in a very short time; a slow-burning building could take a longer time. High buildings should be subdivided by fireproof walls and provided with horizontal exits. All high buildings should be provided with three essentials: (1) fire walls; (2) tower stairs, and (3) automatic sprinklers. There are few buildings of this character in the city at present. Tower stairs enable the firemen to fight a fire on its own level.

Mr. Kenlon said that he regards 6-inch terra-cotta walls with wire glass as excellent fire stops. He stated that such a wall could withstand a temperature of 1600 degrees Fahrenheit for 30 minutes. In high buildings the standpipes should be considered as the primary and not as the auxiliary means of fighting fires. The automatic sprinkler standpipes in buildings could not at present have direct connection with the high-pressure mains, but by proper coordination between the department of water supply and the fire department in the preparation of specifications for the extension of the high-pressure system such a scheme is perfectly feasible.

Mr. Kenlon said that the Yonkers reservoir is 300 feet higher than the lower end of Manhattan Island. This is equal to a pressure of 120 pounds to the square inch in the high-pressure mains. By putting in strong pipes that could be tapped without danger of blow-outs, this pressure could be utilized for a sprinkler supply, thereby relieving taxpayers of the extra expense of tanks and pumping machinery in these buildings.

Districting

Mr. Kenlon said the city authorities should begin now by limiting the height of buildings in the boroughs of Queens, Richmond, The Bronx, and parts of Brooklyn. As to Manhattan, it is just as essential, but very much complicated on account of the many high buildings already erected and the injustice to property owners who purchased land at very high prices. It would seem unfair, he said, to permit one man to erect a 42-story building and compel another, who paid dearly for land on the same block, to keep down to 8 stories high.

Statement by Mr. Charles W. Killam, Professor, School of Architecture, Harvard University, Boston, Mass., October 4, 1913

Cornices and parapet walls

Mr. Killam said that a height limit was incomplete unless it incorporated a limit on the width of cornices and also one on the height of parapet walls. A height limit is sometimes nullified by the erection of high parapet walls.

Tenement house law

Mr. Killam referred to the Massachusetts Tenement House Act for Cities, chapter 786, Acts of 1913, a permissive law which may be adopted by any city except Boston. That law has the following provisions:

A parapet exceeding 3 feet in height is considered as a part of the height of the building.

The number of stories is restricted to one for each 10 feet in width of the street.

Three-story tenements on interior lots to have 15-foot rear yard with addition of 5 feet for each additional story.

An outer court on the lot line extending from the street to the yard is allowed to be narrower than other courts.

Referring to the Brookline law as amended April 10, 1912, Mr. Killam said that for tenements 60 feet in height an inner court inclosed on all four sides shall have a least horizontal dimension of 24 feet.

Statement by S. Adolphus Knopf, M. D., Professor of Medicine, Department of Phthisic-Therapy, New York Post-Graduate Medical School and Hospital, July 29, 1913

High buildings and tuberculosis

As a physician you will pardon me if I leave the consideration of the commercial and esthetic aspect of the situation for others to consider who are more qualified to do this. As a medical man and a sanitarian, I wish to speak merely of the danger to health and life of our fellow citizens which arises from too tall buildings wherever the streets are so narrow as to prevent the necessary natural light, sunshine and pure air to enter the lower stories of the buildings. As a specialist in tuberculosis, I may be permitted to speak principally of this affliction so justly called the "Great White Plague."

Tuberculosis, which is propagated by bad air, foul air and lack of sunlight, causes annually a loss of 200,000 citizens to the United States. This disease could be largely prevented would we live and work in pure air, in air relatively free from mineral and vegetable dust, and last, but not least, would we construct the buildings in which we live and labor so as to allow sunlight to enter more freely. Tuberculosis is far more prevalent among the workers in our downtown tall office buildings than is generally known and much more than should be the case when one considers the wealth which is harbored there and the relatively good pay these bookkeepers and clerks receive as a rule.

Carefully gathered statistics show that in the city of New York the garment workers are afflicted more frequently with tuberculosis than any other class of workers. The majority of these workers do not, as is often thought, work in their homes. They work in the tall crowded buildings, situated in congested districts, 10, 12, 20 or more stories high, where every floor masses hundreds of workers. Many are tuberculous without knowing it. Others know that they are tuberculous, but, perhaps fearing their discharge, hide their disease as long as they can; but in the meantime they disseminate the germ of tuberculosis by coughing in their neighbors' faces, or over the clothing they manufacture, or, what is still more frequent, spread the disease by careless expectoration on the floor. During luncheon hour they crowd streets and avenues and those afflicted with the disease expectorate freely on sidewalks and streets. The infectious sputum dries and pulverizes, and is inhaled with the dust and causes tuberculosis in any susceptible individual who may frequent that street.

Again, the infectious spittle from the consumptive may be carried on the soles of the workers' shoes back into the factory or into their own homes, causing the infection of wife and children. In case of epidemics of pneumonia and la grippe, the same process of infection through spitting and coughing is carried on and both diseases are by no means so infrequent or non-dangerous as is generally supposed.

And now, not content with the many altogether too tall buildings already lining the part of Fifth Avenue south of 23d Street and the adjoining streets, some, let me hope not greedy but only thoughtless, capitalists wish to increase the number of disease-breeding and death-trap sky-scrapers and erect them in the one principal and most beautiful street of New York City where there are as yet relatively few of these unsanitary and unsafe structures. I use the term "unsafe" advisedly. The workers in the tall buildings in narrow streets are, as above described, much exposed to the danger of contracting the various diseases of the respiratory organs (tuberculosis, pneumonia, la grippe, etc.). The same holds good of the people who are obliged to walk these streets who, in addition, are exposed to dangerous drafts and currents of air, which contain, particularly in the lower strata of the atmosphere of these canyon-like streets, a large portion of the noxious gases characteristic of every large city. Where the buildings are low and the streets are wide, these poisonous gases diffuse much more easily and hence are less dangerous.

I trust that your Commission may report favorably on the limitation of the height of buildings regarding the section north of 23d Street on Fifth Avenue. Fifth Avenue is perhaps now and surely will be in the future the street most eagerly sought by strangers visiting the city. In the past it has been admired for its beautiful buildings, which are low, for its width as a thoroughfare, and for the light and air which spell health and beauty. Is all this to be changed because of thoughtlessness or greed?

Statement by Mr. Walter Laidlaw, Executive Secretary New York Federation of Churches, June 12, 1913

Zoning

Mr. Laidlaw said that he was a zonist absolutely; that he was principally interested in the subject from the standpoint of providing homes for wage earners. The mere growth in ten years within a

19-mile radius from the City Hall of New York was greater than the total population of all but seven of the largest cities of the world. There is no need for tenements in New York. All the population of New York City for thirty years to come can be accommodated in two-family houses, 14 to the acre. The factory and house owner should be encouraged to move out from the congested region. More and more immigrants are to-day going to The Bronx, and as many into Brooklyn as into Manhattan.

Statement by Mr. Walter Lindner, Counsel Title Guarantee and Trust Company, July 7, 1913

Districting

I believe that the height of buildings to be erected in the future requires restriction. Under existing constitutional limitations, such restrictions must be justifiable on the ground that they are appropriate to the preservation of the public health, safety or morals —that is to say, that they come under the exercise of the police power. Such limits as are adopted should be reasonable—that is to say, they should be just both to the property owner and the community and should not go further than can be supported by public opinion. An illustration of regulations which have the support of public opinion and therefore are never seriously questioned, is the manner in which the fire limits of the city have been fixed and extended from time to time.

The city could place a flat limitation on the height of all buildings, but if it did, such limitation ought to apply to all boroughs equally. It might also establish a flat limitation with a proviso that certain percentages of the area and, if advisable, portions set off from the sides of the lot, may be carried to greater height. A permission of this kind could be justified on the ground that if the owner went to a greater height within the limits of his own lot, setting off from the sides, front and rear when he goes beyond the flat limitation, he would not be using the light and air belonging to the community but only that within his own lot. In all permissions to erect high buildings, the fire hazard, the panic danger and the ability of the fire department to reach great heights can be taken into account.

I do not believe that the zone system can be adopted under the present constitutional limitations, nor do I believe if it could be adopted that it would be advisable. The zone system based on present land values could be construed by the courts as being based on expediency and not on principles justifiable by the police power.

The difference in social conditions would not justify the exercise of the police power to limit buildings at different heights in different districts.

If health and sanitation warranted limiting buildings in the suburbs at a low height, then these same grounds could be consistently urged in remedying the congestion in the built-up areas. No one has a vested right to maintain an unsanitary condition whether it is in the outlying or in the central part of the city. The unsanitary conditions of old districts cannot be urged in justification of stricter provisions in new districts. This would be to discriminate between the healthfulness of different localities. Legislation cannot be passed to limit buildings at different heights in different districts unless exceptions are made to prevent wholesale destruction of existing buildings; it should be directed toward the abolition of unsanitary conditions in all localities.

It does not seem to me that industries which do not involve special fire hazard, or which do not emit offensive or noxious fumes or fluids, could be restricted to certain districts. Breweries, therefore, could probably be kept out of residential neighborhoods; millinery shops, on the other hand, could not.

Assuming we could have zones, I think the height limit in any particular zone should not be altered by a vote of a certain percentage of lot owners. If this were done, it would deprive the remaining percentage of its protection.

New streets in undeveloped sections might be made narrower. The city might acquire a 30 or 40 foot strip for the roadway and an easement of 15 feet on each side for set-back purposes. This would make the legal width of the street only 30 or 40 feet. This plan, if adopted, would permit different height limits in different sections of the city, provided the buildings facing the street were limited in height to, say, 1½ times the width of the street.

Statement by Mr. Electus D. Litchfield, Representing the New York Chapter of the American Institute of Architects, May 29, 1913

I may present to you one or two suggestions relative to the work which you have in hand which came as the result of a very considerable study which I have given the problem, first as a member of the special committee on Limitation of Heights of Buildings of the Building Code Revision Commission of the years 1906-1907 and since then as one who has come to a very definite conclusion as to the proper course of action in the premises.

History

I do not know just when the agitation for a limitation of the height of buildings in New York City first started. From the first it has been closely allied with the movement for bettering housing conditions and with the enactment of legislation for the conservation to the tenement-house dweller of light and air. Together with this, owing in a great measure to the inadequate architectural solution of the problem of the design of the extremely high building made possible by the invention of the skeleton steel construction, there has arisen a prejudice against the high buildings from the artistic standpoint.

Esthetic side

The successful design of buildings of great height has been so rare that there has developed a distinct artistic prejudice against the high buildings as a class which very probably is not justified. Then, too, the design of individual buildings without any regard for the neighboring conditions has produced even on our most important streets such an irregular and in no sense picturesque cornice and sky line that there has arisen a distinct desire for such a regulation of the heights, or at least of the cornice lines, of the buildings upon such streets as Fifth Avenue as would produce an architectural dignity which is now lacking and which they might well possess.

John M. Carrére's idea

The late John M. Carrére gave voice to a suggestion relative to the limitation of the heights of buildings at the preliminary hearing before the Building Code Commission in 1906. The records of the New York Chapter of the American Institute of Architects show that the matter was under discussion among architects certainly not less than six years prior to this, but so far as I know Mr. Carrére's suggestion was the first one made before an official body in the city of New York. His proposition was that some plan should be worked out by which the taxes upon buildings should be increased in a definite proportion as the buildings increased in height, as the higher the buildings went the more of the necessary light and air they consumed, his idea being that, after the proper tax had been calculated according to the value of building, it be multiplied by a certain factor which would be based upon the recognition of the fact that in so far as the building extended above a reasonable height it absorbed more than its own share of light and air.

Mr. Carrére's idea in regard to the limitation of height through taxation, while not altogether, I think, a practical one, was, I suppose, based on the principle, which must be correct, that the ownership of a building or lands does not carry with it a slice of the atmosphere from the earth to the heavens. Indeed the lawyers will tell us that property rights, being derived from the state, are controllable by the state for the benefit of the public.

Point of view of the courts

The time has not yet arrived when esthetic considerations have controlling weight with the courts at law. In questions involving the health and comfort of the community, sanitary conditions, on the other hand, have long since been considered of the utmost importance. The principle of pro bono publico is a recognized one as regards the right of the state to govern the individual and the courts have set forth unequivocally the principle that the property rights of the individual are subordinate to the rights of the community.

The supreme court of the state of Maine in a recent decision has said: "The right of the public to control and limit the use of private property is peculiarly applicable to property in land because such property is not the result of productive labor but is derived solely from the state itself, the original owner." The court goes on to say: "We do not think the proposed legislation would take private property within the inhibition of the constitution; while it might restrict the owner of lands in his use of them, might delay his anticipated profits, and even thereby might cause him some loss of profit, he would still have a large measure of control and large opportunities to realize values."

Mr. Justice Holmes of the Supreme Court of the United States in delivering the opinion of that Court on April 6, 1908, sustaining the Court of Errors and Appeals of New Jersey in a similar view, has said: "The State as quasi sovereign and representative of the interests of the public has a standing in court to protect the atmosphere, the water and the forests within its territory, irrespective of the assent or dissent of the private owners of the land most immediately concerned."

Method of limiting height

It is clearly within the prerogative of the Board of Estimate and Apportionment together with the Board of Aldermen to provide such regulations as to height and area of buildings as are necessary to maintain the best interests of the community. These regulations must divide themselves into three distinct classes, as there are three distinct interests of the community to be subserved. These are as follows: (1) that all buildings shall have sufficient light and air for the comfort of their occupants; (2) that the streets shall have proper light and ventilation; and (3) that the buildings abutting upon the streets shall not contain more people than the street, the transit facilities and the sewers may properly serve.

There is no doubt that the time has arrived when it is necessary to the protection of each of these interests of the people that the size of buildings shall in some way be regulated. It is also clear that some regulation of the height of cornice lines would be a distinct architectural advantage to the city. Whether such regulation is possible is for your Commission to determine. The regulation, however, which is necessary to protect the light and air of the buildings' tenants, the light and air of the people in the street, and the regulation of the size of buildings so that the population of them shall not be greater than the sewers, streets and transit facilities may properly serve, are clearly matters for which an ordinance may properly be framed. Within certain limits the protection of the light and air of the tenants of the individual building is taken care of by the building and the tenement house laws.

Limit volume, not height

Your problem concerns itself more with the damage which one building may do to the tenants of another and to the protection of the streets. Most cities which have taken up this problem have ended by passing a law setting a flat limit of height for all buildings. The majority of the Building Code Commission of 1906-1907 started out feeling that such a law should be passed in New York City. As the result, however, of the work of our special committee to whom this matter was referred the Building Code Commission finally decided to recommend not a limit of height but a limit of volume. It is perhaps a trifle difficult to grasp easily the meaning of such a law or regulation. Perhaps the easiest way of understanding it is to assume that you have adopted a limit of height. Let us suppose, for instance, you have determined that 200 feet is the greatest height that any building should go in the financial district (you will, I trust, whether you finally decide on limits or height or limits of volume, set different limits for different sections).

Let us suppose, I say, that you have determined upon a maximum height of 200 feet. Take a building 200 feet high on a lot 100 feet deep and say 100 feet in width; provide that a proper percentage of the light be devoted to light court and calculate the volume of the building above the grade line upon the lot. This volume will evidently be less than 200 times the area of the lot. If you will divide the total volume which you have obtained by 200, you will obtain a factor which multiplied by the area of any lot will give you the volume of the building which your regulations will allow.

It was the conclusion of our commission, and it is this point which I wish to place before your Commission to-day, that as far as light and air are concerned the people will be more greatly benefited if, keeping the volume of the building the same, the area of the light courts or the width of the street were increased. There is an infinite space above every building, but there is a very limited space between each building and its neighbor. If, then, while the volume of the building is kept constant, the factor of height be increased, the factors of width and depth must necessarily be decreased. Any increase of a few feet in the width of a street or of a light court justifies more than a proportionate increase in height.

If you set a flat limit of height, commercial interests will tend to make a property owner build as completely as your light court regulations will allow him over his entire lot. On the other hand, if you set an equivalent limit of volume, he will be enabled to leave greater light courts and have a much greater freedom in the design of his building. One of the glories of New York is its towers. One of its shames is that they are built so close together as to cut off necessary light.

Let me urge you to so frame your regulations that we may still build our towers in ever-increasing beauty, but only when we provide about them such space as shall be proper, not only for the health and comfort of the people occupying the building itself, but of those in our neighbors' buildings and of those upon the street.

STATEMENT BY MR. OSCAR LOWINSON, REPRESENTING NEW YORK SOCIETY OF ARCHITECTS, JUNE 30, 1913

Methods of limiting height

As a matter of public policy and under what is known as police regulations, it is advisable to establish standards in reference to regulating the heights of buildings. As a police regulation, the danger in case of fire or panic in a high building should be considered sufficient to require ample means of escape which in themselves would probably stop the construction beyond normal limits. Except in special types of buildings, there is no need of a building being more than 10 or 12 stories in height. The height of the building should be determined from standards which should be established. With our knowledge of the laws of distribution of light, it should not be a serious matter to frame regulations making the height of a wall dependent upon the distance of the opposite wall. Always care should be exercised that this should not work a hardship. The important thing, however, is to establish a standard, if your Commission can accomplish this, combined with recommendations as to size of exits.

It has often been said that if you permit a germ to have free way it will eat itself to death, and this has been said of the high-buildings movement. However, as the constructors of high buildings are almost invariably of the class that have no thought of their moral responsibilities, regulations forcing the stoppage of this class of work should be enacted.

STATEMENT BY MR. WILLIAM O. LUDLOW, ARCHITECT, FROM "RECORD AND GUIDE," APRIL 19, 1913

The regulation of building height

1. The height of any building at the building line, except on corner plots, shall not exceed 12 times the square root of the width of the street upon which it is located; and no part of such building shall extend above the plane formed by the building line at this height and a line normal thereto inclined away from the street at an angle of 60 degrees from the horizontal. Nor shall any part of

the building extend beyond the allowed height of the building at the building line more than 36 feet.

The height limit should, I believe, be a function of the width of the street for obvious reasons, but multiplying this width by a constant, such as one, one and a half, or two, as some have advocated, gives results that are ill-suited to the requirements of New York streets, that vary from 30 to 200 feet in width, as a little calculation will show. For example, if once the width of the street be the height allowed, and the average floor to floor story height be assumed as 12 feet, 30-foot streets, of which there are a number, would have to be confined to two-story buildings, 40-foot streets to three-story buildings, and even the usual 60-foot street would allow only five stories in height. New York City would never tolerate such a drastic restriction.

Again, if the modulus be one and a half, which is even yet a little low for narrow streets, which in New York, on account of their location, are and probably will be used largely for warehouse and storage purposes, yet on the wide streets ranging as high as 200 feet there might as well be no height limit at all, as far as the fire department and the distribution of land values and population go.

The device of using the square root of the street width as the variable and a constant factor of 12 gives a commercially reasonable height to buildings on the narrow as well as the wide streets.

Permitting on the top of buildings three stories stepped back under the 60 degree inclined plane gives a certain latitude to the cube without materially affecting the light and air conditions of the street and opposite buildings.

2. Excepting on corner buildings, no part of any rear exterior wall of a building shall be nearer to the rear lot line than the following:

Above the first story up to 50 feet, 10 per cent of the average depth of the lot. From 50 feet to 100 feet, 15 per cent of the average depth of the lot. From 100 feet to 150 feet, 20 per cent of the average depth of the lot. From 150 feet upward, 25 per cent of the average depth of the lot.

Light and air requirements must be observed on the rear or yard side of buildings as well as the street front, although the space necessary is not so great.

3. Corner plots, *i. e.*, plots which embrace the intersection point of two streets, may be considered as extending from the corner 50 feet on each street front and of not more than 2500 square feet in total area, and may be built upon over the entire area to a vertical height not exceeding 36 feet in excess of the allowed vertical height at the building line of the highest adjoining building.

This paragraph defines a corner plot and provides in effect that corners may be built vertically at the building line as high as the top set-back story of the highest adjoining building. This, I believe, will obviate the difficulty that might otherwise be experienced in bringing stepped-back façades of unequal heights together at a corner, and will make possible a good architectural effect.

On account of the advantages in respect to light and air, it is also quite logical to permit of building to greater height on a corner than elsewhere.

4. Notwithstanding the foregoing, one-fifth of the total area of any plot may be built upon to any height.

Recognizing the usefulness of the occasional tower as an advertising asset and as an object of real interest and possibly of great beauty, I believe they should not be prohibited. Towers, however, should be so restricted that the temptation to build them in great numbers and of great bulk will be small, for in case of fire the fire department is almost powerless, and egress to tenants is most difficult. A city of towers, to my mind, would be a calamity. I do not believe, however, under any scheme this would ever be realized, as the tower is expensive to build and apt to be most uneconomical in returns to the owner.

5. For purposes of computation, all public squares and parks shall be considered as streets of like widths, but in no case shall this width be considered as greater than 200 feet. Streets bordering the waterfront and all streets greater than 200 feet in width shall be considered as 200 feet in width, but all other streets shall be measured from building line to opposite building line.

This paragraph sets an ulterior limit to all buildings, excepting towers, at a height of 170 feet at the cornice line and 36 feet higher for the set-back stories and corners, although, of course, this height is only possible to buildings in the favored locations of park and water fronts or 200-foot streets.

New York reasonably demands a fairly liberal law, due to the intensive development imposed by a long and narrow island, and an idealistic provision, such as might be suitable to a new city in an open territory, is impracticable and impossible here. I prefer to acknowledge the existing conditions, and neither try to get impossibly ideal results nor to hopelessly give up the fight altogether.

Statement by Mr. L. B. Marks, Representing the Illuminating Engineering Society, July 14, 1913

Artificial illumination

Mr. Marks said that artificial lighting when properly designed is no more deleterious to eyesight than natural light. He said that artificial illumination could be supplied without eye-strain. Natural light is very frequently misapplied in office buildings and factories. Unshaded light sources of high intrinsic brightness are very straining to the eye.

Mr. Marks said that in the present state of the art of illumination it is impossible to lay down any exact laws as to what constitutes ideal illumination. He said that as yet we do not know definitely what elements should be considered primal in installing the best lighting system. As an illustration, he cited the building erected five years ago by the Edison Electric Illuminating Company of Boston. A special commission of illuminating engineers of which he was one was appointed to design the lighting of this building with reference mainly to three considerations: (1) physiological conditions; (2) pleasing appearance; and (3) economy. The commission spent almost a year in making the plans for this building, but the art has advanced so rapidly that many changes would be made if the lighting were installed new to-day.

Statement by Mr. Benjamin C. Marsh, Representing the New York Congestion Committee, June 30, 1913

Zoning

Mr. Marsh said that the zoning system was necessary for New York. The city is composed of what was once many separate municipalities. The conditions arising from this fact make it necessary to differentiate the height limit, not only in the different boroughs, but also between different parts of the same borough. The height ought to be limited with reference to the present land value and the present state of development of the respective sections of the city. The height ought also to be regulated according to the kind of building.

Mr. Marsh said that factory districts have to be developed in order to save employees the cost of transportation. In planning the development of South Brooklyn the city should, if necessary, build a railroad to haul freight. Transit lines used to carry passengers during the day might be used to carry freight at night.

Mr. Marsh said that additional height should be allowed a building which does not occupy the maximum lot area permitted under the law.

Congestion

Mr. Marsh said that the city should adopt a policy of social recreation for the suburbs. If the city did this, the population would spread out.

Mr. Marsh said that 50 per cent of the population of The Bronx lives on about 5 per cent of the area of the borough. Multi-family houses are not necessary throughout the city. Practically the whole city, with the exception of the lower part of The Bronx, Manhattan and several districts in Brooklyn, could be developed with two-family detached houses. At an acreage density of 60 to 75 persons, this will house all of the city's population for some time.

Mr. Marsh expressed the opinion that the progressive factory legislation enacted by the last legislature would drive many factories from the city.

Statement by Mr. Nathan Matthews, Chairman of Commission Which Determined the Districts Under the Present Height Limitation in Boston, Mass., October 3, 1913

Adoption of the Boston height limit

Mr. Matthews said that the real estate owners were not awake when the A and B law was passed in 1904. When the commission, appointed by the mayor to district the city, commenced to hold hearings, the real estate men awoke and unanimously opposed any limitation on height. The owners said they could not build a 125-foot building that would pay; but could stand no cross examination. When the 1906 amendment was passed permitting an intermediate height of between 80 and 100 feet in District B, all the real estate owners wished to have their property included within the intermediate height limit and used the same argument over again.

Mr. Matthews said that the land values in District B have increased since the height limit was imposed. The values in District A have remained stationary, except on particular streets. High buildings possess no advantage if they are all of a uniform height and built up solidly. The height of buildings had been limited in Boston with reference to such considerations as health, sunlight, air and ventilation. Esthetic appearance had not been considered.

Mr. Matthews advised the Commission not to be afraid of the real estate owners. He said it should recommend no compromise. It is just as easy to get through a logical and effective measure as an ineffective compromise. He said that the real estate owners who first opposed a height limit in Boston now heartily support it. The height limit should be made perpetual. If there had been no high buildings in Boston at the time the height of buildings was limited, the maximum limit would have been placed at 80 and 100 feet for the entire city.

Mr. Matthews said that under the law a building over 125 feet in height could not be re-erected to a greater height than 125 feet. The height limit had caused no decline in values. He could not say it had caused an increase in values. He did not think that high buildings were a good investment. He said that rentals in Boston had been depressed during the last 20 years by the migration into the suburbs. Suburban development has been made possible by improved transit facilities.

Statement by Mr. Rudolph P. Miller, Superintendent Bureau of Buildings, Borough of Manhattan, September 22, 1913

Administrative questions

Mr. Miller said that a law limiting the number of persons per unit of floor area should be enforced in the same manner as the present law with reference to the overloading of floors. All building inspection should be centralized in one single department. This would result in great economy to the city. The law contains no provisions relative to the use of reenforced concrete construction. There has been no difficulty in enforcing the regulations laid down by the bureau of buildings with reference to it.

Method of limiting height

Mr. Miller said that districting by height was desirable. The limit for the height of buildings should be some function of the street width. Concessions in the way of greater height might be allowed where a greater percentage of the lot area than the required minimum is left unoccupied.

Light and ventilation

Mr. Miller said that adequate light and ventilation were the strongest arguments that could be advanced in favor of limiting the height of buildings. Practicable artificial light and ventilation can be developed to satisfy the eyesight and to provide pure, wholesome air for the lungs, but they cannot fully replace sunlight as a pathogenic agent. Enameled brick walls would greatly benefit the lighting of courts.

Mr. Miller said that buildings covering from 90 to 95 per cent of the lot area do not obtain sufficient light and ventilation. The courts in the new law tenements were about the best that the city could get on the statute books at present. The street width should not have anything to do with the required width of rear courts.

Exits

Mr. Miller said that adequate exit facilities should be provided within the building in each case. The number and size of exits should be proportioned to the number of occupants, due allowance being made for the fireproofness of the building and the character of the exit facilities that are provided.

Fire walls

Mr. Miller said that the most effective safeguard to life against fire is the fire wall. Macy's, he said, is the only department store in the city that is provided with fire walls. When Stern's department store was constructed, Mr. Miller insisted on its being equipped with fire walls dividing it into three sections, but he was overruled by the board of examiners. Mr. Miller said that the building department made concessions, when possible, in other respects to hotels equipped with fireproof doors shutting across its corridors.

Tower stairs

Mr. Miller said that next to the fire wall, the tower stair is the best safeguard to life against fire. Tower stairs should be installed in factories. Tower stairs, in most cases, could be made to take the place of ordinary stairs for every-day use.

STATEMENT BY MR. JOHN J. MURPHY, COMMISSIONER, TENEMENT HOUSE DEPARTMENT, SEPTEMBER 15, 1913

Tenement house law

Mr. Murphy said that the Tenement House Commission did not get what it wanted when the Tenement House Law was enacted. The court areas are inadequate on the lower floors of five and six story and higher buildings.

Mr. Murphy said that he had been mandamused only once since he became commissioner of the tenement house department, and that unsuccessfully. The Tenement House Law is mandatory in practically all its provisions. It allows very little discretion to the department. This condition was described as necessary at the time the law was enacted in order to have it obeyed.

Mr. Murphy said that the city should have more power in controlling the use of property. The Tenement House Law checked building for a time. This was due, however, to the large oversupply of tenements erected in anticipation of the law. The law itself did not lower realty values.

STATEMENT BY MR. JOHN NOLEN, LANDSCAPE ARCHITECT, CAMBRIDGE, MASS., OCTOBER 4, 1913

Mr. Nolen said that the traveler probably enjoys the high buildings in New York more than anything else. Mr. Nolen thought the city should permit towers. He said it would add incentive to building. Towers will add distinctly to the appearance of the city. They will add accent and emphasis to the street. He thought the suggestion of permitting towers on lots with three street fronts, one of which is an entire block, admirable.

STATEMENT BY MR. FREDERICK LAW OLMSTED, CHAIRMAN NATIONAL CITY PLANNING CONFERENCE, JUNE 6, 1913

Method of limiting height

Some of the aspects of the problems of building height limitation now before your Commission lead me to write you at length in regard to two points which have been upon my mind for a long time. I do not claim any originality for either of the ideas, but I feel them to be important enough to urge upon your attention on the chance that your Commission has not yet fully considered them. One concerns an approximate standard of adequate natural lighting for buildings in a city as a basis for fixing limitations on the height of buildings. The other concerns the method of defining such limitations.

Light and ventilation

I do not consider under the first head the relation of other height limitations to the problem of congestion of streets and transportation lines or to the appearance of a city, but only their relation to the proper lighting and ventilation of buildings. I assume that if building heights were so regulated that every room in every building received reasonably good natural illumination in the daytime under normal weather conditions, the basis for good natural ventilation would also be assured, although some special additional regulations directed specifically toward maintaining good ventilation might be desirable. I assume also that it is a less hopeless project to attempt to ascertain and define in fairly broad terms what conditions are requisite to good natural lighting, and to support the conclusions by a convincing set of facts, than to make a similar definition of the conditions requisite for good ventilation, since the action of air currents and eddies is almost unfathomably complex as compared with the action of light rays.

I believe that the determination, first, of fairly definite standards of several degrees of tolerably good and intolerably bad natural lighting, and, second, of the conditions of building heights, etc., which under normal circumstances will result in those several standard degrees of lighting, would not only be of great value in arriving at sound conclusions about the proper limitations on the height of buildings, but would be of enormous value in winning public support for those conclusions.

I understand that standards of measurement of the illumination within any room at any given moment can be determined photometrically and that it is known with sufficient accuracy to what practical human requirements of light, for various purposes, these measurable standards correspond. Approximate determination can also be made of the influence upon the lighting of a room of what may be called the interior factors, such as shape and size of room, reflecting power of the surfaces within the room, and size, position and other details of the window openings. If, therefore, normal limiting conditions as to these interior factors be assumed, it should be possible to determine approximately what conditions of exterior lighting—that is to say, what quantities and qualities of light impinging upon the plane of the outside walls in which the windows are set—are necessary to secure the several standard degrees of lighting inside the buildings. Quantities and qualities of light in this connection mean chiefly, I suppose, the direction, angular extent and luminosity, first, of the patches of sky visible from each window, and, second, of walls and other near-by surfaces reflecting any considerable quantity of light.

The hourly changes in the luminosity of the sky can be measured, and allowed for, and reduced to a normal condition representing the darkest sky under which it is reasonable to expect good natural illumination inside of buildings.

The direction and angular extent of the patches of sky visible from each window are determined solely by the height and form of the silhouette of the opposite buildings (or other objects), which in turn is absolutely controllable by building-height limitations. The entire angular extent of the outlook from a given window which does not consist of patches of sky consists of the surfaces of buildings (and other objects) reflecting indirect light to the window; and while it is true that the amount of light coming from this source is largely dependent upon the color and texture of the surfaces themselves, it is primarily dependent upon the amount of direct light impinging upon those surfaces, which in turn is dependent upon the height and form of the silhouette of the buildings (etc.) opposite; in other words, upon the building-height limitations again.

Sufficiently approximate allowances can be made for variations in the reflecting power of the particular walls from which indirect light is returned in any given case, just as allowances can be made for the fluctuations in the luminosity of the sky; and indeed, since the color and texture of wall surfaces may be to some extent controlled in the interest of the public health, a definite determination of the influence of that factor upon the illumination of opposite interiors under various normal conditions as to the other factors would be of great interest and value. It might be entirely proper, for example, to permit a building of light color and high reflecting power to be erected to a greater height than a building of dark color and great light-absorbing power. But aside from that question, and making due allowance for the reflecting power of the building surfaces, as well as for the luminosity of the sky at the time of observation, it is, in theory at least, possible to determine pretty definitely what limitations upon the height of the buildings on both sides of an open space (whether street or otherwise) will insure at the low windows in any of the flanking buildings the quantity and quality of light necessary for the standard degrees of illumination within a normal room behind those windows.

I believe that a careful series of measurements and experiments conducted in some of the office buildings on narrow down-town streets of New York, where the lower floors patently and conspicuously lack sufficient natural illumination for the satisfactory pursuit of any kind of human occupation and where the upper floors are admirably lighted, would afford a sound basis for determining upon a series of building-height limitations calculated to insure, respectively, several standard degrees of natural lighting in buildings, each degree adapted to certain conditions of use. The conditions might vary from those now accepted for the lower stories of many hotels and office buildings in New York, where reliance is placed wholly upon artificial light and forced ventilation, and where natural light is merely a pleasant luxury of which a modicum may be superadded occasionally, to those required for the most satisfactory type of private residence, scientific laboratory, museum, studio or industrial plant where the natural illumination is substantially perfect.

If your Commission should undertake such a scientific investigation of light conditions in relation to building height, it is almost needless to say that the methods of conducting it ought to be worked out with the greatest care, in consultation with, if not under the direction of, the highest scientific authorities in the country. It would be very easy to waste a good deal of money in such an investigation without conclusive results through failure to adopt the right methods early in the course of the work.

Districting

Having arrived at such conclusions, it would be necessary to decide upon districts in each of which would be established a set of building regulations guaranteeing to every prospective improver of real estate, within the district at least, a certain minimum standard of natural lighting, and correspondingly restraining him from depriving his neighbors' property of that minimum of light. Naturally in fixing the boundaries of the several districts and determining upon the regulations suitable to each the highest potential utility of each locality would be considered, and the opinion of the majority of the owners of real estate on that point would have much weight, although the interests of the community as a whole should finally control.

Height on street front

The second point I want to bring before you is in regard to the method of expressing a building-height restriction. There are serious objections to the usual method of a uniform flat regulation upon the total height, even when that height is made to depend upon the width of the street on which a building abuts. So far as concerns protection from excessive obstruction of light, such regulations accomplish no more than others which interfere much less with the freedom of the real estate owner. They may even accomplish less. If a building is set back farther from the street line than another, it would be reasonable to allow it to be carried up to a greater height. This would be accomplished by a rule that a building may not be erected to a height greater than the distance of the front of the building from the opposite side of the street (or some multiple of that distance). Still greater latitude would be permitted without serious injury to the light conditions by a rule prescribing that no part of any building shall be erected to a height greater than the distance of that part of the building from the opposite side of the street (or some multiple of that distance). Under this rule the height of buildings would be limited not by a horizontal plane, as in most rules, but by an inclined plane permitting a much greater volume of building without cutting off any more direct light from the street or lower stories of opposite buildings. On the esthetic side it would tend toward a much more interesting and agreeable architectural treatment of the roofs and upper stories than the flat roof that now prevails, including both the stepping back of upper stories with terraces or balconies and the use of steep-pitched roofs with dormers. But the main point is that it would permit the maximum economic use of the land consistent with a given degree of light for the lower stories.

Rear yards

Thus far I have referred only to the safeguarding of the light conditions for that portion of private property fronting upon streets. Similar regulations, based upon the same principles and stated in a similar way, can and should be applied for safeguarding the access of light to the rear of private property, as by a regulation that no part of any building shall be erected to a height greater than twice (or some other multiple of) the distance of that part from the rear of the lot on which it stands.

It is of course necessary to define explicitly how the " height " of any part of a building is to be measured and to define the meaning of " rear line " of a lot in such a manner as to be applicable in a reasonable way to the most irregular case.

Whether in some classes of districts provisions should be made for a continuous open space through the middle of a block even where a lot runs through from street to street is another question, but clearly such a provision should not be universal, because it would undesirably hamper the economic development of many classes of property.

Towers

I should be disposed, even at the cost of a somewhat complicated supplement to the kind of regulation above proposed, to permit even greater latitude of choice to the property owner by allowing the erection of portions of buildings to an indefinite height above the limit fixed in the law, provided that the top of any structure or structures on other portions of the same lot are kept below the permissible height to a corresponding extent and in such a manner that the adjacent property in the rear and upon the opposite side of the street upon which the lot fronts will receive substantially as much light as if the standard height limitation had been adhered to throughout. I doubt whether any fixed method of measuring such compensatory variations from the rule can be defined in the law itself, but I believe that the duty of passing upon the individual cases could safely be entrusted to a building commission or other permanent judicial body with proper provision for hearings and notifications and with provision for appeal from their decision fo a court of review within a limited period by any aggrieved party. This would permit the construction of towers, etc., to any height in any district provided enough space were left about them to avoid undue curtailment of light from neighboring property.

Classification of buildings

Restrictions such as I have discussed above would protect every land owner from being deprived, by the action of any other land owner, of the allowance of light adopted as the minimum standard for the district in question. They would not in any way interfere with the liberty of an owner of a deep lot to build a deep solid mass containing interior rooms very inadequately lighted or not lighted at all. The protection of the community against such types of buildings as are injurious to the people occupying them is a totally different proposition from the prevention of injury to the owners and occupants of other buildings and must be dealt with by special laws depending upon the character of occupancy, radically different regulations being required for dwellings, factories, theaters and warehouses. That is a subject upon which I will not attempt to enter here although it is obvious that in a city having wide variations in building-height regulations in different districts it might be necessary to recognize these districts in the tenement-house laws and other special building regulations based upon occupancy.

Statement by Mr. Robert Anderson Pope, Landscape Architect, November 28, 1913

Districting

There are three controlling considerations in the determining of proper height of building for a great city, which are, first, utilitarian; second, hygienic; and, third, esthetic. While the foregoing is given in the order of their relative importance for business zones, this order changes for both the residential and the civic zone and becomes for the former, first hygienic; second, esthetic; and, third, utilitarian. For the civic zones the order of the importance of these considerations again changes and becomes, first, esthetic; second, utilitarian, and, third, hygienic.

It is self-evident that for the residential zone hygienic considerations must be the vital and primary consideration in the determination of the proper height of buildings. This, in other words, means the protection of the sources of light and air. This seems to be the phase of the subject which has been given the most scientific consideration, but nevertheless the possibilities of this aspect of the question are far from being exhausted. A paramount consideration, for instance, is that of the angle at which the sun's rays becomes a hygienic factor; but this, however, must be the average angle at which the sun's rays are effective for an entire year. Upon this factor more than any other rests the solution for the proper height limitation of a residential community in a built-up city.

Block orientation

In undeveloped residential zones which are ultimately to become closely built up residential sections the proper direction of streets which determine the orientation of city blocks becomes the most important medium, except that of actual height limitation, for effectively and properly protecting the sources of light and air. An illustration of this contention is found right here in Manhattan Island, where the worst possible block orientation has resulted on account of the desire of the original designers of the city plans to facilitate expeditious access to both the East River and the Hudson River. This undoubtedly was a desirable object, since in the days when the initial plan was made water traffic was the principal means for carrying on trade and commerce. Specifically the outcome of this design has been that approximately half of the residential frontage of New York City is without sunlight during those six months of the year when the need of it is most vital to the health of the citizens.

There is a possible modification of these long east and west blocks which may be effected by the use of height of building regulations. Reference is made to the suggestion of dividing the long blocks with a park and sidewalks and then converting the rear yards into public courts with grass space in the middle. Where this could be advisedly undertaken a higher residential building could probably be hygienically permitted.

Principles of districting

Traffic and esthetic considerations in relation to residential zones are only secondary and minor considerations, because the proper width of street necessary to effectively and permanently secure the essential hygienic results in conjunction with height of building limitation will prove in every instance adequate to meet the utilitarian and esthetic needs of this type of zone. The third main type of zone which has been designated as civic has, as a primary consideration, neither the utilitarian as in the business zone nor the hygienic as in the residential zone, but rather the esthetic. Here it should be explained that the use of the word zone has not been meant to define any one section of the city, but rather an area of influence of a given city function, and as such one zone might be found within another and similar type of zone near by but separated by another type of zone.

In the case of the civic zone the area of influence which the height limitation regulation would effect is likely to be relatively restricted, although its influence should extend considerably beyond the group of buildings comprising such a zone.

The primary functions of such a zone must be the furnishing of such sites for public and semi-public institutions as will give the most beautiful and dignified results. Such provision will invariably provide sufficient space for all traffic needs and will at the same time meet the hygienic demands.

The proper extent of the setting most desirable for a group of public buildings depends upon the scientific phase of the question, which has been given but little attention. Reference is made to that optic angle at which a group as a whole of important buildings may be most effectively viewed. As this angle varies more or less with each individual, the average angle must be the one to be used. This has been determined to be approximately 27½ degrees. Of course in the matter of great towers or spires this angle does not need to be considered, since a momentary lifting of the head is anticipated as necessary; but in the mass of buildings comprising a group it should be the esthetic goal that these buildings may be conceived with their greatest effectiveness without involving a conscious effort.

A great esthetic loss has hitherto been caused by failure to give due consideration to this aspect of this problem. Much expenditure has been made for esthetic effect of important buildings, but has been entirely lost through inadequate site, which fails to give the view-point with the optical angle herein asserted as essential. In the permanently built-up sections of the city, such as City Hall Square, this principle can only be applied in part to the height of entrances or to the treatment of the first few stories of the building on account of the excessive height and the lack of the proper amount of setting to perceive the building or buildings as a whole or in a group. This, however, will not prove true of the proposed civic center, which should be designed in a manner conforming to the scientific principles herein stated, as should all other newly developed civic groups such as come under this heading.

Conclusions

1. The height of buildings must be limited.

2. The extent of the limitation must vary according to the functions of the different parts of the city.

3. The maximum economic traffic load which the business zones of a city and their arteries can carry will determine the various heights of the commercial, industrial, wholesale and retail sections.

4. This in turn depends upon anticipating all the possible mediums for increasing traffic capacity, such as traffic regulation,

the designing of the considered section, and the final width of the street.

5. Higher buildings may be permited in a given street when abutting property owners will agree to widen the street sufficiently to accommodate the increased traffic of higher buildings.

6. The angle at which the sun's rays become an effective hygienic factor is the dominant factor in determining the proper height of buildings in closely built-up residential districts.

7. In unbuilt-up districts the orientation of the block in conjunction with the effective angle of the sun's rays will be found the controlling principle in determining the height limitation to be established for such a section when fully developed.

8. Esthetic motives must be the dominant factor in determining the height of buildings for public or semi-public groups. The most important factors in the limitation of the heights of such groups of buildings is the vertical optical angle at which the average individual readily conceives an object.

9. The units of traffic capacity of congested zones should be determined in relation to a unit amount of floor space.

10. An investigation should be made into all possibly advantageous traffic regulations.

STATEMENT BY MR. WILLIAM H. SAYWARD, SECRETARY MASTER BUILDERS ASSOCIATION, BOSTON, MASS., OCTOBER 3, 1913

Mr. Sayward said the height limit was a benefit to Boston. He said that there would always be a certain number of owners who would object to any height limit. He said that at the time of its passage the Boston height limit had been attacked most vigorously. Many of those who then opposed it are now heartily in favor of it.

STATEMENT BY MR. BERNARD L. SHIENTAG, ASSISTANT COUNSEL NEW YORK FACTORY INVESTIGATION COMMISSION, JUNE 26, 1913

Height of commercial buildings

On the subject of the limitation of the height of commercial buildings I have but little evidence to offer. I know practically nothing about the esthetic phase of the problem. As a result of that ignorance, I suppose that I have very little sympathy for any movement to limit the height of commercial buildings simply for esthetic reasons.

Light and ventilation in factories

As to lighting and ventilation, it appeared from the investigations conducted by the Factory Commission that the lighting and ventilation was much better in the high modern loft buildings than in the old type of low factory buildings. True, the latter were for most part of antiquated construction or were converted tenement houses, so the height of the building could not be considered a criterion. The point should be emphasized, however, that every expert who appeared before the commission testified that natural ventilation was entirely insufficient and that the only way proper ventilation can be secured is by mechanical means. That being the case, it would hardly seem to be necessary to resort to the drastic measure of limiting the height of factory buildings in order to bring about better ventilation therein.

Fire hazard in factories

We come now to what is more doubtful ground, and that is the problem of the fire hazard in these high buildings. It has been established beyond question that the higher the building the greater the hazard to life in the event of fire. This is due to the fact that the extension ladders of the fire department do not reach beyond the seventh floor, and that life nets and other devices for the saving of life are useless when a fire occurs above that height. The higher the building, moreover, the longer it would take (assuming that there were no horizontal exits) the occupants to reach a zone of safety. The fact that a high loft building is of fireproof construction does not materially lessen the life hazard. No matter how fireproof the building itself may be, the contents of a factory building are more or less inflammable, and it is the burning of these contents that places the lives of the occupants of the building in peril. As Chief Croker has well said: " The term fireproof, when applied to our factory buildings, does not mean death-proof and conflagration-proof."

Is it necessary, however, to limit the height of buildings because of this increased life hazard? The opinion of practically every expert who testified before the commission was to the effect that such limitation was unnecessary and would be unwise; that where there was a special hazard due to the height at which manufacturing was carried on, that hazard could be successfully overcome by special requirements, such as installation of automatic sprinklers, the construction of a fire wall or other horizontal means of exit, the reduction in the number of occupants permitted to be employed, the use of fireproof windows to prevent the spread of fire from one story to another, and other similar measures and devices.

I believe that the proper enforcement of laws passed as a result of the Factory Commission's recommendations will prevent destruction of human life in the event of fire in many present type buildings regardless of heights. To summarize, these laws require:

1. That every possible precaution be taken to prevent the occurrence of fire (removal of rubbish, prohibition of smoking, fireproof receptacles).

2. That measures be taken to prevent the spread of fire; in the case of high buildings automatic sprinklers are mandatory.

3. That there be a fire alarm system to notify the occupants of the building of the occurrence of a fire and of its location.

4. A periodical fire drill of the occupants of every factory building is required. Where there is more than one factory in a building, there must be a cooperative fire drill.

5. That proper exit facilities be provided. The emphasis here is placed upon interior exits and fire walls rather than the antiquated and useless forms of outside ladder fire-escapes.

6. The limitation of the number of occupants in factory buildings. No greater number of persons may be employed on any one floor than can escape in safety, in the event of fire, by means of the exits provided for that floor.

Statement by Mr. Arthur A. Shurtleff, Landscape Architect, Boston, Mass., October 3, 1913

In my opinion a low building limit like that in Boston will, in time, produce a monotonous skyline, as most buildings will reach the low limit. In case a very high limit were established, it is fair to say that only a few buildings would reach the high limit, others would fall short of it by a small degree, but the bulk of buildings would not attempt to reach it. Under this arrangement a skyline of great variety would result. Doubtless the difficulty of fire control under such a limit would increase. In my opinion the present irregular skyline of New York is exceedingly attractive, and it would seem to me a pity to establish the limit at such a low level that all the buildings of the city would soon reach that uniform plane.

Statement by Mr. Robert E. Simon, Vice-President Henry Morgenthau Co., September 26, 1913

Argument for height limitation

Mr. Simon said a height limit was fundamental and essential to the city. High buildings make for congestion and increase the cost of policing the city and protecting it against fire. He would limit the height of all buildings. An effective height limit would probably reduce real estate values in the beginning in certain sections where high buildings have already been erected. The present owners of high buildings would have an unfair advantage over other owners if the height of buildings were limited. High buildings might be subjected to a surtax above a certain height.

He said that New York has to be made an attractive place for visitors or they won't come here. The Fifth Avenue shops cannot exist on local trade. The erection of tall buildings in the center of residential blocks has destroyed property worth hundreds of millions. The fact that homes are not protected in New York is driving the people out into the suburbs. The unregulated height of buildings has made real estate an unstable investment in New York.

Fifth Avenue—loft buildings

He said that the tall loft buildings were a mistake from beginning to end. They were bad for the manufacturer in that they were situated far from the river front and the railways. This results in great loss in trucking. The freight elevators are always congested and occasion long waits. The old loft district on the lower West Side with its three to six story lofts save most of this waste.

Zoning

Mr. Simon said he never saw a zoning scheme that would permit a city to develop in a normal manner. There is not a man living who could discount the future and say what land should be included in the different zones. He said he would make residential districts. Mr. Simon said a court of appeals to lift the restrictions in the zones when it became necessary would be desirable.

Statement by Mr. Henry Atterbury Smith, Representing New York Chapter of the American Institute of Architects, November 3, 1913

Tenement houses

Our present tenement law already limits the height of the building and regulates the portion of the lot that must be uncovered. This is a health measure, not due to esthetics or convenience. As a result the majority of tenements are five or six stories high and cover 70 per cent of an interior lot. The uncovered area is distributed among rear yards, interior courts and courts that open to the street or yard. These restrictions are less burdensome and more effectively beneficial in the case of large wide properties than of smaller narrower ones.

It would seem that the best solution of a six-story tenement as to uncovered areas and court arrangements should be found among the properties of the City and Suburban Homes Co., or Model Fireproof Tenement Co., or the various economic open-stair tenement types, owing to the fact of their unusual opportunity to study all forms and to the fact that they selected large properties most advantageous to housing results. In these there are units of 100 feet frontage or over and all are of the hollow block type—that is, the rooms not facing a street or a yard are arranged about a large interior court.

It is only necessary, however, to visit any of these buildings to come to the conclusion that the lower apartments facing the court have inadequate light, and yet it is to be remembered that these are the best types for light and ventilation; what obtains in narrower properties is worse.

Therefore to better light and ventilate the less desirable lower rooms it is obvious that the height of the building should be decreased or the amount of the lot that may be covered should be further restricted, or both.

But by making these restrictions most desirable, from the health point of view, the income of the property is reduced, or the rent increased in proportion to the amount of the restriction. Soon a point would be reached when the commercial builder would be no longer attracted and tenements would cease to be erected. Housing the poor in many European cities has to be performed by the municipality at public expense. We may be approaching such a state of affairs in New York; surely we will be if we make too many or too radical restrictions. So we should consider these matters with a due knowledge of their effect.

Improvements in the tenement house law

There is among tenement house owners already a feeling that our tenement department as at present administered is unnecessarily interfering with property rights. It would be well to weigh the advisability of reconsidering our tenement law, of reducing the rigor and burden in some places and of directing attention to some more lasting and meritorious regulations.

For instance, by examining the three groups above mentioned there will be found some buildings wherein the entrance to the 100-foot unit is through an open passage to the court. This materially helps the ventilation, but not the light. Again, some used a construction which would obviate the necessity of light-obstructing, theft-inviting fire-escapes. Again, some used exterior open stairs, thus reducing the dangers of contagious and infectious diseases and also adding a considerable volume of fresh air to the uncovered space. Now the building containing all these advantages from an average health point of view might be more acceptable to the city and to the commercial builder (upon whom we have to look for the majority of our tenements) than one of a less healthful type, for instance, a story lower or of less covered area.

It would doubtless be a benefit to the tenement dwellers, which would show in our city's death rate, if the average height of tenements were reduced two stories or the amount of lot that could be covered restricted to about 50 per cent; but before such a hardship upon the commercial building enterprise is approached we should carefully consider whether or not our present tenement law has already entertained all the health measures available which will not upset values.

STATEMENT BY MR. HOWARD C. SMITH, REPRESENTING THE CHAMBER OF COMMERCE, JUNE 12, 1913

Assessment of damages

Mr. Smith suggested that in place of a restriction as to height, a scheme of damages to adjoining property be evolved, the amount to be determined by the height of the building, the proximity of property damaged, and the value of the property affected, and to this end he suggested that it might be possible to run an imaginary angle, say at 45 degrees, from the top of any building and in every direction, and to award damages to such property as fell within that angle, the amount to be dependent upon the mean height of the imaginary line extending over the property.

Mr. Smith has not yet had an opportunity to find out whether such a law could be made constitutional or not, and has merely made this as a suggestion offered for consideration, and which from his point of view will come nearer to securing fair treatment to land owners generally.

It is probable that such a rule could not be made applicable to buildings now erected, or whose plans have been already filed with the building department, but if some method of graduated damage, payable over a term of years, could be devised to ameliorate the position of those property owners whose property has already suffered in value by reason of adjacent high buildings it would be eminently desirable.

STATEMENT BY MR. JOHN H. STORER, REPRESENTING WOOD, HARMON & CO., BOSTON, MASS., OCTOBER 3, 1913

Mr. Storer said he favored the height limit. It made for stability in land values. The height limit in Boston he considered a wise one. It has been advantageous to most owners.

STATEMENT BY MR. R. CLIPSTON STURGIS, PRESIDENT BOSTON SOCIETY OF ARCHITECTS, BOSTON, MASS., OCTOBER 3, 1913

Boston height limits

Mr. Sturgis said that Boston had felt its way to limiting the height of buildings, and had gone from one step to another. The progress made in height limitation, he said, had been prompted by injury. The present height limit is too high in the narrow streets.

Mr. Sturgis said that if an indefinite height were permitted, the owners of one-fourth of a block could by erecting high buildings detrimentally affect the values of the other three-fourths.

Mr. Sturgis said there was no doubt that the height limit in District B could in the light of past experience be improved upon, but how he could not say. Buildings higher than 125 feet would undoubtedly have been erected in District A had it not been for the height limit. The buildings erected in this district since the height limit was enacted have practically all been erected to a height of 125 feet. The height limit has certainly not affected the values in any detrimental way in District B.

Towers

Mr. Sturgis said that a fairly definite economic height limit existed in the case of towers. Towers will not bring in a financial return above a certain height. The number of elevators has to be considerably increased above a certain height; as the amount of space occupied by these elevators on the ground floor would be very large, the height of towers would be determined by an economic limit. Mr. Sturgis saw no particular reason why towers covering 20 or 25 per cent of the lot area should not be permitted provided they would not injure neighboring property.

Statement by Mr. Frank D. Veiller, Representing the Fifth Avenue Association, June 19, 1913

Fifth Avenue

The high-class retail business for which Fifth Avenue is so well known is the most sensitive and delicate organism imaginable, depending, first, on the exclusiveness of the neighborhood; second, on its nearness to the homes of the rich and the large hotels; and, third, on its lack of congestion, especially on the sidewalks, so that the customers may not be crowded or jammed in a hurlyburly crowd on their way to and from the different shops.

The wholesale section, on the other hand, is crowding the retail section as closely as the retail invades the residence section, the desire being to be as close as possible to the exclusive retail shops.

Fifth Avenue, below 34th Street as far as 23d Street, is already doomed. Below 23d Street it is irretrievably lost. Of prime importance is the preserving of Fifth Avenue from 42d Street to 59th Street. The loft buildings have already invaded the side streets with their hordes of factory employees. If an adequate move were made restricting the occupancy of the buildings so that no manufacturing could be done either on Fifth Avenue or from Madison Avenue over to Sixth Avenue, the matter would be solved. The employees from these loft buildings cannot be controlled. They spend their time—lunch hour and before business—on the avenue, congregating in crowds that are doing more than any other thing to destroy the exclusiveness of Fifth Avenue. If the exclusiveness and desirability of Fifth Avenue are destroyed, the value of real estate on Fifth Avenue will depreciate immediately. As a concrete example of this take the property on the west side of Fifth Avenue between 30th and 31st Streets. About three or four years ago this property was actually sold for $380,000, and to-day the property cannot be sold for $240,000.

This is not a plea entirely for the property owners, but for the preservation of Fifth Avenue, which is the most wonderful shopping street in this country, and in many respects more wonderful than anything in Paris or London. It is certainly of national importance, and we are only doing our obvious duty in preserving it.

In case the occupancy of the building cannot be regulated either through the factory commission or otherwise, the next best step would be in the limitation of the height of buildings in this zone, thereby diminishing the volume of operatives and making a uniform skyline. From a business standpoint this would be no hardship on the owners of property, for the most paying investment to-day for the section under discussion is a six-story building. A large office building and a large hotel, owing to the nature of their occupancy, are no disadvantage. A first-class hotel, on the contrary, is a decided advantage.

If the scope of this Commission is broad enough, I would recommend the limitation of the height of buildings through the city into zones, so that the different sections may be treated in a manner that will comply with the various local problems. For instance, if the Greenwich section and the old dry-goods section above Chambers Street were treated as a manufacturing center, this would work out to the salvation of the neighborhood. The tenements of the East Side are furnishing the operatives for the manufactures of this city, and if the factories could be in the neighborhood more convenient to their homes, which this would do, it would furnish tenants for buildings that are now nine-tenths vacant.

Comparison of values north of 42d Street on the side streets between Fifth and Madison Avenues as opposed to those between Fifth and Sixth Avenues will indicate the value of property occupied for exclusive business and that occupied for loft buildings. Between Fifth and Madison Avenues property is worth $4500 and up a front foot, for in these blocks there are practically no loft buildings. The buildings are for retail businesses, while between Fifth and Sixth Avenues there are a number of loft buildings already in, which have determined the occupancy of the balance of these blocks, and the value of real estate is from $2700 a front foot to as high as $5000, depending on its nearness to Fifth Avenue.

These are the conditions as they exist to-day, and if something is not done speedily to check further inroads the condition that now exists below 23d Street will in a few years prevail on Fifth Avenue north of 34th Street, and Fifth Avenue, as now known, will be lost to this city forever.

Statement by Mr. Leslie C. Wead, Representing the Chamber of Commerce, Boston, Mass., October 3, 1913

Boston height limits

The limitation of the height of buildings was first made in consequence of the erection of certain buildings in the financial district to a height that seemed to be excessive and it was realized that if no limitation were made the result would be serious congestion in the narrow streets and the shutting off of light and air from existing buildings and from the lower portions of other buildings which might be erected.

The subsequent limitation on Beacon Hill was in order to avoid the complete shutting off of the view of the State House dome, which was threatened by the erection of one high apartment house on the southwesterly slope of the hill. The law which authorized the division of the city into districts, known as A and B, in which the limitations were respectively 125 feet and 80 feet, was passed in consequence of the erection of a few buildings in the residential section to the former limit of 125 feet and fear that other high buildings might be erected which would injure neighboring property. The height limit of 80 feet in District B is not too low when the value of the land is taken into consideration, as the building value should not be more than twice the land value.

Effect on fireproof buildings

In District B, having a limit of 80 feet, the general building law requires buildings more than 75 feet in height to be fireproof. Many owners, therefore, prefer to build of second-class construction to a height of 75 feet rather than of first-class (fireproof) construction where the limit is 80 feet, although in the latter by reducing the height of stories one more story might be obtained. The difference in cost would be very substantial, some types of buildings being nearly double for the fireproof construction, thus requiring a larger investment without a corresponding increase in rental values.

The residential section of the city known as District B includes the Back Bay section, which is all filled land, and it is necessary to drive piles to support the foundations. It is therefore necessary to use special precautions in the erection of high buildings to have sufficient piling, as otherwise the buildings would be insecure. An illustration of this is seen in the tower of the Old South Church which was built without sufficient piling and is said to be three feet out of plumb.

Height limit a benefit to real estate values

A reasonable restriction in the limit of height does not affect land values detrimentally if it is applied uniformly to all buildings within the district.

Land values in District A vary from $25 or $30 per square foot in the outlying sections, while in the heart of the retail and financial district values are generally from $100 to $200 per square foot and in a few instances specially desirable corners have been valued at $300 per square foot.

STATEMENT BY MR. W. B. P. WEEKS, BOSTON, MASS., SEPTEMBER 29, 1913

I think the height of buildings law in the city of Boston is a very fair one and for the interests of the city. I should oppose any increase in the height or any change in the present law. I think it is a great mistake to allow buildings above the height established in Boston. It is bound to prove a great injury in the end to any city that allows unlimited height, and it is proving so in New York. A height limit should have been established there years ago. The Massachusetts law is a good one and has proved so here in Boston. I see no reason for changing it.

STATEMENT BY MR. FRANKLIN H. WENTWORTH, BOSTON, MASS., AUGUST 14, 1913

Replying to your letter of August 11th requesting a statement of opinion in the matter of limitation of the heights of buildings in the city of New York, I would state that I have long been on record as in favor of such action. The limitation of building heights in the city of Boston is already demonstrating its advantages, in distributing desirable and beautiful new buildings over a considerable area, thus preventing undue congestion and lessening the fire hazard, and in inducing the architects to give especial attention to beautifying façades.

Argument for a height limitation

The esthetic values are obviously not those paramount, however, in the consideration of this problem respecting New York City. Manhattan Island is of limited area, and such necessary features as light, air, sanitation (capacity of sewers, etc.) and transportation facilities cannot be adequately provided if buildings of unlimited height providing accommodations for thousands under one roof continue to be erected without restriction. The lower stories of many buildings are already undesirable through lack of sufficient light and air and it is conceivable that the continued "canyonizing" of the streets may eventually operate to injure the permanent commercial value of the sky-scraper.

Your problem is complicated by the fact that your landlords have already been permitted to go so far in the erection of these high buildings, and those prospective builders who have invested in unimproved or poorly improved real estate under past and present conditions will oppose restriction. I assume that whatever may be done will be largely the result of a compromise between public servants and conflicting private interests, and that therefore all the suggestions you desire from me are those relating to technical phases of the subject.

Several methods are advocated by engineers who have given thought to the subject of regulating building heights. An absolute limit of height is the easiest solution, but it may not be the best. Many American cities have adopted it.

Set-backs

The offsetting or "stepping" of the façades with each increase in height finds favor with some. This plan admits more light and air to the street, but does not effectually limit building heights nor relieve congestion. These objections, though in a lesser degree, apply to the proposition to permit a portion of the building to exceed the established limit of height in the form of a tower.

Districting

The ideal plan is to regulate the height of all buildings in a zone or district to the limit best suited to that particular section and to limit within such district itself the height of each building in proportion to the width of the street or plaza upon which it fronts. This plan is obviously more difficult to administer than the others, and might require a permanent commission with more or less arbitrary powers; but all the values, both common and esthetic, might be conserved under it, the entire city being considered, all parts in relation to the others.

Fire hazard of sky-scrapers

I do not consider the sky-scraper especially hazardous from the standpoint of fire, if it is built and finished entirely of fire-resistive materials and fully equipped with modern fire-extinguishing apparatus; but I do consider it hazardous from the human standpoint when it is multiplied, as in lower Manhattan, to a degree producing a congestion which visits daily discomfort upon the citizens and may under special conditions result in untold horror and loss of life.

Statement by Mr. Alfred T. White, Member Tenement House Commission and Tenement Owner, September 16, 1913

Tenement house law

Mr. White said that the Tenement House Commission of 1901 was obliged to confine its attention to tenement houses; in his opinion there was no reason why hotels and apartment hotels should not be subjected to similar restrictions. His suggestion was that the Heights of Buildings Commission should include all residential buildings in one class and should not undertake to recommend special changes in the Tenement House Law or affecting tenement houses alone.

Effect of the tenement house law on mortality

Mr. White attributed one-third to one-half of the decrease in the death rate of the city to the successive tenement house laws. He credited the remainder of the gain to the work of the health department, to cleaner streets and the cooperative work of private benevolence.

Other effects of present laws

Almost of necessity the courts required under the present law are paved. This deprives children of necessary playgrounds and results in an increased demand for public parks and public playgrounds. Builders should be encouraged to cover less of the lot and leave more open space. He stated that the Brooklyn buildings in which he was interested, housing over five hundred families, covered a little less than half of the lot area and left liberal yard space.

Frame tenements

Mr. White stated that in his opinion no frame tenements whatever should be erected within the city limits. Such tenements pay very trifling taxes, while each family residing in them requires the same expenditure for schools, fire protection, police, etc.; so that each family brought to the city and thus housed adds to the city's burdens.

Rentals

Mr. White said there were districts in Brooklyn in which rents had remained nearly stationary for twenty years, while in some districts of Manhattan rents have doubled in the same period. In Brooklyn the stagnation was largely in the waterfront districts and owing to the discontinuance of some of the ferries. Thousands of families in the crowded districts of Manhattan could be much better housed at much lower rents in Brooklyn within walking distance of the present subway.

Set-backs

On narrow streets, Mr. White said, owners should be obliged to set their buildings back from the street so that the effective width would in no case be less than 60 feet.

Districting

The present limitation of heights, so far as he knew, is confined to non-fireproof tenement houses, is uniform for the whole of

Greater New York and was evolved almost entirely, if not entirely, from the development of the most crowded districts of Manhattan Island.

The proper development of all the boroughs outside of Manhattan requires a stricter limitation of tenement houses and, in his judgment, this limitation should be different in different zones or districts of the same borough; for instance, the height limit which would be appropriate to East New York would be entirely out of place on Brooklyn Heights. Some arrangement should be provided for changing the zones or districts and the limitations, but the power to change should be so checked and guarded that changes would not be easy, or great injustice might result.

Height limits and area limits in any zone or district should apply to all buildings; and especially to all residential buildings, including hotels and apartment hotels and private dwellings as well as tenement houses. To permit the erection of spires and towers some provision could be made, as, for instance, that on non-residential buildings a spire or tower not covering more than a certain percentage of the area of the building might be carried to twice the height of the building.

He would urge the provision under which in any zone or district a building covering less than the permitted percentage of the lot could be increased in height; for instance, in a district where buildings might be limited to four stories, or the equivalent in feet, if covering 70 per cent of the lot; another story might be permitted if only 60 per cent of the lot were covered, and still another story if only 50 per cent were covered. His experience of over thirty years as an owner of tenement houses convinces him that a six-story building covering less than half the lot, and therefore with all sunlighted rooms, is better for the tenants than a building with rooms opening upon courts four stories in height covering 70 per cent of the lot. It is evident also that the whole neighborhood profits by the increased open area, and the necessity for public parks is somewhat diminished.

Statement by Mr. Ira H. Woolson, Representing the National Board of Fire Underwriters, and Mr. F. J. Stewart, Representing the New York Board of Fire Underwriters, October 6, 1913

Argument for height limitation

A reasonable limitation in the heights of buildings along the main thoroughfares and congested districts of our city will produce the following results: the conflagration hazard will be lessened; the danger to life and property due to isolated fires will be largely reduced; the real property values more equitably distributed; and the beauty, health and comfort of the city promoted.

Fire hazard of high buildings

The impossibility of the fire department, even with its best apparatus and high-pressure water system, successfully combating from the street a fire which occurs at a height of 100 feet or more above the street level is generally acknowledged. Therefore the only protection available for such fires is that afforded by hose streams carried up from the street level, interior standpipe connections, or automatic sprinkler equipment. As the latter is seldom used except in mercantile and manufacturing buildings, we must depend upon the first two mentioned means of extinguishment for fires in the upper floors of the majority of high buildings. Both of these methods have their limitations, and in case of a sweeping fire causing severe exterior exposure they might become crippled or inefficient.

A strict classification of most of our high buildings would rate them only as of *fairly efficient fire resistive construction,* because of the unreasonable opposition to the use of wired glass or shutters to protect against exterior exposures, combined with various other prevalent structural defects. This fact, coupled with the large amount of combustible contents which such buildings always house, would not only render them quite susceptible to simultaneous fires on many floors when attacked by the intense hot blast created by the burning of a block of near-by low-grade buildings, but also makes them weak in resisting a spread of fire within their own walls.

The possibilities of a fearful holocaust in the burning of such a building is apparent. The condition of several hundred or more people caught in the upper stories with several floors below them belching flame and smoke at every crack and opening is not pleasant to contemplate. Even though the building were constructed in the best manner possible, with enclosed elevators and stairways or smokeproof towers, the danger to life would still be very great. Suppose that the elevator boys quit operating their cars either from fear or because the shafts were filled with smoke and untenable. Either condition might easily occur. The occupants would then have to depend upon the enclosed stairways as their only means of escape. Think of this mass of frightened humanity fleeing for their lives down narrow stairways from the twentieth or fortieth story. The physical effort involved in such a flight would be very great. The chances are that many would be overcome by physical or nervous exhaustion and their helpless bodies would block the passage for those behind. Panic would then result with all its attendant horrors. Fire or smoke might easily be added to this frightful condition if the building were not of the highest grade construction.

We do not think this forecast is overdrawn or chimerical. We believe the conditions stated are well founded possibilities which have been greatly underestimated.

Should two or more such high buildings get fully aflame from either of the causes mentioned, the chances of controlling the fire within them or of preventing the spread of fire from them is correspondingly lessened, and would thus create a great general hazard to both life and property.

Limit at which height should be fixed

In view of the highly congested population and values in the area being considered, and the vital necessity of protecting this area in order to safeguard the lives and property of the city as a whole, we feel we are fully justified in suggesting that the height of all buildings be limited to at most 125 feet, except that buildings subdivided by numerous partitions, such as office buildings and the like, might be allowed as high as 150 feet. We would favor the limitation of factory buildings to 85 feet in height.

Mercantile buildings

We feel it our duty to direct special attention to the life and fire hazard existing in large mercantile establishments, and trust it may receive careful consideration.

In support of unlimited height and area in such buildings, the argument was recently presented before the Building Committee of the Board of Aldermen that such stores in this city were really very safe, because we have no record of large fires in them.

Statement was made that it is unjust to enact special legislation restricting the size of such establishments until events had demonstrated that distinctive control is necessary. The logic of such argument is fallacious. The required proof would doubtless exist after a fire had swept through one of those buildings during busy hours, and probably the result would shock humanity.

Certain facts exist in connection with such buildings which are undeniable. They are usually excessive in height and area. They are filled with highly combustible material, piled upon tables, hung in the air, and displayed upon rows of shelving extending one-third the distance to the ceilings; added to this is the natural accumulation of refuse behind and under the counters. In some of these establishments several thousand employees are scattered over the various floors, and at times many thousand customers, mostly women and children, crowd the narrow aisles. It is evident that a fire once beyond control would spread with frightful rapidity. These assertions must be conceded.

To say that the loss of life in such a fire would be appalling is mere conjecture, but we believe the facts warrant the supposition.

The installation of automatic sprinklers greatly lessens the danger of spread of fire through inflammable stock of this character. In fact, many of our large mercantile buildings of this type are already equipped with sprinklers, but the life hazard due to panic still exists and is augmented by excessive floor areas.

Limitation on the area of high buildings

Therefore, if this subject be within the province of your Commission, we urge that it give particular attention to limitation in size of this class of buildings.

Regarding your inquiry as to a proper limitation of undivided floor area, we would recommend as follows:

Tenement houses when not fireproof, 3000 square feet.

All other non-fireproof buildings:

Fronting on one street.................... 5,000 sq. ft.
Fronting on two streets................... 7,500 sq. ft.
Fronting on three or more streets..........10,000 sq. ft.

Armories, churches, auditoriums, hotels, light and power stations, office buildings, railway stations, school buildings and colleges, tenements, theaters, when fireproof, no restrictions as to area.

Car barns, when fireproof, 20,000 square feet.

All other fireproof buildings:

Fronting on one street.................... 7,500 sq. ft.
Fronting on two streets...................10,000 sq. ft.
Fronting on three or more streets..........12,500 sq. ft.

Except that on the first story only of every fireproof building, hereafter erected or occupied as a store, the floor area may be 20,000 square feet.

Except in car barns, all allowable floor areas mentioned in this section may be increased 50 per cent when a standard equipment of automatic sprinklers is installed.

INDEX

M. B.
BROWN
PRINTING
&
BINDING
CO.
NEW YORK

www.ingramcontent.com/pod-product-compliance
Lightning Source LLC
LaVergne TN
LVHW020607110826
845149LV00002B/400